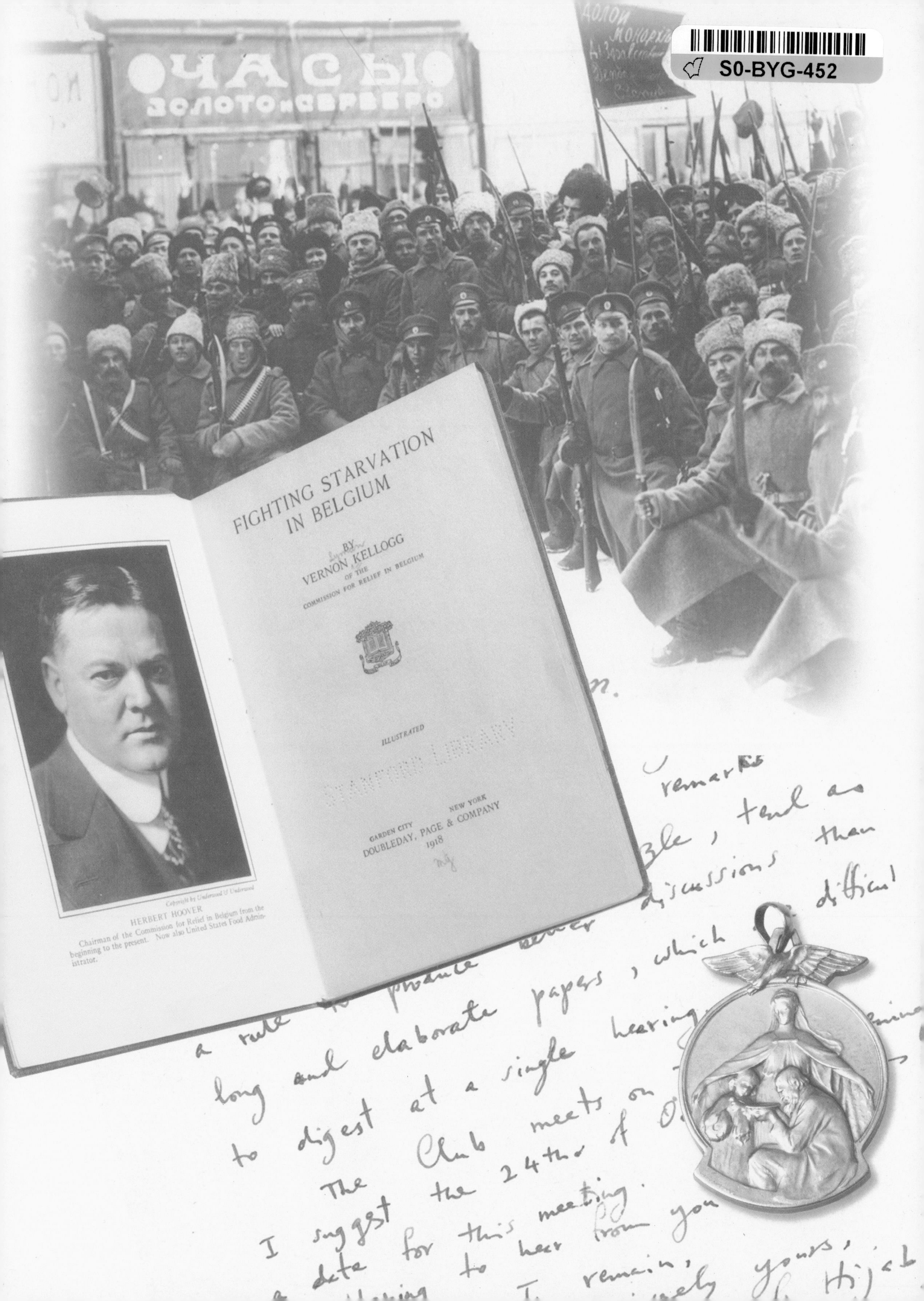

ЧАСЫ
ЗОЛОТО и СЕРЕБРО
FIGHTING STARVATION
IN BELGIUM
BY
VERNON KELLOGG
OF THE
COMMISSION FOR RELIEF IN BELGIUM
ILLUSTRATED
STANFORD LIBRARY
GARDEN CITY NEW YORK
DOUBLEDAY, PAGE & COMPANY
1918
Copyright by Underwood & Underwood
HERBERT HOOVER
Chairman of the Commission for Relief in Belgium from the beginning to the present. Now also United States Food Administrator.
remarks
tend as
discussions than
difficult
papers, which
long and elaborate papers, which
to digest at a single hearing
The Club meets on
I suggest the 24th of
a date for this meeting
to hear from you
I remain,
yours,

Государства
тъ. Въ
ками порядкомъ
СЫНУ НАШЕМУ
КНЯЗЮ АЛЕК
вступленiе
на 6
ИЧА обяза
同盟軍中國戰區統帥部任職令
特派美國陸軍中
將史蒂威爾為本
部參謀長此令
最高統帥蔣中正
盟軍字第一號
RSA 1994
RSA
PAN AFRICANIST CONGRESS OF AZANIA
SPORTS ORGANISATION FOR COLLECTIVE CONTRIBUTIONS AND EQUAL RIGHTS
THE KEEP IT STRAIGHT AND SIMPLE PARTY
VRYHEIDSFRONT - FREEDOM FRONT
WOMEN'S RIGHTS PEACE PARTY
WORKERS' LIST PARTY
XIMOKO PROGRESSIVE PARTY
AFRICA MUSLIM PARTY
AFRICAN CHRISTIAN DEMOCRATIC PARTY
AFRICAN DEMOCRATIC MOVEMENT
AFRICAN MODERATES CONGRESS PARTY
AFRICAN NATIONAL CONGRESS
DEMOCRATIC PARTY - DEMOKRATIESE PARTY
DIKWANKWETLA PARTY OF SOUTH AFRICA
FEDERAL PARTY
LUSO - SOUTH AFRICAN PARTY
MINORITY FRONT
NATIONAL PARTY - NASIONALE PARTY
INKATHA FREEDOM PARTY
KISS
VF-FF
WRPP
WLP
XPP
AMP
ACDP
ADM
AMCP
ANC
DP
DPSA
FP
LUSAP
MF
NP
IFP

A Wealth of Ideas

This volume was made possible by a generous grant from Bill and Jean Lane.

A Wealth of Ideas

REVELATIONS FROM THE HOOVER INSTITUTION ARCHIVES

Bertrand M. Patenaude

STANFORD GENERAL BOOKS
An imprint of Stanford University Press
Stanford, California
2006

Stanford University Press
Stanford, California

Printed in Canada on acid-free, archival-quality paper

Library of Congress Cataloging-in-Publication Data

Patenaude, Bertrand M., date–
A wealth of ideas: Revelations from the Hoover Institution Archives / Bertrand M. Patenaude.
p. cm.
Includes bibliographical references and index.
ISBN 0-8047-4727-X (cloth : alk. paper)
1. Hoover Institution Archives. 2. World politics—20th century—Sources. I. Title.

CD3119.S77P37 2006
016.90982—dc22 2005010868

Original Printing 2006

Last figure below indicates year of this printing:
15 14 13 12 11 10 09 08 07 06

Designed and typeset by Gordon Chun Design
in 11/17 point Kepler for main text.

For the staff of the Hoover Library and Archives,
past and present

CONTENTS

FOREWORD

In 1897, at age twenty-two, as a recently graduated geology major from Stanford University, Herbert Hoover left for Australia to evaluate gold mines. Later, while managing the largest coal mine in the world, he was stranded in the siege of the Boxer Rebellion in China. He eventually established a mining office in London. Even during this period of frenzied activity and restless travel, he stayed in touch with his university.

As early as 1907 Mr. Hoover was buying books for the Stanford faculty and the university library. By 1910 he had become a confirmed bibliophile and compulsive collector, specializing in rare books on the history of mining, including valuable incunabula. Alfred Chester Beatty, a business partner and fellow American mining engineer based in London, accompanied Mr. Hoover on a long trip in late 1911 to examine the copper and iron mines of the Kyshtym region in the Urals of tsarist Russia. Beatty, who was also fascinated by rare manuscripts, went on to build a library of remarkable antiquities, including some of the oldest manuscripts on paper and papyrus. Mr. Hoover, however, focused on materials that researchers could use for contemporary studies. In 1913, having donated his library of books on China to Stanford, he began supporting the transcription of documents from the British Public Records Office for Stanford historian E. D. Adams.

When the new technology that had been used to open up the world was then used to wreak unprecedented destruction in World War I, Mr. Hoover's passion shifted to manuscripts that helped evaluate the treacherous political developments of the twentieth century. By 1919 Mr. Hoover had founded his own collection at Stanford dedicated to the pursuit of peace. With his good friend Ambassador Hugh Gibson, Mr. Hoover wrote about the lessons to be learned from those records in *The Basis of Lasting Peace.* For Mr. Hoover, documents would continue to serve as metaphorical ore samples with which to survey political movements and history for their wealth of ideas.

As the collections continued to grow in both quantity and scope, the Hoover Institution became an international center for documentation and research on modern history and politics. The historical developments of the Soviet Union, modern China, and Central Europe were documented in great detail, as would be expected from the interests of the founder. In addition, political movements in Latin America, Africa, and the Middle East were also covered. As a result, cold war studies can be examined from all angles in the reading room of the Hoover Institution Archives. Often the curators collected obscure pamphlets, such as those issued by the Muslim Brotherhood of Egypt in the late 1940s, which turned out to have enormous political relevance decades later. The archives frequently preserves documents that would not survive in their own countries. Curators acquire materials that represent diametrically opposed points of view, so historians have as many perspectives as possible for analyzing modern history. The result has been a flood of books and articles based on the sources gathered in the Hoover Institution Archives.

At the February 2001 meeting of the Hoover Institution Board of Overseers, Deputy Director Charles G. Palm articulated the case for a book to provide an overview of the treasures of the Hoover Institution Archives and survey its wealth of sources. He envisioned an illustrated volume that would offer a visual sense of the historical artifacts in the holdings, in addition to revealing their intellectual content. Without hesitation, Overseer Bill Lane offered to support such a volume.

To implement the concept developed by Palm and Lane, Hoover Institution Fellow Bertrand Patenaude was asked to comb the archives, select images, and author the volume from the perspective of a professional historian. In 1992 Patenaude had coedited (with Stanford historian Terence Emmons) the diaries of Frank Golder, the founding curator of the Hoover Institution Russian collections. Ten years later Patenaude published a detailed history of the American relief expedition to Soviet Russia during the famine of 1921, *The Big Show in Bololand* (Stanford University Press), again based on the Hoover Institution Archives. Years of intense archival research on those books thus made Patenaude uniquely qualified to provide an overview of the archival treasures. The resulting text and images both highlight interesting aspects of the holdings and demonstrate how a trained historian can use those primary sources to reconstruct an accurate account of political movements and historical turning points.

Book designer Gordon Chun, using the text and images, created this attractive volume from the standpoint of an artist with extensive museum experience and visually captured the rich material culture in the documents, photographs, and artifacts. The collaboration of Patenaude, who worked with the archives staff to find the most representative materials from an estimated sixty-five million items, and Chun has thus resulted in a greater understanding of numerous documents preserved in the stacks at the Hoover Institution. Elena Danielson, the director of the Hoover Institution Library and Archives, shepherded this project from its outset and deserves significant credit for the quality of this pleasing product.

That Mr. Hoover, an ambitious and harried businessman in his twenties, would see wealth in terms of knowledge and begin building an institution to promote scholarship for later generations, says something about him and about the culture that produced such a library.

John Raisian
Director
Hoover Institution
Stanford University

INTRODUCTION

This book draws on the extraordinarily rich collections of the Hoover Institution Archives to illuminate and illustrate some of the most important ideas, individuals, movements, and events of the twentieth century. As suggested by its title, the book's unifying theme is the power of ideas. Its aim is to present a representative profile of the extraordinary wealth of ideas that emerges from the various documentary materials in the archives.

Each of the eight chapters is organized around a particular theme, yet the chapters are arranged in roughly chronological order, starting with the movement for peace at the turn of the twentieth century and ending with the free-market consensus at the turn of the twenty-first century. Along the way there are chapters covering the century's major wars, revolutions, and communist and fascist tyrannies. These explore the ideas and actions of such political leaders as Hitler, Stalin, and Mao, and American military officers such as generals Marshall, Stilwell, and Wedemeyer. There are also chapters devoted to liberal philosophers Sidney Hook and Karl Popper, and economists Friedrich von Hayek and Milton Friedman.

An illustrated book—or any single book—can only hope to suggest the scope and richness of the Hoover's holdings. Deciding on the particular topics to feature in such a volume presents a historian with agonizingly difficult choices, so vast are the archival collections and so varied are the types of material from which to choose: official correspondence, personal letters and diaries, typed and holograph public and private manuscripts, political posters, photographs, film stills, and original artwork, as well as rare books and newspapers from the Hoover Library. In selecting the illustrations, an attempt has been made to provide a cross-section of the various kinds of material researchers generally work with in the archives, including film and microfilm, though for obvious reasons audio archives could not be represented. The Hoover poster collection is the subject of its own chapter.

The archives staff guided the author to the Hoover's many documentary treasures. Some of these extremely rare items would be included in any volume on the Hoover Archives: for example, the abdication letter of Tsar Nicholas II, the diary of Joseph Goebbels, and the ink sketches made by a colleague of Mao Zedong during the Long March. Once one moves beyond such obvious candidates, however, choosing what to include necessarily becomes more subjective. The basic criteria for selection were the historical importance and interest of the documents, their representativeness of the Hoover's particular areas of strength, and, critically important for a book of this kind, their visual accessibility. Inevitably, the documents and images included here reflect the author's particular research interests and experiences in the Hoover Archives over a period of twenty-five years, as well as his more wide-ranging investigations during the eighteen months devoted to the preparation of this volume.

The bibliography includes the most important secondary literature used in the research and preparation of the text, though the author was also greatly assisted by the many unpublished items prepared by the Hoover Archives staff, past and present, as descriptive material for the individual collections. These provided much useful background. Also helpful in this way were the texts written to accompany Hoover Archives exhibits over the years. An invaluable resource were the Hoover Institution's internal records, which were made available to the author for the duration of the project.

How and why the Hoover Archives came into existence in 1919 and within a short time was able to establish itself as one of the leading research centers in the world is the special subject of Chapter 3, "The Tower"—though in fact the story is told throughout the book, whose text often discloses how individual documents or entire collections from around the world ended up on the Stanford campus. The intention of the founder, Herbert Hoover, was to build up a documentary collection whose scope and reputation for excellence would in turn serve to attract to itself "valuable additions." He succeeded, and these additions, in the form of new collections and increments to existing collections, continue to accumulate and add to the richness of the Hoover Archives.

A Wealth of Ideas

KEEP COOL
Don't be Stampeded into War
Come to a
PEACE
MASS MEETING
Monday, 8 P.M.
APRIL 2, 1917
AT THE
Convention Hall, 5th and L Sts., N.W.

Chapter One

PEACE AND WAR

The Hoover Institution began as the Hoover War History Collection, established as a gathering point for documentation on the causes and course of the Great War. Indeed, the collections on World War I remain one of the greatest strengths of the archives. The great power rivalries, the arms races, the secret treaties, the military war plans, the maneuvers of autocrats, officials, and soldiers, from the famous to the obscure—these are impressively documented in numerous archival collections accumulated over the course of many decades. This is to be expected of an institution whose founding was occasioned by the War. It comes as something of a surprise, therefore, to discover the depth of the Hoover's coverage of the great peace movement that gathered force in Europe and America toward the end of the nineteenth century. The Hoover Institution is dedicated, as its formal name indicates, to the study of war, revolution, and peace; yet in the story of the twentieth century, as it unfolds in the archives, peace comes first.

A PASSION FOR PEACE

In 1889 the first International Peace Congress was held in Paris. Peace advocacy has probably been around for as long as there has been war, but in the 1890s for the first time it began to take the form of an organized movement—multifarious and hodgepodge, but a movement nonetheless. Religious and moral pacifists and humanitarians began to find in their company scholars, statesmen, lawyers, and businessmen, even millionaires such as the industrialist Andrew Carnegie. These recruits brought the peace movement a new sense of legitimacy and credibility, along with financial backing. When the Swedish munitions manufacturer Alfred Nobel died in 1896, he left a fortune toward the establishment of several scientific and literary prizes, and most famously the peace prize given in his name.

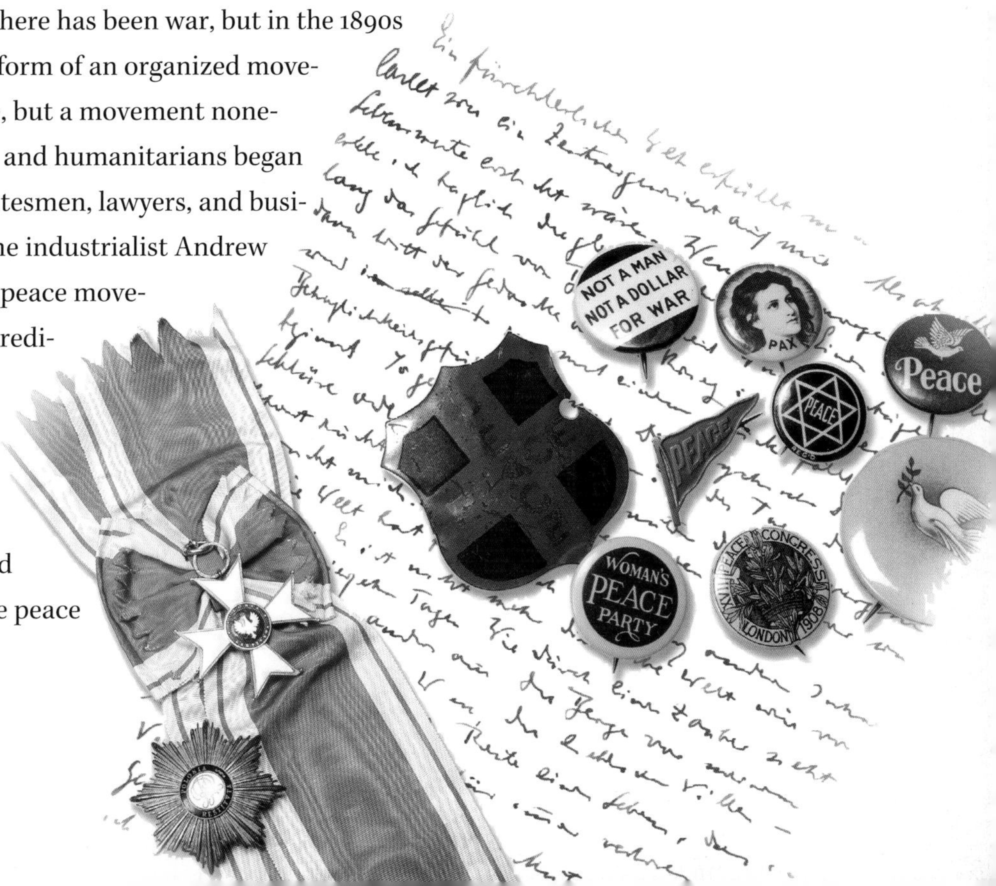

The first truly international (as opposed to European) diplomatic conference convened in 1899 at The Hague, where representatives of twenty-six states met to discuss ways to achieve disarmament and regulate relations among states. The Hague conferences (a second, even larger gathering took place in 1907) marked the first time in history that statesmen came together to discuss the prevention of war at a time when war did not threaten. The Hague conferences failed to halt the arms races that helped precipitate the First World War, but they advanced the development of international law, particularly the laws of war and the concept of international arbitration, and established a Permanent Court of Justice at The Hague.

It was in part their willingness and ability to champion the practice of international arbitration and mediation that won the Nobel Peace Prize for President Theodore Roosevelt (1906) and former Secretary of State Elihu Root (1912). As secretary of state under Woodrow Wilson from 1913 to 1915, William Jennings Bryan took special pride in the fact that, under his stewardship, the United States negotiated more than two dozen "cooling off" treaties: arbitration agreements by which the signatories consented to refrain from fighting for one year while their disagreement was investigated by a neutral party. "The international peace movement praised these legal instruments as another sign of the inevitability of peace through reason," writes historian Barbara Kraft, "and Bryan thought them his greatest achievement. Each time a treaty was concluded he sent the participating ambassador a plowshare paperweight that had been 'beaten' from an obsolete sword supplied by the War Department."

In America the spirit of the peace movement was very much in keeping with the Progressive Era's faith in progress and in the power of citizens' initiatives to achieve what elected officials failed even to attempt. A better life was possible, even the elimination of war, if citizens stepped forward where statesmen did not dare. The weapons of choice in the pursuit of these goals were petitions, pamphlets, mass meetings, demonstrations, and parades. It was a time of great activism and idealism, and the cause of peace attracted many eager recruits.

Peace advocates represented a whole spectrum of points of view, from the idealistic to the realistic. Some believed in the power of moral suasion and appeals to reason to eliminate the scourge of war. Among the more legal-minded of the peace activists, some were apt to believe that simply creating the right institutions, such as the Permanent Court at The Hague, would be enough to prevent war. Still others became convinced that the growing economic interdependence of states meant that statesmen and capitalists would increasingly come to understand that war was not profitable and therefore was unthinkable.

Lay Down Your Arms!

Bertha von Suttner, 1886. *(Die Friedenswarte)*

In America as in Europe, women took the lead in the struggle for peace. The women's suffrage movement, then in full blossom, served to energize the peace movement, leading suffragists doubling as passionate advocates for peace. The woman regarded as the "mother" of the movement was a native of Prague, Bertha von Suttner, who in 1889 leapt to great fame with the publication of her antiwar novel, *Die Waffen nieder!* (translated as *Lay Down Your Arms!*). In the nineteenth century, only *Uncle Tom's Cabin* had a larger readership, and as Harriet Beecher Stowe's novel did for the antislavery movement von Suttner's novel popularized the movement for peace. By 1905 it had been translated into thirteen languages. It prepared the ground for the peace organizations that began to spring into existence in the final decade of the century.

Lay Down Your Arms! brought von Suttner accolades from prominent men of every land. Stanford University President David Starr Jordan said of her book, "It gives the vision of a better world, one ruled by ideas, not by guns, bayonets, and poison gas." The novel made believers of many influential individuals who had been skeptical of the cause of peace, among them Alfred Nobel. It so happens that in 1876 von Suttner (née Bertha von Kinsky) had briefly been hired by Nobel as his secretary-housekeeper. Now he had the pleasure of writing to congratulate the first-time novelist, whom he addressed as "Dear Baroness and Friend":

> *I have just finished reading your admirable masterpiece. We are told that there are two thousand languages—1,999 too many—but certainly there is not one into which your delightful work should not be translated, read, and studied. How long did it take you to write this marvel? You shall tell me when next I have the honor and happiness of pressing your hand—that Amazonian hand which so valiantly makes war on war.*

It is generally assumed that it was von Suttner who persuaded Nobel to establish his peace prize, which was awarded for the first time in 1901 and which von Suttner herself received in 1905. Alone the extraordinary and enduring influence of her book might have won her this honor, but it was her subsequent work in behalf of the movement that secured it for her. In

1891, two years after the publication of her novel, she began to edit a monthly journal of the same name, *Die Waffen Nieder!*, published in Berlin and Vienna by a Viennese named Alfred Fried. In 1899, von Suttner handed over the editorial reins to Fried, who changed the journal's name to *Die Friedenswarte (The Peace Watch)*, which began its existence as a weekly. In 1911, when awarding Fried the Peace Prize, the Nobel Committee praised him for putting out "the best journal in the peace movement."

Die Friedenswarte served as a forum for the often lively disagreements within the peace movement as to how best to prevent war—debates that took on an increasing urgency as war's shadow lengthened in the twilight of old Europe. As editor, Fried liked to portray his own brand of pacifism as especially hard-headed, while he criticized "romantic pacifists" such as Leo Tolstoy for placing too much faith in the power of morality. The beginning of wisdom in matters of war and peace, Fried believed, was to recognize that the root cause of war was the anarchy of international relations. He placed more reliance on economic cooperation and political organization among nations as bases for peace, and less on the limitation of armaments and on international law: "If we wish to substitute for war the settlement of disputes by justice, we must first substitute for the condition of international anarchy a condition of international order." The slogan on the masthead of his journal read, "Organize the World!"

Fried's self-styled realistic pacifism left him hardly better prepared to cope with the coming of war in the summer of 1914—and a death in the family must have seemed like an omen for the entire peace movement: on June 21 Bertha von Suttner died at her home in Vienna. One week later, Archduke Franz Ferdinand, heir to the throne of the Austro-Hungarian Empire, was assassinated in Sarajevo. This triggered a series of events that produced a conflagration: on July 28 Austria-Hungary declared war on Serbia; on August 1 Germany declared war on Russia; on August 3 Germany declared war on France; on August 4 Germany invaded neutral Belgium, which prompted Great Britain to declare war on Germany; on August 6 Austria-Hungary declared war on Russia. Treaty obligations and rigid war plans left no time or room for mediation efforts or cooling-off periods. A third Hague Conference, scheduled for 1915, would never take place.

When war broke out, Fried was in Vienna, where all pacifist activities were subject to the control of the government censor and the hostility of an inflamed public. He moved to Switzerland, where he continued to publish *Die Friedenswarte* as a rallying point for international peace efforts. Accused of treason by the Austrian government, he was unable to return to Vienna until the war's end. From the first days of the war, Fried kept a diary, which he serialized in his journal and which was published after the war as *Mein Kriegstagebuch (My War Journal)*. In it he recorded his thoughts and activities, as well as those of his fellow peace activists.

Alfred Fried's "ex libris" book plate. Fried chose for his book plate the design he proposed in 1906 for the international peace movement and that he used on the masthead of his journal, *Die Friedenswarte.* He explained that he had purposely rejected the obvious symbols—olive branch, dove, angel, white flag, broken sword, plowshare—which, he felt, did not accurately represent the philosophy of the movement as espoused by his journal. Instead he chose a series of interconnected gears. As he wrote to his readers upon introducing the design: "This shows cooperation toward a common goal; this shows the part in relation to the whole, the whole in relation to the part, the calm, certain progress through organization." Such symbolism, he wrote, should be embraced by peace activists everywhere: "Let the peace movement in every land adopt these gears as their symbol and put aside the sentimentality of the existing symbolism, as well as the sentimentality of the pacifism that persists in certain minds."

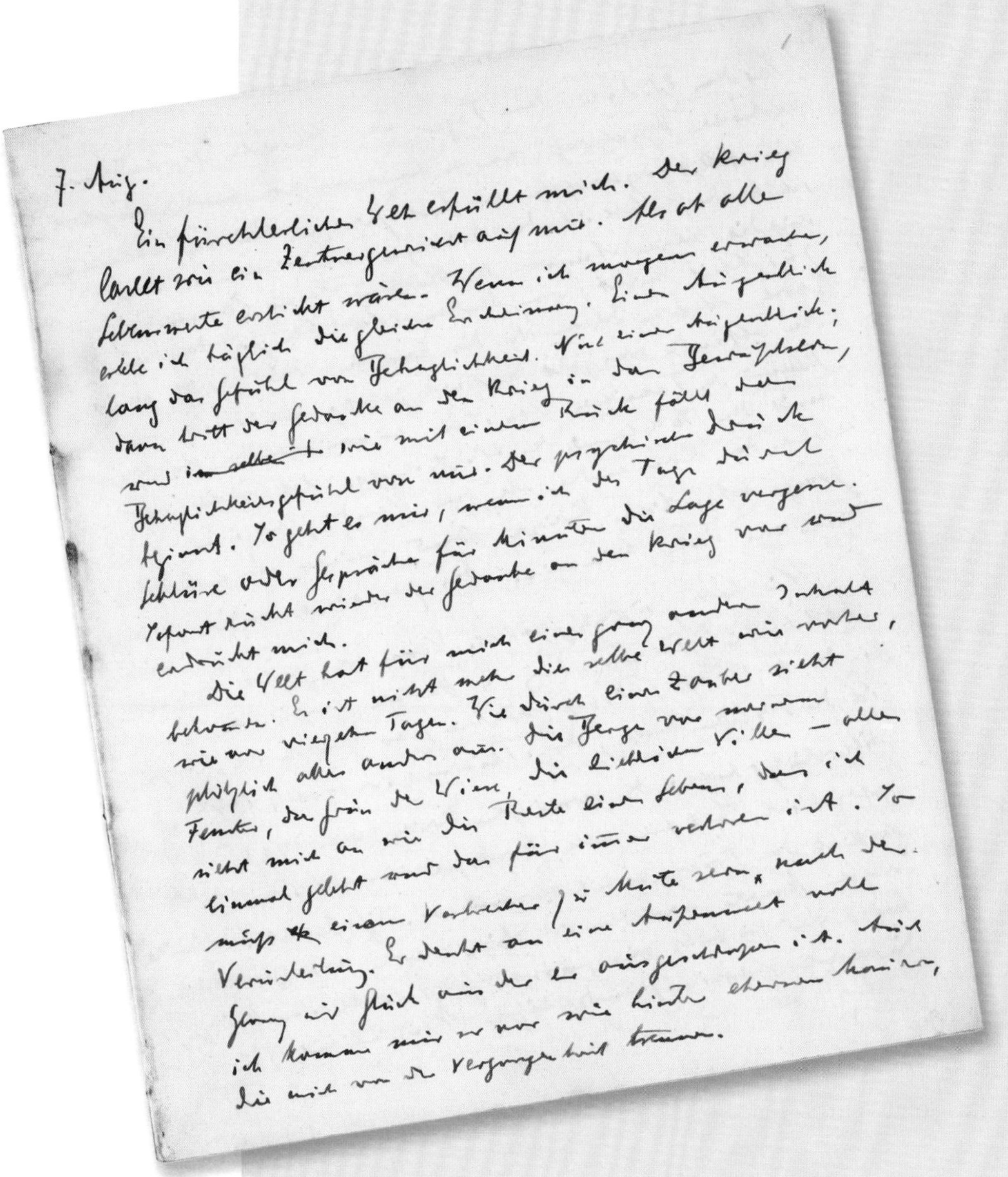

The first page of Alfred Fried's wartime diary, dated August 7, 1914. "I am filled with a terrible pain. The war weighs on me like a heavy weight. As if everything worth living for were suffocating. When I wake up in the morning, I experience every day the same symptom: for a moment long the feeling of comfort. Only for a moment; then the memory of the war enters my consciousness, and as though with a shove the comfort falls away from me. The psychological pressure begins. So it goes for me if during the day, while lecturing or in conversation, I forget the situation for a few minutes. Immediately the memory of the war returns and oppresses me.

"The world has taken on a completely different meaning for me. It is no longer the same world as before, as fourteen days ago. As if a spell had been cast, everything suddenly looks different. . . ." (Alfred Fried Papers)

Fried hoped that the catastrophe and the evident futility of the war would serve to vindicate the arguments of reasonable pacifists like himself and give their voices greater authority when the war ended. But of course this was not to be the case. Fried lost whatever wealth he possessed in the collapse of Austria-Hungary and died in poverty of a lung infection in Vienna, in 1921, at the age of fifty-seven.

Ford's Peace Ship

It is a curious fact that when a war that had been so anxiously anticipated for so long finally arrived, it nonetheless came as something of a shock. Many American pacifists instantly blamed secret diplomacy and arms manufacturers. Some preferred to keep silent, or they took sides against the Kaiser's Germany. The die-hard activists urged President Wilson, as leader of the "greatest neutral nation," to arrange an open-ended conference of neutral countries with the goal of "continuous mediation" toward peace. After the sinking of the *Lusitania,* on May 7, 1915, as submarine warfare turned American public opinion increasingly against Germany, American pacifists became more and more preoccupied with keeping the United States out of the war.

Women remained in the forefront of the movement for peace. The International Congress of Women, meeting at The Hague in the spring of 1915, had peace at the top of its agenda. One participant was the American suffragist and social worker Jane Addams, who as president of the Women's Peace Party sought, in the fall of 1915, to organize a conference of neutral countries—Norway, Sweden, Denmark, Holland, Switzerland, and Spain—under U.S. sponsorship. The White House resisted such proposals, but one of the leaders of the international women's congress, the Hungarian feminist and peace activist Rosika Schwimmer, had better success. Returning to the United States, where she had lectured against the war in 1914, she took up the cause of a neutral conference in a series of speaking appearances that brought her to Detroit and, on November 17, to a meeting with Henry Ford. In conversation with Mme Schwimmer, Ford indicated a willingness to finance a neutral conference and promised to come to New York to help organize the undertaking in person.

Ford arrived in New York City a few days later, and at an informal press conference on November 24, 1915, he astonished reporters with the statement: "We're going to get the boys out of the trenches by Christmas." Ford had chartered a ship, the *Oscar II,* and his intention, as he now announced, was to sail to Europe and establish a conference of neutral nations that would seek to bring about peace through continuous mediation. However sincere were Ford's motivations, his penchant for self-advertising immediately laid him and his peace ship open to ridicule. "Out of the trenches by Christmas"—overnight this promise

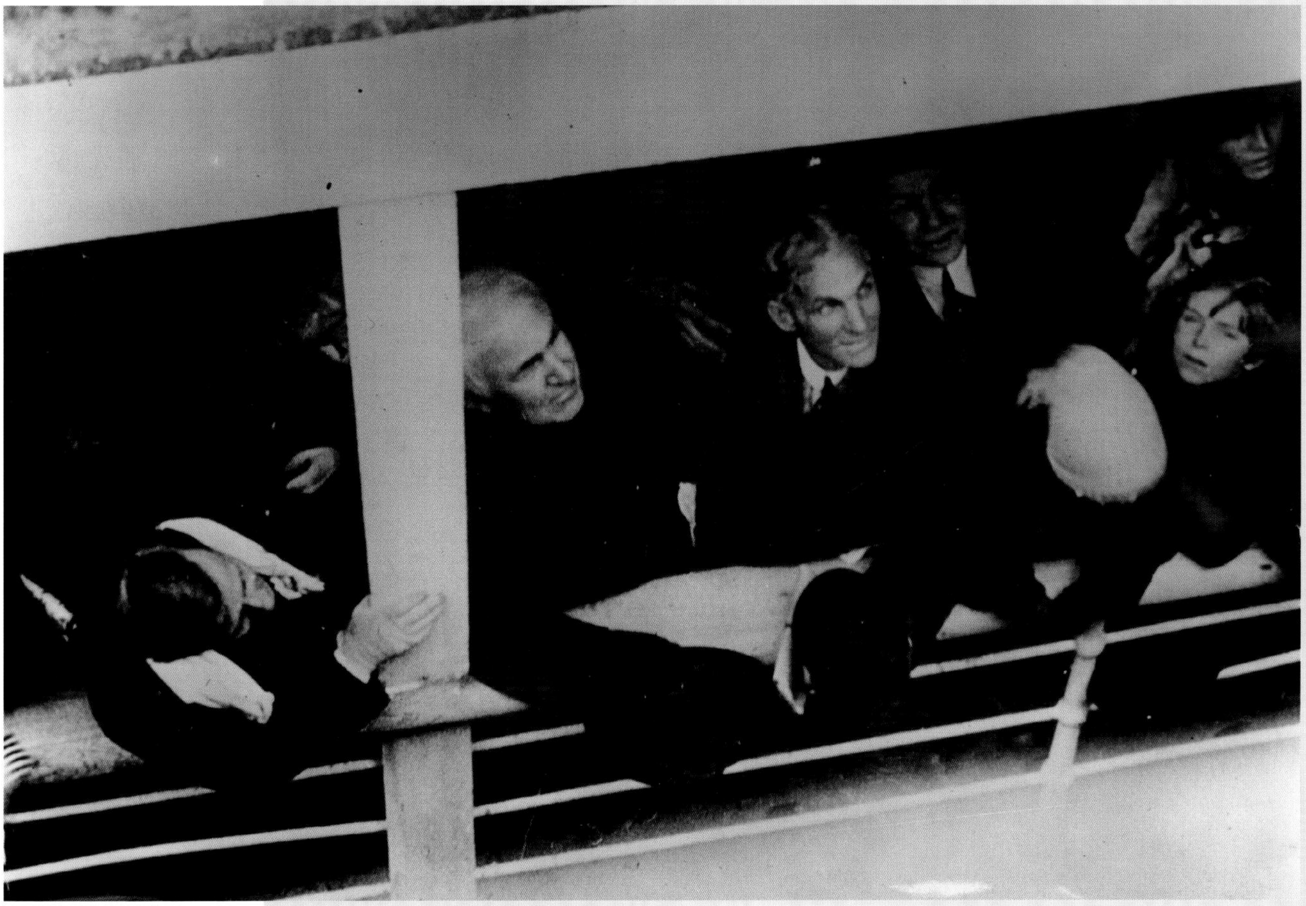

Henry Ford, aboard the *Oscar II,* shortly before it sailed from Hoboken; the white-haired man to his right is Thomas Edison, who came to see Ford off. (Ada Grose Papers)

FORD PEACE EXPEDITION

IDENTIFICATION CARD

MEMBER

Mrs. Alice Park

PLEASE SHOW THIS CARD WHEN REQUESTED

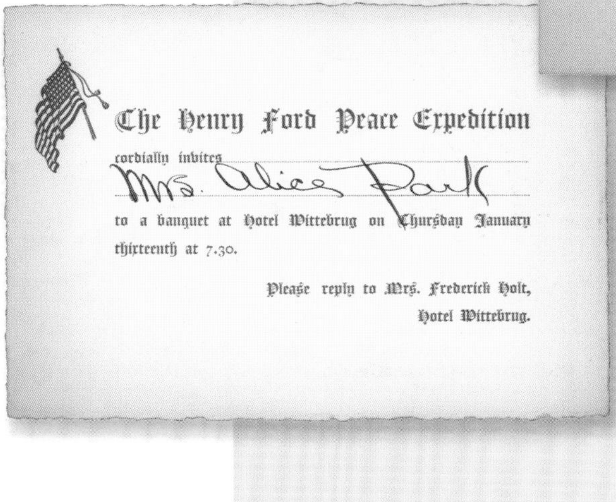

The Henry Ford Peace Expedition

cordially invites

Mrs. Alice Park

to a banquet at Hotel Wittebrug on Thursday January thirteenth at 7.30.

Please reply to Mrs. Frederick Holt,
Hotel Wittebrug.

Ford Peace Expedition documents of Alice Park, a suffragist and pacifist from San Francisco. (Alice Park Papers)

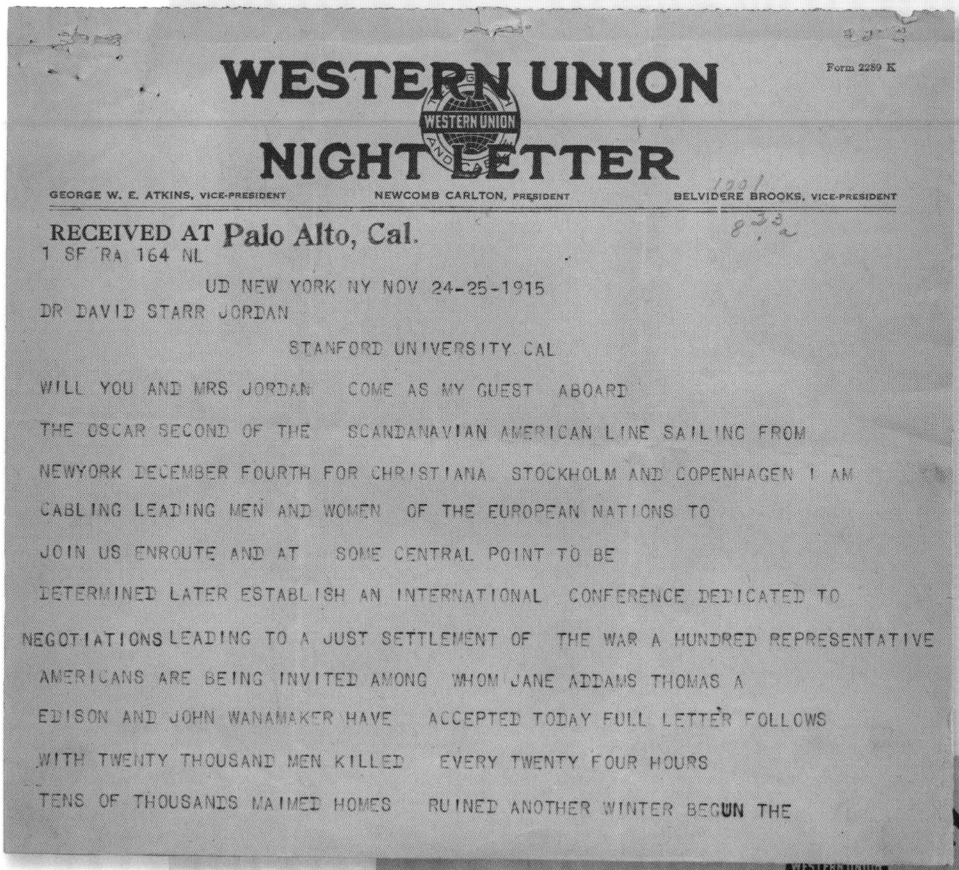

WESTERN UNION
NIGHT LETTER

Form 2289 K

GEORGE W. E. ATKINS, VICE-PRESIDENT NEWCOMB CARLTON, PRESIDENT BELVIDERE BROOKS, VICE-PRESIDENT

RECEIVED AT Palo Alto, Cal.

1 SF RA 164 NL

UD NEW YORK NY NOV 24-25-1915

DR DAVID STARR JORDAN

STANFORD UNIVERSITY CAL

WILL YOU AND MRS JORDAN COME AS MY GUEST ABOARD
THE OSCAR SECOND OF THE SCANDANAVIAN AMERICAN LINE SAILING FROM
NEWYORK DECEMBER FOURTH FOR CHRISTIANA STOCKHOLM AND COPENHAGEN I AM
CABLING LEADING MEN AND WOMEN OF THE EUROPEAN NATIONS TO
JOIN US ENROUTE AND AT SOME CENTRAL POINT TO BE
DETERMINED LATER ESTABLISH AN INTERNATIONAL CONFERENCE DEDICATED TO
NEGOTIATIONS LEADING TO A JUST SETTLEMENT OF THE WAR A HUNDRED REPRESENTATIVE
AMERICANS ARE BEING INVITED AMONG WHOM JANE ADDAMS THOMAS A
EDISON AND JOHN WANAMAKER HAVE ACCEPTED TODAY FULL LETTER FOLLOWS
WITH TWENTY THOUSAND MEN KILLED EVERY TWENTY FOUR HOURS
TENS OF THOUSANDS MAIMED HOMES RUINED ANOTHER WINTER BEGUN THE

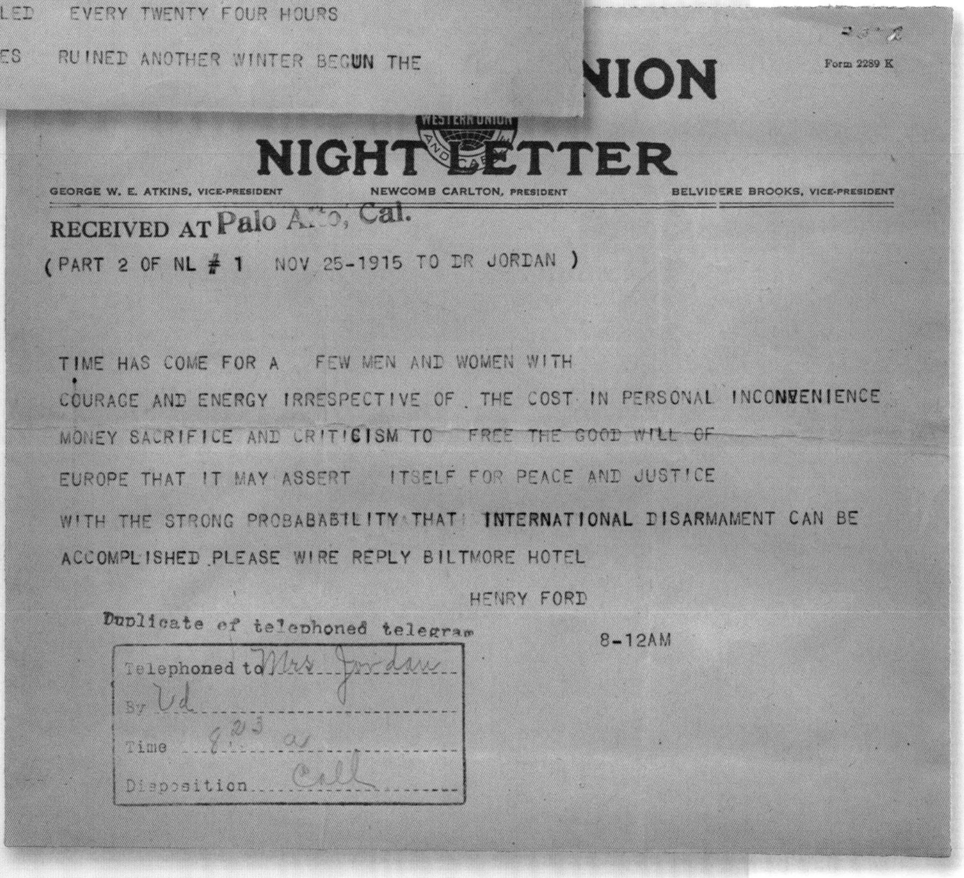

NIGHT LETTER

Form 2289 K

GEORGE W. E. ATKINS, VICE-PRESIDENT NEWCOMB CARLTON, PRESIDENT BELVIDERE BROOKS, VICE-PRESIDENT

RECEIVED AT Palo Alto, Cal.

(PART 2 OF NL # 1 NOV 25-1915 TO DR JORDAN)

TIME HAS COME FOR A FEW MEN AND WOMEN WITH
COURAGE AND ENERGY IRRESPECTIVE OF THE COST IN PERSONAL INCONVENIENCE
MONEY SACRIFICE AND CRITICISM TO FREE THE GOOD WILL OF
EUROPE THAT IT MAY ASSERT ITSELF FOR PEACE AND JUSTICE
WITH THE STRONG PROBABABILITY THAT INTERNATIONAL DISARMAMENT CAN BE
ACCOMPLISHED PLEASE WIRE REPLY BILTMORE HOTEL

HENRY FORD

Duplicate of telephoned telegram 8-12AM

Telephoned to Mrs Jordan
By Ud
Time 8:23 a
Disposition Call

Ford telegram to David Starr Jordan, November 24/25, 1915. This was among the first telegrams of invitation Henry Ford sent to 115 people, announcing, prematurely and erroneously, that Thomas Edison and John Wanamaker, the Philadelphia department store mogul, had accepted his invitation to join the peace expedition. Edison told Ford he was too busy, though privately he expressed skepticism about the endeavor. Wanamaker backed out in the face of all the bad press. Jane Addams was prevented from sailing by illness. (David Starr Jordan Papers) became a national punch line. "GREAT WAR ENDS CHRISTMAS DAY; FORD TO STOP IT," read the headlines in the next morning's *New York Tribune*. The press portrayed the expedition as a "wild-goose chase," "Ford's folly," a "peace-junket," a "peace-joy-ride," "more innocents abroad," "fantastical," "ridiculous," "Quixotic."

This was only the beginning of what Jane Addams called "a season of great hilarity." Yet not everyone was laughing. Some public figures, including many peace activists, saw the endeavor as a reckless exercise in amateur diplomacy that was bound to hinder serious efforts to negotiate an end to the fighting. Addams, for one, lamented that Ford's expedition served only to draw attention away from the vital task of arranging a conference of neutrals. Theodore Roosevelt, who wanted his countrymen to take a firm stand against the evils of German militarism, expressed disgust: "Mr. Ford's visit to Europe will not be mischievous only because it is so ridiculous, but because it is a most discreditable thing to the country."

On December 4, 1915, Henry Ford and more than one hundred delegates sailed from Hoboken, New Jersey, aboard the steamship *Oscar II* bound for Christiania (Oslo), Norway. This was to be the first stop in what was planned as a series of peace meetings in neutral Europe, ending up at The Hague, where the conference of neutrals would be organized. Believing that publicity was vital to his cause—that even bad publicity was better than none at all—Ford invited a large number of newspaper "boys" to make the voyage at his expense, and more than fifty reporters accepted the invitation. The nearly one hundred "peace pilgrims" on board were a motley collection that included twenty-five college boys and a few coeds. Scrutinizing the passenger list, Addams discovered "a group of very eccentric people."

The *Oscar II* had an especially rough crossing, not only on account of severe weather. Shortly after the peace ship left New York, President Wilson delivered an address to Congress on American preparedness. In the past year, Wilson said, "the whole face of international affairs" had been so altered that he now felt compelled to ask Congress to strengthen America's armed forces so that the nation could "care for its own security." One of the reporters had brought an advance press copy of the president's message on board the ship. This was read aloud to the assembled delegates and provoked an emotional discussion that lasted through the night. In the end, the expedition members voted to draw up a resolution condemning Wilson's action, but the drafting of the text opened an unhealable rift among the delegates. Ford himself, confined to his cabin with a heavy cold, was able to avoid this unpleasantness. Back home, meanwhile, there was hardly any letup to the press ridicule, fed by reports of the shipboard antics of the peace pilgrims, notably the political machinations of the manipulative Mme Schwimmer.

On the morning of December 19, after fifteen days at sea, the *Oscar II* arrived at Christiania, in the midst of the city's worst snowstorm in a decade. Upon arrival, Ford remarked ominously to Schwimmer, "I think I'd better go home to Mother"—by which he meant his wife. On December 25, the deadline he had set for getting the boys out of the trenches, Ford set sail for the United States. The man who prized publicity would long be unavailable for comment.

The Henry Ford Peace Expedition continued without Henry Ford. The delegates visited Stockholm and Copenhagen and then traveled to The Hague, where delegates from other neutral countries were waiting to take part in the peace conference. But after Ford's sensational defection, the neutral conference, such as it was, was hardly noticed. In February 1917, after spending upwards of a half million dollars in the cause of peace, Ford withdrew his support. Several months later, as the United States entered the war, Ford's factories were converted to the manufacture of war supplies.

Campus Radical

One of the seasoned pacifists who was singularly unenthusiastic about Ford's initiative was David Starr Jordan, chancellor of Stanford University, whom Ford had invited aboard his peace ship. In the wake of the fiasco, Jordan wrote privately to Jane Addams that there had never been any question whether he would accept an invitation to cross the Atlantic with a "shipload of amateurs and students." More diplomatically, he wrote to Ford that the delicate diplomacy involved in arranging a neutral conference, to which publicity is a hindrance, should have been separated from the public demonstration intended by the peace expedition, to which publicity meant everything. Serious mediation, Jordan instructed, could be achieved only by experienced diplomats, who were not to be found among the "commission of enthusiasts" aboard the *Oscar II.*

Jordan could speak about such matters with some authority. One of the giants of American education, he was an internationally renowned pacifist, having served as chief director (1910–14) of the World Peace Foundation, and president of the 1915 International Peace Congress. A graduate of Cornell's pioneer class of 1872, Jordan was an ichthyologist by training. In 1885, at age thirty-four, he was named president of Indiana University, making him the country's youngest college president. Six years later he became the founding president of Stanford, which position he filled until 1913, at which point for the next three years he occupied the newly created and largely honorary position of chancellor.

A tall man in black hat and loose-fitting clothes, Jordan was familiar throughout the land as Stanford's Grand Old Man, a kind of Tolstoy on the Farm. In his pacifist writings and speeches, Jordan the scientist emphasized war's biological costs: "War takes the best men that nations produce. It kills them off and leaves the inferior ones to perpetuate the

David Starr Jordan, 1921. (American Pictorial Collection)

Bronze bust of Jordan, by Elizabeth Norton, 1920.

race." As for war's causes, Jordan was inclined, beginning with the Spanish-American War, to see war profiteers in the shadows.

As the prospect of a general European conflict began to loom large, Jordan preached the insanity of war among the Great Powers. Like many pacifists of his day, he wrote things that within a short time would leave him open to the charge of naiveté or worse. In September 1912, in an address delivered to the Harvard Union, Jordan declared: "What shall we say of the Great War of Europe, ever threatening, ever impending, and which never comes? We shall say that it will never come. Humanly speaking, it is impossible."

When war came nonetheless, Jordan devoted considerable energy to stopping it and keeping America out of it. On the eve of Ford's expedition in November 1915, Jordan met privately with Woodrow Wilson, attempting, without success, to convince the president to arrange a conference of neutral nations. Yet his pacifism had a sharp edge (he was no "agent of human uplift"), and by the beginning of 1917, as American opinion turned solidly against Germany and in favor of America's entry into the war, a speech by David Starr Jordan, that pacifist agitator, might cause a riot, especially on a college campus.

KEEP COOL
Don't be Stampeded into War
Come to a
PEACE
MASS MEETING
Monday, 8 P.M.
APRIL 2, 1917
AT THE
Convention Hall, 5th and L Sts., N.W.
SPEAKERS
DR. DAVID STARR JORDAN, Chancellor
Stanford University, Cal.
RABBI JUDAH MAGNES, of New York
HERBERT BIGELOW, of Ohio
And other Noted Men and Women

Announcement poster for an antiwar meeting in Washington, D.C., with David Starr Jordan as the headliner. Four days later the United States entered the Great War. (David Starr Jordan Papers)

At Yale, a student audience hooted and jeered him. At Princeton, after the university president refused to make a building available for an appearance by Jordan, local opinion swung in his favor and it was arranged for him to deliver his address in a church on campus. When, however, Jordan's remarks turned critical of President Wilson, as the *Nation* described the scene, "a storm of censure burst upon him, expressing itself in hisses, and ready to proceed to further extremes but for the fact that the meeting was in a church." At the Baltimore Academy of Music, he was almost mobbed by a crowd singing "Hang David Jordan on a Sour Apple Tree!"

Although Jordan's pacifism would remain a subject of controversy, once the United States entered the war, in April 1917, Jordan the Peacemaker supported President Wilson and directed his thunder instead at the German autocracy, which put him back squarely in the American mainstream. "I abhor war and distrust its results," he wrote. "I tried to believe that we could keep out of this war. I do not believe now that it could have been done, and the President chose the right time to enter it."

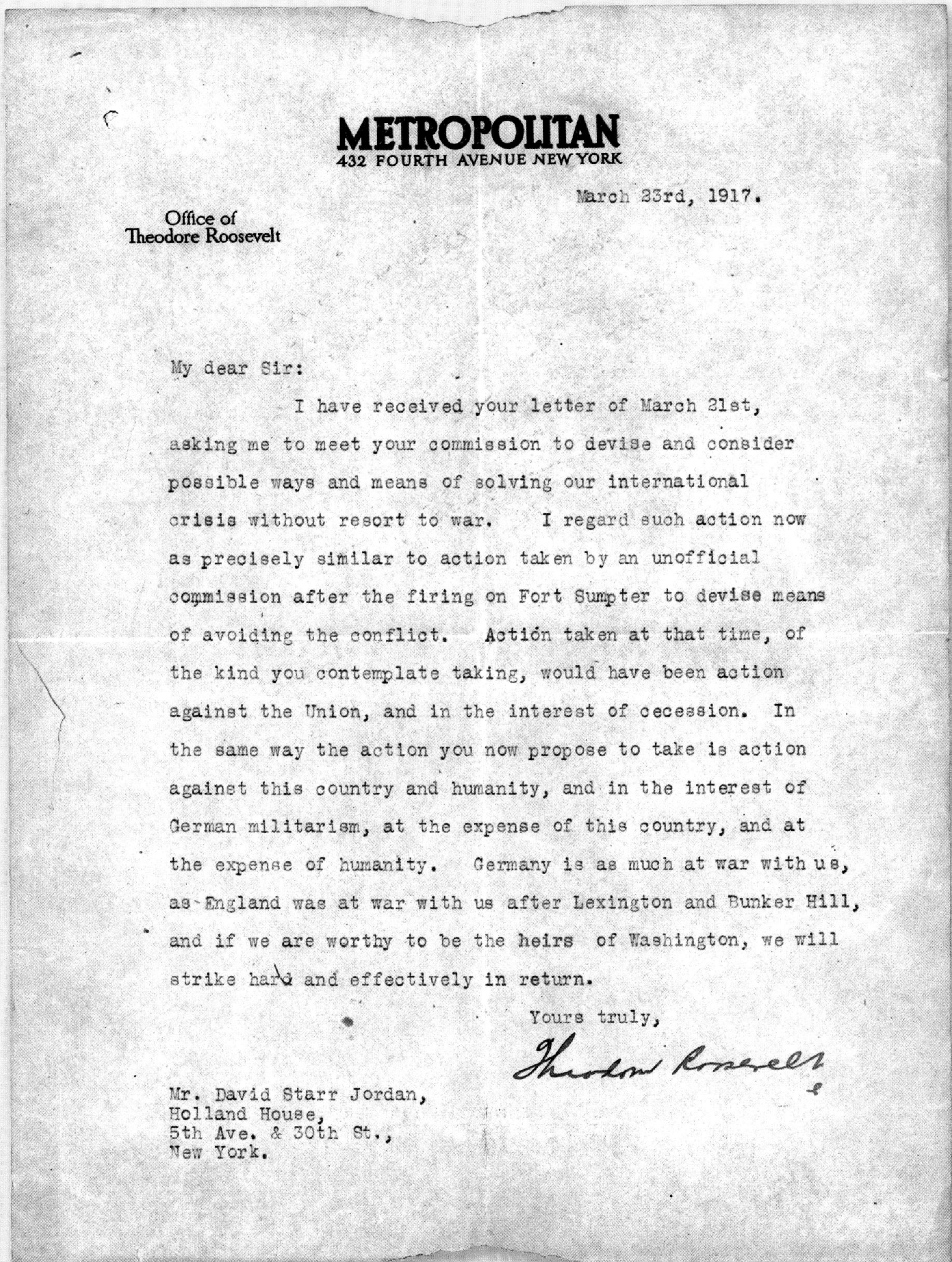

METROPOLITAN
432 FOURTH AVENUE NEW YORK

Office of
Theodore Roosevelt

March 23rd, 1917.

My dear Sir:

I have received your letter of March 21st, asking me to meet your commission to devise and consider possible ways and means of solving our international crisis without resort to war. I regard such action now as precisely similar to action taken by an unofficial commission after the firing on Fort Sumpter to devise means of avoiding the conflict. Action taken at that time, of the kind you contemplate taking, would have been action against the Union, and in the interest of cecession. In the same way the action you now propose to take is action against this country and humanity, and in the interest of German militarism, at the expense of this country, and at the expense of humanity. Germany is as much at war with us, as England was at war with us after Lexington and Bunker Hill, and if we are worthy to be the heirs of Washington, we will strike hard and effectively in return.

Yours truly,

Theodore Roosevelt

Mr. David Starr Jordan,
Holland House,
5th Ave. & 30th St.,
New York.

Letter from Theodore Roosevelt to David Starr Jordan, March 23, 1917 (David Starr Jordan Papers). On April 6, 1917, the date of America's entry into the war, Roosevelt wrote, "The whole professional pacifist movement in the United States has been really a movement in the interest of the evil militarism of Germany."

MAISON FISCHMA
WALTER BARTH BANQ

THE GREAT WAR

Belgium 1914

The German war plan, known as the Schlieffen Plan, called for a two-front war, against France and Russia. Success depended on a rapid defeat of France by means of an overwhelming attack through Belgium. Once this goal was achieved, the bulk of the German Army would be turned against Russia, which, it was assumed, would be slow to mount an attack because of its enormous size and inadequate railway network.

On August 3, Germany declared war on France; on the following day its troops poured into Belgium. Taking the route through Belgium, essential for the swift defeat of France, ensured that Great Britain, sworn by treaty to defend Belgium's neutrality, would enter the war against Germany. Britain probably would in any case have come to the defense of France, though its treaty obligations were ambiguous. The German invasion of Belgium, which outraged the British public, ensured a general European conflict.

opposite:
German troops marching into Brussels, August 1914. (Oliver B. Zimmerman Photograph)

Cathedral at Rheims. This photograph of the war's most famous ruin was taken by Captain Alexander Edouart, head of the American Red Cross motion picture service. The Cathedral at Rheims was one of the finest examples of Gothic architecture in the world until it was severely damaged early in the war by German shells. Numerous visitors to the city remarked on the deceptive appearance of the cathedral when approached from the front: the façade gave the impression that the structure, rising above the city's ruins, had come through unscathed. A closer inspection even of this photograph indicates otherwise. (Alexander F. Edouart Papers)

Total War

In his account of the First World War, historian Gordon Craig records that, "On February 10, 1916, a panic broke out along the east coast of England because of a rumor that a German Zeppelin had appeared over the resort town of Scarborough; and public indignation over this outrage was so great in the weeks that followed that the government found it expedient to appease it by creating ten home-defense squadrons of the Royal Flying Corps." Craig recalls this incident in order to illustrate the fact that the Great War was the first total war in modern history. Ordinary citizens of the combatant countries, no matter how far removed they were from the battlefields, could not count on escaping the war's hardships or even its horrors. As H. G. Wells wrote in his *A Short History of the World:*

> *The old distinction maintained in civilized warfare between the civilian and combatant population disappeared. Everyone who grew food or who sewed a garment, everyone who felled a tree or repaired a house, every railway station and every warehouse was held to be fair game for destruction.*

Most directly in harm's way were the residents of northeast France, Belgium, and Poland, and of other territories that were overrun or fought over. But new kinds of weapons brought the war home to noncombatants living outside the occupied lands and the battle zones. Among the new agents of warfare, one is associated with an airship named Zeppelin, another with a munitions works named Krupp.

The Zeppelin might not have left its mark on the First World War—and therefore on *any* war—had it not been for the perseverance of its namesake, Count Ferdinand von Zeppelin (1838–1917). In 1863, as a military observer for the King of Württemburg, Zeppelin accompanied the Union Army during the American Civil War. It was during his sojourn in the United States that he made his first and only ascent in a balloon, on August 19, 1863, in St. Paul, Minnesota, courtesy of one John Steiner, a former Union Army civilian balloonist. Whatever effect this little adventure in a tethered balloon had on him, after Brigadier General Zeppelin retired from the army in 1890 he began a quest to create giant flying "ships." When the German government rejected his proposals for a lighter-than-air flying machine, Zeppelin founded his own company to produce the airships.

Zeppelin was not alone in his pursuit. By the end of the century, others were experimenting with attaching motors and propellers onto balloons in order to travel by air. But Zeppelin's particular design, which solved the instability and unwieldiness of earlier models, put him ahead of his competitors. His first rigid, power-driven airship, the Luftschiff *Zeppelin 1*, made its initial flight in July 1900. Crashes and other setbacks followed, but

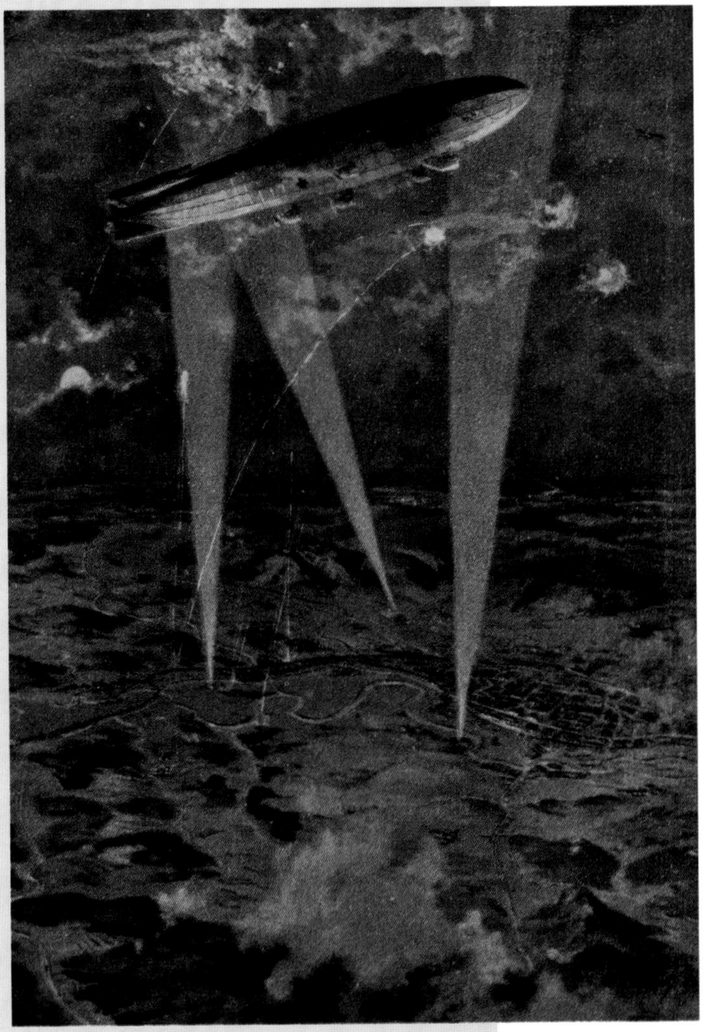

German propaganda postcards of Zeppelin attacks on (clockwise from top left) London, Antwerp, and Lunéville. (World War I Pictorial Collection)

The Hoover Archives holds thousands of such postcards, many of them inscribed by the sender, which were produced in large quantities by the European belligerents, especially Germany and France.

Zeppelin was intrepid, and soon his name became synonymous with all such German airships, no matter which company had produced them. In time, Zeppelin became a national hero. The kaiser awarded him the Prussian Order of the Black Eagle, an honor normally bestowed only on high nobility. For Germans, the Zeppelin became an icon, a source of national pride.

When war came, Germany used Zeppelins in battle and for bombing raids over cities far beyond the Western Front. As an instrument of war, the Zeppelin proved to be cumbersome and vulnerable (four were brought down by ground fire in the Battle of Verdun), and its moment as a warship in the sky was destined to be brief, but as a terror weapon it had no peer in the first years of the war. The first such episode occurred when a Zeppelin bombed the Belgian city of Liège on August 6, 1914, though it was forced to land after drawing artillery fire. The first Zeppelin attack on London took place on May 31, 1915, killing twenty-eight people and injuring sixty. England would be subject to these bombing raids until June 1917.

Late in the war, Paris experienced a unique threat in the form of the long-range Paris Gun. This supercannon, developed by the Krupp munitions works, is often incorrectly called Big Bertha, after the howitzer used with devastating effect against the Belgians at the start of the war (and, incidentally, named for the Krupp heiress). As its name implies, the Paris Gun was designed to demoralize the residents of Paris. A cannon thirty-four meters in length with a twenty-one-centimeter bore, it could fire a shell a distance of seventy-five miles, reaching a maximum altitude of more than twenty-six miles, with a flight time of some three minutes. This would be the highest altitude attained by a manmade object until Nazi Germany developed the V-2 rocket during World War II. The gun's payload (fifteen pounds) and accuracy (it could hit Paris, but not a specific target) were less impressive. Yet targeting was improved with the help of German spies serving as spotters on the ground, relaying reports by telegram through Switzerland.

At first, the weapon struck terror in the residents of Paris (who initially believed that the shells had been dropped by a high-altitude airplane), but after the initial shock Parisians adjusted to the new circumstances and their resistance hardened. A British officer sent to Paris in March 1918 to investigate wrote of the Paris Gun: "The whole enterprise savoured slightly of the 'stunt.' And in many respects it recalled the ingenuity, the scientific skill, the huge expenditure of money that was all lavished on the Zeppelin campaign against London. The latter was defeated and abandoned in favor of the cheaper and fundamentally more deadly aeroplane raid." As the accompanying photograph shows, however, the Paris Gun could achieve deadly results. From March through August 1918, three of the guns fired 351 rounds, killing 256 people and wounding 620.

Interior of the Church of St. Gervais in Paris after it was struck by a shell fired from a Paris Gun on Good Friday, March 29, 1918, killing eight-eight and injuring one hundred, most of them women and children. The devastation resulted not from the explosion of the shell, but rather from its impact, which caused part of the vaulted roof to collapse on those attending the service. (Loring Phillips Papers)

Gallipoli 1915

The most controversial military campaign of the First World War was Gallipoli, which historian John Keegan calls "one of the Great War's most terrible battles but also its only epic." The idea to force the Dardanelles, the narrow strip of water linking the Mediterranean to the Black Sea, arose when the Russian government, alarmed by the advance of the Ottoman armies into the Caucasus, appealed to the British and French to stage a diversion in order to draw off the Turks.

The proposal was eagerly taken up by the First Lord of the Admiralty, Winston Churchill, who envisioned seizing Constantinople and bringing down the Turkish government, thereby exposing the flank of Germany and Austria-Hungary and opening the sea supply lanes through the Black Sea to Russia, which could then turn the tide on the eastern front. That was the idea. In the end, what was intended as a rapid assault turned into a nightmarish reprise of the trench warfare on the western front.

"The grand advance began on 18 March," Keegan relates, "with sixteen battleships, twelve British, four French, mostly pre-Dreadnoughts, but including the battlecruiser *Inflexible* and the almost irreplaceable super-Dreadnought *Queen Elizabeth,* arrayed in three lines abreast. They were preceded by a swarm of minesweepers and accompanied by flotillas of cruisers and destroyers. Even in the long naval history of the Dardanelles, such an armada had never been seen there before." Little went according to plan, however, as mines sank three battleships and disabled three cruisers, while inflicting damage on others. The warships withdrew; the Turkish defenses held.

The problem for the attacking navy was that the mobile Turkish batteries on the heights could fire at the exposed and vulnerable minesweepers. So the decision was made to land troops on the Gallipoli peninsula in order to put the Turkish artillery out of action so that the minesweepers could clear the way for the Allied ships to sail up to Constantinople.

On April 25, British forces landed at Cape Helles, on the tip of the peninsula, yet although they made a successful landing they were unable to move up to take the heavily defended crests. Meanwhile, thirteen miles farther up the west coast of the peninsula, the Australian and New Zealand (ANZAC) forces came ashore at what would from then on become known as ANZAC Cove. They fared no better than the forces at Cape Helles, advancing only a mile and a half up steep, rugged terrain before coming under heavy fire from the Turkish defenders. By evening, there had been 2,000 Allied casualties at Cape Helles and 2,000 more at ANZAC Cove, out of a total force of 30,000 men put ashore. These numbers were now set to rise as the Turks organized their defenses and launched counterattacks. The invaders were stuck in place—and with mounting discomfort as spring turned into summer.

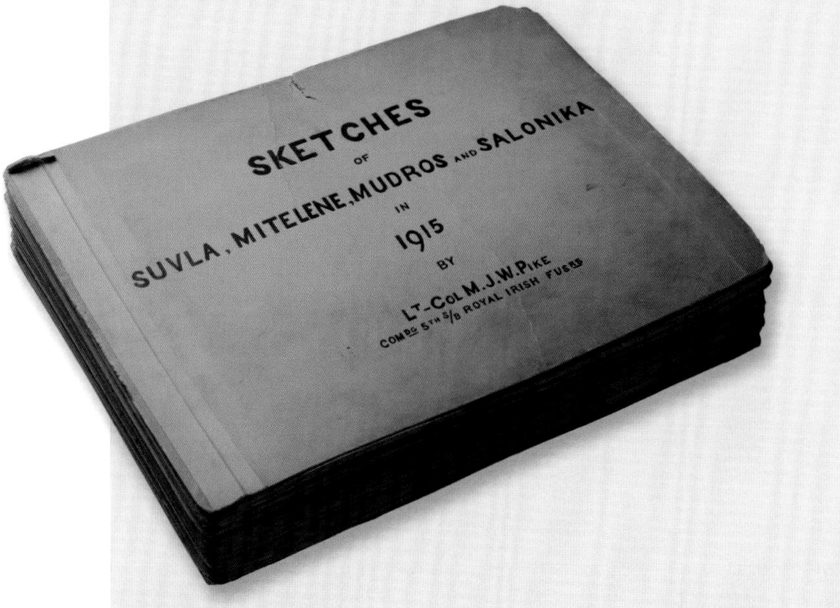

above:
Gallipoli sketchbook of Lt. Col. M.J.W. Pike, containing his own elaborate captions.

below:
Map of Suvla Bay: "This map shows the ground occupied by the troops after forcing the landing at SUVLA on Augt 7th 1915 and held until the evacuation. The high hills on the east were not held by us and only a portion of KIRITCH TEPE SIRT was in our possession. The route taken by the 31st inf[antr]y B[riga]de for the attack and capture of CHOCOLATE HILL on the day of landing is marked in blue."

Portion of a Trench. "On taking over enemy trenches, the first thing to be done is to adapt them to their new requirements. The little bit of trench here shown was the entrance to a communication trench in a part of the Turkish line that had not been completed when we took them and being enfiladed by the new line occupied by the enemy did not suit us at all. Two or three men were killed and an officer and several men wounded just round the corner of it. The line of our trenches prolonging to the right of Green hill and on the plains below can be seen. It is not a good thing to make such alterations in a line of trenches that the enemy cannot fail to notice them, it gives things away[;] consequently our end (that shown in sketch) was blocked up and the trench left as it was but MINED thus ensuring a warm welcome to any of the enemy who might try and creep up to pay a visit."

A Dugout. "The dug-out here shown was on CHOCOLATE HILL and the head quarters of one of the battalions defending that place and GREEN HILL. It was part of the original Turkish trenches and as regards to the protection which it gave against shell-fire was of but little practical use. The portion in the foreground was the commanding officer's quarters, the centre was used as the battalion head quarter mess, and the further end was occupied by the adjutant of the battalion, each portion being about 12 feet square. Roofing was made of corrugated iron, an old door, and a few sandbags covered with earth and s[c]rub for the sake of extra protection and to make it less conspicuous. It was proof against shrapnell bullets and no more while the breadth of the [dugout] rendered it liable at any time to the visit from a shell."

In August, in an attempt to break the deadlock, the British made another landing further north at Suvla Bay. Here the same scenario played out: the amphibious landing was generally successful, but the inexperienced soldiers were unable to move off the beach and seize the high ground while they had the advantage of surprise. It was on this occasion that, to the south near ANZAC Cove, successive waves of Australian soldiers were slaughtered in a fruitless attempt to divert Turkish forces away from Suvla Bay. Commanding the defenders was a young officer by the name of Mustapha Kemal. Gallipoli made him a national hero; he would go on, as Kemal Ataturk, to become the founding president of modern Turkey.

As was the case farther south, after a few days of indecisive fighting, which cost the British nearly 8,000 casualties, the British and Turkish forces at Suvla Bay hunkered down, occasionally launching costly attacks and counterattacks. The stalemate on Gallipoli dragged on for the remainder of the year until a decision was made to withdraw. Some consolation was taken from the success of the evacuation, which might have been very costly in lives. The forces at all three enclaves were removed slowly and by stealth, without alerting the Turks to the fact that a complete evacuation was under way. On January 9, 1916, the Turks discovered that the British positions at Cape Helles, ANZAC Cove, and Suvla Bay were empty.

The Gallipoli campaign had lasted eight and a half months and cost the Allies as many as 265,000 casualties, of whom some 46,000 were killed in action or died from wounds or disease. The Turks, who were less meticulous about counting their dead, probably suffered 300,000 total casualties. Yet for the Turks, Gallipoli was, as it remains, a great military victory. They had thwarted the world's greatest navy and won a victory over the world's greatest empire.

Chocolate Hill

On August 7, 1915, just as darkness was falling at Suvla Bay, British forces succeeded in capturing Hill 50 and Hill 53, which they soon renamed Green Hill and Chocolate Hill. This would be their home for the next five months—those who managed to stay alive. Among the forces that landed at Suvla Bay were two brigades of the 10th (Irish) Division, and among their number was Lt. Col. M.J.W. Pike, commander of the 5th Service Battalion, Royal Irish Fusiliers, with the 31st Infantry Brigade.

As the accompanying illustrations will testify, Pike was a sketch artist in uniform. With time on his hands during five months on Chocolate Hill (so renamed for its prevailing odor), he managed to produce some two dozen drawings. His artwork in the possession of the Hoover Archives consists of copies of drawings he made on the spot; the originals he submitted to headquarters after the campaign ended. Pike's drawings and accompanying text present a stunning contrast between the visual beauty of the surroundings and the macabre human ordeal to which they played host.

Pike tells of the severe strain on soldiers who were constantly vulnerable to shell fire ("such an awful trial to the nerves"). He describes the inhospitality of the soil (sandy near the water, stony on the hills) to the digging of trenches, which effort was in any case frustrated by inadequate supplies of sandbags, barbed wire, and wood—"in fact everything necessary for a trench if it is to be held for any length of time." Among the unpleasantries of trench life on Gallipoli were the intrusions of fleas, lice, and bugs, especially the "plague of flies," which made eating meals "a most trying and exhausting proceeding entailing terrific energy not only in the disposing of the food as quickly as possible, but in the frantic waving of the arms necessary to dispel the clouds of undesired but pressing guests."

At first glance, none of this intrudes upon the sedate landscapes and interior trench scenes Pike presents in his series of sketches. Yet there is menace and death and the stench of rotting corpses on Pike's Gallipoli. Even his text can be read between the lines, though in his final judgment on the campaign—written, in two rambling sentences, while his countrymen were still digging trenches along the western front—his bitterness is in plain view.

> *All those who fought in the abandoned Gallipoli Peninsular have left behind them many dear friends and comrades, in common with all other present survivors who have been engaged in this world conflict no matter where serving but perhaps we may be pardoned if, in our memories of the past, the many gallant deeds and loyal services done by our comrades in the Peninsular appear at first sight to such as were engaged there to have been of little or no avail and hardly to have been appreciated in the way they should have been. The description of these operations as "A legitimate war gamble" has not been considered by those engaged in them as a satisfactory explanation of their origin but it is now realized that the work done there, far from being of little use had indeed a far reaching and important effect on events as a whole, so let it rest at that.*

The Western Front

Expectations in the summer of 1914 were for a short war. No one, least of all the German General Staff, had expected or prepared for the four-year war of attrition that became the Great War. In the first weeks after the Germans launched their invasion into Belgium and France, their armies advanced with awesome speed. The German war plan, which called for fighting a two-front war one front at a time and which depended on a swift victory in the west, unfolded as it was designed.

But as the German armies extended their supply lines over hundreds of miles, they were unable to maintain the speed required to deliver France a knockout blow. Meanwhile, Russia's armies were able to mobilize more quickly than anticipated and began to push westward into East Prussia. To meet this threat, on August 26 the Germans transferred troops from along the right wing of their invading forces in France. The French army, together with a small British force, took advantage of this opening by launching an attack along the Marne River that put the Germans on the defensive. The Battle of the Marne, fought from September 3 to 12, was a decisive moment in the war.

During the weeks that followed, in what has become known as the "Race for the Sea," the sides fought a succession of indecisive short-range flanking battles until the trenches of the western front extended to the sea. As John Keegan describes, the war in the west had become deadlocked: "The prospect of any offensive, either by the Allies or the Germans, looked far away as winter fell in France at the end of 1914. A continuous line of trenches, 475 miles long, ran from the North Sea to the mountain frontier of neutral Switzerland."

opposite:

Trenches on the front in France. Stereoscopic glass slides. The Hoover Archives pictorial collection of the First World War includes several hundred high-quality slides showing battlefield and other scenes along the western front. (World War I Pictorial Collection)

DOUAUMONT TRANCHEES DE
DEPART

NIEUPORT RUINES DU
PHARE. 8748

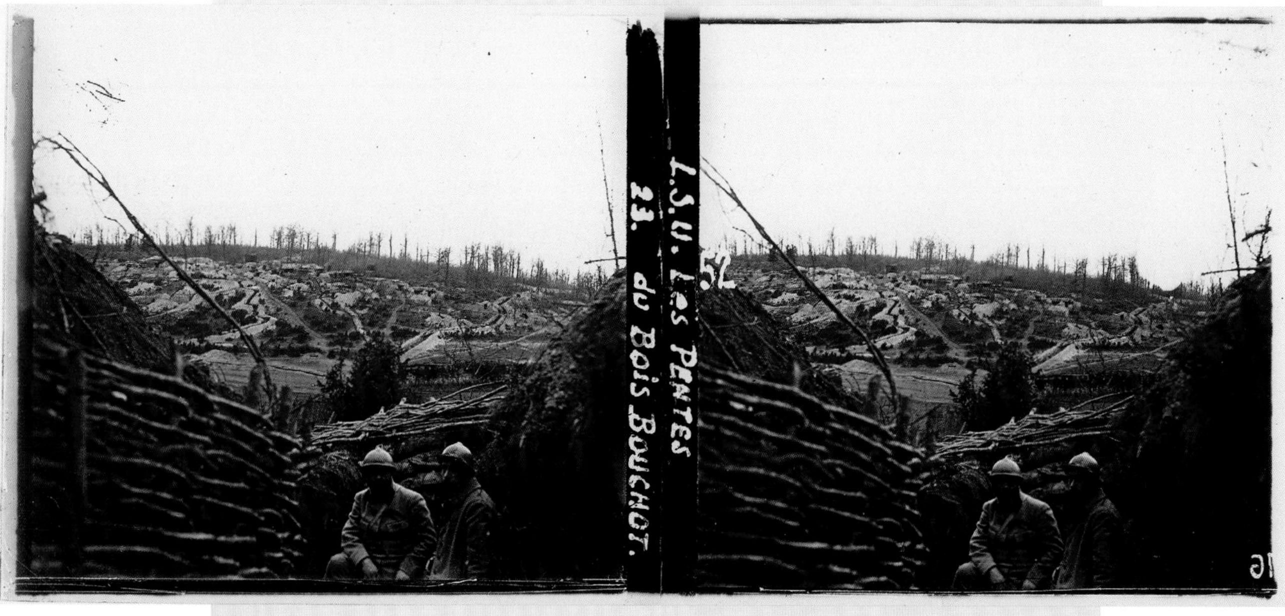
L.S.U. Les PENTES
23. du Bois BOUCHOT.

The year 1915 saw Germany, together with Austria-Hungary, concentrate its main efforts on knocking Russia out of the war, and although their forces advanced deep into the tsarist empire, decisive victory, for the moment, proved elusive. Meanwhile, the British undertook to break out of the stalemate by taking the war to Turkey, which led to the costly, demoralizing, and ultimately futile campaign at Gallipoli.

In 1916, a series of battles took place on the western front whose human toll is made all the more staggering by the indecisiveness of their outcomes. From February to August, the French defended Verdun at a cost of 350,000 casualties, to 330,000 for the Germans. From July to October, the Allied offensive along the Somme cost the Germans more than 600,000 men, while the British took more than 400,000 casualties and the French nearly 200,000—and all for a few miles of wasteland. Late in 1917, in the Battle of Passchendaele, the British would advance a distance of five miles while suffering nearly 70,000 battlefield deaths and more than 170,000 wounded, with a similar toll for the Germans. The machine gun was the infantryman's deadliest enemy, though artillery fire claimed many lives and limbs, as did bayonets and grenades in fighting at close quarters, while poison gas provided its own special brand of horror.

In March 1917, the Romanov dynasty fell, raising the prospect that the eastern front might collapse with it. Yet the formation of a Provisional Government in Petrograd raised hopes in Western capitals that a democratic Russia would prove to be a more effective military ally. The timing of these events was especially fortunate for Woodrow Wilson, who the following month would bolster his case for bringing America into Europe's war by portraying Russia as a "fit partner in a league of honour" and the war itself as a fight to "make the world safe for democracy." Yet, far from improving Russia's fighting capacity, the revolution brought only further political and economic turmoil, clearing the way for the Bolsheviks to seize power in the October Revolution. In March 1918, Lenin's government signed a separate peace with Germany.

Germany's victory in the east enabled it to bring all its force to bear to a final great offensive in the west in the spring of 1918—and just in time, because the soldiers of the American Expeditionary Force, led by Gen. John Pershing, had begun to arrive in France. Two million of them were expected by the end of 1918. The Germans needed to act before the American presence tipped the scales toward the Allies. The German armies reached their farthest point on July 15, along the Marne. At that moment there were nine American divisions in the Allied line serving in a unified Allied command under French Gen. Ferdinand Foch. Foch deployed these Americans in his successful counterattack on the Marne on July 18. The tide had now turned, and after the final Allied offensive in September in the Argonne forest, the Germans were forced to sue for peace. An armistice went into effect on November 11.

...And it was not a dream!...

Ce n'était pas un rêve.... And it was not a dream.

"Ce n'était pas un rêve!" ("And it was not a dream!") Sketch by Parisian artist Jean Jacques Berne-Bellecour (Paris, 1918) depicting the arrival of American troops under the Stars and Stripes; the soldiers walk past a young girl meant to represent France. (World War I Pictorial Collection)

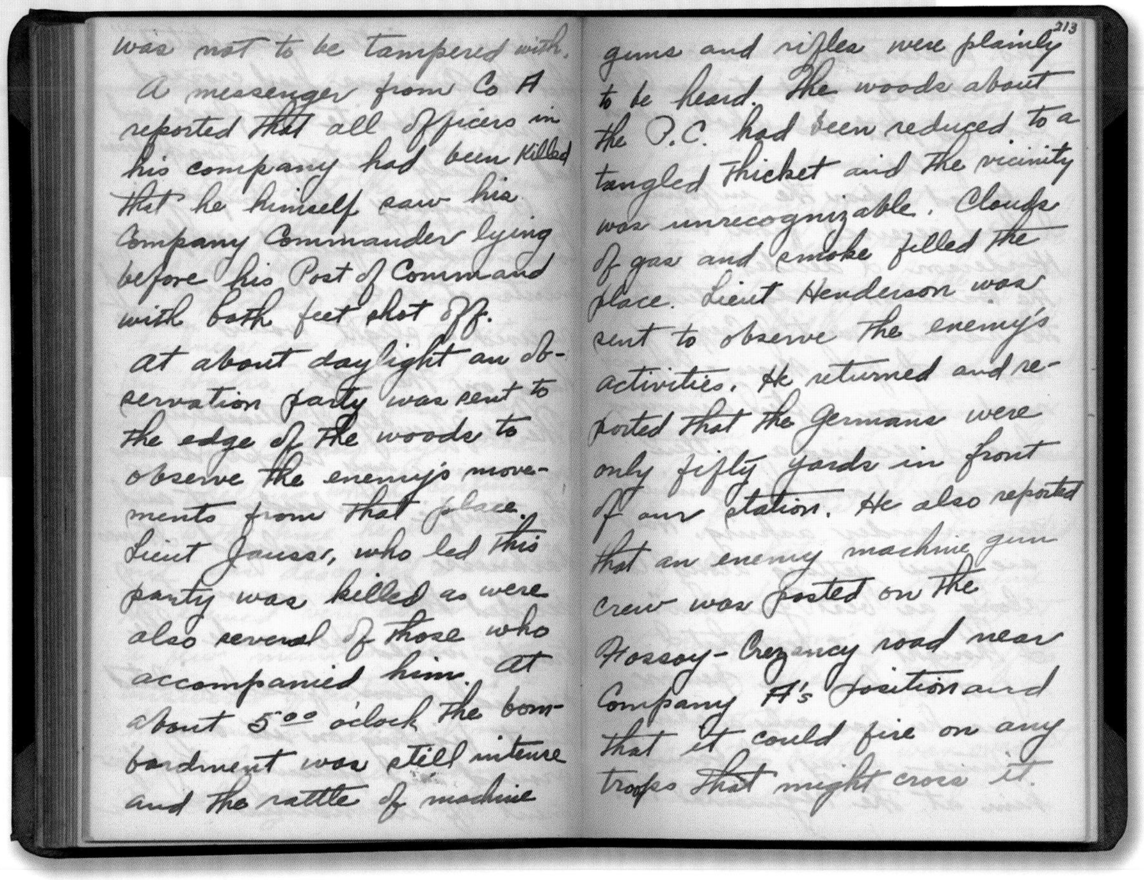
was not to be tampered with.
A messenger from Co A
reported that all officers in
his company had been killed
that he himself saw his
Company Commander lying
before his Post of Command
with both feet shot off.
At about daylight an ob-
servation party was sent to
the edge of the woods to
observe the enemy's move-
ments from that place.
Lieut Jauss, who led this
party was killed as were
also several of those who
accompanied him. At
about 5:00 o'clock the bom-
bardment was still intense
and the rattle of machine

213
guns and rifles were plainly
to be heard. The woods about
the P.C. had been reduced to a
tangled thicket and the vicinity
was unrecognizable. Clouds
of gas and smoke filled the
place. Lieut Henderson was
sent to observe the enemy's
activities. He returned and reported that the Germans were
only fifty yards in front
of our station. He also reported
that an enemy machine gun
crew was posted on the
Fossoy-Crezancy road near
Company A's position and
that it could fire on any
troops that might cross it.

The war journal of Maj. Fred Walker. Walker served with the 30th Infantry Battalion, 3rd Division, in the Marne defense of July 1918. The Germans attacked on July 15, but their advance was thwarted, and they were forced to withdraw back across the river. For his role in this battle, Walker was awarded the Distinguished Service Cross for extraordinary heroism. According to the citation, Walker's battalion faced the main thrust of the German attack along a sector of the Marne front, yet managed to inflict great losses on the German troops as they came across the river. "Those who succeeded in crossing were thrown in such confusion that they were unable to follow the barrage; and, through the effective leadership of this officer, no Germans remained in his sector south of the river at the end of the day's action." This passage from Walker's journal, written not long after the battle, captures the terrifying confusion and horrific violence in the midst of the battle. Wounded in action on July 21, 1918, Walker received the Purple Heart. (Fred Walker Papers)

The total number of military deaths in the Great War is estimated at nearly ten million. A remarkable fact about the final stage of the conflict is how the entry of the United States proved decisive even though America's time on the battlefield was relatively brief (four months) and its casualties relatively few. Some 50,000 Americans were killed in battle, and another 60,000 died of disease; of the latter, as many as 25,000 soldiers in the American army died from influenza, a worldwide epidemic that took half a million American lives overall. The total number of American casualties was 330,000. As historians point out, these American losses are smaller than those suffered by their allies in individual battles such as Verdun, the Somme, and Passchendaele. Yet the arrival of America's doughboys at the front, after the sides had fought themselves to exhaustion, quickly made the difference.

Louis Raemaekers: The Biting Cartoonist

Louis Raemaekers was the Great Cartoonist of the Great War. His name is not as well remembered as those of the great statesmen and generals, but in those years Raemaekers enjoyed wide popularity and, more to the point, enormous influence. His obituary in the London *Times*, published in August 1956, which must have raised eyebrows among younger readers, ranked him among the greats: "There were a dozen or so people—Emperors, Kings, statesmen, and commanders-in-chief—who obviously, and notoriously, shaped policies and guided events. Outside that circle of the great, Louis Raemaekers stands conspicuous as the one man who, without any assistance of title or office, indubitably swayed the destinies of peoples."

Raemaekers had been a political cartoonist and caricaturist on the staff of the Amsterdam *Telegraaf* since 1907, unknown outside his country until the outbreak of the war inspired him to create the wickedly anti-German cartoons that would make him famous. In the early months of the conflict, when Raemaekers's influence was confined to neutral Holland, it took courage for the editors of *De Telegraaf* to resist German pressure to suppress his work. Gradually, his drawings attracted the attention of newspaper editors in other countries, and by early 1915 albums reproducing his first wartime cartoons made their way into the Allied and neutral countries of Europe.

Raemaekers's breakthrough came in December 1915, when an exhibition of his work in London produced a sensation, drawing large crowds, even well into the Christmas season when it was assumed that Londoners would prefer to block out the war and the Germans. In January the exhibition moved to Paris, where it was received with equal enthusiasm. In 1917, Raemaekers toured America, drawing cartoons for various newspapers; with the United States going to war, he was treated as something of a hero. By the end of 1917 Raemaekers had published more than a thousand cartoons, reproduced in hundreds of newspapers on both sides of the Atlantic.

Kaiser Wilhelm, General von Hindenburg, and an assortment of menacing German officers in spiked helmets were Raemaekers's favorite victims. Should anyone question the acutely anti-German content of his cartoons, Raemaekers liked to point out that his mother was German. He drew his inspiration mainly from the newspapers, but he had several opportunities to observe his subject firsthand, slipping into occupied Belgium to look and listen for himself.

Seldom a week went by during the course of the war when Raemaekers did not produce at least four cartoons for the newspapers, in addition to the large number of drawings he made for posters and programs used for charitable purposes as part of the war effort. What is remarkable, considering this output, is that his work sustained its high quality

"The Widows of Belgium"

through the end of the war, and that the drawings he produced in the second half of 1918 were considered to be among the finest he ever produced.

The Raemaekers collection at the Hoover Institution, acquired in 1944, includes hundreds of original drawings, consisting mostly of his bitingly satirical cartoons, including later works sending up Hitler, Mussolini, and Stalin. During the war he made frequent trips to the French front; the collection contains numerous rough sketches made during these visits. His papers, especially his personal correspondence, testify to his outsize celebrity and the attention he received from statesmen such as Winston Churchill, Woodrow Wilson, Theodore Roosevelt, and David Lloyd George.

After the war Raemaekers moved to Belgium (perhaps because the kaiser was allowed to take refuge in Holland) and used his art to champion the League of Nations and, beginning a decade later, sound the alarm against German fascism. Not long after the Nazis came to power in Germany, he emigrated to the United States, where he was a regular contributor of cartoons for the New York *Herald Tribune* and the afternoon tabloid *PM.* His glory days had ended long before, when the Germans surrendered to the Allies, and the kaiser fled Berlin.

"Seduction: 'Ain't I a lovable fellow?' "

The "Big Four" negotiators at the Paris Peace Conference: from left to right, David Lloyd George, Vittorio Orlando, Georges Clemenceau, and Woodrow Wilson. (George E. Stone Papers)

Herbert Hoover in his Paris office, 1919. The peace activist Jane Addams, who as an associate of the Food Administration visited Paris during the Armistice, wrote after her return to the United States, "Mr. Hoover's office seemed to be the one reasonable spot in the midst of the widespread confusion; the great maps upon the wall recorded the available food resources and indicated fleets of ships carrying wheat from Australia to Finland or corn from the port of New York to Fiume." (World War I Pictorial Collection)

PEACE AND BREAD

As the guns of war fell silent, all attention seemed to focus on the American president, Woodrow Wilson. When the Armistice was signed in November 1918, Wilson announced that he would go to Paris to negotiate the peace. He reached Europe in January 1919, and huge throngs of enthusiasts greeted him in several cities, capped by an extraordinary outpouring of public acclaim and emotion upon his arrival in Paris.

Wilson had captured the popular imagination in January 1918 with the announcement of his Fourteen Points, which called for a new world of openness, freedom, and permanent peace. They demanded an end to secret treaties and secret diplomacy in favor of "open covenants openly arrived at," freedom of the seas, free trade, arms reductions, the "impartial adjustment of all colonial claims," the withdrawal of armies of occupation, and the self-determination of nations, which entailed redrawing the internal boundaries of Europe along national lines. The fourteenth point called for the formation of "a general association of nations," a permanent international body devoted to preserving peace. Wilson had persuaded the Allies to agree that the Fourteen Points would serve as the basis of the peace talks; yet, as events in Paris would demonstrate, this was no guarantee that his lofty principles would actually shape the peace treaty.

Historians have tended to be harsh on the negotiators at Paris, not least on the author of the Fourteen Points. Two aspects of the talks, and of the treaty, are invariably subject to the closest scrutiny. The first is the principle of self-determination, which prescribed that each European people or nation, as defined by language, should be able to establish its own sovereign nation-state. This was inspired by the twin assumptions that nationalism was a natural counterpart of democracy and that national self-determination in practice would remove a fundamental cause of past European wars. In this case, the power of principle was encouraged by the force of events, as the Russian, Austro-Hungarian, and Ottoman empires had collapsed under the strain of war and their component parts were now struggling to sort themselves out.

To Wilson's dismay, however, self-determination turned out to be very complicated to put into practice: ethnonational groups in Central and Southeastern Europe were intermixed and remained so even after the peacemakers created seven new "nation-states." Perfect separation would have required the physical relocation of millions of people. In any case, the peacemakers were not prepared to treat all nations equally: for example, one-third of all Hungarians ended up residing outside the new state of Hungary. So the potential problem of ethnonational irredentism was not resolved once and for all at Paris, but merely shifted down to the next level. In these highly imperfect arrangements historians have identified the seeds of the next European conflagration.

A more immediate disappointment for Wilson was the fate of his League of Nations, the project closest to his heart and the one with which he will forever be most closely identified. Only the establishment of an international body like the league, he believed, could keep the world truly safe for democracy. Wilson's enthusiasm was not shared by all of his fellow peacemakers at Paris, including his key partners, the British and the French. Georges Clemenceau, the French premier, famously remarked of Wilson's points that even Almighty God had issued only ten commandments. The result was that although Wilson succeeded in having the League's "covenant" written into the Treaty of Versailles, the concessions he had to make in order to achieve this compromised the idealism of the Fourteen Points.

The terms set by the victors on defeated Germany—reparations payments, partial military occupation, the infamous "war guilt" clause—were harsh, even humiliating. Wilson had promised a just peace unlike any before it, one that would serve as the foundation for the new world order he envisioned. The Treaty of Versailles was greeted with bitter disillusionment by the American public, especially Wilson's liberal supporters. Meanwhile, Wilson's league met with stiff opposition from Republican isolationists on Capitol Hill. These circumstances, plus party politics and the physical exhaustion and obduracy of the president, led the Senate to reject Wilson's treaty by a narrow margin, which prevented the United States from joining the League of Nations.

The shortsightedness of the peacemakers in 1919 is standard fare in history textbooks, which tend to draw a straight line from Versailles through the rise of a revanchist Germany to the outbreak of the Second World War. This kind of historical determinism not only simplifies the storyteller's job; it relieves the interwar statesmen and nations of responsibility for how the story turned out. The fact that peace had any kind of chance at all after 1919 was due in no small measure to a different dimension of America's postwar diplomacy, no less important than Wilson's moderating role at the peace conference, and one that the textbooks almost always overlook: namely, the vital role of American food relief, which sped Europe's economic recovery and stabilized its politics. The importance of this American contribution was recognized at the time by all Europeans, even if some of their statesmen were resentful of it, especially of the muscularly American way the food relief was administered.

The responsibility for Europe's economic recovery, which began even before the peace talks got under way and continued well after they concluded, belonged to another American statesman in Paris, Herbert Hoover. Hoover had achieved international recognition at the start of the war when he organized the relief of German-occupied Belgium, and later as head of the U.S. Food Administration, which was charged with sustaining the allied war

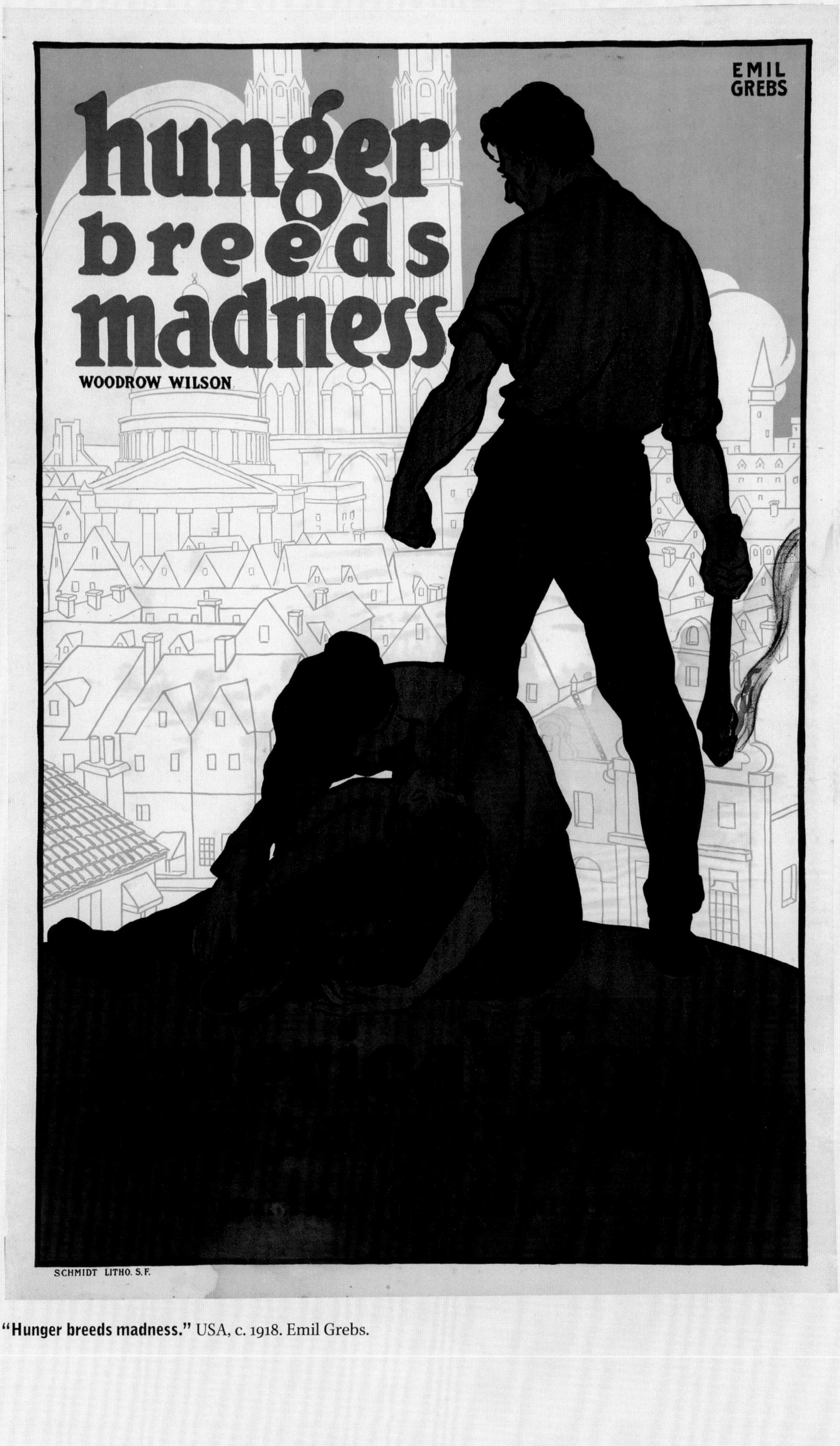

"Hunger breeds madness." USA, c. 1918. Emil Grebs.

American food relief operations were established in 1919 in twenty-two countries in Europe and the Near East. (American Relief Administration, European Operations Records)

Cup made from emptied can of condensed milk, a staple of American food relief to Europe after the First World War. Many such cans were used as drinking cups for years after the war.

effort. In wartime America, the verb "to Hooverize" just about became synonymous with "economize," as the public was urged to conserve food supplies as a contribution to the war effort. "Food Will Win the War" was the most popular hortatory slogan of Hoover's Food Administration during the war. Now its job was to win the peace.

In Paris, Hoover became something like the food administrator for the world. During the nine months following the Armistice, he organized the distribution of more than $1 billion in relief, which translates into more than four million tons of food and other supplies delivered to children and adults across Europe, all the way to the inconstant borders of Bolshevik Russia. Hoover wore many administrative hats in Paris, but the principal agency of American assistance was the American Relief Administration (ARA), staffed by some 1,500 demobilized U.S. Army and Navy officers. In 1919 Hoover converted the ARA into a quasi-private relief organization. Over the next four years—often in conjunction with other private American relief organizations—it would distribute several hundreds of millions of dollars in food and medicine to twenty-two countries in Europe and the Near East. The ARA's largest undertaking was its final operation: a two-year rescue mission to Soviet Russia to fight the Great Famine of 1921.

Much like its post–World War II successor, the Marshall Plan, American aid as orchestrated by Hoover was inspired by a combination of interrelated motives. The most apparent was humanitarianism, which was by then becoming a peculiarly American vocation. Central as well was a concern to accelerate the economic and political reconstruction of Europe, not least in order to revive the market for U.S. goods. Less elevated, but not inconsiderable, was the desire to unload America's huge agricultural surpluses, whose accumulation was largely attributable to the successful policies of Food Administrator Hoover. Inseparable from these considerations, and suffusing the distribution of food aid with a crusading spirit, was a determination, as Hoover phrased it, "to stem the tide of Bolshevism."

The common perception of the day—certainly among Wilson and the peacemakers in Paris—was that Bolshevism was the product of anarchy, the handmaiden of hunger. It had taken power in Russia, had briefly controlled Budapest in 1919, and was threatening the stability of Germany, Austria, and all the rest of Central Europe. The cure for the "disease of Bolshevism" was food, and the United States was the one country that could deliver it. In the months before the peace treaty was signed, Hoover's urgent insistence on the importance of extending food relief to the "enemy nations," principally Germany, ran into opposition from the French and the British, as well as congressmen and senators back home. But Hoover found ways to make sure that food got through. Whatever the ultimate verdict historians render on the diplomacy that produced the Treaty of Versailles, by 1920 it was generally assumed on both sides of the Atlantic that American food had kept the postwar crisis in Central Europe from sliding into anarchy and had given the Peace of Paris a chance.

1917г.
Царское Село.
Моя горячо любимая
Мама,
Какъ давно
не
1911

Chapter Two

REVOLUTIONS

Among all the upheavals of the twentieth century documented in the Hoover Institution Archives and Library, the revolutions in Russia and China stand out. The materials on the 1917 Russian Revolution are, taken together, the Hoover's greatest single documentary resource. These materials cover the Russian Revolution broadly understood, from its roots in the nineteenth century—the Hoover holds an original copy of the 1848 *Communist Manifesto* by Karl Marx and Friedrich Engels—through the tumultuous events of 1917 and of the Civil War and the Great Famine that followed. One of the notable features of these records is the role played in their preservation by émigrés from Russia, some of whom were exiled by the Revolution.

By comparison with the Russian experience, the Chinese revolutions of 1911, which saw the overthrow of the Manchu dynasty, and 1949, which marked the ascent to power of Mao Zedong's Communists, feel like one long revolution played out in slow motion. China did not have a stable ruling government after the declaration of a republic in 1911. Instead there was internal fragmentation, a prolonged and bloody war with Japan, and civil war. Only in 1949 was mainland China united politically, under Communist rule. Most of the Hoover Institution's key collections on China, in striking contrast to those on Russia, were brought together by Americans who were themselves actors in the historic events they helped document.

THE RUSSIAN REVOLUTION

The Last Tsar

In March 1917, the Romanov dynasty collapsed unexpectedly and with little bloodshed. This event is remembered as the February Revolution because it fell within that month according to the Russian calendar at the time, which was thirteen days behind that of the West. The Revolution began with workers' protests against food shortages, which then turned into industrial strikes and escalated into mass political demonstrations against the war and the autocracy. Soldiers began to kill their officers and mutiny. The refusal of the Petrograd garrison to fire on crowds of protesters signaled the end of imperial authority. Tsar Nicholas II, returning to the capital from his personal command of Russia's crumbling war effort at the front, was pressed to abdicate, which he did in favor of his brother, who refused the throne. Quite suddenly Russia was no longer an absolute monarchy.

Particular documents in the Hoover Archives allow one to get right up close to the fall of the Romanovs, as a handful of individuals scramble to stay ahead of events. One of those men was Nicolas de Basily, who drafted the text of the tsar's act of abdication. He preserved his abdication drafts and other, related documents and left behind a memoir of those fateful days. They provide a fascinating account of the agonizing and calculating that went on behind the scenes as de Basily and his colleagues maneuvered to save the Russian monarchy, and with it the Russian empire, from collapse.

At the time of the February Revolution, de Basily was chief of the diplomatic chancellery at the imperial army headquarters at Mogilev. Nicholas had departed headquarters by train to join his family at Tsarskoe Selo, the royal palace near Petrograd, but his train was diverted to Pskov when his safety could not be guaranteed because of the presence along the route of hostile troops. On March 14, Gen. Mikhail V. Alekseev, chief of staff of the High Command of the Russian Army in Mogilev, on the basis of information received from Petrograd about the progress of the revolution in that city and in Moscow, decided to appeal to the emperor for the appointment of a government responsible to the legislative bodies, in particular the lower house, the Duma.

As General Alekseev showed de Basily the draft of his telegram to Nicholas, they decided that with it should be forwarded the text of a manifesto from the emperor to the people of Russia announcing his decision. The hope was that, just as during the Revolution of 1905, when the autocracy took the steam out of the revolution by issuing a manifesto that led to the creation of the Duma, the announcement now of a similar manifesto, one offering more significant concessions, would be enough to turn the tide. At General Alekseev's behest, de Basily drafted the imperial manifesto, which was telegraphed to Pskov, where the tsar's train arrived at seven on the evening of March 14. The emperor accepted the solution proposed by General Alekseev and signed the manifesto at about 2:00 A.M. on March 15.

Events during that night preempted the publication of the manifesto, however. The news from Petrograd told of large street demonstrations against the war and the autocracy, and everywhere troops were declaring allegiance to the Duma and the people. There were growing demands that the tsar abdicate in favor of his son, the hemophiliac Alexei, with the tsar's brother, the Grand Duke Michael [Mikhail], serving as regent.

When General Alekseev learned of this ominous drift of events, he consulted with de Basily, a lawyer by training, as to the constitutional protocol for the monarch's abdication. As de Basily later recalled, he had to use a bit of finesse in order to provide a legal justification for the desired solution:

> *I consulted the lawbooks to refresh my memory and immediately drew up the brief the general had requested. I explained that the Fundamental Laws of the Empire did not foresee the abandonment of power by a reigning monarch; however these laws did authorize members of the imperial family so desiring to renounce their rights of succession in expectation of a situation whereby they might be called upon to ascend the throne. There was no reason to refuse that right of renunciation to a member of the reigning family already invested with power.*

There was no ambiguity regarding the line of succession, however: if the reigning monarch had a male heir or heirs, the eldest son, no matter what age, was the legal successor to the throne. "Thus Nicholas II could legally abdicate only in favor of his legitimate heir, his young son Alexei. Since the latter was then only twelve and a half years old, a regency would be required until he reached majority."

The law having been clarified, de Basily's principal challenge, as he sat down to compose the abdication statement, was to provide the document with an appropriately poised and dignified tone and context. The first drafts were written on telegram blanks and other scraps of paper. To de Basily's fifth draft General Alekseev contributed some minor editing, including an introductory sentence that coupled Russia's revolution with its war for survival: "In these days of great struggle with the external foe, who has been striving for almost three years to enslave our native land, it has been God's will to visit upon Russia a new grievous trial." The tsar's abdication was presented as a selfless gesture on the part of the sovereign to unite his people against the foreign nemesis. The final draft was telegraphed to the tsar aboard his train in Pskov, and he signed it shortly before midnight on March 15.

Back at army headquarters, Basily recalls the agonizing wait that continued into the night, until, "Toward half past one in the morning—it was the night of March 15–16—we

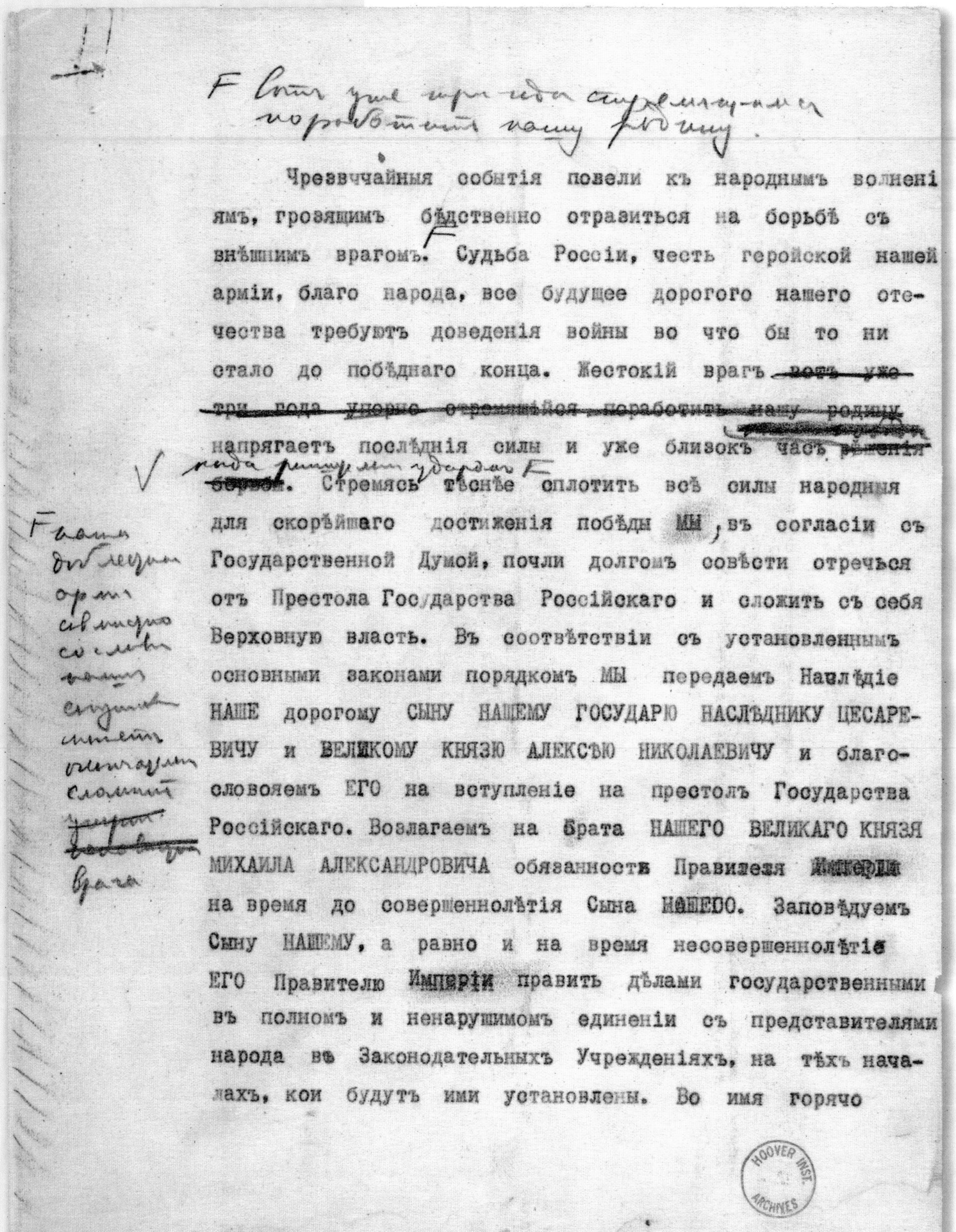

Чрезвычайныя событія повели къ народнымъ волненіямъ, грозящимъ бѣдственно отразиться на борьбѣ съ внѣшнимъ врагомъ. Судьба Россіи, честь геройской нашей арміи, благо народа, все будущее дорогого нашего отечества требуютъ доведенія войны во что бы то ни стало до побѣднаго конца. Жестокій врагъ ~~вотъ уже три года упорно стремящійся поработить нашу родину~~ напрягаетъ послѣднія силы и уже близокъ часъ ~~рѣшенія борьбы~~. Стремясь тѣснѣе сплотить всѣ силы народныя для скорѣйшаго достиженія побѣды МЫ, въ согласіи съ Государственной Думой, почли долгомъ совѣсти отречься отъ Престола Государства Россійскаго и сложить съ себя Верховную власть. Въ соотвѣтствіи съ установленнымъ основными законами порядкомъ МЫ передаемъ Наслѣдіе НАШЕ дорогому СЫНУ НАШЕМУ ГОСУДАРЮ НАСЛѢДНИКУ ЦЕСАРЕВИЧУ и ВЕЛИКОМУ КНЯЗЮ АЛЕКСѢЮ НИКОЛАЕВИЧУ и благословляемъ ЕГО на вступленіе на престолъ Государства Россійскаго. Возлагаемъ на Брата НАШЕГО ВЕЛИКАГО КНЯЗЯ МИХАИЛА АЛЕКСАНДРОВИЧА обязанности Правителя Имперіи на время до совершеннолѣтія Сына НАШЕГО. Заповѣдуемъ Сыну НАШЕМУ, а равно и на время несовершеннолѣтія ЕГО Правителю Имперіи править дѣлами государственными въ полномъ и ненарушимомъ единеніи съ представителями народа въ Законодательныхъ Учрежденіяхъ, на тѣхъ началахъ, кои будутъ ими установлены. Во имя горячо

Tsar Nicholas II's abdication letter, draft no. 5. The handwritten changes made by General Alekseev, together with an introductory sentence he contributed, were incorporated into this version, which was retyped and became the final draft of the act of abdication, until Nicholas altered it. This draft has the tsar ceding the throne to his son, with his brother Michael as regent (the words in capital letters denote their names and titles); instead, the tsar abdicated in favor of his brother. The various drafts were retained by de Basily and, after his death in 1963, were donated by his widow to the Hoover Institution. (Nikolai Aleksandrovich Bazili Papers) were advised that a communication would be transmitted from Pskov. We rushed to the telegraph. My eyes never left the ribbon of paper covered with Russian print emerging from the machine. I immediately recognized my text of the abdication manifesto. At first I saw no change, then suddenly I was stupefied to see that the name of the Emperor's son, the young Alexei, had been replaced by that of the Grand Duke Mikhail, brother of Nicholas II. . . . The abdication of Nicholas II in favor of his brother instead of his son was a crushing blow indeed."

Nicholas II and his son, Alexei. (Nikolai Aleksandrovich Bazili Papers)

As it happened, when Nicholas was told that he might have to leave his son behind in Russia and live in exile, he decided to alter the abdication text and name his ineffectual younger brother, the Grand Duke Michael, as his successor. De Basily's stupefaction was shared by the Duma leaders who had come to Pskov from Petrograd to urge the tsar to abdicate. Legal questions aside, they understood that the only chance to retain the monarchy and arrest the revolution was to place Alexei, an innocent child, on the throne. Announcing the Grand Duke Michael's accession, far from calming the situation, would inflame the army and the public. In the event, when the Duma leaders informed Michael that his safety could not be ensured, the newly designated tsar renounced the throne. The 300-year reign of the Romanovs had come to an abrupt end. Territories attached to the Russian Empire through the person of the tsar soon began to declare their independence.

Perhaps Russia's descent into anarchy in 1917 would have continued even had the tsar had the good sense, and the emotional fortitude, to cede the throne to his son. Whatever the case, his little bit of editing sealed the fate of a dynasty and an empire. De Basily's fascinating personal testimony does not end with the abdication. On the afternoon of March 16, General Alekseev requested that he go to meet the imperial train, on its way to Mogilev from Pskov, in order to brief the former emperor in person on the latest events in Petrograd. De Basily carried with him a small notebook bound in black leather, in which he had kept detailed notes of the communications received and sent by headquarters since the beginning of the Revolution. At about six that evening, boarding the imperial train at a little station along the route, he met privately with the tsar. "Referring to the notes in my small notebook, I summed up for him, as briefly as possible, the news that had reached us during the last few days describing a situation that was becoming more and more desperate. Everything was collapsing. The capital had refused to accept the succession of the Grand Duke Mikhail to the throne. The dynasty was in danger of falling; the country was adrift."

Later in the evening, at a somber dinner aboard the train with the tsar and his entourage, de Basily answered the questions of his dinner companions about the latest events in Petrograd. There was naturally a great deal of curiosity as to the composition of the Provisional Government, the interim ruling body selected from among the leading figures of the Duma, and de Basily had made a list of the new cabinet of ministers. "The Emperor paid attention to our discourse, and we passed to him my little black notebook in which he read the names of the members of the Provisional Government. He questioned me about them, particularly those he had not met or about whom he desired to be better informed."

The Provisional Government was supposed to hold power until a constituent assembly of nationally and democratically elected delegates could meet and draw up a constitution. However, further revolutionary events intervened to spoil this scenario. The Provisional Government, its authority challenged from the start by a rival body, the Soviet of Workers' and Soldiers' Deputies in Petrograd, steadily squandered its legitimacy in a series of increasingly leftward-leaning cabinets, each in turn undermined by its failure to reverse the Russian army's fortunes at the front and to manage the economic distress related to the prosecution of the war, especially a deepening food crisis. Workers and soldiers became increasingly radicalized as Russian politics as a whole slid to the left.

Lenin's Bolsheviks capitalized on this chaos and took power, in the name of the Soviet, in what would become known in the Soviet Union as the Great October Socialist Revolution. Eight months later, on July 17, 1918, at their place of internal exile near the Ural Mountains, the tsar, his wife, and their children, along with their servants, were murdered on orders of the local Bolsheviks. The road back was now sealed off.

Russian troops posing in the snowy streets in Petrograd during the February Revolution of 1917. (Russian Pictorial Collection)

Members of the Russian Provisional Government, March 1917. (Russian Pictorial Collection)

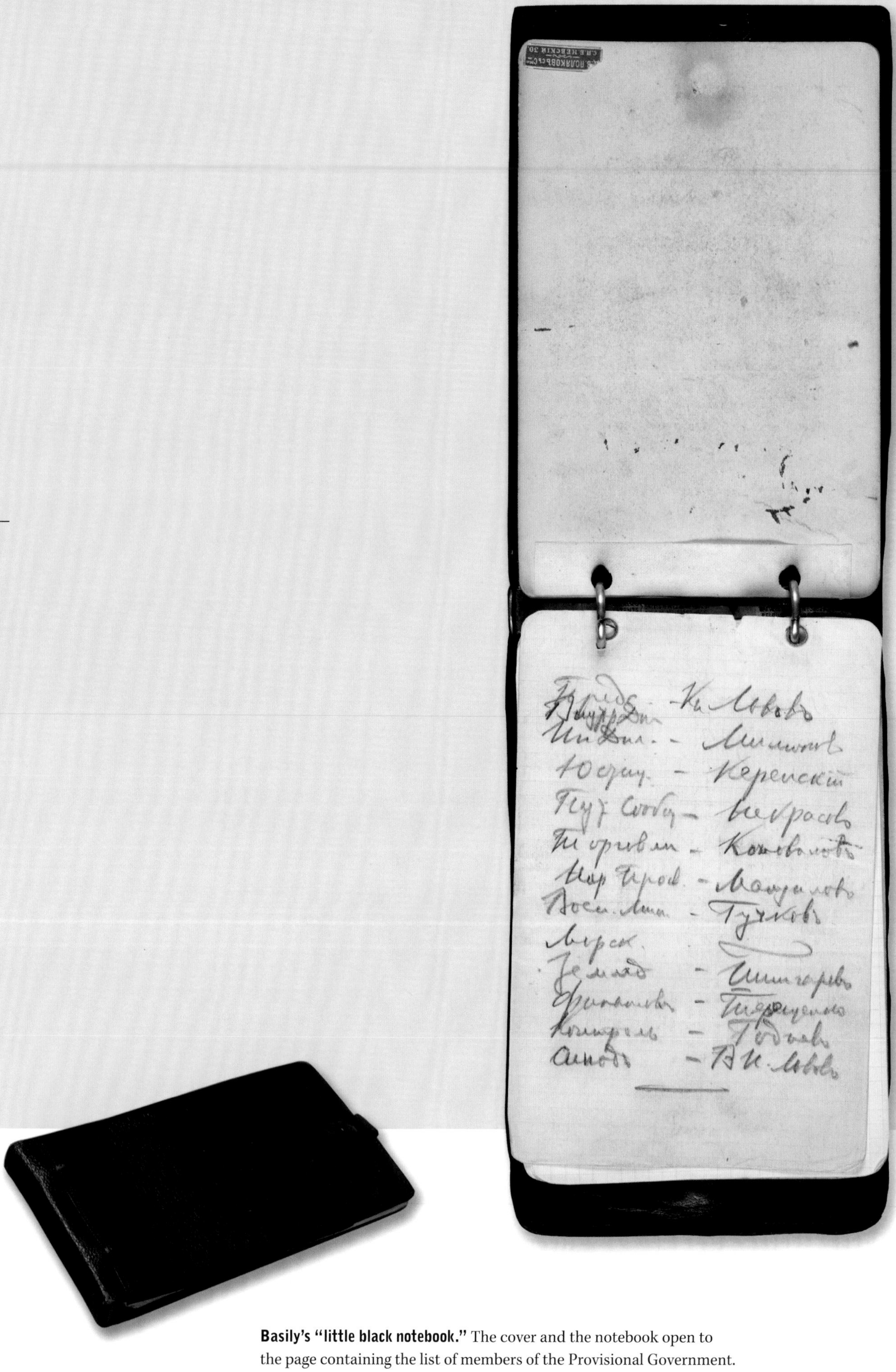

Basily's "little black notebook." The cover and the notebook open to the page containing the list of members of the Provisional Government. (Nikolai Aleksandrovich Bazili Papers)

The Truth About *Pravda*

In 1917, the new Soviet regime declared itself to be the "dictatorship of the proletariat." In fact what emerged was the dictatorship of a single party, as Lenin's Bolsheviks moved to suppress their political rivals and consolidate power. By 1922, the members of all political parties and groupings had fled the country, been driven into exile, or, if they remained in Soviet Russia, one way or another been silenced. The Mensheviks, archrivals of the Bolsheviks, ended up haunting the very same cafés in the capitals of Central Europe—Berlin, Prague, Vienna—where they once debated ideological and organizational questions with their former comrades who now ruled Russia.

Once upon a time, at the start of the twentieth century, the Bolsheviks and Mensheviks all belonged to the Russian Social Democratic Workers' Party, most of whose leaders were veterans of tsarist prison and internal exile before their escape to Europe and the life of the political émigré. At one of the Social Democrats' contentious congresses, which met in Brussels and then London in the summer of 1903, the delegates had a falling out over revolutionary strategy and tactics, as a faction around Vladimir Lenin desired to make the party more selective in its membership and more conspiratorial in its methods. An initial vote gave Lenin's faction a majority and thus its name, "bolshevik," or "majoritarian." Many historians of the revolutionary movement have found it telling, if not bizarre, that the faction that lost this vote—the "mensheviks," or "minoritarians"—chose to retain this designation even though soon afterward they commanded a majority within the party.

In any case, the story of the road to October 1917 is often cast as the triumph of the Bolsheviks' tough, uncompromising revolutionary politics against the Mensheviks' milder, more "European" brand. Yet the divorce was not final in 1903, and there were repeated attempts to bring the two groups together. One who tried to play the role of matchmaker was Leon [Lev] Trotsky, who had originally sided with the Mensheviks before striking out on his own. Eventually, in the heady days of 1917, he would join forces with Lenin, but in the meantime he frequently clashed with the Bolshevik leader and his comrades in polemical battles whose details would be resurrected by Trotsky's rivals in the power struggle after Lenin's death.

One of these disputes involved the origins of *Pravda* (Truth), that most famous of Communist newspapers. The official Soviet histories credited Lenin and the Bolsheviks with launching *Pravda,* in 1912. Not surprisingly, the truth is more complicated.

The *Pravda* in question in fact originated in 1905 as a modest publication put out by a minor Ukrainian Menshevik group called Spilka. In 1908, the publishers were running low on funds and proposed to Trotsky, then living in Vienna, that he take it over. The first issue under his editorship appeared in October 1908, published in Lvov, in Austrian Galicia. This and the next few issues that he edited still carried the Spilka name on the masthead; but at the end of 1908 that group disbanded and left Trotsky as *Pravda*'s sole owner. In November 1909, with its sixth issue, it was transferred to Vienna.

Trotsky's paper would later be remembered as "Viennese *Pravda*," which might mislead one to think that its target readership sat in the crowded coffee houses of the Habsburg capital. In fact, *Pravda* was produced primarily for illegal circulation inside Russia. Arranging for its transportation clandestinely into Russia greatly added to the cost of publication, and because Trotsky had trouble raising the necessary funds only five issues of *Pravda* appeared in the first year of his editorship. Yet despite the infrequency of its appearance, the paper became popular in socialist circles inside the Russian empire. This was due largely to *Pravda*'s focus on the problems of workers and its attempts to find common ground between the Bolsheviks and the Mensheviks, whose harsh polemical tone the paper avoided. Predictably, Trotsky's *Pravda* came under attack from the newspapers under the control of Lenin, who, except for brief periods of truce when it suited his immediate purposes, ruled out compromise with the Mensheviks.

The split was made final in January 1912, at a conference in Prague, where Lenin declared that the Bolsheviks alone constituted the Social Democratic Party. Trotsky furiously denounced Lenin's move in the pages of *Pravda*. He had reason to be more furious still when, three months later, he learned that the Bolsheviks in St. Petersburg had begun to publish a daily newspaper called *Pravda*. This was clearly an attempt to capitalize on the good name of Trotsky's publication, which remained the most popular of the newspapers imported illegally from abroad. Trotsky cried theft and threatened, in print, to take unspecified "further steps," yet there was really nothing else he could do but shut down his paper.

The first issue of the Bolshevik *Pravda* appeared on April 22 (May 5 on the Western calendar), 1912. It continued to appear until the outbreak of the war and then resumed publication in 1917, when it began its long, distinguished career as the official organ of Soviet Communism. Eventually, Trotsky would once again find himself the target of its polemical attacks, first as a rival in the Kremlin's succession struggles and later, in the 1930s, as a political exile in Mexico. Back in 1912, during his moment of outrage, it is believed that he sent an ultimatum directly to the Bolshevik editorial offices in St. Petersburg. He was unaware at the time that the man who organized the rival paper in the Russian capital and put out its first issue was the little-known Georgian Bolshevik Iosif Dzhugashvili, who went by the name of Stalin, and who, a decade later as the General Secretary of the Soviet Communist Party, would be in a position to relieve Trotsky of much more than intellectual property.

Россійская Соціаль-Демократическая Рабочая Партія

№ 1

ПРАВДА

Пролетаріи всѣхъ странъ соединяйтесь!

3 (16) октября 1908 г.

Цѣна отдѣльнаго номера 5 коп.

Рабочая Газета

Органъ Украинскаго Союза „Спілки".

„Правда своимъ читателямъ".

Опять — подполье!

Нашу газету, предназначенную для рабочихъ города и деревни, намъ приходится печатать заграницей и тайно перевозить въ Россію. Черныя сотни могутъ свободно издавать свои погромные призывы; но сознательные рабочіе не могутъ открыто высказать правду о своей нуждѣ и своей борьбѣ.

Въ концѣ 1905 года было иначе. Тогда погромныя изданія ютились въ тайникахъ департамента полиціи, а честная рабочая печать безпрепятственно выходила въ свѣтъ подъ защитой пролетарскихъ организацій.

Царское правительство твердо знало, гдѣ его главный врагъ. Какъ только оно оправилось послѣ октябрьской стачки, оно всей тяжестью своей военно-полицейской машины обрушилось на голову пролетаріата. Капиталисты поддержали правительство противъ насъ, либеральная буржуазія трусливо отошла къ сторонкѣ, крестьянскія массы не съумѣли оказать намъ необходимую поддержку, царизмъ нашелъ въ своей арміи достаточно темныхъ и развращенныхъ полковъ, — и пролетаріатъ былъ разбитъ. На пролетарскія организаціи и на рабочую прессу (газеты) правительство накинуло петлю.

При первой и второй думахъ петля эта затягивалась все туже. Либералы (кадеты), которые господствовали въ думахъ благодаря избирательному закону Витте, обѣщали народу взять лаской все то, чего пролетаріатъ не добился силой. Либералы призывали народъ къ спокойствію и терпѣнію. Но они оказались безсильны обезпечить народу тѣ свободы, которыми мы пользовались въ концѣ 1905 года подъ защитой нашихъ собственныхъ организацій. Соціалдемократическая пресса ко времени первой и второй думы была почти невозможна: каждое изданіе подвергалось полицейской конфискаціи.

Послѣ разгона второй думы правительство открыто и окончательно утверждаетъ въ странѣ господство штыка и пулемета. Манифестъ 17 октября разрывается на части и превращается въ пыжи для патроновъ. Вся страна отдается на растерзаніе отдѣльнымъ царькамъ. Собранія не допускаются. Организаціи раздавлены. Профессіональные союзы преслѣдуются по пятамъ. Рабочая пресса (газеты), не только политическая, но и профессіональная, подвергается истребленію.

Третья дума не внесла въ это положеніе никакихъ перемѣнъ. И она не собирается ихъ вносить. Въ пролетаріатѣ она видитъ врага, а въ свободѣ рабочей прессы — лютую опасность.

И вотъ теперь во времена столыпинской „конституціи" — точно такъ же, какъ и до начала революціи — рабочую газету приходится ставить за предѣлами Россіи и тайно перевозить черезъ царскую границу. **Слово правды** снова становится самой запретной контрабандой.

Худшее время позади.

Страшное декабрьское кровопусканіе и дальнѣйшій правительственный терроръ (разстрѣлы, казни, аресты, высылки) обезсилили массу. Соціалдемократическія организаціи подверглись опустошенію. Связи ослабѣли.

Правда, въ 1906 и 7 годахъ могущественно развертываются *профессіональные союзы*. Но не надолго. Разгулъ контръреволюціи, военный разгромъ городовъ и селъ, голодъ въ деревнѣ, міровой кризисъ (застой въ промышленности и торговлѣ) — все это нанесло жестокіе удары русской промышленности. Новые десятки тысячъ безработныхъ были выброшены на улицы и непосильнымъ грузомъ навалились на молодыя плечи профессіональныхъ союзовъ. Преслѣдованія полицейскихъ башибузуковъ додѣлали дѣло. Союзы терпятъ жестокій уронъ и вмѣстѣ съ партіей загоняются въ подполье.

Нетерпѣливыя одиночки отрываются отъ массы и сжигаютъ свои силы въ безплодныхъ схваткахъ и экспропріаціяхъ... Въ рабочихъ кварталахъ воцаряется угнетенное настроеніе... Самое глухое время приходится на конецъ прошлаго года.

Но постепенно рабочіе сбрасываютъ съ себя оцѣпенѣніе. Подъ двойнымъ кнутомъ кризиса и реакціи они снова начинаютъ искать средствъ и путей отпора. По общему свидѣтельству жизнь на фабрикахъ и заводахъ въ настоящее время оживляется, настроеніе крѣпнетъ, ослабѣвшія партійныя связи возстанавливаются. Лучшіе рабочіе, искавшіе выхода своей энергіи въ образовательныхъ кружкахъ и клубахъ, испытываютъ острое чувство неудовлетворенности. Они еще разъ убѣждаются, что однѣхъ лекцій, даже самыхъ лучшихъ, недостаточно: рабочіе успѣшнѣе всего *учатся* тогда, когда *борются*.

Рабочіе смѣняютъ интеллигенцію.

Партійная жизнь возстановляется, но формы ея другія.

Интеллигенція, которая въ дореволюціонную эпоху занимала господствующее положеніе въ партійныхъ организаціяхъ, теперь ходомъ вещей отодвигается на задній планъ. Большинство старыхъ работниковъ разсѣяно по тюрьмамъ, въ ссылкѣ, въ эмиграціи, многіе отстали отъ партіи. Притокъ *новыхъ* изъ среды интеллигенціи почти совершенно прекратился. *Рабочимъ приходится дѣло своей партіи брать цѣликомъ въ свои собственныя руки.*

Есть ли необходимыя силы? Мы не колеблясь отвѣчаемъ: *есть*!

Еще до революціи сотни рабочихъ прошли серьезную школу *соціалистической пропаганды*. Въ великихъ событіяхъ послѣднихъ лѣтъ они нашли незамѣнимую *политическую* школу. Въ Совѣтахъ Депутатовъ и особенно въ профессіональныхъ союзахъ они пріобрѣли неоцѣнимый опытъ *организаціоннаго строительства* и классоваго *самоуправленія*. Со стиснутыми зубами эти передовые рабочіе покидаютъ надежду удержаться на открытомъ полѣ и берутся за возстановленіе нелегальной соціалдемократической организаціи. Они пришли къ убѣжденію, что безъ этого аппарата нельзя теперь шагу ступить ни въ политической ни въ экономической борьбѣ,—нельзя не только завоевать новыя легальныя позиціи, но и использовать тѣ, которыя остались.

Съ полнымъ довѣріемъ взираемъ мы на совершающееся теперь возрожденіе и перерожденіе партіи. Мы не сомнѣваемся, что партія выйдетъ изъ него окрѣпшей душой и тѣломъ. Она окончательно сброситъ съ себя организаціонную и матеріально-финансовую зависимость отъ буржуазной интеллигенціи, — и во главѣ пролетарскихъ организацій станутъ рабочіе—вожди. Нашей газетой мы постараемся оказать посильную помощь возсозданію партіи на этихъ новыхъ основахъ.

The first issue of Trotsky's *Pravda.*

The Dustbin of History

It was Trotsky who uttered one of the most famous lines of the Russian Revolution, when he dismissed his Menshevik and other rivals with the words, "Go now where you belong, into the dustbin of history." And so they did, most of them. But one man's dustbin is another man's archive, and one of the Mensheviks Trotsky sent packing, Boris Ivanovich Nicolaevsky, would go on to become the great archivist of the Russian Revolution, from its roots in the revolutionary emigration and underground to its Soviet-era aftermath inside the USSR and among its outcasts abroad.

The Boris Nicolaevsky Papers is arguably the single most important collection on Russia in the Hoover Archives. The product of more than forty years of vigorous collecting, it contains, in some 800 manuscript boxes, a wealth of primary documents from many diverse sources and of various kinds, including correspondence, speeches, memoirs, writings, minutes of meetings, and photographs. Its chronological breadth is remarkable, extending back to the middle of the nineteenth century and encompassing such revolutionary legends as Mikhail Bakunin, rival of Marx and father of Russian anarchism, and the early populist Petr Lavrov. It covers political, social, and economic conditions and developments in late tsarist Russia and in Soviet Russia under Lenin and Stalin. A list of individuals whose papers are in the Nicolaevsky collection would read like a Who's Who of the Russian revolutionary movement, as well as of the international socialist movement.

Nicolaevsky was a natural archivist, but his biography shows that his life might have turned out very differently. He was born in Russia in 1887, the son of an Orthodox priest, in the small town of Belebei, in what is now the Bashkir Republic. At an early age he got caught up in left-wing politics, and in 1904 he formally joined the Social Democratic Party, siding at first with its Bolshevik wing but soon gravitating toward the Mensheviks. Over the next years, Nicolaevsky's activity as a revolutionary organizer (he played a leading role in the 1905 revolution in Samara) and journalist was interrupted by arrests and long sentences in prison or internal exile; in all he spent some thirty-one months in tsarist jails and another seven years in exile in the frozen north and in eastern Siberia. This allowed him plenty of time to engage his passion for the printed word, and he read widely and deeply.

Following the Revolution of 1917, as the Bolsheviks moved to restrict and then outlaw their rivals, Nicolaevsky's interest turned increasingly in the direction of archival work. He helped to set up an official Soviet archive and served for two years as director of the Historical Revolutionary Archive in Moscow, in which capacity he traveled around the country collecting documents of historical significance. In February 1921, in the days of the mutiny of the Kronstadt sailors and widespread worker and peasant unrest, Nicolaevsky was among a number of leading Mensheviks arrested by the Soviet police. After a year in prison, he was expelled from the country and settled in Berlin.

Mensheviks in exile. Former leaders of the Menshevik Party, photographed in Vienna in 1931. Seated front row center, second from left, Petr Garvi, Fedor Dan, Isai Iudin (Aizenshtat), and Rafael Abramovich. Boris Nicolaevsky stands at the center in the back of the group. (Boris Nicolaevsky Papers)

As an exile, Nicolaevsky now applied much of his feverish energy and endless resourcefulness to collecting documents. Ever the networker, he maintained his connections with Soviet archives, serving from 1924 to 1931 as Berlin representative of the Marx-Engels Institute in Moscow, for which he collected materials in Europe. Émigré politics also preoccupied Nicolaevsky, who became a steady contributor to the Menshevik newspaper in exile, *Sotsialisticheskii vestnik (Socialist Herald).* He published scholarly articles and books; his first book in English, *Aseff the Spy,* published in 1934, is considered a classic account of the career of this notorious police spy and terrorist. And his "Letter from an Old Bolshevik," based on his conversations with Nikolai Bukharin in Paris in the spring of 1936, achieved cult status as an essential document on the purges of the 1930s.

With the Nazi advent to power in Germany in 1933, Nicolaevsky moved on to Paris, where he continued his collecting work. When Nazi Germany invaded France, he fell back on the conspiratorial techniques learned in his youth in an attempt to rescue his and other archives (part of which for a time he concealed in a chicken coop); all things considered, he was mostly successful. He fled to New York at the end of 1940 to take charge of papers he had sent out of the country ahead of him. His future wife, Anna Mikhailovna Bourguina, placed her own life in danger by remaining in France in order to safeguard the collections left behind. Some of these materials were indeed reclaimed at the end of the war. Another portion, however, fell into Nazi and later Soviet hands and were never recovered.

In the United States, Nicolaevsky continued his collecting activities, as well as his journalistic and scholarly writing. He became a kind of mentor to the entire Slavic field in America, allowing scholars to research his materials and offering them his encyclopedic knowledge of and unique insights into Russia. The bulk of his collection was acquired by the Hoover Institution at the end of 1963. Nicolaevsky himself served as curator of his collection at the Hoover Institution until his death in 1966.

Boris Nicolaevsky's presence at the Hoover can be felt not only in the collection under his name but throughout the Hoover Library, in the form of Russian books, newspapers, and journals from before the Revolution. It is thanks to him that the Hoover Institution holds a complete run of Trotsky's *Pravda* (1908–1912), as it does of many other extremely rare prerevolutionary Russian newspapers and journals, extending across the spectrum of liberal, socialist, anarchist, and populist opinion, published both inside Russia and abroad. Most of the periodicals brought to the Hoover by Nicolaevsky were long ago integrated into the Hoover Library's holdings.

Not surprisingly, the Nicolaevsky Papers are the best source outside Russia for documentation on the Menshevik Party, from its earliest days as a political faction to its postrevolutionary emigration. In fact, Nicolaevsky obtained roughly a quarter of his collection from fellow Mensheviks. The existence of one of the collection's jewels, uncovered only in the 1980s, is owed to a former fellow Menshevik: the private papers of Trotsky, from the period after his expulsion from the Soviet Union in 1929, when Stalin consigned him to the dustbin of history.

The Tsar's Secret Police

Researchers at the Hoover Archives can study the Russian revolutionary movement from the perspective of the Okhrana, the tsarist secret police, whose records disappeared after the Revolution, only to surface on the Stanford campus forty years later. The rescue of this archive was due to the remarkable determination and resourcefulness of Basil Maklakoff (Vasilii Maklakov), ambassador to France of the Russian Provisional Government in 1917.

After the February Revolution, the Provisional Government appointed a mixed-party commission to investigate the files of the Paris branch of the Okhrana, mainly in order to expose the identities of secret agents among the Russian émigrés. This commission, which managed to accomplish little during its brief existence, was dissolved after the Bolsheviks took power. Ambassador Maklakoff then closed and sealed the files. When France recog-

Hoover staff members Witold Sworakowski and Marina Tinkoff opening the first crates of the Okhrana collection, at the Hoover Institution, October 1957. (Hoover Institution Records)

nized the Soviet Union in 1924, it was obliged by international law to turn over the former Russian embassy building and all its contents to the Soviets. Maklakoff secretly arranged—through Nikolai Golovin, a former Imperial Russian officer—for the files to be shipped to the Hoover Library. To put the Soviets off his trail, he signed a statement stating that he had burned the records.

In 1926, seventeen large wooden packing cases containing the Okhrana files arrived on the Stanford campus. Maklakoff had stipulated that the cases were to remain sealed for thirty years. They were kept first in the basement of the Stanford Museum and then, after the Hoover Tower was constructed, transferred to a storage room on the Tower's top floor. When the thirty-year term expired, in 1956, Maklakoff—who may not have counted on living a long life, and who apparently had no desire to go out with a bang—requested that the crates remain sealed until three months after his death, which came on July 15, 1957. On October 28, a press conference at the Hoover Institution made headlines in announcing the existence of the Okhrana archive.

The Paris branch of the imperial secret police was established in the Russian embassy in Paris in 1883. By 1905, the Paris Okhrana office had absorbed all other tsarist police bureaus abroad and become the principal repository of all of Russia's intelligence information on the revolutionary movements abroad. The records kept in Paris in many ways surpassed those at headquarters in St. Petersburg, particularly with regard to Russian revolutionary émigrés and their foreign supporters.

Short-term visitors to the Hoover Archives will delve into the Okhrana files at their peril, so captivating are their contents. The files cover the years 1883–1917 and are especially complete for the period from 1901 to the February Revolution. A summary of the archive's rich contents is in itself staggering. The bulk of the material includes the entire correspondence between the Paris and St. Petersburg offices for the years 1901–1917, containing seventy volumes of "incoming" (from St. Petersburg) letters (about 35,000 items) and thirty bundles (about 30,000 items) of "outgoing" letters (carbon copies). As well, there is a vast

Single page from Okhrana album of mug shots, including (upper right) those of Lev Bronstein (Trotsky), who was eighteen years old when the photograph was taken. (Okhrana Collection)

collection of printed and multigraphed "circulars" for the period 1899–1917, ordering the investigation, shadowing, or arrest of suspicious revolutionaries or foreign agents. Another large collection contains about 40,000 reports of some 450 agents and informers at various times in twelve countries (Sweden, Denmark, Germany, Belgium, England, Italy, France, Switzerland, Austria, Turkey, Romania, and the United States).

Beyond this, there are complete accounting records, with receipts, of the agents' and informers' salaries and expenses (about 100 folders), personal files of about 160 agents, complete codes, photographs, and photographic plates of intercepted correspondence, foreign code books and other illicit materials secured by agents, and other once-secret records. A collection of as many as 4,000 photographs served as the principal tool for identifying suspects; twenty-three large volumes contain addresses of Russian citizens living abroad.

The Okhrana archive is unique as a complete record, over a period of many years, of the operations of a national intelligence service. As a window on the personalities, methods, and activities of tsarist Russia's revolutionary adversaries and its police enforcers, it has no parallel.

St. Petersburg, c. 1914. (World War I Pictorial Collection)

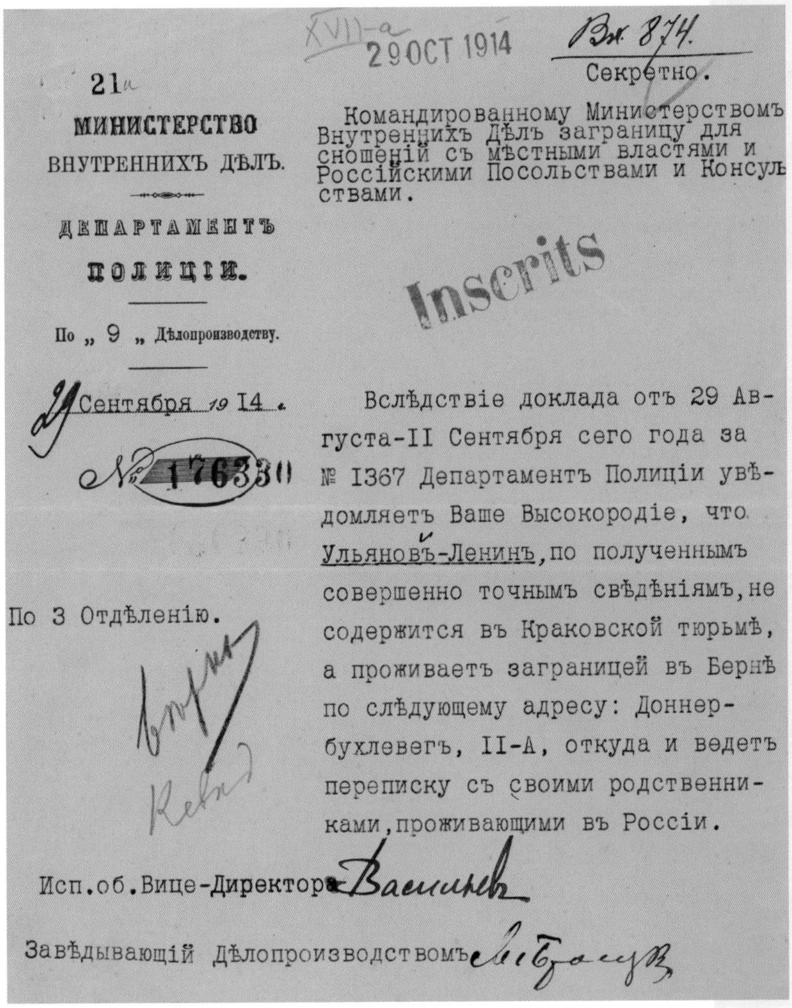

XVII-а 29 OCT 1914 Вх. 874.

21а
МИНИСТЕРСТВО
ВНУТРЕННИХЪ ДѢЛЪ.
ДЕПАРТАМЕНТЪ
ПОЛИЦІИ.
По „ 9 „ Дѣлопроизводству.
29 Сентября 1914.
№ 176330

Секретно.

Командированному Министерствомъ Внутреннихъ Дѣлъ заграницу для сношеній съ мѣстными властями и Россійскими Посольствами и Консульствами.

Inscrits

Вслѣдствіе доклада отъ 29 Августа-II Сентября сего года за № 1367 Департаментъ Полиціи увѣдомляетъ Ваше Высокородіе, что Ульяновъ-Ленинъ, по полученнымъ совершенно точнымъ свѣдѣніямъ, не содержится въ Краковской тюрьмѣ, а проживаетъ заграницей въ Бернѣ по слѣдующему адресу: Доннербухлевегъ, II-А, откуда и ведетъ переписку съ своими родственниками, проживающими въ Россіи.

По 3 Отдѣленію.

Исп.об.Вице-Директора Васильев

Завѣдывающій Дѣлопроизводствомъ

Where's Lenin? In 1914, Vladimir Lenin (born Ulyanov) was living in Cracow, in Austrian Poland. When Austria declared war on Russia on August 6, Lenin and his wife were on vacation in the Tatra range of the Carpathian Mountains. On August 8, after jittery locals reported his behavior as suspicious, Lenin was arrested as a spy for tsarist Russia. With the Russian army poised to invade Austria, Lenin had to worry he would fall into Russian hands.

Seeking help, Lenin sent a telegram to Victor Adler, the internationally renowned Austrian Social Democrat, in Vienna. Adler was able to convince the Habsburg minister of interior that, far from being a spy for the tsarist government, Lenin was its implacable enemy, capable of rendering great service in the anti-Russian cause. This argument had the desired effect. On August 19, Lenin was released from prison and given a pass to travel from Cracow to Vienna, whence he made his way to Bern, Switzerland.

The letter shown here, dated September 29, 1914 (according to the Russian calendar at that time; October 12 on the Western calendar) clarified Lenin's whereabouts. The director of the Department of Police in St. Petersburg informed the chief of the Paris Okhrana that "Ulyanov-Lenin, according to absolutely precise information received here, is not being held in a Cracow prison, but is living abroad in Bern at the following address . . . from where he is corresponding with his relatives in Russia." (Okhrana Collection)

Shadowing Savinkov

The Okhrana files document the extraordinary lengths to which Russia's police agents in Europe would go in order to infiltrate and otherwise monitor émigré political circles. Once on the inside, undercover operatives attended the conferences of conspiratorial groups and associated with their leaders, from the likes of Lenin and Trotsky to the conspirators engaged in assassination and banditry. Among the individuals who commanded special attention, which can be judged by the thickness of his police dossier, was the notorious left-wing terrorist Boris Savinkov.

Savinkov's story reads almost like a caricature of revolutionary biography; as a character in a novel he would be dismissed as a preposterous figure. Himself a novelist and friend of Russian poets, he is aptly described in the introduction to his posthumously published *Memoirs* as "much more fighter and terrorist than socialist, much more the romantic Nietzscheian of the 'superman' type than theoretician and propagandist."

Born in Warsaw in 1879, Savinkov attended St. Petersburg University, from which, in 1899, he was expelled for his part in student disturbances. Arrested in 1903 for his role in underground socialist activities, he was exiled to Vologda, from where he escaped to Western Europe, landing in Geneva. There, still in 1903, he joined the Socialist Revolutionary (SR) Party, signing on to its Combat Organization. Between 1902 and 1905 the Combat Organization carried out a number of spectacular assassinations, two of the most dramatic directed by Savinkov from inside Russia: those of Interior Minister V. K. Plehve, on July 15, 1904, and of the Governor-General of Moscow, Grand Duke Sergei Alexandrovich, on February 4, 1905.

The success of these and other such operations increased the prestige of the SR party and Savinkov's standing within it, until, in December 1908, scandal struck when the head of the Combat Organization, Evno Azev, was exposed as a tsarist police spy. Azev had long been under a cloud of suspicion, but his exposure—which, as the Okhrana files demonstrate, rocked the Russian political establishment—nearly destroyed the Socialist Revolutionary Party. It instantly discredited the practice of revolutionary terrorism, forcing Savinkov to

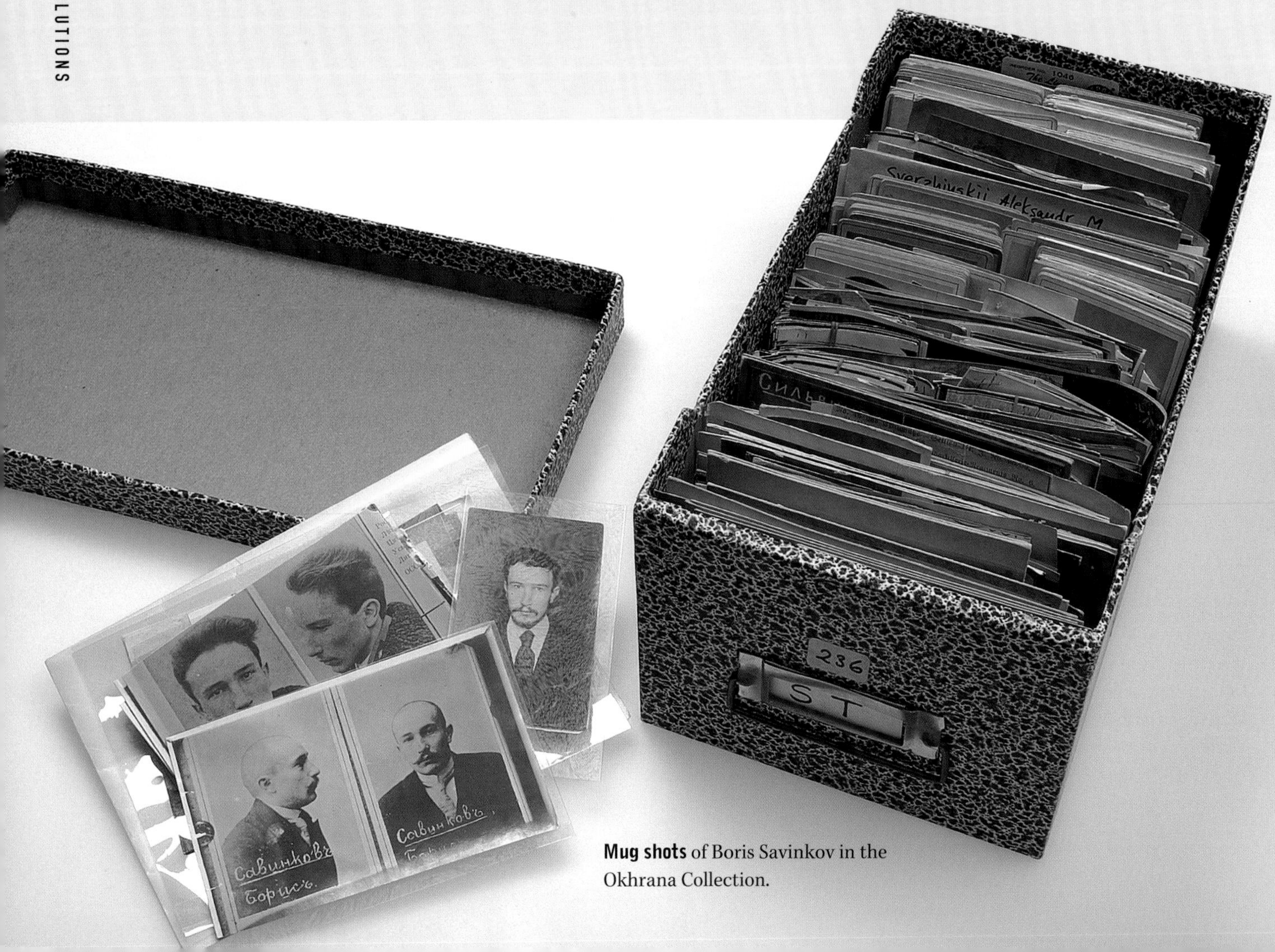

Mug shots of Boris Savinkov in the Okhrana Collection.

seek other, less sensational outlets for his conspiratorial talents, and indeed he began to devote more energy to literary pursuits.

At the outbreak of World War I, he joined the French army as a volunteer. When the Russian autocracy collapsed, he made his way into Russia and was appointed commissar to the Seventh Army on the southwestern front. In July 1917 he was named assistant war minister under Alexander Kerensky, but this rapid ascent was cut short in August when he was discredited in the so-called Kornilov affair, named for the Russian army general who turned his troops toward Petrograd in an attempted coup d'état. Kornilov's drive toward the capital fizzled out, but it ended up compromising the Provisional Government and giving the Bolsheviks an opening. In its immediate aftermath, Savinkov was expelled from the SR party for refusing to explain his role in the affair.

After the Bolsheviks took power, Savinkov applied his considerable talents to the White cause, most dramatically by leading an anti-Communist uprising in the city of Yaroslavl in July 1918. These and other such ventures failed, of course, and with the White armies folding in 1920 Savinkov ended up in Poland trying to raise an anti-Bolshevik army there, until the Polish government asked him to leave the country. Frustrated in his attempts to direct subversive operations against the Bolshevik regime from Paris, he decided to return to Soviet Russia. This sounds like a form of suicide, though the circumstances are obscure. The Soviets claimed that he was arrested crossing the Polish frontier on August 15, 1924, after his conspiratorial organization had been penetrated by the Soviet secret police. Western sources have speculated that he connived in this operation.

Whatever the case, the infamous Boris Savinkov, being one of a kind, was given his very own show trial, pronounced guilty of conspiracy, and sentenced to death—a sentence commuted to a maximum of ten years' imprisonment. Whatever calculations had inspired his return to Soviet Russia, for the ultimate revolutionary romantic there was now only one way out. In May 1925, Savinkov jumped to his death from a fifth-floor window of the Lubianka prison in Moscow.

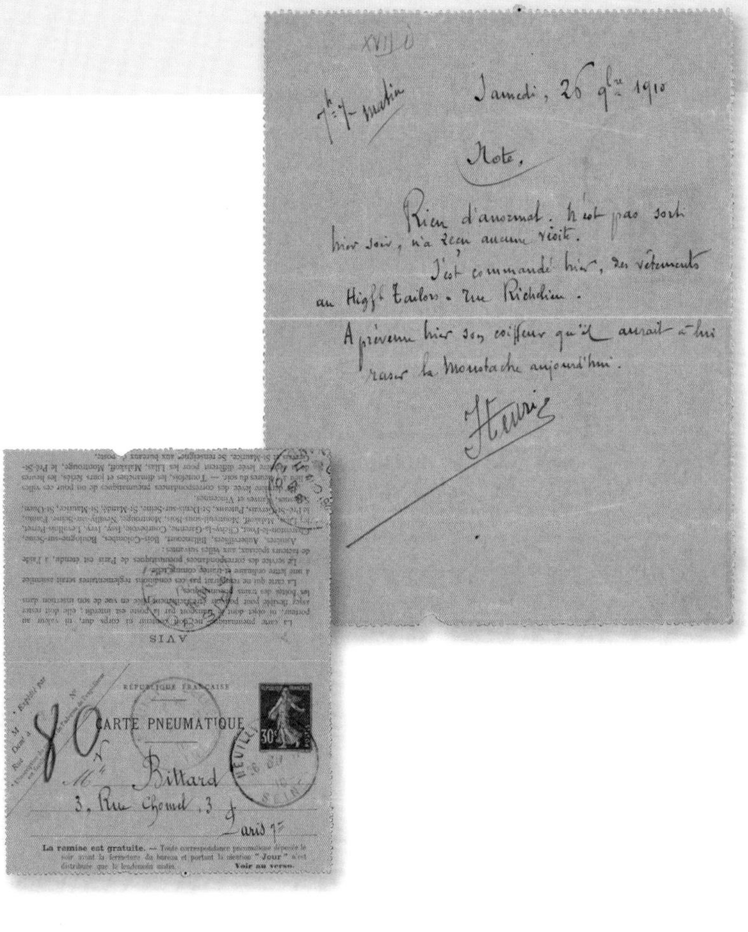

Postcard, with text in French, sent by an Okhrana agent shadowing Savinkov in Paris, dated September 26, 1910. Savinkov's file contains dozens of such surveillance records, which are especially detailed during the period 1910–11. The researcher can observe his movements around Paris, throughout France, and, except when the trail goes cold, across Europe.

The text of this postcard, sent by agent Henri During on September 26, 1910, is rather typical. It reports "Nothing abnormal": Savinkov had not gone out during the previous evening; nor had he received any visitors; he had dropped off some clothing at "High Tailors," on Richelieu Street. "He warned his barber yesterday that he would have to shave his moustache today." (Okhrana Collection)

True Diarist

One of the genuine archival gems at the Hoover is a diary of the Russian Revolution that went undiscovered for more than sixty years. That this manuscript ended up at Stanford at all is due to an extraordinary confluence of events at the end of the Russian Civil War, when a major famine descended on the country. The Soviet government was forced to accept outside assistance in the form of a massive influx of food and medicine provided by Herbert Hoover's American Relief Administration (ARA), which entered Soviet Russia in the summer of 1921 to fight the famine, and which fed and saved millions of people over the next two years.

Among the American relief workers was a historian by the name of Frank A. Golder, who had come to Stanford in 1920 to teach summer school and was enlisted to go to Europe as a curator for the newly founded Hoover War Collection. Thus began his association with Stanford, which would last until his death. In 1921 he was made associate professor and in 1924 professor of Russian history, at which time he also became a director of the Hoover Library. Born near Odessa in 1877 and trained as a historian at Harvard, Golder had a facility in Russian and German and ample experience traveling and researching inside Russia. He was in St. Petersburg in 1914 when Russia entered the Great War, and again in 1917 at the time of the February Revolution.

On being hired as a curator for the Hoover Collection, Golder departed in August 1920 on his first collecting trip, a journey of three years that would have an enduring effect on the field of Slavic studies in America. Relying on the good offices of the ARA in the places he visited, Golder traveled during the next year throughout central, eastern, and southeastern Europe and the Near East, collecting books, manuscripts, periodicals, government documents, personal papers, and posters, and arranging for their shipment to Stanford. All the while, Golder was impatient to get into Russia.

His opportunity came in August 1921, when the ARA signed an agreement with the Soviet government to fight the Great Famine. Golder entered Soviet Russia with one of the first ARA parties at the end of August and remained there for most of the next twenty-one months, often contributing his services to the American relief effort. His collecting achievement during this period was Golder's most important professional accomplishment. Thanks to his effort, the Hoover Institution's holdings on modern Russia and early Soviet history are unsurpassed in the West.

Golder drew on past contacts with Russian archivists, scholars, and librarians, and he also made new connections within the Bolshevik establishment, most important with the Marxist historian and Deputy People's Commissar of Enlightenment Mikhail Pokrovksy, who assisted him in collecting, free of charge, most official publications since 1917, including complete runs of many newspapers and journals. Book prices were very low when Golder

Vladimir Lenin, flanked by Trotsky (left) and Lev Kamenev, Moscow 1919. (Bertram D. Wolfe Papers)

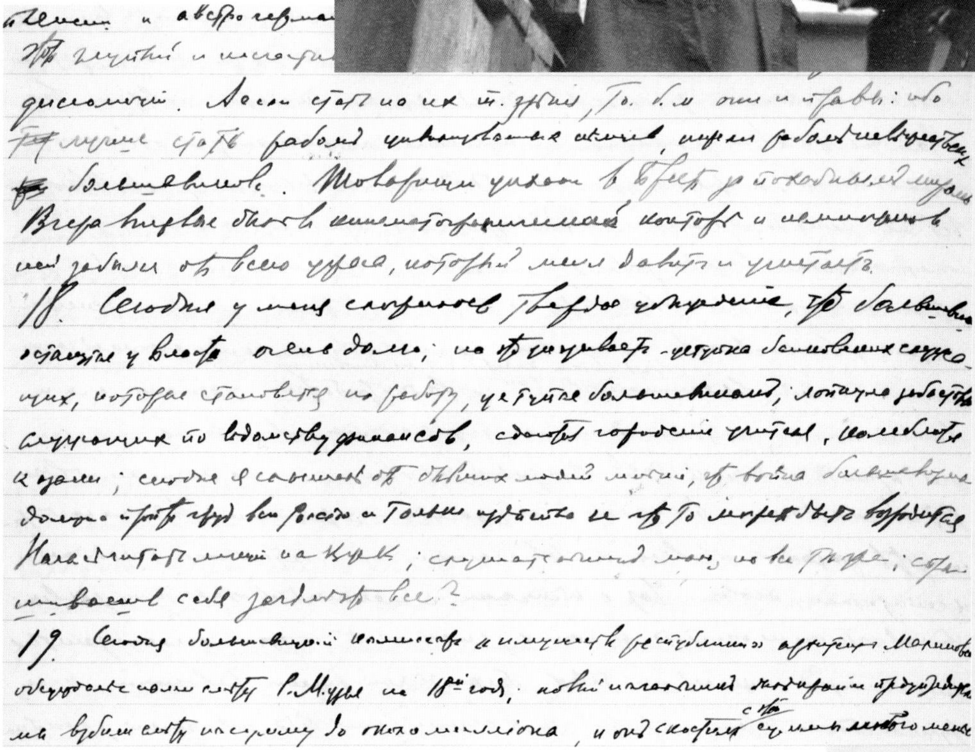

Got'e diary entry for January 18, 1918: "Today I reached the firm conclusion that the bolsheviks are going to remain in power for a very long time. Evidence of this is the compromise of the bank employees, who are yielding to the bolsheviks and going back to work; the collapse of the strike of the finance-administration employees and of the city teachers; and the wavering of the cossacks. Today I heard the opinion from some former people that the war of bolshevism must sweep over all of Russia, and that something can grow again, perhaps, only on her ashes. I began to give lectures at the Higher Women's Courses; there were few auditors, but they were all the same ones as before; you ask yourself, what is it all for?" (Frank A. Golder Papers)

arrived in Russia, and he purchased aggressively. In addition, he also acquired the personal papers of several individuals, including a manuscript of singular importance: the diary of a Moscow historian by the name of Yuri Got'e.

True diaries are extremely rare, and only a very few diaries appear to have been kept in Russia during the Revolution and Civil War. Got'e recorded his first entry on July 8, 1917, and his final entry on July 23, 1922. What he produced during those five years is, Terence Emmons attests, "a nearly perfect example of the true diary: unlike many—perhaps most—personal journals that are eventually published, this one was never revised, censored, or embellished at a later time by its author. His entries are never separated from the events and experiences they describe by more than a few days; usually they were recorded the same day." Got'e faithfully wrote down his observations and impressions of Russia's agony during its "time of troubles," with a special sensitivity for the fate of his own kind: the intellectuals and the former well-to-do whom the new order had reduced to "former people."

Nor is there any evidence that the diarist wrote with an eye toward future publication. On the contrary, as Emmons observes, "For Got'e, his diary may have been above all a means of bringing order into the ongoing chaos of events, and thus of exercising a kind of control over them." The result is a work that, perhaps better than any single primary document of its kind, makes sense of how a relatively small group of revolutionaries, numbering at most 150,000 when they seized power in October 1917, were able to retain their grip on power and secure their rule over Russia.

Got'e would survive Stalin's regime of terror (arrested in 1929, he was sentenced to five years in a labor camp), but his diary might not have been preserved had Frank Golder not arrived in Russia in 1921 and succeeded in persuading its author to entrust it to him for safekeeping—another of the qualities that made Golder a great collector.

Golder died of lung cancer in January 1929, after a brief illness. He had been especially careful, in shipping the diary from Moscow to Stanford, to hide the identity of its author. As a result, the diary was something of an archival mystery until 1982, when its authorship was determined by Edward Kasinec, director of the Slavonic Division of the New York Public Library. Its hundreds of pages of handwriting were then deciphered and its text turned into typescript. It was published under the title *Time of Troubles* in 1988, on the eve of the next Russian revolution.

Bolshevik Icons

An urgent priority for the new Bolshevik regime was to make its ideology and its program known to the Russian people. The regime's social base was primarily among urban groups and, to a lesser extent, soldiers in Petrograd and at the front, most of them peasant draftees. The Bolshevik Party—renamed the Communist Party in February 1918—could claim very little support from the vast rural population. It portrayed itself as the vanguard of the proletariat, the workers being the chosen class according to the teachings of Marx and Lenin. Yet Russia's working class in 1917 numbered at most two million out of a total population of 120 million. Thus, the goal—and the challenge—of Bolshevism in power was not merely to spread the word about its ideology but to establish its legitimacy.

The obstacles were formidable, beginning with the fact that the majority of the Russian population was illiterate, especially outside the major cities. Even reaching literate Russians became increasingly difficult with the disruption of the publishing industry and the transportation system, which sharply curtailed the publication and distribution of newspapers. The Bolsheviks' solution was visual propaganda, at which they proved to be extremely adept, in particular the propaganda poster, which they pioneered and which enabled them to get their message out to all classes of Russians. The result was very impressive; before long symbols like the hammer and sickle, the red star, and the heroic worker became Bolshevik icons.

The first political posters appeared in August 1918, as the Civil War was getting under way. The next three years saw the production of some 3,000 posters by more than 450 organizations and institutions. Although the quality ranged from the innovative to the crude, the ubiquitous presence of these posters was a new fact of Soviet life. According to Berkeley sociologist and historian Victoria Bonnell, "All manner of public spaces were decorated with posters, whose color, design, and imaginative imagery enlivened an otherwise drab society."

Bonnell researched the extensive collection of Bolshevik posters at the Hoover Institution for her 1997 book *Iconography of Power: Soviet Political Posters under Lenin and Stalin.* Bonnell's study explains how Bolshevik visual propaganda, whose messages aimed to transform traditional Russian ways, exploited Russia's highly visual traditional culture. Just as the Russian Orthodox icon occupied a central place in Russian religious practice, so did the new Bolshevik iconography herald the communist religion.

"A Year of Proletarian Dictatorship, October 1917–October 1918" (1918). This lithograph was made for the first anniversary of the October Revolution. It shows a worker (left) and a peasant standing on the broken chains and other symbols of the old regime and guarding the entrance to a utopian scene of economic prosperity. Dozens of posters with similar imagery appeared during the Civil War, beginning with this famous poster by Aleksandr Apsit (1880–1944), one of the earliest and most influential political artists of the Revolution. Trained as an icon painter, Apsit had been a political artist before the Revolution.

From the very outset, Soviet political art portrayed the Revolution's social base as a worker-peasant alliance. The reality was utterly different. Marxist ideology instructed that the proletariat was the chosen class; the backward peasantry was viewed with suspicion and hostility. During the period of so-called War Communism, from 1918 to 1921, the government requisitioned food by force, which eventually provoked the peasants to violent resistance. These Bolshevik policies, on top of the dislocations of seven years of war and revolution, left the peasants with little or no reserve of food to fall back on. So, when a severe drought led to a crop failure in 1920, the result was mass starvation. The Great Famine that began in the summer of 1921 would claim five million lives, mostly in the countryside. Thus the symbolism of worker–peasant harmony was at best wishful thinking. More telling is the pride of place given the slogan along the top, "Proletarians of all countries, unite!"

"First of May" (1919). The heading reads, "Russian Socialist Federative Soviet Republic"; the slogan on the flag reads, "Proletarians of all countries, unite!"; below the title is a quote attributed to Marx and Engels: "Workers have nothing to lose but their chains, and they will acquire the whole world." The international dimension of the Communist revolutionary enterprise is depicted in this poster, designed by Apsit in 1919. True Marxists assumed that the proletarian, or socialist, revolution was supposed to occur first in advanced industrialized societies. The Bolsheviks justified taking power in backward Russia by presenting their revolution as the detonator for a worldwide revolutionary conflagration—the theme symbolized in Apsit's poster. By May Day 1919, when this poster was created, the prospects for world revolution still appeared promising to the true believers in Russia and their comrades in the international communist movement. Within a year, however, it was apparent that the master narrative was not going to unfold as planned, at least not anytime soon. Socialism would have to be built in Russia first.

"**Russian peasants** returning home after pillaging a country house of a rich landlord (near Pskaff [Pskov], 1919)."

The Hunger Artist

A most unusual visual record of the Russian Revolution can be found in the paintings of Ivan Vladimirov—not those displayed in the museums of St. Petersburg and Moscow, but those that ended up at the Hoover Institution. Vladimirov's name is listed in the standard Soviet biographical dictionaries as a celebrated artist of the Revolution. His most famous painting, *Down with the Eagle* (1917), depicts peasant soldiers tearing down the imperial emblem from atop the roof of an apothecary shop during the February Revolution. Like many Soviet artists, Vladimirov later contributed to the cults of Lenin and Stalin.

Yet to judge from the collection of his paintings in the Hoover Archives, Vladimirov was not an uncritical observer of life under the new regime. In these works—forty in all, most of them watercolors—we see the Revolution's unheroic side: the brutality and vulgarity of the winners, the poverty and humiliation of the losers. Many are of Petrograd street scenes, under leaden gray skies, where the desperate search for food and fuel takes many forms, including, in a scene familiar during the years 1919 and 1920, a house being dismantled for use as firewood. There are village dramas—a landlord and a priest are sentenced to death; thuggish Bolsheviks come to requisition cattle and wood from distraught peasants—but Vladimirov's main theme here is the tragic fate of former aristocrats and bourgeois, hungry and cold and struggling to stay alive.

"Miserable life of Russian nobles and persons of high rank during the revolution. (Drawn from nature in the home of General Buturline, 1919.)"

"Hungry ones in Petrograd dividing a dead horse in the street (1919)." Note the red flags in the demonstration taking place in the far background, across the canal.

That Vladimirov, who was born in Vilna (present-day Vilnius, Lithuania) in 1869, should evince sympathy for the dispossessed is not at all suprising, given his own bourgeois (and cosmopolitan) background. His parents, who met and married in England, both belonged to the Russian intelligentsia. His artistic inclinations were encouraged by his mother, herself a watercolorist, and his art was shaped by formal training in Vilna, St. Petersburg, and Paris. He liked to paint action scenes and found inspiration serving as an artist-correspondent at the front in the Russo-Japanese War, the Balkan War of 1912, and the First World War. His work also traveled well, as his sketches appeared in the Russian *Niva*, British *Graphic*, and French *Illustration*.

Vladimirov is credited with having painted some of the earliest works inspired by the October Revolution, and he seems to have had no difficulty fitting into the Bolshevik establishment, exhibiting his works in major shows and teaching art courses in Leningrad. His Soviet-era paintings—like those at the Hoover, strictly middlebrow—romanticized the military battles of the Great War, the Russian Civil War, and, in the last years of his life, the Second World War. He died in Leningrad in 1947.

Vladimirov's paintings, which were procured for the Hoover by Frank Golder in 1922, do not add up to evidence that the artist was secretly anti-Communist. The circumstances of their creation would caution against drawing any such conclusion. Most of the paintings were commissioned by Golder, who was introduced to Vladimirov by American relief workers in Petrograd (whose beneficence is the subject of one of the paintings). The artist was paid for his work, most likely in the form of American food packages. These were highly coveted in those hungry times, even by establishment artists.

Motion Picture Men

Herman Axelbank spent more than a half-century compiling a motion picture film record of the twilight years of Imperial Russia, the Russian Revolution, and the Soviet Union. The fruit of his efforts—266 reels containing more than 250,000 feet of film, most of it raw footage—constitutes the single most impressive collection of its kind outside Russia.

Axelbank's is yet another of those Russian émigré success stories behind the Hoover Archives. He was born in 1900 in the Ukrainian village of Novo-Konstantinov. In 1909 his family moved to New York City, where, several years later, Axelbank got a job as an office boy for Samuel Goldfish (later Goldwyn), at Goldwyn Pictures on 42nd Street in Manhattan. As the story is told, not long after the Bolsheviks took power, Axelbank hired a cameraman with experience working in Eastern Europe to go to Russia to film Lenin and Trotsky. Axelbank must truly have caught the film bug, because it is said that he pawned his possessions and borrowed from friends in order to pay the cameraman's advance. In 1922 this man returned with scenes he had "captured" in the land of the Bolsheviks, including film of the 1922 Moscow trial of the Socialist Revolutionaries, and Axelbank's film archive was begun and quickly expanded.

Axelbank's collection stayed contemporary by accumulating motion picture coverage of events in Soviet Russia as they unfolded—in the 1920s the Pathé, International, and Fox news services each purchased film from him—but he also set out to fill in the chronological background of the Revolution, purchasing film of the First World War on the eastern front, of the Romanov family relaxing and in official ceremonies, and of scenes of daily life in provincial Russia, as well as in St. Petersburg and Moscow. Among the treasures of the prerevolutionary period is a sequence of Tsar Nicholas II and his entourage skinny-dipping and generally acting silly for the camera, the way people tend to do in home movies. The

Film reel of "Tsar to Lenin," with original case. (Herman Axelbank Film Collection)

Series of frames taken from one sequence of film from the Axelbank Collection showing Lenin speaking at the Second Congress of the Communist International, July 1920.

tsar himself took a turn behind the camera, which makes Nicholas one of scores of cameramen, most of their identities long forgotten, whose work is preserved in Axelbank's collection.

The collection's enormous cast of famous characters includes many of the key figures of the Russian Revolution. There are, as well, battle scenes from the Russian Civil War, ceremonial events marking May Day and the anniversary of Great October, and the inevitable funerals of prominent figures, among them Tolstoy and Lenin. The coverage extends into the 1970s, but it is the footage on the first forty-four reels, shot from about 1901 to 1937, that is extremely rare and that puts the Herman Axelbank Film Collection in a class of its own.

In the 1920s, Axelbank began to edit documentary sequences from the footage in his collection. Eventually this led to the production of the classic documentary film "Tsar to Lenin," which premiered at New York's Filmarte Theater on March 6, 1937. The film's editor and narrator was Max Eastman, the American biographer of Trotsky and sometime Trotskyite, whose nervous, hectoring voice supplied the film's narrative arc. The scenes of the tsar and his entourage in the buff served to suggest frivolous indifference to a population seething with discontent. Crowds gathered before the camera become "the masses." In other places Eastman's coaching is unnecessary, as when Alexander Kerensky, the last head of the Provisional Government, appears on the screen, the personification of vainglory.

At the time of its release, the most controversial thing about "Tsar to Lenin" was its portrayal of Trotsky as the key organizer of the October putsch and the founder and leader of the victorious Red Army. This was all quite accurate, but in the Soviet Union Trotsky's name had been removed from the official histories of the Revolution. He was then being tried in absentia—along with many of Lenin's Old Bolshevik comrades in the dock—for sensational crimes such as treason, sabotage, espionage, and assassination in the macabre show trials then taking place in Moscow. So his mere presence in the film was enough to upset American Communists loyal to Stalin, and they picketed the theater.

Axelbank's collection still bears the scars of "Tsar to Lenin," his only serious venture into documentary film. It is evident from the editing and arrangement of certain film and still sequences. Every once in a while the sensibility of 1937 announces itself with a blast of Eastman's narration, delivered, in that strangely agitated voice, like a ghost from the past. As the name implies, "Tsar to Lenin" ends with Lenin and the Bolsheviks firmly in power. But the film foreshadows the revolution's betrayal. At one point Stalin appears on the screen, seen as a dark, blurry figure at the edge of a still photograph of a group of revolutionaries. Eastman convulses, "Nobody then dreamed . . ."

CHINA IN REVOLUTION

Rivalry and Struggle

The standard historical accounts tell us that China underwent two revolutions in the first half of the twentieth century: in 1911 and in 1949. Yet China's tumultuous half-century is perhaps better understood as an extended time of troubles.

The Chinese Revolution began in 1911 with the overthrow of the Manchu dynasty. The principal figure was Sun Yat-sen, who for years had plotted to bring down the Manchus. Unrest spread across the country, punctuated by several uprisings orchestrated by Sun's Revolutionary Alliance, a loose confederation of subversive groups. An army revolt in Wuchang on October 10, 1911, was the decisive event, sounding the death knell of the monarchy and marking the birth of a republic. October 10 became China's Independence Day. But who would lead this republic? Though Sun Yat-sen had many supporters, he lacked the kind of organized military force needed to rule China. According to historian Jonathan Spence, "Sun himself was fund-raising in the United States during the events of late 1911; he read the news of the Wuchang uprising in a Denver newspaper while en route to Kansas City."

Sun returned to China on Christmas Day, 1911, and was promptly chosen by delegates from sixteen provincial assemblies who had gathered in Nanking [Nanjing] to be "provisional president" of the Chinese republic. He assumed office in Nanking on January 1, 1912. But despite these formalities, a genuine Chinese republic failed to materialize. In just over a month's time, Sun, recognizing that he lacked the experience and especially the military power to rule the country, relinquished his claim on the presidency, giving way to a military general, Yuan Shikai, who had close ties to the Manchus. On February 13, the day after the abdication of the Manchu boy emperor Puyi, Yuan Shikai replaced Sun as provisional president. Sun hoped that Yuan would use his army and authority to realize the goals of the republic, but Yuan's methods were those of a military dictator.

In December 1912, China held its first national elections, in preparation for which the Revolutionary Alliance transformed itself into a political party and was renamed the National People's Party, or Kuomintang [Guomindang]. The election results, announced in January 1913, gave the Kuomintang a clear victory. But as he was waiting to board a train in Shanghai that would take him to Peking [Beijing] to assume the premiership of China, Kuomintang leader Song Jiaoren was shot to death. Yuan was widely believed to have arranged the assassination; in any case, his armies now openly moved against those of the Kuomintang, which were easily routed. Sun was forced to flee to Japan. On January 1, 1916, Yuan declared himself emperor, a move that alienated his closest political allies as well as

"National Army Soldiers Entering Taiping Gate in Nanking" (Shanghai, 1912). Text in Chinese: "Picture of battles won by the Republic of China." In early December 1911, after several weeks of fighting, Manchu loyalist troops were defeated in Nanking, which had been China's capital in the fourteenth century and held a special symbolic importance in the minds of the Chinese.

Sun Yat-sen. Among several collections containing interesting materials on Sun Yat-sen and the early Republic is that of Paul Linebarger, former justice in the U.S. Court of the Philippines, who was legal adviser to Sun Yat-sen from 1907, when the two men first met, to Sun's death in 1925. As Linebarger tells the story, during a visit to China, after his cook was kidnapped and tortured by bandits, Linebarger went to see "the archrevolutionist" Sun, "who impressed me so favorably with his personality and character and with the nature of his revolution that I resigned as United States District judge and determined to follow him in his efforts to overthrow the imperial dragon throne of 4,000 years duration." Linebarger describes this photograph of Sun and Mme Sun (née Soong Ch'ing-ling, who autographed it) as one of the last photographs taken of Sun. Linebarger supplied his own caption: "The sword cane carried by the reformer, with a heavy three foot steel blade, concealed within, was presented to him by the author, who obtained it as a formidable relic of the French Revolution, in Paris, France." (P.M.W. Linebarger Papers)

the foreign powers whose recognition he sought. After attempting unsuccessfully to repair the political damage, he died that June.

After Yuan's death, China entered the so-called warlord period. The country became fractionalized as regional military leaders arose to fill the power vacuum at the center. The term "warlords" described a variety of figures with diverse profiles, from local bandits to commanders of large armies and territories, and with divergent political views and ambitions. They supported themselves by taxing their populations and, when their authority was challenged, used force of arms against their rivals. Despite the breakdown of central authority, by the early 1920s an arrangement among warlords in and around Peking led to that city's recognition by foreign governments as the capital of China.

Meanwhile, Sun Yat-sen returned to China in 1916, establishing the Kuomintang's headquarters in the southern city of Canton. But Sun's power over the southern provinces was nominal, and he died in 1925 without seeing China unified. Yet his influence would endure in the form of his ideas on Chinese politics and society, ideas that were shaped in part by his experience in America.

Born in China in 1867, Sun was educated in the Hawaiian Islands and later earned a medical degree in Hong Kong. A charismatic figure and effective speaker, Sun developed a following among overseas Chinese, and this made him a successful fundraiser for the

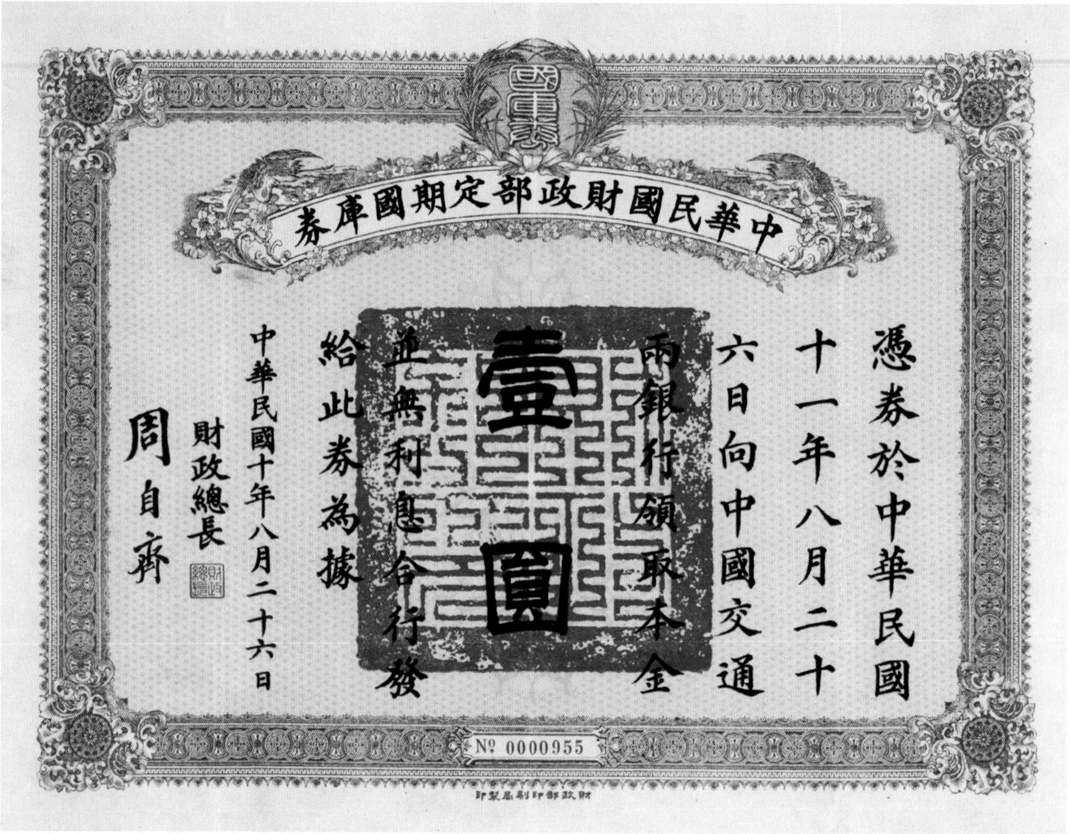

Certificate of National Bonds issued by the Ministry of Finance, Republic of China, in 1921. (P.M.W. Linebarger Papers)

revolutionary cause, especially in the United States, Canada, and Singapore, where he could count on the generous support of several wealthy Chinese businessmen. Before the revolution, Sun had expressed only a vaguely formulated political ideology, which was vigorously anti-Manchu and prorepublican, and broadly socialist. Above all, Sun's goal was to transform China into a strong modern state. It was only after the fall of the Manchus, in particular during his period of exile in Japan, that Sun was able to formulate a relatively coherent political program and plan of organization. Sun believed that China's path to modernity should unfold in three stages, beginning with successive periods of military and then party rule, after which could come a genuinely republican constitution. Sun made clear his belief that China was not ready for democracy, but he was unclear about the length of the transition period to democratic self-rule.

Shortly before his death in 1925, Sun collected his political ideas into a book, *The Three Principles of the People,* arguably the most influential Chinese text until the publication in the 1960s of Mao's incendiary Little Red Book. Sun's three principles of the people were democracy, nationalism, and livelihood. *People's democracy* meant sovereignty of the people and implied a constitutional order, though Sun had in mind a government run initially by elites; his text could easily be read as making a case for a benevolent dictatorship. *People's nationalism* meant anti-imperialism, with the goal of supplanting family and clan loyalty in order to create a unified China that could become a great power. *People's livelihood* meant economic reform that would distribute wealth, especially land, more equitably and bring a gradual end to poverty.

It all sounds quite reasonable, and Sun's three principles were defined ambiguously enough to be invoked by the Kuomintang, under Chiang Kai-shek, and the Communist Party, under Mao Zedong. Sun's economic ideas were generally socialist, but although he expressed a general sympathy for the Bolshevik Revolution he was not a Marxist. To Sun, China had to be selective in borrowing and adapting the ideas of Marx and Lenin, or any other strand of Western thought.

Besides, China hardly fit the Marxist model for a socialist revolution. The only "capitalists" in China were landowners, most of them foreigners living in the cities. Thus, in the Chinese context, anticapitalism was tantamount to anti-imperialism, a sacred cause to most Chinese. (Witness the Chinese reaction in 1919 to the Versailles Treaty, whose neglect of China set off the mass protests of May 4 in Peking, followed by similar demonstrations throughout China.) And since China had no genuine capitalists, once the imperialists had been expelled the state would itself have to take the lead in industrializing the country.

Whatever his political philosophy had in common with that of Soviet Communism, political reality moved Sun toward relations with Moscow in his struggle to defeat the regional warlords and build a national government. In his efforts to secure financial support, he turned to Lenin's government, which, its revolutionary aspirations in Europe having been thwarted, was ready to champion the cause of the developing world by stoking the fires of anti-imperialism in Asia. In 1923, Moscow instructed the recently established Chinese Communist Party to join forces with the Kuomintang, whom the Soviets provided with military equipment and instructors and political organizers. Among the latter was the veteran revolutionary Mikhail Borodin, whom Sun Yat-sen had met years before in the United States. Borodin set to work bringing discipline to the ranks of the Kuomintang and strengthening Sun's leadership position. Sun's Three Principles of the People were endorsed as the Kuomintang's official ideology, and Sun himself was named party leader for life.

The Kuomintang, its armies thus reorganized and rejuvenated with the help of Soviet equipment and advisers and the alliance with the Chinese Communists, launched a new political and military offensive in 1924, the Northern Expedition, led by Sun's successor, Chiang Kai-shek. Chiang's main objective was to bring the warlords to heel and centralize power in China under a single Nationalist government. And in fact, during the next few years, as his armies swept northward Chiang would go a long distance toward achieving his aims.

A major casualty of Chiang's unfolding triumph was the alliance of his Nationalists and the Chinese Communists. Much of the success of his Northern Expedition had depended on the Communists, whose role was to prepare the ground ahead for the Kuomintang armies through propaganda and by organizing strikes and demonstrations. But Chiang grew wary of his Bolshevik advisers, whose long-term goals, he knew, were not his own. Their class-war tactics were alien to his own middle-class supporters, and he had to wonder if ultimately these workers' organizations might reemerge as local soviets, which would be replicated in other cities throughout China—the same kind of chain reaction that brought the Bolsheviks to power. The breaking point was reached in Shanghai.

On April 12, 1927, after a Communist-organized general strike and armed insurrection had cleared the way for the fall of Shanghai to the Kuomintang, Chiang's forces entered the city and carried out a bloody purge of the Communists and their Russian advisers. Those who escaped, Borodin among them, were forced into hiding. The reverberations of the Shanghai massacre were felt in Moscow, where Trotsky and the Left Opposition, then making their last stand, used it to attack Stalin, who had championed the alliance of Communists and Nationalists.

Chiang's armies continued northward and by the end of 1928 had occupied Peking and established a seat of government at Nanking, which won the recognition of the major foreign powers. And yet, things were not entirely what they seemed from a distance. Chiang's control over the territories under the Kuomintang flag was far from undisputed, and on several occasions he had to deal with defections and manifestations of warlordism. Chiang had yet to consolidate his regime when, in 1931, Japan invaded Manchuria. Thus began the long torment of China by the Japanese army, which would eventually serve to reverse the balance of power in Chinese politics and make possible the improbable comeback and eventual triumph of the Communists.

Red Epic

After Chiang Kai-shek's purge, a number of armed Communist contingents fled to the southeast and the safety of the mountains. Among them was Mao Zedong, a former librarian, teacher, newspaper editor, and union organizer, and one of the founding members of the party. The Communists, who in 1931 established a Chinese Soviet Republic at Jiangxi, drew their support almost entirely from the poorer peasantry and the rural underclass, attracted by the Communist policy of expropriation and redistribution of large landed estates and vulnerable to their intensive propaganda. But soon after taking refuge in the south, Mao and the other Communist leaders realized that if the party were to survive it would need to organize its own army. And so, under the leadership of Zhu De, a former high-ranking officer in the Kuomintang who specialized in guerrilla tactics, they created the Red Army as a disciplined guerrilla force to offset the enormous advantage in numbers enjoyed by the Kuomintang forces.

After the Red Army's initial success in fending off the Kuomintang forces, Chiang launched a campaign that put 700,000 troops in the field against the Communists' 150,000. In order to escape certain destruction and to establish a territorial base safe from the incursions of the Nationalists and the harassment of local warlords, in 1934 the Red Army broke out of their Kuomintang encirclement and undertook what became known as the Long March. Their route took them northward around the western periphery of China. Over the course of one year, the marchers traveled some 6,000 miles across often treacherous terrain, struggling against hunger, disease, and freezing cold, and battling hostile forces along the way. Even reliable sources disagree on the exact numbers, but a reasonable estimate is that some 80,000 men and women undertook the journey, and that of these about 8,000 to 9,000 made it to the final destination, in northern Shaanxi province, on October 20, 1935. There the Red forces established themselves and set out to build a base of support among the local peasants. The city of Yenan [Yan'an] was to be the de facto capital of the Chinese Communists almost uninterruptedly until the 1949 revolution.

The Long March was, as it remains, the Great Red Epic. The world first learned about it from the American journalist Edgar Snow, the first outsider to visit Mao and the Communists in their new sanctuary near Yenan in 1936. In fact, most Chinese learned of it from reading the Chinese edition of Snow's book *Red Star over China*. It was the crucible of the Chinese Revolution. It forged a sense of unbreakable unity among the survivors, many of whom went on to occupy positions of power and prestige in the Communist government. And it sealed the status of the forty-year-old Mao Zedong, who emerged as the undisputed political and military leader of the Chinese Communist Party, with Zhou En-lai as his indispensable lieutenant.

The Long March Sketches

The Hoover Institution Archives holds a collection of twenty-four black ink sketches of the Long March, drawings made along the route by one of its survivors. The artist, Huang Zhen, was one of Mao's cadres in the 1930s; he rose to the rank of general in the Red Army. After the revolution he became a diplomat, serving as China's ambassador to Hungary, Indonesia, and France, before heading up China's Liaison Office in the United States in the 1970s. He returned to China in 1977 to become minister of culture.

Huang Zhen's unique artwork ended up at the Hoover Archives thanks to Edgar Snow and his wife, "Peg," to whom Huang entrusted his sketches in 1937, most likely in order to preserve them. The sketches were published, anonymously, in book form in Shanghai in 1938, using photographic reproductions of the originals. The book was titled *Sketches on the Journey to the West* to complement Snow's *Red Star over China* (1937), which had just been published under the Chinese title *Notes on the Journey to the West.* Only two thousand copies of the book were printed, and all but a few copies were lost or destroyed during the subsequent decade of Sino-Japanese and civil war.

In 1958, a reader in the Peking Library came across the book and recognized its singularity, and soon a new edition was in preparation, with a copy of the original publication serving as the master copy. The artist had not been identified in the original edition, and no one could now remember who it was. By coincidence, just at this time Huang Zhen returned from a diplomatic assignment abroad and someone mentioned the project to him, at which point he cleared up the mystery. He had drawn his sketches en route, using scraps of paper of different kinds, sizes, and colors—anything he could lay his hand on at that time. For the new edition of the book, Huang provided elaborate and informative captions for each image.

The Chinese government twice reprinted the book and then published a new edition in 1982. Huang Zhen was still alive, though Chairman Mao had been dead for six years and official enthusiasm for his undertakings in power had certainly waned. But the Long March retained its mystique. The editors, affirming the uniqueness of Huang's sketches, lamented that his original artwork could not be located. "We sincerely hope that the missing originals can also be found some day so that more splendour can be added to our historical documents."

Crossing the Luding Bridge. The most famous incident of the Long March also involved the greatest act of heroism: the crossing of the Luding Bridge, a suspension bridge high above the Dadu River, by twenty-two Red Army men, in what amounted to a suicide mission.

The Luding Bridge, built in 1701, is a chain structure about 100 meters (329 feet) long and 2.8 meters (9.2 feet) wide and made of thirteen chains, nine forming the floor, covered with planking, with two chains on either side as railings. As Huang Zhen relates: "People walking across the middle are often scared out of their wits as the bridge sways badly from left to right above the roaring water below."

On May 29, 1935, the Red Army arrived at the bridge and found that its planks had been removed. Despite heavy gunfire from the enemy troops stationed at the other end of the bridge and in the hills above, the Red Army assault team of twenty-two men, selected from the Second Company of the Fourth Regiment, moved forward. Behind them, laying planks, came troops of the Third Company.

As the story is told, the twenty-two Red warriors, each armed with a pistol, a sword, and hand grenades, negotiated the chains and overcame the Kuomintang forces, who as a last resort set fire to the blockhouse they had been occupying. After a two-hour firefight, the bridge was secured. Eighteen of the twenty-two raiders survived the assault. Over the years, the Communist Chinese paid tribute to these Luding heroes in many books and feature films. (Nym Wales Papers)

Climbing the Jiajin Mountains. After crossing the Dadu, the Red Army forces came to the Western Sichuan Plateau, where they gazed up at the snowy peaks of the Jiajin Mountains, a fourteen-thousand-foot pass in the Great Snow Mountain Range. The survivors would remember the trek through the Snowies as the worst experience of the Long March. Mao was ill with recurrent malaria and at times had to be carried in a litter. Many of the marchers were from the warm, semitropical regions of southern China and had little experience with snow and cold or with the thinness of the air at such a high altitude. There were many victims of frostbite. Huang Zhen recalled:

> *As we went up higher and the paths became narrower and the mountains steeper, the going grew more difficult. A careless step would end your climb by sending you to the depths of the surrounding gorges. Meanwhile the cold wind kicked up the snow which swirled around us. In the clouds and fog, the Red Army soldiers marched on in thin clothes which offered no protection against a cold snowstorm. The wind, as sharp as a knife, cut our faces. The air grew thinner and many of us, scarcely able to breathe, began to feel dizzy and weak. Our legs trembled. For every step we took, we stooped and panted. Many weak and ill comrades died on the way.*

The original caption along the left side of the drawing reads: "The Snow Mountains are high, but the morale of the iron-hewn Red Army is higher still." (Nym Wales Papers)

Carrying Grains Across the Grasslands. The landscape in this sketch appears benign, but only because its perils are not apparent. Huang's caption speaks of the "painful struggles and hardships" endured in the crossing of the misleadingly labeled Great Grasslands, a treacherous swampland just south of the Yellow River. Huang describes the driving winds, rain, hail, and sleet that slowed the soldiers' progress, and the dense fog that distorted their sense of direction.

> *We could hardly tell where we were going. Hidden ditches and rivers criss-crossed the wild grass, and dark stagnant water gave off a foul smell. Trudging through sodden quagmires covered with rotten grass and stems required great attention. If not careful, you could easily sink in so deep that it was difficult to pull your legs out. . . . Some mules and horses dropped into quagmires. They tried desperately to get out while sinking deeper and deeper until they disappeared in the marsh. People could do nothing to save them. The evil quagmires quickly resumed their original appearance.*

Each of the soldiers carried a grain sack containing either fried or powdered barley, weighing, as Huang's caption notes, a little more than 20 catties (about 1.3 pounds) for fifteen days. "If someone fell down, dropping his grain sack into poisonous water," Huang recalled, "he was faced with a hard dilemma: if he did not want to eat the barley, he went hungry. However, if he did, he risked suffering a bloated and aching stomach. Some people saw their grain spill into dirty mud after their sacks had gotten caught and torn on grass-roots. They could do nothing but rely on other people's support." Nighttime brought freezing cold. Thousands died from illness or exhaustion. "Every time we continued our march after a cold and hungry night, we left some comrades lying forever on the ground where we had camped together." (Nym Wales Papers)

Gung Ho over Mao

The end of the Long March found the remnants of Mao's army in northern Shaanxi province. The year they arrived, 1935, the world Comintern line swung to the "popular front" policy of solidarity among all antifascist forces. Once again, political calculations made in Moscow would influence the course of events in China. Stalin insisted that Mao and the Communists form an alliance with Chiang Kai-shek's government, based at Nanking, in a united front against the Japanese. The force of Moscow's authority in internal Chinese politics was given a vivid demonstration in December 1936, when Chiang was kidnapped during a visit to Sian, in northwestern China, by a disaffected warlord sympathetic to the Communists. Moscow pressured Mao into arranging Chiang's release so that he could lead China's struggle against the Japanese.

An uneasy alliance was now in place, with the Communists as the junior partners. In the summer of 1937 came the Japanese invasion and the fall of Shanghai and Nanking, forcing Chiang's government to retreat to the inland city of Chungking. The toll on Chiang's armies was terrific. He had ordered that Shanghai be held at all costs, with the result that up to 250,000 of his troops—more than half of his best soldiers—were killed or wounded at Shanghai (as compared to 40,000 or more casualties for the Japanese).

By an arrangement reached between Chungking and Yenan in late 1937, the Red Army was now redesignated as the Eighth Route Army and placed under the nominal command of the Kuomintang. The two sides pledged to work toward the realization of Sun Yat-sen's Three Principles of the People. In fact, however, despite their common interest in repelling the Japanese each side now acted with a keen eye on its own long-term interests. The Communists conducted their own brand of guerrilla warfare against the Japanese and meanwhile tempered their doctrine and policies in the countryside in order to accommodate their Kuomintang allies. As historian Spence writes:

> *Participation in the united front inevitably forced on many radicals a sharp break with their earlier ideological goals and aspirations: rent reduction and limited land redistribution had to replace the expropriation of wealthy landlords' holdings that had been practiced in Jiangxi and the other soviets. Gradualist approaches to education and indoctrination were substituted for confrontational strike action, and a cautious economic program of rural credits and development of local industries was designed to avoid alienating the wealthier farmers or townspeople in border regions.*

United front leadership poster. This Chinese poster from 1937 takes a hopeful view of the new anti-Japanese alliance of Nationalists, Communists, and others. The images are of various political and military leaders, including Chiang Kai-shek (upper right) and Mao Zedong (at center, third row from bottom), with Sun Yat-sen (top), who had died in 1925, portrayed as modern China's spiritual leader. The poster's captions exhort these leaders and their followers to combine forces in a national effort to repel and eliminate the Japanese "dwarf bandits." (Joseph W. Stilwell Papers)

Edgar and Helen Foster Snow, China, 1930s. (Randall Gould Papers)

The Nationalists, meanwhile, as an urban-based movement with little to offer the peasantry in the way of a reform program, had been cut off by the Japanese armies from their mainstay of support in the urban centers of eastern China. Economically, the effect was devastating and led to rampant inflation. Chiang's regime became increasingly corrupt and authoritarian.

By 1941, in the face of these circumstances and with both sides chafing under the constraints of their arrangement, the united front was on the verge of collapse. Chiang's forces lashed out against the Communists. The confrontation might have escalated into all-out war, but for the Japanese attack on Pearl Harbor in December. As long as Japan remained undefeated, Chiang could not afford to antagonize the United States by renewing the civil war. But the Kuomintang government effectively blockaded the Communists in their northern outpost and otherwise sought to isolate them until the military campaign could be renewed. That Chiang's government did not succeed in this was due in large part to the efforts of a few enterprising American journalists, soldiers, and diplomats.

Owing largely to the American presence in China, both before and after Pearl Harbor, researchers in the Hoover Archives are able to get a close-up view of the Chinese Communist ascent from their nadir in 1935 to their triumph in 1949.

It was a journalist, Edgar Snow, who reached the Communists first, spending four months in 1936 at their headquarters in the caves of Bao'an, outside Yenan, in Shaanxi province. His series of articles, published in the *China Weekly Review*, recounting his sympathetic interviews with Mao and other Communist leaders and describing what he saw and heard while he was among them—including the first news of the heroic Long March—caused a sensation, and a great deal of consternation in Nanking. Snow's portrait muted the Communists' revolutionary ideology, highlighting instead their determination to cast the Japanese out of China and introduce agrarian reform. The following year, Snow turned this material into a book, *Red Star over China*, which became an international best seller.

Other American journalists followed in Snow's footsteps and invariably presented a similar picture of their Red hosts as genial, disciplined, earnest, brave, egalitarian, and unpretentious. Typically there were strikingly unfavorable contrasts drawn to the ruling

Mao Zedong, in 1936, at the caves of Bao'an, in Northern Shaanxi province (photograph by Edgar Snow). (Nym Wales Papers)

The "Big Four": left to right, Po Ku, Zhou En-lai, Zhu De, and Mao Zedong, Yenan, 1937 (photograph by Helen Foster Snow). (Nym Wales Papers)

Mao Zedong and Zhu De, Yenan, 1937 (photograph by Helen Foster Snow). (Nym Wales Papers)

Kuomintang. If these foreign journalists did not all, like Snow, explicitly predict the eventual victory of the Communists, the impression was left that Mao & Co. were serious contenders.

One of these journalists was Snow's wife, Helen Foster, known as Peg. She had come to China at the age of twenty-four, in 1931, with the promise of a mining company secretarial job secured through her father, a Utah lawyer with connections to the state's mining industry. She met Snow in Shanghai; they married the following year and moved to Peking, where they set about reporting the Chinese civil war and the student movement. It was the Snows' contacts with Peking's student movement and with the Communist agents who had infiltrated it that led to Edgar receiving the invitation to Bao'an to meet Mao Zedong.

Upon her husband's return, Peg Snow undertook a similar journey, at considerable risk to her life, venturing to the Communist headquarters in Yenan, where she spent four months in 1937. She too interviewed and photographed Mao and his comrades and, upon her return to Peking, published articles and eventually a book, *Inside Red China* (1939), under the pen name Nym Wales. She described Mao as "the Chinese Lenin" and rhapsodized about the dedication and discipline of leaders such as Zhou En-lai and Zhu De. Some would say she was a better writer than her husband. She was certainly the better archivist; the Nym Wales Papers constitute one of the most important collections in the Hoover Archives.

Helen Foster Snow's most lasting influence in China was the creation, together with her husband and several others, of the Gung Ho movement of industrial cooperatives in Shanghai in the 1930s—"gung ho" being the Chinese equivalent of "work together." The idea caught on all over China—and the term itself became a permanent part of the American vocabulary thanks to Marine Capt. Evans Carlson, assistant naval attaché in China and friend of the Snows, who adopted it as the motto for his famous World War II battalion, Carlson's Raiders. For a time the Gung Ho cooperatives enjoyed the support of both Mao and Chiang Kai-shek. In 1958, these cooperatives were, like much else, coopted by the Communists, who merged them into state-run communes.

THE DIXIE MISSION

When the United States entered the Second World War, its chief focus was on defeating Hitler first; the war in Asia would have to wait. But in the meantime it was important to keep China from falling to the Japanese. As a way of bolstering the military effort of Generalissimo Chiang Kai-shek, whose government had retreated to a new capital at Chungking, President Roosevelt designated Lt. Gen. Joseph Stilwell to serve as Chiang's chief of staff. Relations between these two men—Stilwell and Chiang—were to become poisonous, famously so, but beyond the clash of their personalities, in the course of the war the Americans stationed in China—and increasingly their superiors in Washington—came to believe in the wisdom of establishing official contact with the Communists in Yenan in order to explore the potential for collaboration in the war against Japan. Naturally, this idea was unpopular in Chungking, and it would become scandalous in Washington after China was "lost" to communism in 1949.

The idea to send an American observer mission to Yenan originated with a report written for Stilwell by his political officer, John Paton Davies, in June 1943. In making his case for an American mission, Davies emphasized the military importance of Shaanxi province, particularly in connection with a future Soviet entry into the war against Japan. Stilwell was convinced, and Davies managed to persuade U.S. Army Chief of Staff George Marshall of the wisdom of such an undertaking. A second report by Davies, written in January 1944, requested Chiang's permission to send such a mission. Chiang gave his approval but then stalled. Meanwhile, after months of lobbying, in May a group of three newspaper correspondents was allowed to travel to Yenan. Yet despite Washington's repeated requests, including one from President Roosevelt in April, the U.S. mission remained stalled. It took the personal intervention in Chungking of Vice President Henry Wallace to force Chiang to make good on his promise.

Stilwell named Col. David D. Barrett, his assistant military attaché, as chief of mission, with the State Department's John Service as his political assistant. The Military Observers Mission—given the name Dixie for the rebel side—reached Yenan on July 23. The group's nine members, augmented by a second contingent sent a month later, represented the air corps, medical corps, signal corps, and infantry. As historian Barbara Tuchman recounts, the American visitors found much to like in Yenan. The correspondents who preceded the mission had humanized the Communist leaders for their readers and written favorable descriptions of the spartan yet cheerful existence inside the Communist zone. Reporting for the Dixie Mission, John Service, who spoke Chinese, was similarly impressed: "He found morale high and the people serious with a sense of mission and a purposeful program under competent leadership." If there was political repression or control, it was not evident. There

Col. David Barrett: Enfant Terrible

The Dixie Mission is thoroughly documented in several Hoover collections, notably the papers of Col. David Barrett, its first chief; Gen. Joseph Stilwell, the commanding officer in China who tapped Barrett for the mission; and Col. Wilbur Peterkin, Dixie's executive officer and later commanding officer, whose collection contains an extensive photographic record of the Communist headquarters in Yenan in 1944 and 1945, as well as motion picture film of Mao and other leading Communists.

By personality, Col. Barrett seems an unlikely figure to head up a diplomatic mission. He was a blunt-spoken man, at least in English; in his fluent Chinese he may have been more prone to subtlety. Tuchman says he was "the only American who could tell jokes convincingly in Chinese to Chinese." This was a result of his long professional experience in China, beginning in the 1930s. After the war, from the summer of 1947, he served as assistant military attaché at the U.S. embassy in Peking, which he departed for Formosa (Taiwan) on February 6, 1950, shortly after all American officials had been ordered out of what then became known as Red China.

Like the members of the Dixie Mission under his command, Barrett developed a preference for Mao and the Communists over Chiang and the Kuomintang. Over time, and especially in the two decades after the 1949 Revolution, these men had to revise their judgment of the Communists, and quite radically. Barrett's transition from enthusiast to enemy was expedited by the new Communist regime, which in 1951 accused him of having masterminded a daring American plot to assassinate Mao Zedong in October 1950. The alleged plan was to fire a trench mortar at the reviewing stand set up in front of the Tienanmen, the main south gate of the Forbidden City, during the celebration of the anniversary of the founding of the Communist regime in China. The accused all confessed to the charges, resulting in the execution of two of Barrett's foreign acquaintances and the imprisonment of five others (all non-Americans) in China.

Barrett could do nothing but issue a detailed statement refuting the official story of a plot, despite its obvious absurdity: "The Communists must rate me very low as a mastermind if they think I would try to assassinate anyone with a trench mortar." This rough treatment at the hands of his former hosts in Yenan did not, however, endear Barrett to Chiang Kai-shek's government on Formosa, where the Kuomintang established its headquarters in 1949 and where memories were long. When Barrett retired in 1952, he applied for permission to live in the Republic of China. Permission was denied, evidently by Chiang personally. When the American ambassador queried Chiang on the subject, all he would say was, "I have my reasons."

In 1970, on the eve of the Sino-American rapprochement, Barrett published a short account of the Dixie Mission, in which he was alternatingly bitter about Dixie's conservative critics in America, with their "perfect hindsight," and regretful about his former enthusiasm for the Communists in opposition. By then, after two tumultuous decades marked by political repression and mass starvation in Communist China, there was a lot to regret.

> *As I see it now, in the clear light of hindsight, the mistake I made in 1944 was in not considering the Chinese Communists as enemies of the United States. I thought of them primarily as allied with us in fighting the Japanese. "The enemy of my enemy, my friend." Communism as a political doctrine was just as much anathema to me then as it is now, but I was naive to the extent that I thought of the Chinese members of the Party as Chinese first and communists afterwards, a belief which I later realized was woefully wrong. If someone tried to tell me in the summer of 1944 that the time would ever come when Chinese boys and girls would stand up in a mass trial and ask that their parents be shot as counter-revolutionaries, I would have laughed at him.*

David Barrett cracking wise to Zhu De (foreground) and cracking up Mao Zedong, August 1944. (David D. Barrett Papers)

Col. David Barrett flanked by Mao (right) and Zhu De, Yenan, 1944. (David D. Barrett Papers)

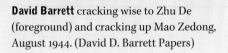

Dixie Mission, outfitted in uniforms tailored by the Red Army in Yenan, September 6, 1944. Barrett stands at the center of the front row; on his left is Col. Wilbur Peterkin; behind Peterkin, peering over his right shoulder, is John Service. Barrett wrote on the back of this photograph: "THE WELSH COAL MINERS' CHORUS, JUST UP FROM THE PITS: This real dilley, which might yet hang us all, shows the U.S. Army Liaison Group, Yenan, in the Communist suits coopered to our individual forms and presented to us by our genial hosts in Yenan." (David D. Barrett Papers)

were no gendarmes, no bureaucracy, no limousine caravans—in other words, none of the "clap-trap of Chungking" and certainly none of its defeatism.

These favorable American assessments must to some extent have been influenced by the geniality of the Communist hosts—at least that is the impression one is left with after studying dozens of photographs taken during the Dixie Mission. In retrospect, of course, it all seems like part of a charm offensive aimed at seducing the gullible Americans. The members of the mission had their photograph taken in the specially tailored uniforms of the Eighth Route Army, whose soldiers, according to the *New York Times* correspondent, were "among the best-clothed and best-fed the writer has seen anywhere in China." Long afterward, Dixie's chief, Col. Barrett, recalled joking to Zhou En-lai that Yenan was the Communists' "Potemkin village."

The Dixie Mission was sent to evaluate the Communist potential for military collaboration against the Japanese, and to assess "the most effective means of assisting the Communists to increase the value of their war effort." It was this prospect of direct American military assistance to his foes that alarmed Chiang and was the reason he had tried to prevent the mission. After 1949, Davies, Service, and other young diplomats like them would lose their jobs during the McCarthy period for having concluded, like Edgar Snow in 1936, that the Communists were a better bet than the Nationalists, and for advising the State Department to keep lines open to both sides.

These American emissaries did not believe that the Chinese Communists were *real* Communists. As Tuchman explains, "This negative assumption was derived from the syllogism that while Communism was known to be a bad thing, it seemed to operate in many ways as a good thing in China; therefore it could not be orthodox Communism." In Washington, it became routine in official correspondence to refer to the Communists, following President Roosevelt's example, as "so-called Communists."

Later, Service, Davies, and the others would be ridiculed for having believed that the Chinese Communists were mere "agrarian reformers." The fact is, however, the Communists of the united front period had modified their agrarian and educational policies and toned down their propaganda. It was only after the war that they reverted to their earlier radicalism, promoting land confiscation and other forms of class warfare. At the same time, the priority of the American military was the Japanese occupation army in Manchuria and northern China and the prospects of a drawn-out resistance that would cost thousands of American lives. Considering all these circumstances—not least, the genuine American doubts about the effectiveness and reliability of Chiang's Nationalists—throwing a line out to the Communists seemed to make sense.

Barrett

FOR INTER-DEPARTMENTAL USE
STANFORD UNIVERSITY

OFFICE OF

....

November 28, 1952

Easton:

Colonel Barrett (see attached) might just turn up in your office before I have a chance to perform introductions. He has given the Library quite a lot over a period of six years, and he arranged a lot of Kuomintang connections for me when I was collecting in 1946-7. He also had me to some fine parties. He is quite a character. Twenty-four years of China duty as an army attache. He is steeped in language, area, and the ins and outs of politics over a long period of time--but has always been something of an enfant terrible. Back in the thirties he used to know a lot of communists and observed them more carefully than most officials. Later he was a violent anti-communist. Last year, a number of his alleged "agents" were executed in Peking for an alleged Barrett-manipulated plot to assassinate Mao Tse-tung. He is now retired, much against his will and is hot-footing it back to Formosa to spend the rest of his days in what is left of his kind of China. We should persuade him to spend a good part of his future leisure helping us collect.

Mary
Mary Wright

MCW:mo

Memo from Mary Wright, the Hoover Library's curator of Chinese and South East Asian Collection, to Hoover Library Director Rothwell Easton, November 28, 1952 (Hoover Institution Records). From 1946 until the spring of 1947, the Hoover Library's principal representatives in China were Mary Wright and Arthur Wright, both students of China. Using Tokyo as a base, the Wrights traveled extensively throughout China, collecting materials on the Chinese Communists and on the civil war. Thanks to the U.S. Air Force, Mary Wright succeeded in flying to Yenan, the capital of the Chinese Communists, before it fell to Nationalist troops on March 19, 1947. The newspapers, pamphlets, and books she packed up and sent to the Hoover Library form a vital part of the Hoover's exceptionally rich coverage of China between the revolutions.

Mary and Arthur Wright left Stanford in 1959 for teaching positions at Yale, where she became the first tenured woman in the arts and sciences, and where her teaching inspired Jonathan Spence, later one of America's premier China scholars, to become a historian of modern China.

Last Chance in Manchuria?

At the behest of the United States, and as arranged at the Yalta Conference in February 1945, the Soviet Army entered the war against Japan by invading Manchuria in August 1945. This Russo-Japanese war lasted only one week, cut short, along with the entire war in Asia, by the dropping of the atomic bombs on Hiroshima and Nagasaki. The United States, in overestimating the length of the war by about one and a quarter years, and with the goal of saving American lives, had rewarded the USSR with dominance over Manchuria, which the Soviet Army had managed to conquer with little difficulty by the time the Japanese surrendered on August 14, 1945.

In the autumn, Chinese Communist forces under Lin Biao reached Manchuria, where they made contact with the Soviets, who allowed stockpiles of Japanese weapons and equipment to fall into Communist hands, while preventing the Nationalists from rapidly moving their troops into the region. Yet, for the time being, the Soviet leadership did not openly commit itself to the Communist side in China's imminent civil war.

The United States now began its ill-fated attempt to mediate an agreement between Chiang and Mao, which had the unintended effect of giving the Communists further time to strengthen their military position. In August, U.S. special envoy Patrick Hurley personally escorted a reluctant Mao to Chungking for talks with Chiang. Hurley's role as peacemaker was soon taken over by Gen. George Marshall, now retired from active duty and enlisted by President Truman for this especially delicate diplomatic assignment. Marshall quickly concluded that Chiang was the chief obstacle to a peaceful resolution of civil war and demanded that Chiang accept an immediate cease-fire, which Marshall succeeded in arranging and which went into effect on January 10, 1946.

Meanwhile, the fate of Manchuria had become the vital question for the Nationalist government. Chiang understood Manchuria's potential as the industrial heartland of East Asia. It was a region rich in natural resources, such as coal, iron, and timber, with a population of more than forty-five million, large industrial cities, and extensive food reserves. Manchuria was essential to China's future as a modern industrialized country. The Japanese had invested heavily in the region since their occupation in 1931, and the Soviet Army availed itself of large quantities of industrial machinery, from machine tools to power-generating equipment and transformers.

Chiang believed that since the United States was not about to expel the Soviets from China, the only way he could secure their withdrawal was to negotiate. With tens of thousands of Chinese Communist guerrillas pouring into Manchuria, Chiang sought to persuade the Soviets to withdraw from Manchuria at the earliest possible date and in a way that would allow control of the region to pass to the Nationalists and not the Communists. Indeed, until May 1946, when the Soviets finally pulled their troops out of Manchuria, they left open the possibility of reaching an agreement with the Nationalist government on the future status of Manchuria and the disposition of its Japanese assets.

And so, without the knowledge of the U.S. government or of the Chinese public, in the autumn of 1945 the Nationalists conducted secret negotiations in Manchuria's capital, Ch'ang-ch'un, with the Soviet authorities led by Marshal Rodion Malinovsky, commander of the Soviet occupation army. On the Chinese side, the highest-ranking negotiator was General Hsiung Shih-hui, chairman of the Nationalist Military Affairs Commission for Manchuria, but the most important members of the mission were Chiang's son and Chang Kia-ngau (1889–1979), an economist, scholar, diplomat, founder of the Central Bank of China, and later minister of railroads and communication. He spent the last decade of his life as a senior research fellow at the Hoover Institution, where he deposited his private papers, including his diary of the Sino-Soviet negotiations over Manchuria.

Chiang Kai-shek, undated (early 1930s). (Oliver J. Todd Papers)

Chang's diary spans the period from October 12, 1945, through April 30, 1946. Its key revelation is that Chang and other leading Kuomintang officials, including perhaps Chiang Kai-shek, believed that the Nationalist government, by making significant concessions to the Soviets, could reach an early accord with the Soviets on economic cooperation in Manchuria after the Soviet withdrawal, with the result that Nationalist troops might be able to occupy Manchuria's cities as early as January 1946, before the civil war resumed in earnest.

In the end, no agreement was reached. Most students of Soviet history would conclude that this was because Stalin was never sincere about reaching an accord with the Kuomintang, and that negotiations were meant at most to buy time—at a minimum to see what the Soviets could get away with (literally and otherwise) and at a maximum to give the Chinese Communists time to prepare for the resumption of the Civil War. Chang's diary blames the failure of the negotiations not on Soviet duplicity but on ambivalence toward the talks of Nationalist officials in Chungking who thought that the issue could be forced militarily and who took actions that undercut the efforts of the Chinese negotiators.

The larger debate over these negotiations (beyond the question of Soviet motives) is really a debate about the viability of the Nationalist government in the face of the rising Communist tide. Was the Kuomintang really a spent force, as the U.S. State Department became convinced? For those who dispute this point of view, the role of American diplomacy in 1945–46 was entirely negative. It kept Chiang's Nationalists from an early military victory,

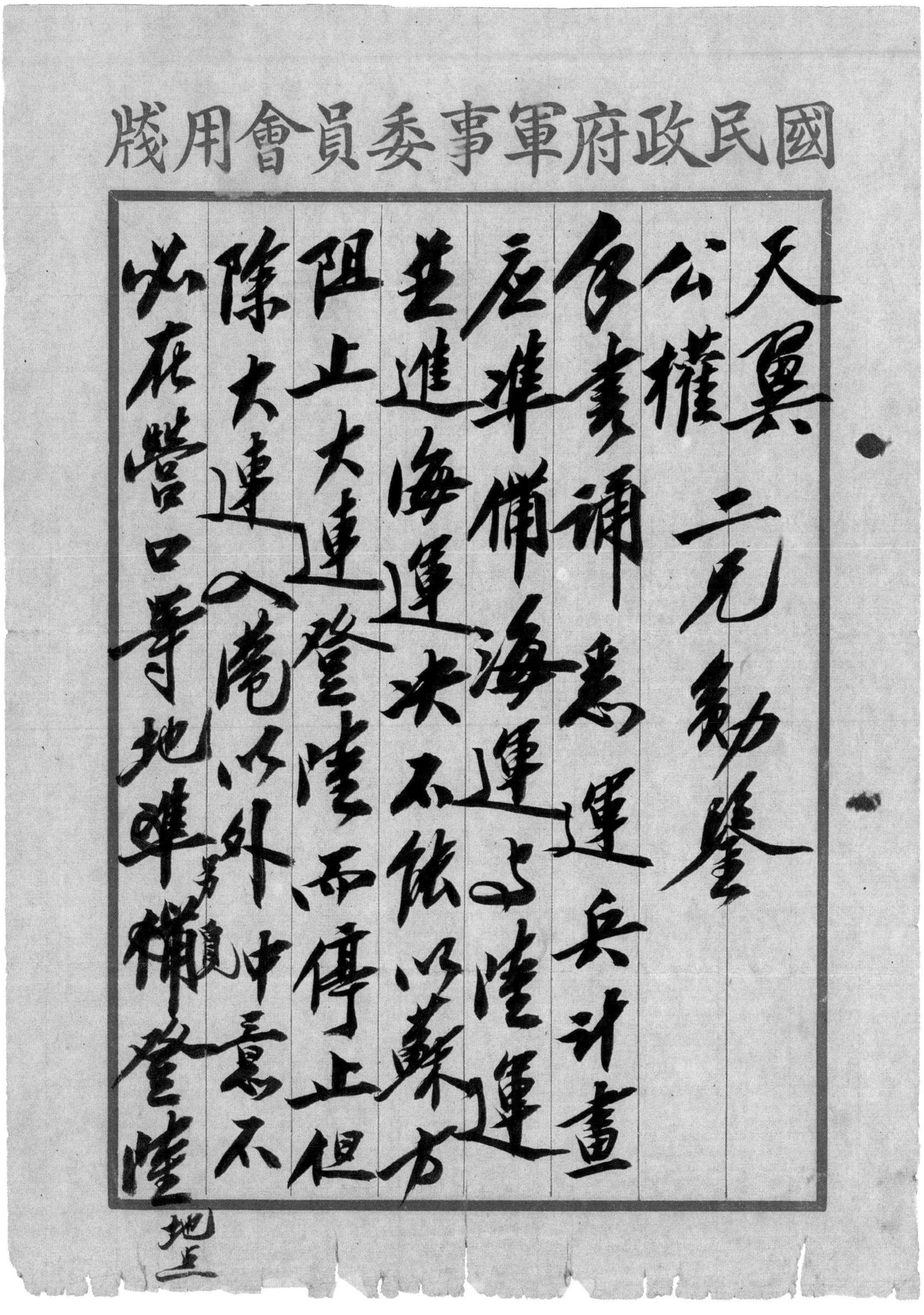
國民政府軍事委員會用牋

天翼
公權 二兄勛鑒

Handwritten letter of instruction from President Chiang Kai-shek to Hsiung Shih-hui and Chang Kia-ngau, October 16, 1945, concerning negotiations with the Soviet Union over the disposition of Manchuria. As his letter shows, Chiang took seriously the possibility of reaching an accord with Moscow, but he also understood that many things could go wrong: "As for Soviet apprehensions about certain events and persons hindering cooperation between our two countries, we must give special attention to this and do our utmost to avoid such a situation; generally we must not allow room for the slightest misunderstanding." (Chang Kia-ngau Papers) giving the Communists a breathing spell; and it signaled to the Soviets that the United States was not going to act to prevent a Chinese Communist victory in China. Even many of those who find America's diplomacy misguided and naïve, however, believe that no matter how hard a line the United States might have taken there was no stopping the Communists.

Whatever Moscow's motivations, the drawn-out negotiations (and other delaying tactics) had enabled the Chinese Communist forces to move more than half a million troops into Manchuria by January 1946. As Stalin withdrew Soviet troops in April and May, each side made preparations to take their place: the Communists from their bases in the countryside, the Nationalists from the cities. (The terrain, forested and mountainous, favored guerrilla armies.) In June, Marshall managed to negotiate a cease-fire in Manchuria, but it was ineffective and bound to be short-lived. The civil war erupted in Manchuria, lasting until the fall of 1948, when the Nationalist forces were routed. As Spence observes, other forces worked to undermine the authority of Chiang Kai-shek in China proper, notably a "catastrophic inflation" and "the defection from his side of a majority of China's intellectuals, students, professional classes, and urban workers."

By the autumn of 1949 the People's Liberation Army had triumphed over the Kuomintang throughout China. On October 1, 1949, in Peking, the People's Republic of China was founded. Chiang withdrew his crippled armies to the island of Formosa (Taiwan)—and to the lesser islands of Matsu and Quemoy—where he established the small but soon prospering Republic of China, which until 1971 continued to occupy China's seat in the United Nations. During the 1990s, economic prosperity was accompanied by political democracy, which served to strengthen the Republic of China's claim to direct descendancy from Sun Yat-sen and his Three Principles of the People.

PURPOSE OF THIS INSTITUTION IS TO
STAND AS A CHALLENGE TO THOSE WHO PROMOTE
ATTRACT THOSE WHO SEARCH FOR PEACE.
DEDICATE THIS BUILDING TO THESE PURPOSES.
HERBERT HOOVER
ENCYCLOPEDIAS

Chapter Three

THE TOWER

Herbert Hoover—engineer, humanitarian, statesman—was for a great many years Stanford University's most influential alumnus, trustee, and benefactor.* The first resident student to arrive at the new campus in 1891, he studied engineering and went on to achieve phenomenal success and great fortune as a businessman in the mining industry, which took him all over the world. The food campaigns he organized in wartime and postwar Europe and America earned him worldwide admiration and respect and set him on a path toward the White House. His wealth and celebrity, together with a forceful personality and his commitment to excellence at Stanford, gave him an extraordinary influence at his alma mater, second only to that of its founders, Leland and Jane Stanford.

Hoover died in 1964, yet in essential ways he remains Stanford's Big Man on Campus. His influence is manifest in the university's institutions and is visible in its architecture, including the home that he and his wife, Lou Henry, built in the hillside above campus and that now serves as the residence of the university president. Hoover's greatest legacy to Stanford is the library and archives that bear his name and the monumental structure he built to house them. Above all, the Hoover Tower.

FOUNDATIONS

In a memoir written many years after the founding of the Hoover Library, Herbert Hoover cited as its inspiration a passage from the autobiography of Andrew D. White, the distinguished historian and diplomat and the first president of Cornell University. It was the winter of 1915, and Hoover, who had undertaken to deliver lifesaving food to Belgian citizens through his neutral Commission for Relief in Belgium (CRB), was crossing the English Channel. In the passage in question, White recounted how, beginning in his student days in Paris in the 1850s, he assembled a vast collection of primary documents on the French Revolution, documents that a colleague used to write one of the best books in English on the subject. Reading about this, Hoover recalled, resolved him to undertake the systematic collection of contemporary documents on the European war that had been under way for several months.

* The text of this chapter draws extensively on George H. Nash's essential *Herbert Hoover and Stanford University* (1988).

However well Hoover's memory served him in 1951, the contemporary documents record that the particular source of his inspiration was a Stanford history professor named Ephraim Adams. In February 1915, Adams wrote to Hoover in London asking that the records of the CRB be preserved and expressing the hope that these records could eventually be deposited at Stanford. Hoover replied that he found Adams's suggestion to be of "extreme value," promised him that "every atom of material" would be saved, and agreed that it was a "fine idea to store them at Stanford University." As it happened, the CRB's files would become what Adams later called "the first item of importance in our collection" at Stanford. For now, though, there was no mention of a larger plan.

At the end of the war, in January 1919, Adams again wrote to Hoover, now in Paris administering America's massive postwar food relief campaign across Europe, reminding him of his earlier pledge regarding the CRB's records. Three months later came Hoover's reply, in the form of a telegram to his wife at Stanford, asking her to inform university President Ray Lyman Wilbur and Professor Adams that he would provide $50,000 for the establishment of "an historical collection on the Great War." Hoover instructed that the collecting work should begin immediately, and that a "suitable commission" should be sent to Paris promptly for this purpose. A return cable from Stanford requesting details elicited a terse reply from Hoover: "My idea is to simply collect library material on war generally."

Adams and his wife—as the most "suitable commission" then available for the job—started for Paris on May 22, 1919. The immediate aim was to use the occasion of the Peace Conference to collect the so-called delegation propaganda from the seventy states and nations that had sent representatives to Paris, in the rush for recognition encouraged by Woodrow Wilson's call for "the self-determination of peoples." Soon after Adams arrived, he realized that Hoover's name, "at that moment the most applauded in Europe," would open all kinds of doors. He later called Hoover's good name "the one greatest asset in our enterprise."

This would be the case across Europe, where Hoover established headquarters for his American Relief Administration (ARA), an official U.S. agency that began operating as a private relief organization from July 1919. Adams hired two former students, Robert Binkley and Ralph Lutz, the latter a professor at the University of Washington, as his agents in Central and Eastern Europe. Lutz would prove to be an especially resourceful collector and a blessing to the entire enterprise. While Adams mostly remained in Paris, collecting government documents, propaganda pamphlets, and other "fugitive literature" generated by the delegations to the Peace Conference, Lutz traveled across the continent, acquiring books, pamphlets, newspapers, private papers, and documents and arranging for their shipment to Stanford. By 1920, Lutz was joined by another Stanford historian, Frank Golder, and together they laid the foundations of the Hoover Institution's unparalleled Eastern European and Russian collections.

Ephraim D. Adams (right) and **Ralph H. Lutz**, standing alongside unopened materials at the Hoover Library, c. 1924. (Hoover Institution Records)

From the first, the collecting was broad in scope, as indicated by the categories Adams used in his first report on the Hoover collection, published in 1921: society publications; government documents; ordinary books; posters, proclamations, and orders; newspapers and periodicals; war propaganda. After the first $50,000 had been spent, Hoover continued to finance the collecting with large grants. As he explained to President Wilbur in 1924, in words that have become part of Hoover lore, "There will be a thousand years to catalogue this library but only ten years in which to acquire the most valuable of material."

Today this sounds like common sense, but in fact in those days the systematic collecting of archival material was not as well understood in the United States as we might assume. (The National Archives was founded only in 1934.) Hoover and his collectors were the leading edge. The sense of improvisation and ambition is captured in the changing names of the enterprise, which started out, in 1919, as the Hoover War History Collection, a name soon shortened to the Hoover War Collection. The collection expanded so rapidly that it soon outgrew its designation as a "special collection" within the university library, and in 1922 the university administration named it the Hoover War Library and assigned it an entire wing of the university library. Adams was its chairman from 1920 to 1925; Lutz then headed the institution until 1944.

Hoover resisted every attempt to dilute his collection's singularity, as when, in 1921, a close associate proposed its partial merger with the general library in the name of cutting expenses. Hoover's reply was firm. He understood the desire to keep down costs. "I do feel strongly, however, that in upbuilding a collection of this kind we must have the psychology of a separate body of material. Its mere exhibition and the knowledge of it in its physical situation attracts to itself valuable additions. . . ." Time would demonstrate the wisdom of Hoover's insistence that his library stand apart.

And yet, physically it did not stand apart. The Hoover Library materials were located inside the university library, and the competition for limited space, along with ambiguous lines of administrative authority, inevitably created tensions between the Hoover and university library staffs. These tensions were exacerbated by a fundamental disagreement between the Hoover Library directors and the university librarian, George Clark, over the role of the library. Clark, a book collector, believed that the library ought to devote its resources chiefly to the accumulation of published records, while Adams and Lutz wished to emphasize primary sources such as newspapers, handbills, pamphlets, posters, proclamations, private papers, and photographs.

These tensions only grew worse as the Hoover War Library's acquisitions policy became increasingly open-ended, especially after the triumph of National Socialism in Germany, which, against the background of the Great Depression, seemed to forbode another great crisis for Europe and the world. On Herbert Hoover's own initiative, in October 1933 the scope of the library's collecting was significantly broadened to include such subject categories as Nazism, taxation and national debts, and the New Deal.

At the same time, the library was expanding in other ways. In 1932 it offered its first course of instruction, eventually adding several more. Also in 1932 the Hoover Library Publications series was launched with two scholarly volumes based on primary documents in the library; seven more volumes followed in 1934–35. Research scholars from across the country came to Stanford to use the Hoover's archival and library materials. What had started out as a collection of documents on the Great War grew into a major research library on twentieth-century history.

To reflect the broader interests and activities, in 1938 Hoover proposed that the library be renamed the Hoover Library on War, Revolution, and Peace. "This will transform it from a dead collection to a live one," he said. "It has been suggested that we use the title—'War, Peace, and Revolution.' This is a little less optimistic. Perhaps we had better have the title wind up with Peace." The designation would change again in 1947, to the Hoover Institute and Library on War, Revolution, and Peace; and again in 1956 to the one it bears today, the Hoover Institution on War, Revolution and Peace.

The Savior of Belgium

The story of the Hoover Institution's origins and first two decades is closely bound up with Herbert Hoover's special relationship with Belgium, which began in 1914 with an undertaking unprecedented in history: the rescue of the entire Belgian nation from starvation, thanks in large part to Hoover's energy and enterprise.

By September 1914, as the trench warfare on the western front settled into a stalemate, German-occupied Belgium was threatened with famine. A densely populated and highly industrialized country, Belgium depended on imports for half its food, including three-quarters of its grain. The German occupation authorities refused to assume responsibility for feeding the Belgians and blamed the British naval blockade for preventing the country from being able to feed itself. On its part, the British government, which sought to tighten the economic noose around Germany and its armies, declared that feeding the Belgians was the responsibility of their German occupiers, and that in any case the German authorities were likely to seize imported food to support their own armies.

As the situation began to appear dire, Hoover stepped forward and agreed to head up a neutral commission to deliver food supplies to Belgium. At the time, Hoover was a businessman living in London. He had made a name for himself beyond the business world in August 1914 when he arranged to furnish nearly 200,000 American tourists stranded in England by the war with emergency funds and transportation to the United States. After weeks of negotiations, on October 22 his Commission for Relief of Belgium (CRB) was established. Great Britain agreed to let food relief pass through its naval blockade, while Germany promised not to requisition the food once it arrived in Belgium.

On paper the arrangement was straightforward enough, but putting the plan into action proved to be enormously complicated. Initially no one expected the war to last more than a few months; when it did, and as the months became years, the task of securing the necessary funds became formidable. Money raised from charitable appeals sustained operations in the early period, and as the war dragged on, the slack was picked up by subsidies from the Allied governments, which eventually covered more than three-quarters of the total funding. The CRB used this money to purchase wheat and other foodstuffs from all over the world, which it then arranged to ship into Belgium using its own fleet of some sixty ships. Their destination was the neutral Dutch port of Rotterdam, where they unloaded their cargo for shipment by canal, rail, and cart into Belgium (and, in time, northern France). In his contemporary account of the CRB, Vernon Kellogg provides a sense of the big picture:

> *Rice from Rangoon, corn from Argentina, beans from Manchuria, wheat and meat and fats from America; and all, with the other things of the regular programme,*

such as sugar, condensed milk, coffee and cocoa, salt, salad oil, yeast, dried fish, etc., in great quantities, to be brought across wide oceans, through the dangerous mine-strewn Channel, and landed safely and regularly in Rotterdam, to be there speedily transferred from ocean vessels into canal boats and urged on into Belgium and Northern France, and from these taken again by railroad cars and horse-drawn carts to the communal warehouses and soup kitchens; and always and ever, through all the months, to get there in time*—these were the buying and transporting problems of the Commission.*

One hundred thousand tons of foodstuffs per month were prepared in mills, dairies, and bakeries and then distributed to more than seven million Belgians over an area covering 19,500 square miles—"all held in the close grip of a hungry enemy army." Hoover and his American staff, which never numbered more than forty, administered relief through a network of 40,000 Belgian volunteers led by a committee of some of Belgium's most prominent businessmen. When the United States entered the war in 1917, the American relief workers were withdrawn and operations on the ground were handed over to a neutral Spanish-Dutch committee. Otherwise, the enterprise continued to be directed by Hoover and his American colleagues of the CRB.

The CRB was dogged by controversy. The diplomacy behind the scenes of the relief mission was extremely delicate, with the various belligerent governments ready to believe that the Commission's humanitarianism was working to the benefit of the enemy side. The resulting strain on all the responsible officials—from Hoover in London to the directors in the field—was considerable. Adding to the complexity of the undertaking, in the winter of 1914–15 the CRB extended its operations behind the German lines into northern France, an industrialized region more than 8,000 square miles in area between the war zone and the Belgian frontier, with a population of about two and a quarter million French civilians.

In the end, over its four-and-a-half-year existence, the CRB provided relief worth more than $880 million. The mission launched Hoover's wartime and early postwar career as the Master of Emergencies, in an epithet of that era, whose philanthropy was grounded in hardheaded business principles (he was also called the Master of Efficiency) and muscular diplomacy. Nowhere was he more revered than in tiny Belgium. In August 1918, when Hoover visited the fragment of Belgium not under German occupation, King Albert presented him with the title created exclusively for him: "Ami de la Nation belge" (Friend of the Belgian Nation).

This was merely the beginning of a special relationship. Hoover conducted the operations of the CRB, as he would all his subsequent relief missions, along the same lines as his mining operations, employing the same creatively aggressive financing strategies and

S.S. Lynorta. "Virginia Relief Ship to Rotterdam." Relief ships used for Belgium (whose port of call was neutral Rotterdam) were often identified with a sponsor-state in the United States. (Raymond Bland Papers)

Belgians in St. Gilles, a suburb of Brussels, express their gratitude to the CRB, with banners and, in the foreground, a photograph of President Wilson. (Commission for Relief in Belgium Records)

commercial principles, strict accounting methods, and efficient administration. Kellogg called it "engineering efficiency," and indeed many of the principal figures Hoover drafted for service in the CRB were fellow mining engineers. The result, as Hoover biographer George Nash reports, is that when the CRB liquidated it had a surplus of $35 million:

> *Of this sum the CRB distributed more than $18 million in outright gifts to the Universities of Brussels, Ghent, Liège, Louvain, and other educational institutions. The remainder of the money was divided between two foundations created in 1920: the CRB Educational Foundation [later renamed the Belgian American Educational Foundation] in the United States, and the Fondation Universitaire in Belgium.... During the 1920s Hoover's foundation granted over $2 million to the Fondation Universitaire and over $1.6 million for the rebuilding of the University of Louvain, so terribly ravaged during the German occupation.*

Hoover's Belgian connection and the special Belgian-American bonds it helped to forge would influence the development of his library at Stanford in several ways: from the conversation, begun in 1915, about the CRB's records that helped inspire the library's founding, to the deposit of the vast CRB archive as the library's founding collection in 1919, to the construction of its tower building twenty years later, and the ringing of its bells ever since.

Vernon Kellogg, *Fighting Starvation in Belgium* (1918).

Kellogg was from 1894 to 1920 a Stanford professor of entomology. He went to work as a diplomat and administrator for Hoover's CRB, the U.S. Food Administration, and the postwar American Relief Administration in Poland, before becoming the first permanent secretary of the National Research Council. A leading public intellectual of his day who served as trustee and executive board member of some of the nation's premier foundations and academic associations, Kellogg authored many books and published numerous articles on science, government, and international affairs in the popular press. He is an excellent example of Herbert Hoover's gift for attracting brilliant talent to his enterprise.

"Food ship for Belgium." USA, c. 1915, b/w.

Hoover Library book plate. Before the Hoover Tower was built, the Hoover Library's book plate featured a bronze statue of the goddess Isis, the most important god in Egyptian mythology, symbolizing life, motherhood, healing, and magic, among other things. The statue itself was a gift to Herbert Hoover from the Belgian people in gratitude for his humanitarian undertaking in their behalf during World War I. Belgian sculptor Auguste Puttemans cast this piece and had it shipped to the United States in 1922. The statue was located on the Stanford campus until 1939, when it was moved to the vicinity of Hoover's birthplace, on what are now the grounds of the Herbert Hoover Presidential Library, in West Branch, Iowa. The text at the base of the statue reads: "Je suis ce qui a été, ce qui est, et ce qui sera, et nul mortel n'a encore levé le voile qui me couvre." ("I am that which was, that which is, and that which will be, and no mortal has yet lifted the veil that covers me.")

Belgian Lace

One of the subplots of the CRB rescue mission—and an outstanding example of Hoover's innovative approach to philanthropy—is the story of Belgium's celebrated lace workers under the German occupation. Belgian lace had long been a symbol of the nation. Queen Elisabeth served as matron of the country's lace industry, and nationally famous artists vied with each other to create the most beautiful designs. There were nearly 50,000 lace workers—women and girls—in Belgium in 1914, supporting themselves and some of their families. When war came and the blockade kept out the fine thread essential to their trade, Belgian's lace workers faced destitution and their entire industry was threatened with ruin.

In early 1915, the Commission for Relief in Belgium came up with a plan to head off this threat. The Commission arranged to import the thread needed to make lace, in exchange for which an equivalent weight in lace was to be turned over by the lace workers to the CRB for sale in Paris, London, and New York. A portion of the earnings from these sales was used to pay the wages of the lace workers, with the rest held in London for payment at the end of the war. In some cases, the CRB paid women in advance for their as-yet-unsold lace products, on the understanding that they would return these payments when they were able to sell their products after the war. This arrangement enabled more than forty thousand lace workers to engage in half-time work for the duration of the war and thereby ensured the continued vitality of Belgium's lace industry.

Belgian lace became part of the symbolism of the Allied cause, as the plight of the lace workers and the sale of lace products were used to rally public opinion in behalf of "little Belgium." The Germans always suspected that the lace operation had a political dimension, and it turns out that in one way their suspicions were well founded: some of the designs of lace products brought to Britain and America, such as tablecloths and runners of needle and bobbin laces, included national emblems and flags of the Allied powers.

Vernon Kellogg's wife, Charlotte, a tireless promoter of the Belgian cause in America, reported in her 1920 book *Bobbins of Belgium* that "old patterns were restored and improved and by the end of the war 2,237 new designs had been added." Thanks to Lou Henry Hoover, an especially influential champion of the women of Belgium and northern France, samples of this lace ended up at Stanford. Articles from her collection of Belgian needlepoint are on display in the Lou Henry Hoover Room, on the ground floor of the Hoover Tower.

Belgian relief poster (UK, 1915–1918).

Charlotte Kellogg, *The Women of Belgium* (1917).

Building the Tower

By 1929 the Hoover War Library had accumulated more than 1.4 million items—both archival and published materials—and the need for additional space was acute. The idea of creating a separate facility had first been proposed by Director Ephraim Adams in the early 1920s. In 1924, Hoover suggested that his library be combined with the proposed Stanford War Memorial building, for which $100,000 had already been raised. The plan for that building called for a small lecture hall and a central lobby featuring memorial displays honoring the men of Stanford University who died serving in the Great War. Hoover had the idea to attach to this design the stacks, reading rooms, offices, and archive and film vaults required for his library.

An early architectural sketch, prepared by the firm Bakewell and Brown and circulated to potential donors in 1926, reflected Hoover's concept: a two-story building with two wings and a memorial tower rising twice as high at its center. At the start of Hoover's presidency in 1929, the fundraising efforts for such a structure seemed close to success, but in October came the stock market crash, and before long the Great Depression set in. The fundraisers and the Hoover War Library's directors were forced to reconsider their plans, and for a time in 1930 they even considered constructing an inexpensive "utilitarian building" connected to the university library. One result of the delay—felicitous, in retrospect—was the separation of the Hoover War Library from the proposed Stanford War Memorial building, which was completed in 1937, without a tower, and is today known as Memorial Auditorium.

The funds for a library building were finally secured in 1938, thanks largely to Herbert Hoover's foundations. The major breakthrough came in May 1937, when the American Relief Administration finally liquidated and endowed more than $140,000 to Stanford for the erection of a building to house the Hoover War Library. In late 1938 the Belgian American Educational Foundation donated $300,000 toward construction of the proposed building, with the proviso that the university cover the $100,000 still outstanding and assume the costs of maintenance. The university's trustees agreed. John D. Rockefeller, Jr., gave $50,000, and the balance of the funding came from numerous smaller individual donations.

The design was contracted to Arthur Brown, Jr., of the firm Bakewell and Brown, who had designed several buildings on campus, including one of its architectural gems, the University Library, as well as San Francisco's beaux arts city hall (after the original was destroyed in the 1906 earthquake) and its art deco Coit Tower. Incorporating the tower motif that had been abandoned for the Stanford War Memorial but that Hoover still favored for his library, Brown designed a monumental structure that, as Hoover understated the matter, "would add to the ornamentation of an open space campus."

On December 8, 1938, Stanford President Ray Lyman Wilbur publicly unveiled the plan for the $600,000 building. On the Stanford campus and in the local community, the building's harshest critics spoke the loudest—which is often the way radically new architecture is received (Coit Tower, designed to resemble the nozzle of a firehose, is a well-known example). In the case of Hoover Tower, conspicuousness itself was the key bone of contention on a campus whose core was a two-story quadrangle in the Spanish Mission style. *The Stanford Daily* editorialized that the new structure would violate Stanford's aesthetic integrity in "an apparent purposeless departure from traditional Quad architecture." Letters to the *Daily*'s editor called it a "tower of Babel" and "a monument to wounded vanity." A student theatrical production lampooned it as the "Boulder War Library."

The design that aroused this criticism was soon altered, though not in order to appease the critics. Brown's original plan envisioned a spacious entrance hall and two stories of offices, from which would arise a tall tower with a sloping red-tiled roof. In early 1939 the design was changed from a sloping roof to a dome in order to allow for the installation of a carillon, which had just become available. The revised blueprint increased the height of the tower and capped it with a red-tiled domed belvedere. Aside from its functional utility in accommodating the bells, the dome had the advantage of resembling the (much smaller) twin domes atop the Stanford Union building. This and the fact that the redesign was said to have been modeled on the sixteenth-century cathedral in Salamanca, thereby clinching the building's Spanish pedigree, may have helped soothe local opinion.

Two weeks after the library's groundbreaking in mid-August 1939, war broke out in Europe. Hoover had acted in anticipation of these events. In the spring of 1939, on the strength of $100,000 he was able to raise from another of his foundations, Hoover sent Ralph Lutz, now the library's director, on a collecting mission to Europe. "I didn't want to go," Lutz later recalled, "but he just had me up to the house one day and he said, 'You've got to get back there.' He said, 'There's imminence of war and this time I want you to collect materials from the totalitarian states.' He told me, 'Go to every country.'"

Lutz was in Europe when the war began. For several months he traveled across the continent collecting materials for the library. As he went, Lutz established a network of contacts among book dealers, librarians, and government officials, enlisting them to collect propaganda and other materials for the Hoover Library during the war. Lutz promised to compensate them for their acquisitions and their efforts at war's end. On his journey, Lutz must have paused to reflect on how his current assignment was a kind of mirror image of his collecting work twenty years earlier, in immediate postwar Europe. As Nash writes of this undertaking, "It was a brilliant innovation. No other library had ever employed such a strategy; no other even had representatives in Europe at the time. Once again, thanks to the founder's farsightedness and timely financial support, and to Lutz's own astuteness and

Artist's sketch of the Hoover Tower, December 1938. This original design envisioned a reading room at the top of the Tower, with tall windows providing plenty of natural light and a scenic view; the redesign placed the reading room on the ground floor. (Hoover Institution Records)

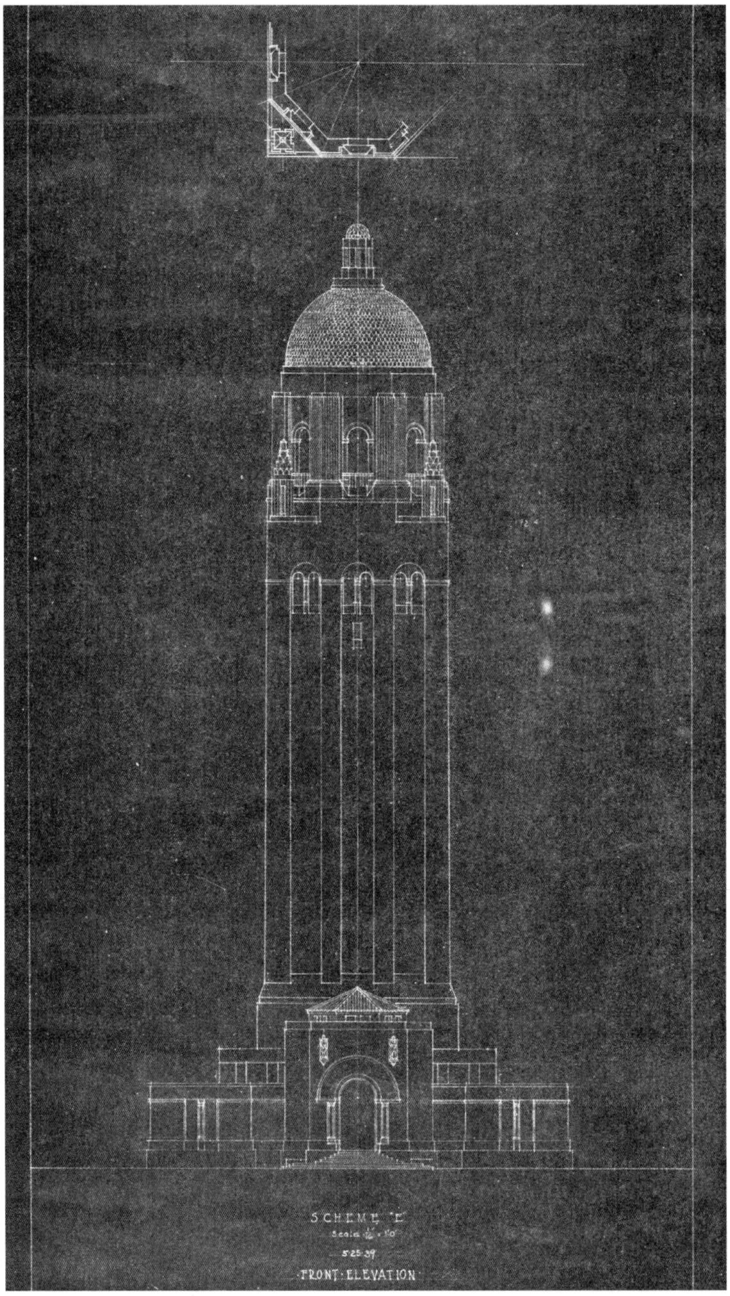

zeal, the Hoover Library would reap a historical bonanza and remain unchallenged in its field."

Meanwhile, back at Stanford, construction of the Hoover Library building proceeded apace. Its skeletal girders rose above the plane of the central campus skyline, eventually reaching a height of 285 feet above the basement floor. As the Tower was nearing completion early in 1941, Hoover asked that the formal dedication of his library building be made part of the university's fiftieth anniversary celebrations, and of course his request was granted. The dedication of the Hoover Tower took place on June 20. In his remarks, Hoover declared, "The purpose of this institution is to promote peace. Its records stand as a challenge to those who promote war." Two days later, Nazi Germany invaded the Soviet Union; six months after that came Pearl Harbor and America's entry into the Second World War.

Hoover Tower under construction. (Berton W. Crandall Photographs)

Herbert Hoover standing in front of the newly completed Hoover Tower, c. 1941. The Tower was later joined by two adjacent structures, the Lou Henry Hoover Building (1967) and the Hoover Memorial Building (1978). In 1978, the archives, which had been located on the tenth floor of the Tower, were moved to their own facility, on the basement floor off the central courtyard between the Lou Henry Hoover and Hoover Memorial buildings. (Herbert Hoover Papers)

Bells in the Tower

On May 19, 1939, three months prior to groundbreaking for the construction of Hoover Tower, Stanford President Ray Lyman Wilbur received a telegram from Herbert Hoover in New York, informing him that "the carillon of thirty-five bells in the Belgian Tower of the World's Fair might be obtained for the library building. The bells weigh eighteen thousand pounds including electric clock which operates timing of bells." The total cost would be at most $15,000. Hoover had two questions for Wilbur: "First is construction of tower such that bells could be installed and second do you want bells at all?"

The answers, it turned out, were yes to the second and no to the first. Architect Arthur Brown, Jr., immediately began redesigning the tower to accommodate an 18,000 pound carillon. His revised plans changed the sloping rectangular roof to a dome, moved the reading room down to the first floor, and turned the fourteenth floor into a belvedere just large enough to serve as a belfry. Details about the carillon were late in coming, and the architect and builders had to make last-minute improvisations in order to make everything fit.

The 1,350 pound main bell, or bourdon, bears an inscription in Latin: "Because I am called Leopold the Royal, For peace alone do I ring over the waves of the Atlantic."

Arriving at Stanford along with the bells was Kamiel Lefevere, a Belgian-American carillonneur and composer, later carillonneur at Riverside Church in Manhattan. Lefevere dismantled the carillon in New York, oversaw its transport by ship from Brooklyn to San Francisco, and reassembled it inside the Hoover Tower. Before coming to Stanford, Lefevere wrote to the university requesting the music for songs familiar to the Stanford community, that "a choice of well known American songs and possibly one or two Stanford college songs will make the automatic playing better understood." University President Wilbur suggested "America the Beautiful." Warren D. Allen, university organist, provided the music for such student favorites as "Hail, Alma Mater," "Stanford Loyalty Hymn," and "Hail, Stanford, Hail."

Ralph Lutz outside the front door of the Tower, as workmen wheel in one of the large bells for the carillon, 1941. (Berton W. Crandall Photographs)

On March 17, 1941, Lefevere gave the bells their first sound test, which, he was able to report, made a distinct impression on the campus: "The introduction of the carillon during the first tryout certainly got a rousing welcome from the student body, who sang and shouted with the music and roared in unison between the numbers 'more, more, more.'" Two evening concerts, announced in the local papers, attracted large audiences. It was said that the bells could be heard three miles away and that drivers in the vicinity began "tooting their automobile horns long and loud between each selection." In this way, even before the Tower was officially opened, the sound of its bells worked to soften objections to its appearance and smooth its reception into the community. Lefevere was invited back to Stanford to perform during the Tower's dedication ceremony, at which he played "America the Beautiful" and "The Star Spangled Banner."

Bell being returned by crane into the belfry of the Hoover Tower, February 19, 2002. (Stanford Visual Art Services)

Over the years, the bells held up especially well, and it took the 1989 Loma Prieta earthquake to disable the driving mechanism for the automatic player. In January 2000, the thirty-five bells were removed and sent to the Netherlands for restoration. Eleven of the bells had to be replaced, though not the bourdon bell. The carillon was augmented by the addition of nine larger and four smaller bells, bringing the total to forty-eight and expanding their range from three octaves to four. The bells were returned to the Tower on February 19, 2002.

Hoover Tower with four footprints descending along its western face. (Stanford News Service)

On May 23, 1950, student climbers of the Stanford Alpine Club descended the Hoover Tower's western face, the second of the so-called Tower trilogy climbing capers. During the previous year the campus awoke to discover four very large, evenly spaced ascending footprints on the Tower's face, said to be the tracks of "the Monster." The descending footprints shown here were the work of three students who managed to sneak into the Tower (in ways since closed off), climb stairs to the observation deck, and then rappel down, leaving the Monster's footprints. During Big Game Week 1951 a student climber made it to the very top of the Tower, placing an expedition pole and banner ("Roses for the Team") at its pinnacle.

The Stanford Trademark

In a letter to Herbert Hoover written in November 1939, Stanford President Ray Lyman Wilbur wrote of the Hoover Tower, then under construction,"The building is going to be the Stanford Trademark within a dozen years." It may have taken a bit longer than that, but today few would argue that Wilbur was wrong in his prediction. Certainly not the casual visitor to the campus, riding the Tower's elevator to the observation platform and its spectacular view of the San Francisco Bay area. From above, the Tower reveals the layout of the campus and the community; from below, it is the campus landmark that orients students and visitors on foot and bike, hikers in the nearby and distant hills, and residents returning to the area by car and even by airplane. As countless photographs attest, the Tower's rising shaft is the perfect foil for the Quad's long low lines of red-tile roofs. It pierces the morning fog, catches the last rays of the setting sun, and situates the rising moon. For all these reasons, the Hoover Tower grows on you.

In time, the source of friction between the university and the Hoover Institution was not architecture but politics. Old questions about the Hoover Library's independence reemerged as a dispute about the university's oversight of Hoover appointments and operations. More in the public eye was the related controversy over Cold War politics, especially after 1959, when Herbert Hoover rededicated his institution to the struggle against "the evils of the doctrines of Karl Marx." Not entirely by coincidence, perhaps, the Stanford-Hoover cold war, which had its harder and softer phases, ended with the collapse of communism, thanks in large part to adept campus diplomacy to resolve questions of administrative authority that had festered for decades.

View of the Stanford University campus, with Lake Lagunita in the foreground and San Francisco Bay in the distance. (Stanford News Service)

Throughout troubled times, the library and archives, uninfluenced by politics, have continued to amass books and documents on political and social ideas and movements across the political spectrum. The collecting work has been conducted as aggressively and innovatively as ever, most impressively in the operation begun in the late 1980s to document the fall of communism and the transition to markets and democracy in Eastern and Central Europe and the former Soviet Union. The remarkable accumulation of materials—including posters, proclamations, periodicals, correspondence, memoirs, and diaries—was achieved largely thanks to old-fashioned legwork and personal networking, in the tradition of the founding collectors, Adams, Lutz, and Golder.

The Hoover Library and Archives will never lose their card-catalogue feel. Yet, as information technology brings new methods of storing and retrieving documentary materials and making them available to researchers and a broader public, the Hoover remains on the cutting edge in its unending quest to document the causes and consequences of war and revolution and efforts to promote world peace. In this sense too, Hoover's Tower never stops growing.

L.p.	Nazwisko i imię.	Stop.	Broń.	R.ur.	Obóz.	Inne dane
189.	Smoczarski Jerzy	ppor.			Star.	
190. 2767	Smoląg Stanisław	przod.	P.P.		Koz.	
191. 2768	Smoleński	kpt.	piech.		"	28 p.p.…
192. 2769	Smoleński	por.			Star.	26 p.a.…
193. 2770	Smolikowski Konstanty	rtm.	kaw.		"	
194.	Smolka Edward	por.			"	
195. 2771	Smolnicki Tadeusz	kpt.	P.P.		Ost.	
196. 2772	Smorawiński Mieczysław	gen.	bryg.		Koz.	
197. 2773	Smulski	por.			"	rez.
198. 2774	Sobański Michał	ppor.	pilot		"	1 p.lotn…
199. 2775	Sobański Roman	por.	lotn.		"	obs.1.p.lot…
200. 2776	Sobczak Jan	plut.	P.P.		Ost.	
201. 2777	Sobczyński Gabryel	kpr.			Koz.	
202. 2778	Sobel	plut.	P.P.		Ost.	
203. 2779	Sobieraj	ppor.		1898	Koz.	Białystok
204. 2780	Sobieraj Wł.	plut.			"	4 p.p.Leg.
205. 2781	Sobieszański (cza)	kpt.	lek.		"	
206. 2782	Sobieszczański Stefan	"	P.P.	1899	Ost.	
207. 2783	Sobieszczyński	plut.	P.P.		"	
208. 2784	Sobkoń Franciszek	"	"		"	
209. 2785	Sobol Władysław dr.	ppor.			Star.	Częstocho…
210. 2786	Sobolak	kpr.	P.P.		Ost.	
211.	Sobkiewicz Zygmunt	ppor.				
212. 2787	Sobolewski Jan	"			Koz.	76 p.p.
213. 2788	Sobolewski Władysław	por.	kaw.	1900	Star.	
214. 2789	Sochocki Tadeusz	kpt.			Koz.	
215. 2790	Sochorowski Feliks	por.	K.O.P.		"	
	~~Soduła Kazimierz~~					
216. 2791	Soduła Kazimierz	plut.	P.P.		Ost.	
217. 2792	Sokalski Ludwik	por.	int.	1885	Koz.	
218.	Sokolewicz	płk.	lek.		Star.	st.sp.
219. 2793	Sokolewicz Wacław	ppłk.			"	aptekarz
220. 2794	Sokolski Eugeniusz	"			"	Baon K.O.…
221. 2795	Sokołowski Wincenty	kpt.	piech.	1886 Lwów		Waków
222.	Sokołowski Leonard	post.	P.P.	1901	Ost.	
223. 2798	Sokołowski Edmund	por.	lek.		Koz.	85 p.p.
224. 2796	Sokołowski Józef	mjr.	kaw.		"	
225. 2797	Sokołowski Anatol	por.	mar.	1902	Star.	W-wa
226. 2799	Sokołowski Feliks	ppor.			Koz.	rez.
227. 2800	Sokołowski Jan	ppłk.			Star.	
228. 2801	Sokołowski Józef	kpt.			Koz.	
229. 2802	Sokołowski Władysław	ppor.			"	rez.62 p.…
230. 2804	Sokólski	mjr.			Star.	
231. 2805	Sokół Michał	pchor.	piech.		Koz.	
232. 2806	Sokół-Szachin Mieczysław	płk.			Star.	K-dt Prz…
233. 2807	Solskiewicz Walenty	podof.			Koz.	
234. 2808	Solarski Zbigniew	ppor. (por.)		1917	Star.	
235.	Solecki Tadeusz	mjr.			"	
236. 2809	Solewski Henryk dr.	por.			Koz.	
237. 2810	Solski Adam	mjr.			"	
238. 2811	Sołchnocki	ppor.			Star.	
239. 2812	Sołtan Adam dypl.	mjr.	kaw.	1898	"	1 p.uł.
240. 2813	Sołtycki Ludwik	por.	pilot		Koz.	S.S.1.p.lo…
241. 2814	Sołtys Tadeusz	"	P.P.		Ost.	
242. 2815	Sołtysik Stanisław	ppor.	lek.		Star.	rez. wet.
243. 2816	Somogyj Roman	por.	lek.		"	1 p.…
244. 2817	[illegible]	mjr.			"	
245. 2818	Sopel	kpr.	P.P.		Ost.	
246. 2819	Sopenhejm I.	ppor.			Star.	Wilno
247. 2820	[illegible] A.	kpt.			"	
2821	[illegible]yl Karol	"			"	67 p.p.
	[illegible]pczyński Ludwik				Koz.	
	[illegible]osenkiewicz Józef	"				

Chapter Four

TYRANNIES

One remarkable aspect of the twentieth century's two greatest tyrannies—Nazi Germany and the Soviet Union—is how their leaders left behind a written record of many of their most notorious plans and deeds. Adolf Hitler laid out his long-term goal of Aryan and German domination in *Mein Kampf,* while Joseph Goebbels boasted about his aspirations and exploits in his elaborate diaries, found among the rubble of the Third Reich. Stalin and the Politburo conducted their grisly business during the Great Terror in top-secret memoranda that remained locked away in the Kremlin until they were revealed to the public upon the collapse of Soviet Communism.

One of the questions that fascinate historians is to what extent the Nazi and Soviet regimes learned from and imitated each other. How was Hitler influenced by the tactics of Lenin's Bolsheviks in seizing and maintaining power? Was Stalin's Great Purge of the Communist elite in 1936–1939 inspired in part by Hitler's move to crush the SA (Sturm Abteilung), his brownshirted stormtroopers, in 1934? Ideological opposites, the Nazis and the Soviets nonetheless practiced similar forms of terror, purge, and propaganda. Contemporaries had trouble perceiving these similarities, which explains the world's stunned reaction when the two regimes signed a treaty of nonaggression and friendship in 1939. Today we understand that the extremes of left and right do indeed come together.

STALIN'S USSR

The Terror and the Gulag

The Great Terror in the Soviet Union took place during the years 1936–1938, when three major show trials were staged in Moscow, mass arrests occurred across the country, and the labor camp system swelled with millions of victims. Yet that was only the greatest of several waves of terror during the Stalin years. The first wave came shortly after he had consolidated his grip on power in 1929, and there were later ones in the years immediately following the Second World War and just before his death in 1953. Historians estimate the death toll from Stalin's terror to run as high as 20 million. But Soviet terror did not originate under Stalin; Lenin was at the helm during the Red Terror of 1918–19, when the first labor camp for political prisoners was established.

Nevertheless, the Great Terror easily deserves its dreaded title. Beyond the heavily scripted show trials of the Old Bolsheviks, who confessed to attempting to undermine the Soviet government through sabotage, espionage, treason, and assassination, there were the sweeping purges of the Party, the government bureaucracy, and the Red Army. From the Communist elite to common workers, no one was immune from arrest, execution, or exile to distant labor camps. The show trials made headlines in the West, but the larger terror was unknown. The arrests in the middle of the night, the crowded prison cells, the millions of prisoners herded into freight cars, the inhuman conditions of the labor camps—these facts were largely hidden from the outside world.

The twentieth century's totalitarian regimes relied on terror to maintain their authority, yet historians are still puzzling over the particular reasons for the Soviet mass purges of the 1930s. Stalin's extreme paranoia about enemies at home and abroad, a threatening or obstructive Soviet bureaucracy, the need to produce scapegoats for the failure to achieve the communist utopia, the example of Hitler's purge of the SA—these and other explanations have been advanced. Whatever their actual causes, there is no doubt that the purges left the Soviet Union severely weakened by the time a halt was called in 1939. Most astonishingly, the Red Army had been virtually decapitated even as the threat of Nazi Germany loomed.

One reason the Great Terror was little known at the time and its origins remain elusive to historians is that the Soviet state became much more secretive in the 1930s. Published sources such as Party and government newspapers, reports, and transcripts of official conferences—extremely valuable resources to students of Soviet politics from 1917 through the 1920s—become more opaque after the victory of the Stalinists. In this environment, and with Soviet archives inaccessible, unofficial sources such as émigré testimony assumed much greater importance for historians seeking to document and analyze the terror. This

ПРОЛЕТАРИИ ВСЕХ СТРАН, СОЕДИНЯЙТЕСЬ!

Всесоюзная Коммунистическая Партия (больш.).

ПРАВДА

Орган Центр. Ком. и Моск. Ком. ВКП (б)

АВГУСТ. 18 1933 г. ПЯТНИЦА. № 227 (5753).

„Из страны слабой и неподготовленной к обороне Советский Союз превратился в страну могучую в смысле обороноспособности, в страну, готовую ко всяким случайностям, в страну, способную производить в массовом масштабе все современные орудия обороны и снабдить ими свою армию в случае нападения извне" (И. СТАЛИН).

На уровень мировой авиационной техники.

ПРИКАЗ РЕВОЛЮЦИОННОГО ВОЕННОГО СОВЕТА СССР.

Народный комиссар по военным и морским делам и председатель РВС СССР ВОРОШИЛОВ.

г. МОСКВА. 18 августа 1933 г.

Обращение Наркомвоенмора тов. ВОРОШИЛОВА

к рабочим, инженерам и техникам авиационной промышленности.

Front page of *Pravda,* August 18, 1933, with photograph of Stalin. A typical example of the cult of Stalin, as it blossomed in the 1930s.

Stalin on vacation in the Caucasus in 1933. To Stalin's left, with an axe in his belt, is Lavrenti Beria, future head of the NKVD, the Soviet secret police. (N. A. Lakoba Papers)

was the approach used by Robert Conquest in his landmark book *The Great Terror,* which was widely acclaimed when it first appeared in 1968 as a brilliantly written work of scholarship. In the 1970s, as Sovietologists grew skeptical of the use of émigrés and dissidents as historical sources, questions were raised about the accuracy of Conquest's book—until the opening of the archives after the collapse of the Soviet Union vindicated his account of the terror.

The Great Terror led to the expansion of the Soviet labor camps into a full-blown economic system of slave labor camps throughout the country, a network that came to be known as the Gulag (the Russian shorthand for the Main Directorate for Corrective Labor Camps), under the administration of the NKVD, the secret police. By the early 1930s, several million inmates were held in the Gulag, where political prisoners were intermixed with murderers and common criminals.

The camps, which were located mainly in remote regions of Siberia and the Far North, became an integral part of the Soviet economy during the Stalin years. Gulag prisoners provided the labor for the gigantic construction projects of the 1930s, such as the White Sea–Baltic Canal and the Moscow–Volga Canal, as well as hydroelectric power stations, strategic roads, and railway lines. Exploitation of natural resources of sparsely populated areas became almost exclusively a Gulag enterprise. The country's lumber industry and its mining of coal, copper, and gold drew heavily on prison camp labor.

Conditions in the camps were extremely harsh, as cold and hungry prisoners were forced to work long hours outdoors in a harsh climate. In all, it is estimated that some 18 million people were sent to the camps, about one-quarter of whom did not survive. After Stalin's death in 1953, many prisoners were released from the camps, and the conditions for those who stayed were improved. Most of the political prisoners were officially "rehabilitated" under Stalin's successors, meaning they were declared innocent of the crimes that had landed them in the Gulag. Although labor camps continued to exist until the end of the Soviet Union, the Gulag was dismantled.

The political thaw in the Soviet Union under Nikita Khrushchev led to public discussion about the terror and the camps, which reached a crescendo with the publication in a Soviet literary journal in November 1962 of Alexander Solzhenitsyn's short novel *One Day in the Life of Ivan Denisovich,* which described a typical day in the life of a camp inmate, based in part on Solzhenitsyn's own experiences in the Gulag. The novel was published in book form the following year, though by then the Kremlin's enthusiasm for "de-Stalinization" was running out.

Solzhenitsyn would publish other (much lengthier) political novels, which won him the Nobel Prize in Literature in 1970, but his name will forever be associated with *The Gulag*

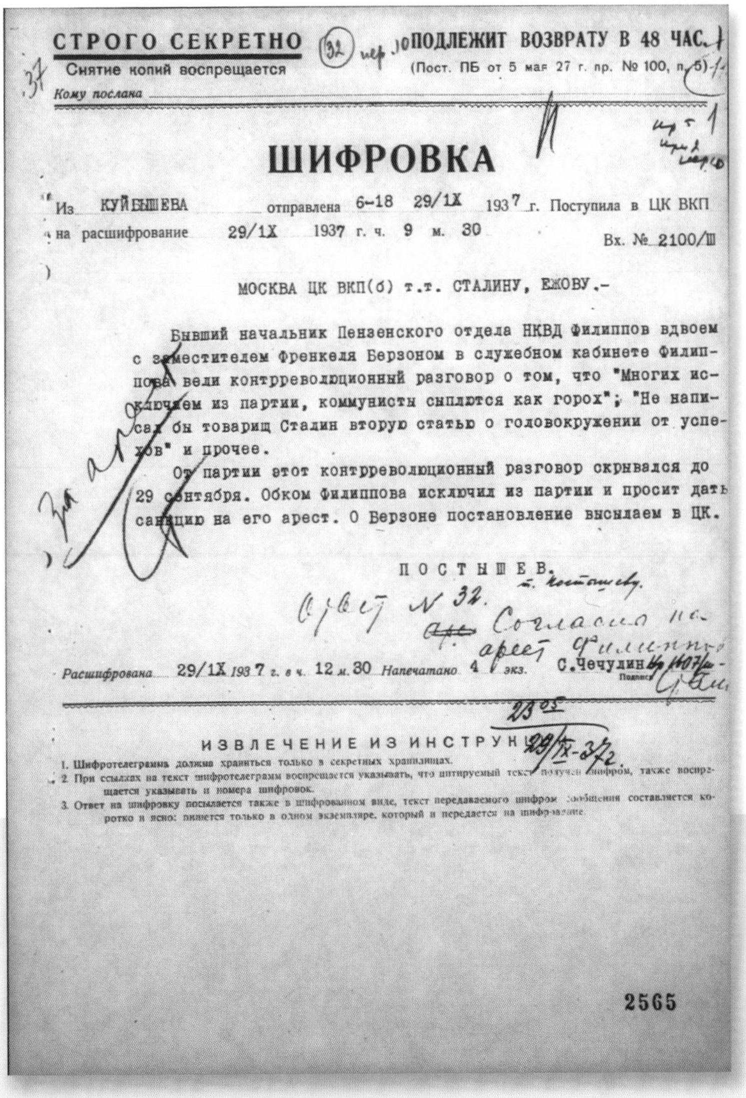

СТРОГО СЕКРЕТНО

Снятие копий воспрещается

ПОДЛЕЖИТ ВОЗВРАТУ В 48 ЧАС.

(Пост. ПБ от 5 мая 27 г. пр. № 100, п. 5)

Кому послана

ШИФРОВКА

Из КУЙБЫШЕВА отправлена 6-18 29/1Х 1937 г. Поступила в ЦК ВКП на расшифрование 29/1Х 1937 г. ч. 9 м. 30

Вх. № 2100/Ш

МОСКВА ЦК ВКП(б) т.т. СТАЛИНУ, ЕЖОВУ.-

Бывший начальник Пензенского отдела НКВД Филиппов вдвоем с заместителем Френкеля Берзоном в служебном кабинете Филиппова вели контрреволюционный разговор о том, что "Многих исключаем из партии, коммунисты сыплются как горох"; "Не написал бы товарищ Сталин вторую статью о головокружении от успехов" и прочее.

От партии этот контрреволюционный разговор скрывался до 29 сентября. Обком Филиппова исключил из партии и просит дать санкцию на его арест. О Берзоне постановление вышлаем в ЦК.

ПОСТЫШЕВ.

Расшифрована 29/1Х 1937 г. в ч. 12 м. 30 Напечатано 4 экз. С.Чечулин

Подпись

ИЗВЛЕЧЕНИЕ ИЗ ИНСТРУКЦИИ

1. Шифротелеграмма должна храниться только в секретных хранилищах.
2. При ссылках на текст шифротелеграммы воспрещается указывать, что цитируемый текст получен шифром, также воспрещается указывать и номера шифровок.
3. Ответ на шифровку посылается также в шифрованном виде, текст передаваемого шифром сообщения составляется коротко и ясно: пишется только в одном экземпляре, который и передается на шифрование.

2565

Ciphered telegram, labeled "Strictly Secret" and dated September 29, 1937, from Pavel Postyshev to Stalin and his police chief, Nikolai Yezhov. Postyshev suggests the arrest of a local secret police official in the Russian city of Penza for having conducted a "counterrevolutionary conversation" in which the policeman complained about the treatment of Party members: "Many are being expelled from the Party, communists are being scattered like peas." Stalin expresses his approval of the suggestion by writing on the telegram "For arrest," and signing "St——."

Before the availability of such evidence, some historians questioned how involved Stalin was in the Terror. Although such documents—and there are many—will not end the debate about Stalin's role, they inculpate him directly in the purges. (Archives of the Soviet Communist Party and Soviet State Microfilm, Fond 89)

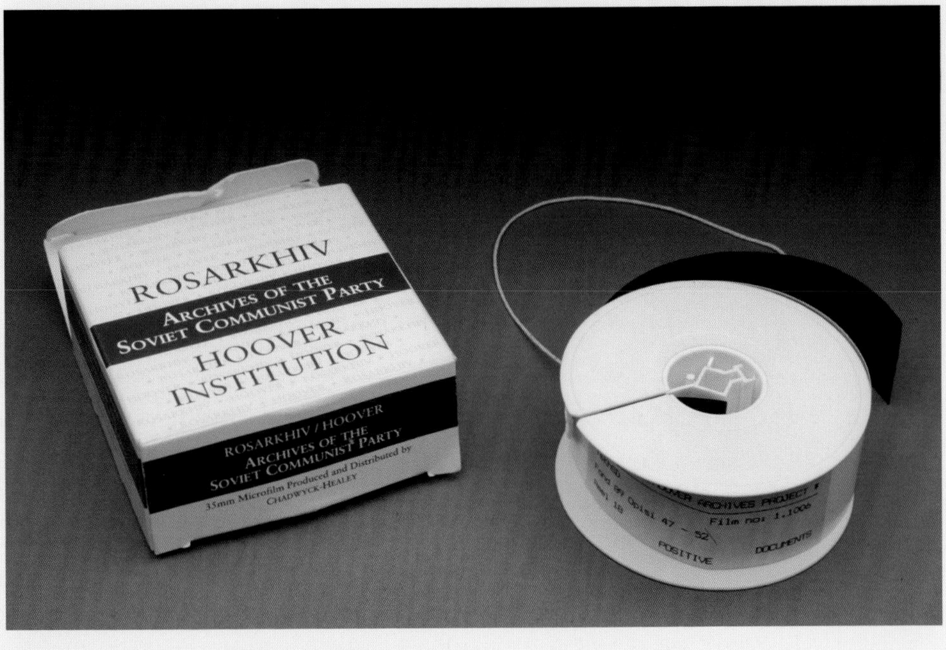

Microfilm reel of Soviet documents. (Fond 89)

Alexander Solzhenitsyn doing research at the Hoover Library, 1976.
(Hoover Institution Records)

Archipelago, which was published in three volumes, in 1973–1975. One of the most important books of the twentieth century, *Gulag* combined oral histories of camp survivors, political analysis, and the author's own recollections of the camps. The publication of volume one, in Paris in 1973, was a landmark event in the history of communism. Solzhenitsyn was denounced in the Soviet press, harassed by the KGB, and expelled from the Soviet Union in 1974.

The Gulag Archipelago energized the human rights campaign inside the Soviet Union, where it was read surreptitiously in *samizdat* (self-published) form or in copies smuggled in from the West. In the West, though many had heard of it, few seem to have read it—and many of the Sovietologists who did were inclined to question its historical accuracy. Solzhenitsyn was, after all, a novelist, not trained in the historian's craft (Conquest, a poet, heard the same skeptical voices). Such skepticism faded out during the final years of Soviet power under Mikhail Gorbachev, when Soviet citizens in every corner of the country came forward with tales from the Gulag that confirmed and amplified Solzhenitsyn's version. In the tumultuous year 1989, portions of *The Gulag Archipelago* were published in the Soviet Union, and all three volumes appeared in print the following year, helping to usher the Soviet Union out of existence.

Since the collapse of communism, once-secret archives have been opened to scholars seeking documentation on the Terror and the Gulag, among many other topics in Soviet history. The process of making primary materials available to Russian and international scholars alike has been greatly facilitated by the pioneering efforts of the Hoover Archives to microfilm Soviet government and Communist Party archives. The first of the collections to be microfilmed, known as Fond 89, includes thousands of once-secret Politburo, Central Committee, and KGB documents, including dozens of hours of Politburo stenograms from the 1960s through the 1980s, offering an inside view of Kremlin decision making from Lenin to Gorbachev. Most remarkable of all is its record of the Communist regime's long history of terror and repression, from the first political prison camp under Lenin, to the Great Terror and Gulag under Stalin, to the KGB's cat-and-mouse games with political dissidents under Stalin's successors.

In June 1998, the Hoover Institution signed an agreement with the State Archives of the Russian Federation to publish the complete records of the Soviet Gulag. This enormous undertaking has produced a microfilm edition consisting of more than 1.5 million pages of documentation from the Soviet archives, covering the history of the Gulag from 1922 to 1960. In keeping with its tradition of documentary publications, the Hoover Institution sponsored the publication in Russia of a series of volumes of key documents from the collection.

An American Survivor

Among the millions swept up in the whirlwind of terror were thousands of foreigners, one of them an American named Thomas Sgovio (1916–1997). Sgovio's father, an Italian radical who had immigrated to the United States but faced deportation for his activities, moved his family from Buffalo to the Soviet Union in the mid-1930s. In 1938, a year after his father's arrest and disappearance into the camps, Sgovio was arrested by the NKVD as he was leaving the U.S. embassy in Moscow, where he had applied for a visa to return to the United States. He ended up serving a five-year sentence in the Kolyma labor camps, one of the inner circles of the Soviet inferno, followed by years of exile.

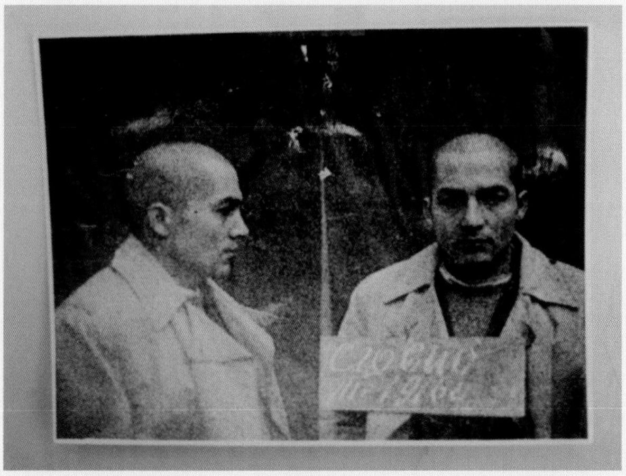

Thomas Sgovio's prison mug shots, 1948. Sgovio's papers in the Hoover Archives include a photocopy of his entire Soviet secret police and court file (1938–1956), including these mug shots. The interrogation transcripts contained in these files make for riveting reading. Sgovio proved to be one tough prisoner, standing up to his interrogators and refusing to cooperate by confessing to the charge of counterrevolutionary behavior.

Sgovio was allowed to return to European Russia in 1948, though forbidden to live in Moscow. He was able to visit his mother and sister, who informed him that his father had, only a few months earlier, returned from the camps after eleven years, a broken man, and died shortly thereafter. Sgovio was arrested again in December 1948 and sent to the central prison in Vladimir, where he remained until July 1949, at which point he was sentenced to exile in the Krasnoyarsk region, where he worked in a lumber camp.

The general amnesty declared shortly after Stalin's death in March 1953 enabled him to return to Moscow, where he went to work for the International Red Cross. In January 1960 he was able to get a visa from the Italian government for his mother and himself. He returned to Buffalo in 1963. Soon after winning his freedom, Sgovio began attempting to write of his experiences in the USSR but found the memories too painful, and in any case realized he did not have the writer's gift. But he had a sense of artistic design (during part of his time in exile he worked as a cartographer), and in the 1970s he created a series of drawings and paintings based on memories of his life as a prisoner in the Soviet camps and prisons. This artwork, which is housed in the Hoover Archives, conveys a sense of the extremes of cold, hunger, and exhaustion endured in the camps and the terror and humiliation experienced in the prisons.

Eventually, Sgovio published a modest memoir through a small publishing house in 1979. He dedicated it to all those who did not survive, those still perishing in communist prisons and labor camps, "and to my Father and others like him who became victims of their own illusions."

"The Work Brigade." "Returning 'home' to the compound after the 12 hour shift in the gold fields of Kolyma—7 days a week—no rest days—even when the thermometer dropped to 70° centigrade below zero. The prisoners were greeted with a sign which hung over the gate: 'Labor in the USSR is a matter of honor, courage and heroism.'"

"To Interrogation." "When a prisoner is being led to interrogation, the escort guard clangs a huge key on his belt buckle or clucks his tongue."

"Vladimir Prison—'Solitary'." "Clad only in underdrawers, the prisoner paces back and forth to keep warm. At night he is given a wooden board to lie on—but he cannot sleep. It's too cold." Sgovio was held in Vladimir prison from the end of 1948 through the first half of 1949.

Breaking with Communism

True Believers

For two decades, two founding members of the American communist movement, Bertram Wolfe and Jay Lovestone, rode the bronco of communist factional politics before making their break with Soviet Communism. Close friends, they brought very different qualities to the movement: Wolfe was the leading theorist and propagandist, and Lovestone was the natural politician and infighter.

Born in Brooklyn in 1896, Wolfe attended City College, where in 1917 he met and married Ella Goldberg, an immigrant from Ukraine. Also at City College he met Jay Lovestone, born Jacob Liebstein in Lithuania in 1898. Both men were pacifists who protested America's entry into the world war and gravitated toward the left wing of the socialist movement. The Bolshevik Revolution drew them to communism and inspired them to help found the American Communist Party in 1919.

Wolfe and Lovestone became confirmed believers in Marxist ideology, with its goals of a classless society and economic abundance, and looked to Soviet Russia as the best hope for putting that ideology into action. When Lenin and the Bolsheviks organized a Communist International (Comintern) of all the world's communist parties, Wolfe and Lovestone were prepared to accept Moscow's leadership in the cause of worldwide revolution. In time, however, they would become wary of Moscow's "guidance" in matters of revolutionary politics.

Bert and Ella Wolfe, undated (1918?). Sidney Hook remarked in his eulogy for Wolfe in 1977, "When one said Bert, one said Ella, too." (Bertram D. Wolfe Papers)

Wolfe visited Moscow for the first time in 1924, during the Fifth Comintern Congress, which he attended as a delegate from the Communist Party of Mexico, where he and Ella had fled to escape an arrest warrant in New York. In Moscow, he saw nothing to shake his faith in communism. A surviving letter he wrote to Lovestone during the congress captures the true believer's enthusiasm for the Soviet experiment. The following year, Wolfe was deported from Mexico and went to New York, where he joined the Workers' Party of America, the latest name for the Communist Party.

Lovestone, the more hardheaded of the two men, poured his considerable energy into the leadership struggles within the American party, struggles that were often taken to Moscow to be settled, if only temporarily.

Bertram Wolfe, Moscow, 1924. Wolfe was in Moscow, attending the Fifth Comintern Congress. (Bertram D. Wolfe Papers)

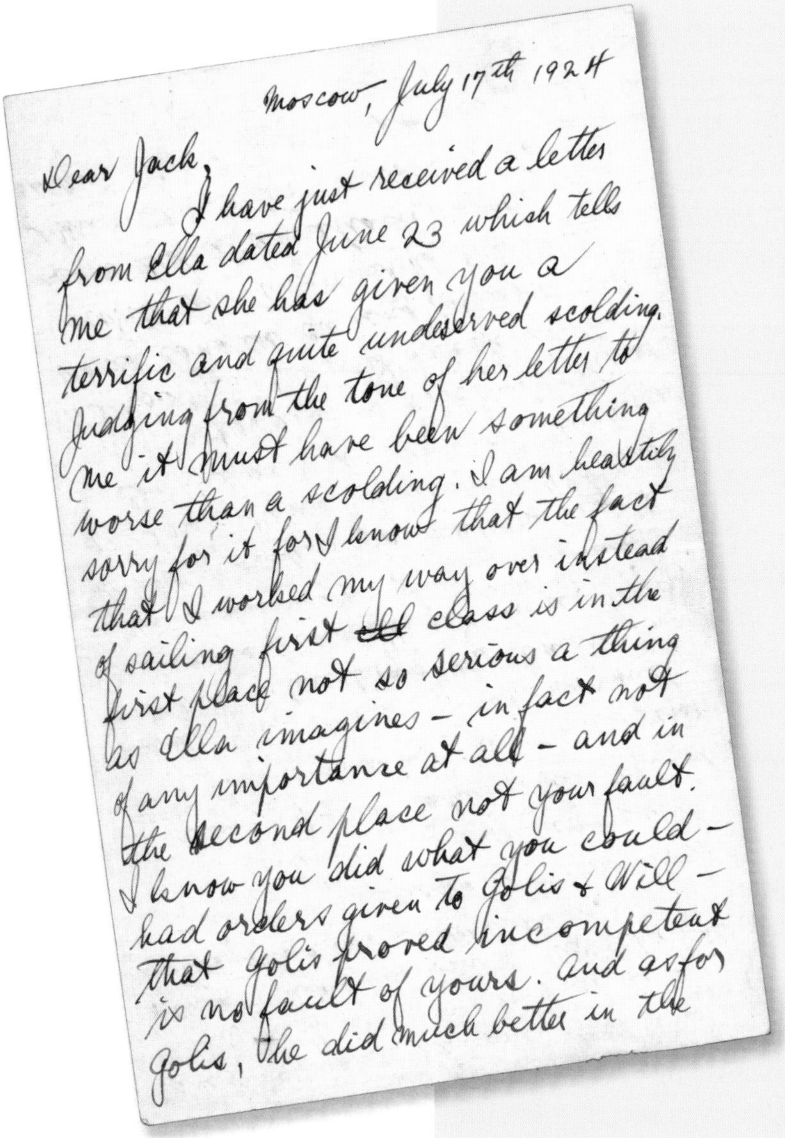

Moscow, July 17th 1924

Dear Jack,
I have just received a letter
from Ella dated June 23 which tells
me that she has given you a
terrific and quite undeserved scolding.
Judging from the tone of her letter to
me it must have been something
worse than a scolding. I am heartily
sorry for it for I know that the fact
that I worked my way over instead
of sailing first ~~cl~~ class is in the
first place not so serious a thing
as Ella imagines – in fact not
of any importance at all – and in
the second place not your fault.
I know you did what you could –
had orders given to Golis & Will –
that Golis proved incompetent
is no fault of yours. And as for
Golis, he did much better in the

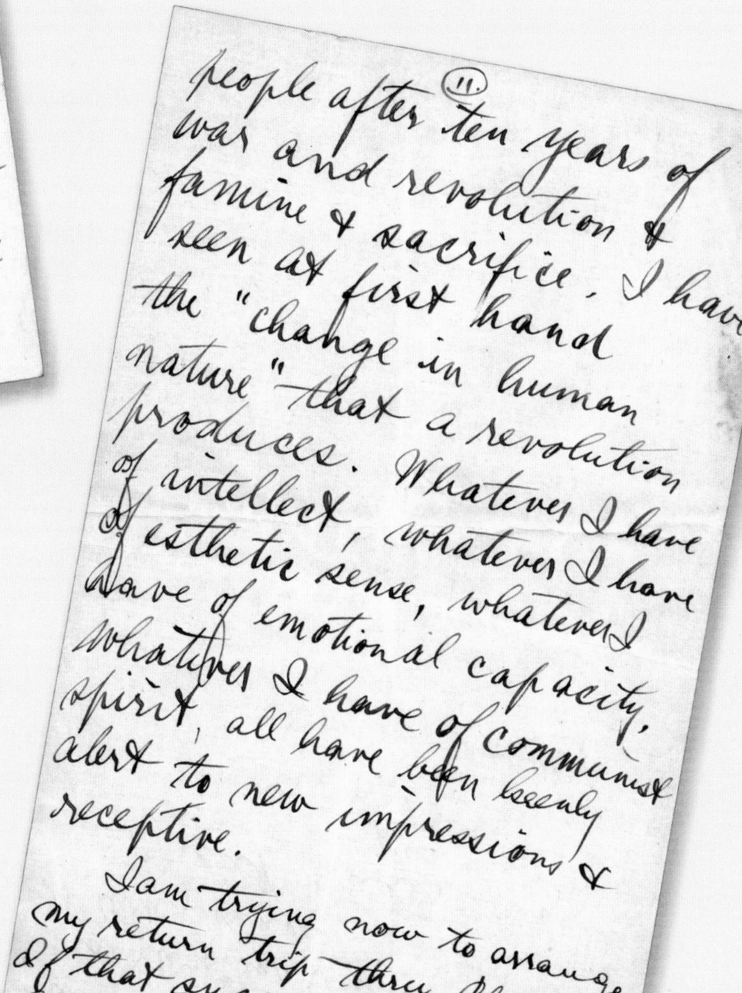

people after ten years of (11)
war and revolution &
famine & sacrifice. I have
seen at first hand
the "change in human
nature" that a revolution
produces. Whatever I have
of intellect, whatever I have
of esthetic sense, whatever I
have of emotional capacity,
whatever I have of communist
spirit, all have been keenly
alert to new impressions &
receptive.
I am trying now to arrange
my return trip thru Chicago.
If that succeeds, I shall
see you there, for I have

Letter from Wolfe, in Moscow, to "Jack" Lovestone, July 17, 1924 (pages 1 and 11). On his first visit to the mecca of world communism, Wolfe's romantic idealism about the Revolution reached a peak. (Jay Lovestone Papers)

Lovestone proved to be a tough and savvy player of party politics. When the head of the American Communist Party, Charles Ruthenberg, died in 1927, Lovestone succeeded him as general secretary. But his tenure was destined to be brief. By then, there was mounting frustration with Moscow's leadership for its limited understanding of the state of affairs in the United States and thus of the appropriate tactics for the American party to employ. Other communist parties were learning the same lesson: the interests of international communism were becoming increasingly incompatible with the advancement of Soviet foreign policy.

Wolfe returned to Moscow for the third time at the beginning of 1929 to attend a meeting of the Executive Committee of the Comintern (his second visit was earlier in 1928 as a delegate to the Sixth Comintern Congress). By now, Stalin was supreme, having vanquished first Trotsky and Zinoviev and the Left Opposition, and then Bukharin and the Right. Wolfe and Lovestone had supported Bukharin's more moderate line and were drawn personally to this most accessible of the Bolshevik leaders. When Wolfe arrived, Stalin was taking steps to erase Bukharin's influence from the Comintern, and that included the Lovestone leadership, which was accused of being insufficiently radical in its stance toward American socialists and trade unions.

Wolfe communicated these mounting difficulties to Lovestone by means of coded telegrams, the last of which urged him to come to Moscow. Lovestone and nine other American party members sailed immediately. The subsequent talks in Moscow failed even to postpone the inevitable. At a final confrontation on May 14, 1929, Stalin demanded that the Lovestone group swear publicly that they would unconditionally obey all directives from the Comintern. Lovestone objected and was removed from the leadership. Stalin attacked Lovestone directly: "And you, who are you? Who do you think you are? Trotsky defied me. Where is he? Zinoviev defied me. Where is he? Bukharin defied me. Where is he? And you! Who are you? Yes, you will go back to America. But when you get there, nobody will know you except your wives." The Americans were allowed to leave—except for Lovestone, who had to make use of a connection at the Latvian embassy in Moscow in order to exit the country. A few years hence, a troublemaker like Lovestone would have disappeared into the Gulag.

Upon their return to the United States, Wolfe and Lovestone were expelled from the party. In 1929, they and their colleagues created an alternative party, the Communist Party of the USA–Majority Group, which in 1931 they renamed Communist Party of the USA–Opposition, before adopting less cumbersome names later on. Unofficially, they were known as the Lovestone group, and they never numbered more than a few hundred members. But for Wolfe and Lovestone this was no break with communism. The Lovestone group still endorsed Marxist principles such as the abolition of private property, Leninist

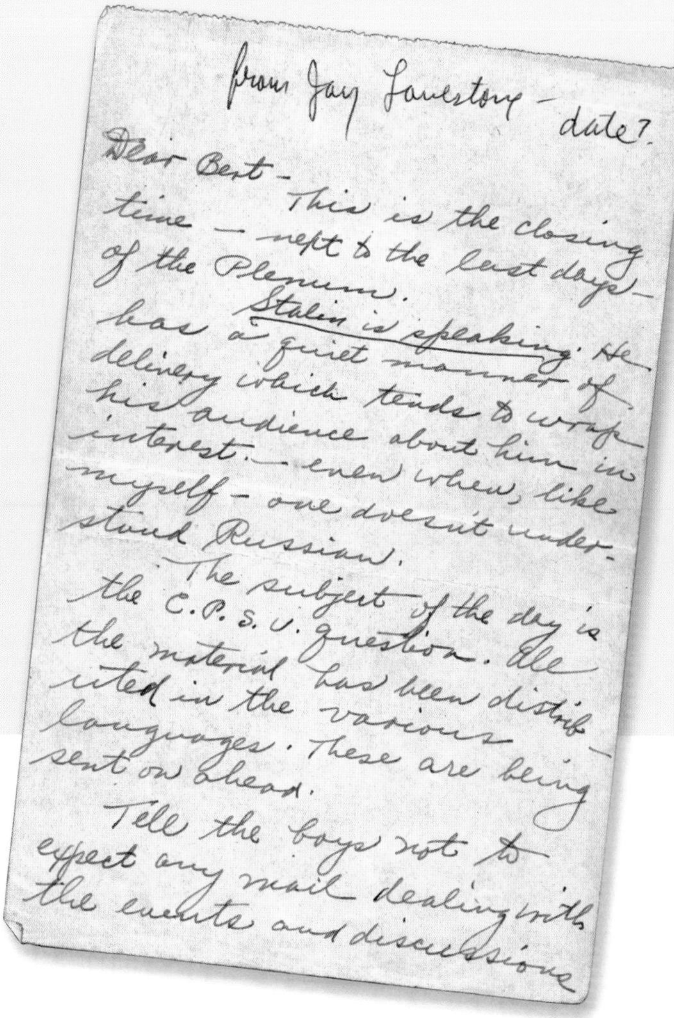
from Jay Lovestone - date?

Dear Bert -
This is the closing
time - next to the last day -
of the Plenum.
Stalin is speaking. He
has a quiet manner of
delivery which tends to wrap
his audience about him in
interest. - even when, like
myself - one doesn't understand Russian.
The subject of the day is
the C.P.S.U. question. All
the material has been distributed in the various
languages. These are being
sent on ahead.
Tell the boys not to
expect any mail dealing with
the events and discussions

First page of a letter (undated [December 1926]) from Lovestone to Wolfe. Lovestone writes as Stalin addresses the plenum of the Central Executive Committee of the Comintern in Moscow in December 1926. In the same letter, which is filled with the latest scorekeeping in the factional struggles among the American Communists, Lovestone remarks, "And Bukh[arin] and yours truly are getting along swimmingly chewing gum, etc." (Bertram D. Wolfe Papers)

tenets such as the dictatorship of the proletariat, and Stalin's insistence that the defense of the USSR from foreign enemies was the movement's top priority. For the next nine years, Lovestone and his followers expected Stalin to return the American party to their control.

During these lean years, Wolfe taught, lectured, and practiced journalism in order to support himself. His connection to Diego Rivera inspired him to publish three books on the Mexican muralist, *Portrait of America* (1934), *Portrait of Mexico* (1937), and *Diego Rivera: His Life and Times* (1939). Lovestone stuck to labor and radical politics, always with a conspiratorial bent (he maintained at least four identities in the 1930s). In fact, recently released documents from the Comintern archives in Moscow show that Lovestone was still doing intelligence work for the Soviet Union as late as 1936, seven years after his expulsion from the Communist Party. Lovestone criticized Wolfe's foray into biography as being unworthy of a serious revolutionary. But developments in Moscow would place a much greater strain on their comradeship and on the entire international communist movement.

The Purge and the Pact

The correspondence between the Wolfes (Bert and Ella) and Lovestone shows the strains on their communist idealism during the 1930s, despite the indictment of capitalism offered by the Great Depression. Part of this, no doubt, was a matter of becoming a little older and wiser. Even though the Soviet Union proclaimed the achievement of socialism in 1936, it became harder to maintain the notion that the USSR was the best model for other countries to follow. For many Western communists, one benchmark on the road to making a break with the movement was the Comintern's policy in the Spanish Civil War. Despite generous Soviet military assistance to the Spanish Republic, reports out of Spain told of Communist moves to crush left-wing forces operating independently of Moscow.

The biggest blow was the three Moscow Trials of 1936, 1937, and 1938. Many American Communists were able to persuade themselves of the authenticity of the first two trials. But the trial of Bukharin in March 1938 was a purge too far: it convinced many Communists and sympathizers, including Wolfe and Lovestone, of the need to make a break. The moment was not sudden: Bukharin's name had been raised during the trial of Karl Radek and sixteen others in January 1937, and when he was arrested a month later it was obvious that Stalin was planning to make him the chief defendant in a third show trial. Doubt began to set in among the Communist faithful.

Wolfe, the journalist, expressed his growing apprehension in print. A breakthrough moment came in his review, in the *New Republic* in November 1937, of the book *The Case of Leon Trotsky,* a transcript of the hearings of the Dewey Commission, the committee of American liberals that had cleared Trotsky of the charges made against him at the Moscow trials. To the surprise of many—including, no doubt, the editors of the *New Republic*—Wolfe examined the evidence and concluded that Trotsky was innocent. Whether or not he understood it, he had reached a point of no return.

Lovestone's state of mind in 1937 is harder to gauge, but when the Bukharin trial opened on March 2, 1938, he felt that the Revolution had truly been betrayed. In a speech one week later under the auspices of the Trotsky Defense Committee, Wolfe called Bukharin's trial an "infamous and murderous farce": "If one word of these charges is credited as true, then the Russian Revolution must have been made by traitors, bandits, imperialists, spies, provocateurs, murderers, and counter-revolutionaries."

Any lingering illusions Wolfe and Lovestone may have still entertained about Stalin's USSR were dispelled by the Nazi-Soviet Pact of August 1939. The outbreak of the war, especially the fall of Paris in May–June 1940, caused a personal break between Lovestone and Wolfe, much as it further fractured the radical left. Lovestone came out in favor of the United States providing aid to Britain, while Wolfe believed, along with many others on the left, that should the United States be drawn into the war American domestic politics would veer toward fascism. To Lovestone, this stance was tantamount to aiding Hitler.

In 1941 Lovestone formally dismantled his communist opposition group. For several more years Wolfe continued to regard Stalinism as an aberration of the project begun by Marx and Lenin. Only in the late 1940s did he stop praising *The Communist Manifesto* as the ultimate expression of his ideals. As Sidney Hook later observed, it required far greater courage for people like Lovestone and Wolfe to break with communism than to embrace it, so great was their emotional investment in it.

Jay Lovestone addressing an antiwar gathering at the New Workers School in the late 1930s. Seated at far right is Bertram Wolfe. The mural on the wall in the background is by Diego Rivera. (Jay Lovestone Papers)

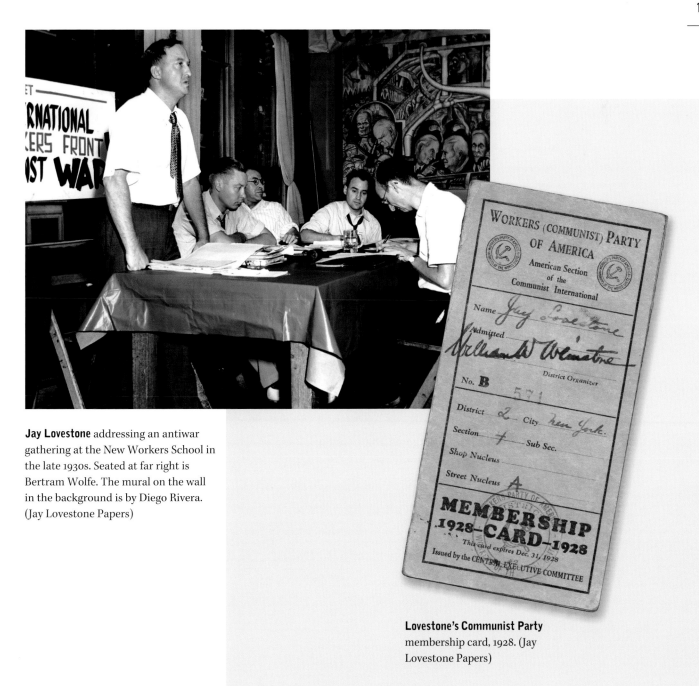

Lovestone's Communist Party membership card, 1928. (Jay Lovestone Papers)

Life After Communism

In their postcommunist afterlives, Lovestone and Wolfe used their distinctive talents and their knowledge as former insiders (and their firm conviction that "it takes one to know one") to warn Americans against, and otherwise work to resist, the totalitarian methods of the Communist bloc.

With his scholarly books on Communism, beginning with the classic *Three Who Made a Revolution,* researched in part at the Hoover Library and published in 1948, as well as his many superbly crafted book reviews and other popular articles on Soviet history, Wolfe was a pioneer of Sovietology. He and Ella returned to the Hoover Institution in 1965, where he was a senior research fellow until his death in 1977 and she his indispensable partner and then literary executor until her own death in 2000.

Lovestone's postcommunist career followed a more unorthodox path, one that allowed him to indulge in his penchant for secrecy and conspiracy. In the 1940s he became affiliated with the International Ladies Garment Workers Union and then assumed a leading role in the American Federation of Labor (AFL). He set up an organization to prevent Soviet penetration of European labor unions, using union funds to expand the international ties of the AFL and later the combined AFL-CIO. His work attracted the attention of the CIA, which began contributing funds in the 1950s. For twenty years, from 1954 to 1974, Lovestone worked in close collaboration with the CIA's counterintelligence chief, James Angleton.

The Hoover Archives acquired Lovestone's papers in 1975—more than seven hundred boxes, documenting the American Communist movement and his own career in great detail. Lovestone stipulated that the collection be closed until five years after his death, which occurred in 1990. The collection served as the basis for *A Covert Life,* Ted Morgan's 1999 biography of Lovestone.

The presence in the Hoover Archives of the papers of both Wolfe and Lovestone offers an interesting opportunity for researchers. An individual's archival collection often contains only one-way correspondence: the original copies of letters received, unless copies of outgoing letters were made and preserved, which was something of a luxury for conspiratorial revolutionaries in the first decades of the twentieth century. In the case of Bertram Wolfe and Jay Lovestone, both of whom left their papers to the Hoover Archives, their original letters are present—in each other's collection.

Stalin's Ghost

Boris Pasternak won the 1958 Nobel Prize in Literature, in the words of the award citation, "for his important achievement both in contemporary lyrical poetry and in the field of the great Russian epic tradition." Pasternak's epic was *Doctor Zhivago,* the great novel of the Russian Revolution that is replete with lyrical poetry. The Soviet authorities treated it as a work of heresy, and Pasternak, after first accepting the prize, was forced by the government to renounce it.

Doctor Zhivago was a long time in the making. In the 1930s, Pasternak all but ceased to write his own poetry, becoming a translator of Georgian verse and of such classic literary works as *Hamlet.* Toward the end of the decade, he turned to prose and began working on his big novel. By the time he completed it, in 1955, the Soviet Union was undergoing a remarkable transition. Stalin's death in March 1953 had inaugurated a "thaw" in politics and in the arts, which received further official encouragement in February 1956 with Nikita Khrushchev's "secret speech" denouncing Stalin's repression.

First edition of *Doctor Zhivago* in Italian translation, published by Feltrinelli Editore, Milan, in November 1957. (Irwin Holtzman Collection)

Boris Pasternak, 1959. (Irwin Holtzman Collection)

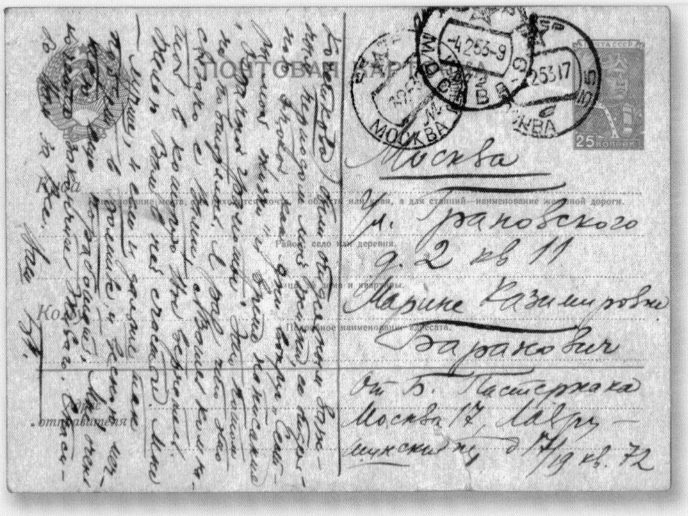
Москва
ул. Грановского
д. 2 кв 11
Марине Казимировне
Баранович
От Б. Пастернака
Москва 17, Лаврушинский пер. д 17/19 кв. 72

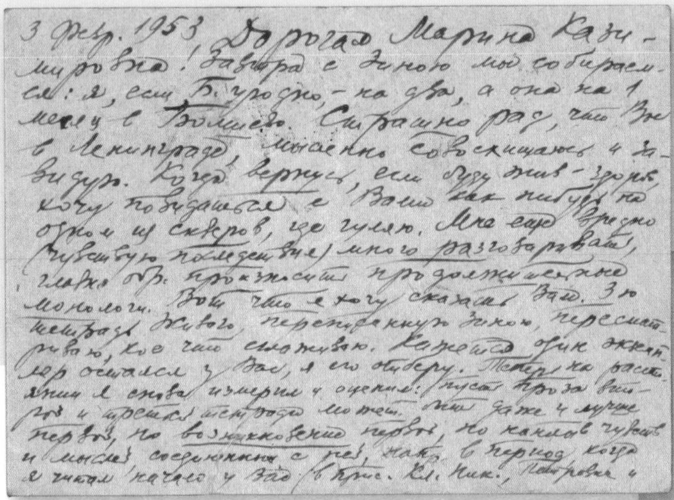

Postcard from Pasternak to Marina Baranovich, February 3, 1953. Among the materials on Pasternak and *Zhivago* in the Hoover Archives are the papers of Marina Baranovich, his longtime friend and typist. They corresponded within Moscow, and he wrote to her also from his home in Peredelkino, the writers colony in the suburbs. At the close of the message he inscribed on this postcard, Pasternak lets out a sigh: "I very much want to finish Zhivago." And for good reason: the year before, he had suffered a massive heart attack and nearly died. On October 21, 1956, Pasternak wrote to Baranovich that there had been "much geographic activity with the novel"—referring to his arrangements to have the book published abroad. (Pasternak Family Papers)

At a family gathering, Pasternak raises a toast in celebration of his Nobel Prize (1958). (Irwin Holtzman Collection)

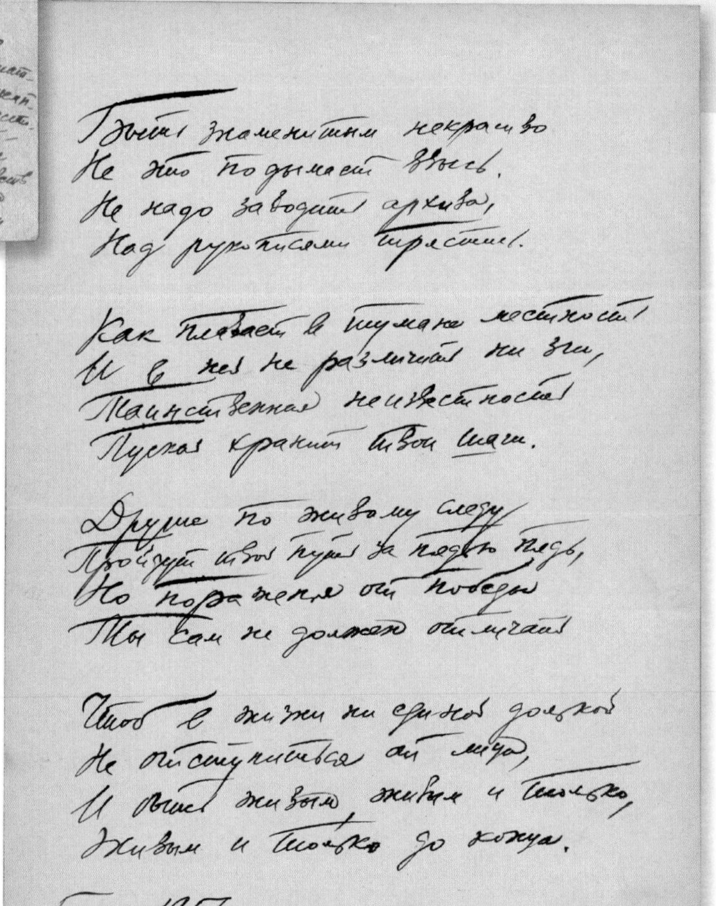
Быть знаменитым некрасиво.
Не это подымает ввысь.
Не надо заводить архива,
Над рукописями трястись.

Как плавает в тумане местность
И в ней не различить ни зги,
Таинственная неизвестность
Пускай хранит твои шаги.

Другие по живому следу
Пройдут твой путь за пядью пядь,
Но пораженья от победы
Ты сам не должен отличать.

Чтоб в жизни ни единой долькой
Не отступиться от лица,
И быть живым, живым и только,
Живым и только до конца.

5 мая 1956

Holograph poem by Pasternak, "To Be Famous Is Unbecoming," dated May 5, 1956. (Pasternak Family Papers)

The Soviet government sought to portray Stalinism as an aberration, but Pasternak's novel invited a reading of history that looked beyond Stalin's "crimes" and his personality cult to the essence of the Bolshevik Revolution. "The novel was devoted to the revolution and the civil war," Lazar Fleishman explains, "but as the first readers noticed, the author showed in telescopic form that the main features of Stalin's time flowed inevitably from the very nature of the Bolshevik Party and Soviet power."

Not surprisingly, the novel was rejected by Soviet publishers. Stymied at home, Pasternak sent his manuscript to Italy, where it was published in November 1957 in Italian translation. The original Russian version was published abroad the following year, and before long the novel would be translated into all the major languages of the world. Pasternak understood the ramifications of this step, jokingly inviting the proxy of his Italian publisher to attend his execution.

The book's publication brought no official reaction, but once the Nobel Prize was announced, in October 1958, the Soviet establishment launched a vicious attack on Pasternak. He was expelled from the Writers' Union and called, among many other unpleasant things, "a pig that fouls its own sty." In the face of this and threats of expulsion from the Soviet Union and retribution against family and friends, Pasternak, who had already sent a telegram to the Swedish academy accepting the prize, sent another one refusing it. In a letter to Khrushchev published in *Pravda* he wrote: "Leaving the motherland will be equivalent to death for me. I am tied to Russia by birth, by life, and by work." He also feared what might befall his loved ones should he be exiled.

In the West, some criticized Pasternak for his apparent penitence. Under the influence of these attacks, he wrote the poem "Nobel Prize," which was published in a London newspaper in February 1959 and caused an international sensation. "Nobel Prize" conveys the poet's sense of isolation and helplessness. Its first stanza reads:

> Like a beast in a pen, I'm cut off
> From my friends, freedom, the sun,
> But the hunters are gaining ground.
> I've nowhere else to run.

Pasternak died the following year of lung cancer. In 1989, as communism was breathing its last, his son accepted his father's Nobel Prize medal at a ceremony in Stockholm.

NAZI GERMANY

Hitler's *Mein Kampf*

As an example of the perils of failing to take ideas seriously enough, it is hard to compete with the story of *Mein Kampf.* Ignored at the time as the ravings of a politician on the lunatic fringe, the book is now routinely referred to as the "blueprint" for the militarism and genocide of the Third Reich.

It is not quite accurate to say that Hitler "wrote" *Mein Kampf,* since he dictated it to Rudolf Hess, beginning in his prison cell in Landsberg, where he was serving time for the failed Beer Hall Putsch in Munich in November 1923. It is said that Hitler wanted to call the book "Four and a Half Years of Struggle Against Lies, Stupidity, and Cowardice," but instead the Nazi publisher talked him into the catchier *Mein Kampf* (My Struggle). Although the

First edition of *Mein Kampf,* volume 1. *Mein Kampf,* published in two volumes (1925 and 1927), both of which are part of the Hoover Library collection, is a considerable rarity.

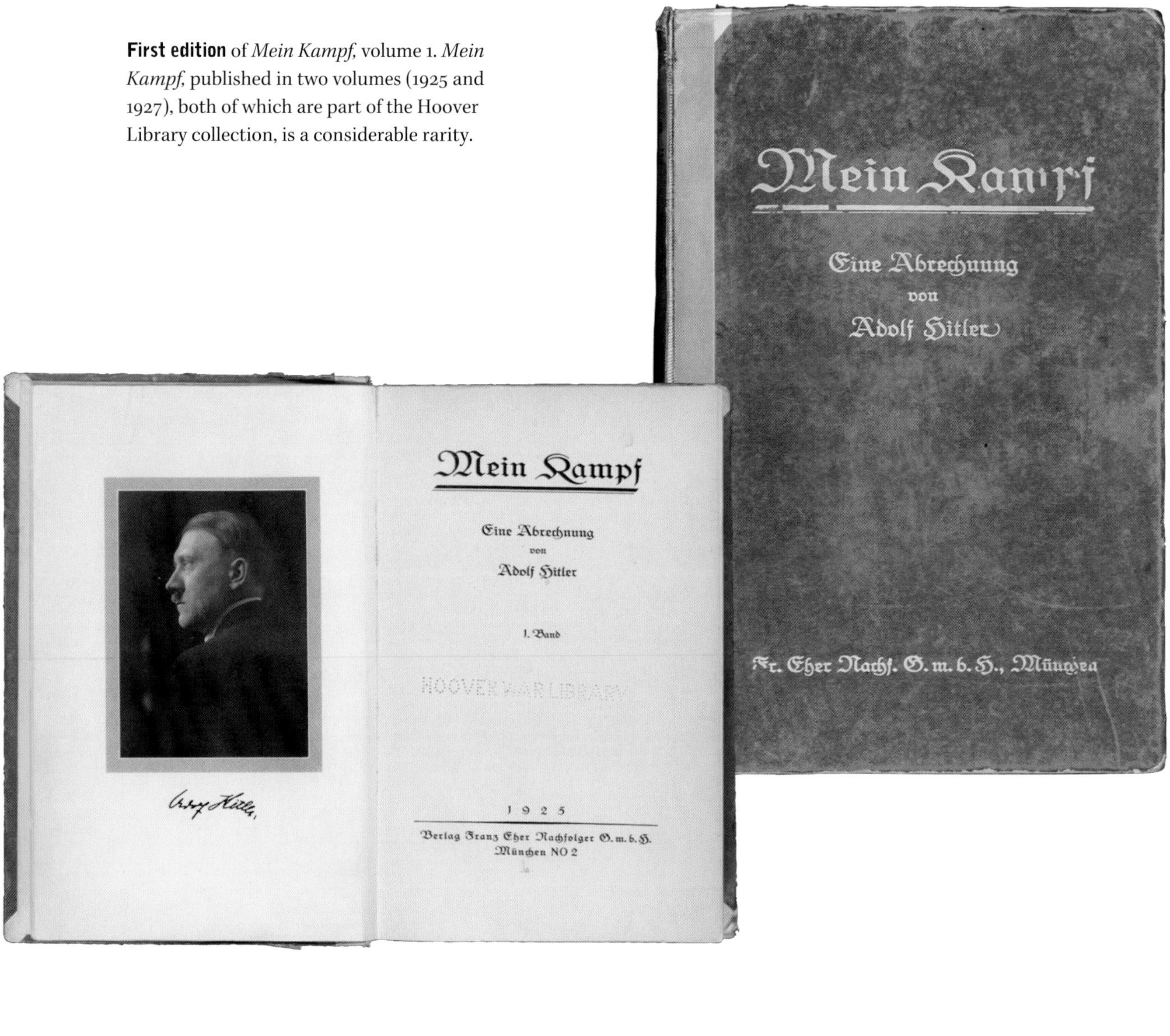

published version was vastly improved by editing—Nazi leader Otto Strasser described the first draft as "a veritable chaos of banalities, schoolboy reminiscences, subjective judgments, and personal hatred"—the book nonetheless reads like a Hitler rant.

Mein Kampf was published in two volumes, in 1925 and 1927. The first volume is Hitler mostly reminiscing on his youth and early days in the Nazi Party. The second volume, which Hitler wrote after getting out of prison, deals with matters of ideology, politics, and Germany's future foreign policy. The book did not outline specific policies, but it laid out his long-term program and his vision for Germany. "Not least," writes Hitler biographer Ian Kershaw, "it established the basis of the Führer myth. For in *Mein Kampf,* Hitler portrayed himself as uniquely qualified to lead Germany from its existing misery to greatness."

Race was at the center of Hitler's view of history, which he portrayed as a struggle between the supreme Aryan and the parasitic Jew. "The racial question," he wrote, "gives the key not only to world history but to all human culture." The Jews were operating an international conspiracy to control world finances and the press and were attempting to undermine the Aryan race by inventing insidious ideologies such as Marxism and liberalism and promoting vices such as prostitution. "Jewish Bolshevism" had taken power in Russia and was subjecting its people to brutal torture and starvation, in the name of a messianic ideology. The mission of the Nazis was to destroy this Jewish Bolshevism by waging war against Russia, and in the process securing *Lebensraum* (living space) for the German people, the master race.

Hitler was disappointed by the sales of *Mein Kampf.* Aside from being dreadfully written, the book was overpriced by the party's publishing house, the Franz Eher-Verlag. By 1929, only about 23,000 copies of the first volume had been sold, and only about 13,000 of the second volume. But after the Nazis came to power, sales took off, so that by 1939 millions of copies of the more modestly priced "people's edition" of *Mein Kampf* had been sold, making Hitler a best-selling author.

Even then, many refused to heed the book's implicit warnings. "Hitler's book was not a prescriptive programme in the sense of a short-term political manifesto," Kershaw writes. "But many contemporaries made a mistake in treating *Mein Kampf* with ridicule and not taking the ideas Hitler expressed there extremely seriously. However base and repellent they were, they amounted to a set of clearly established and rigidly upheld political principles."

Monster Diarist

Joseph Goebbels at a Nazi party rally in Berlin, 1932. (Jay Lovestone Papers)

Although Hitler was a far more effective speaker than writer, Joseph Goebbels, the man who became his propaganda chief, excelled at both. Born in 1897 in the industrial town of Rheydt in the Rhineland, Goebbels contracted osteomyelitis as a boy, which left him with a lame right leg. Unable to take part in athletic activities, he threw himself into books and eventually completed a doctoral degree in literature at Heidelberg University in 1921. As a youth, he tried his hand at poetry, plays, and novels, and he started writing for newspapers in 1922.

In 1924, Goebbels began to keep a diary and continued to do so until his death. He wrote entries by hand, three or four times a week, until 1941, when he began to dictate daily entries, some of which ran up to thirty typescript pages in length. A substantial part of the diaries were recovered after the war, and over the years they have been published. Taken together, the Goebbels diary is, in the assessment of historian Gordon Craig, "clearly the most important document left by the Nazi movement, the richest source of information about the party's internal feuds and debates and crises, as well as, of course, about its author's life, character, and ideas."

Goebbels entered politics after being inspired by Hitler's failed Munich putsch and subsequent trial in 1923. He drifted into Nazi circles in northern Germany dominated by the Strasser bothers, Gregor and Otto. He wrote articles for the populist paper *Völkische Zeitung* before becoming its editor. On November 8, 1924, he devoted an entire issue to Adolf Hitler, whom Goebbels hailed as "our helmsman in need, our apostle of truth, our leader to freedom, our fanatic of love, our voice in battle." In early 1925, after Hitler's release from Landsberg prison, the National Socialist Democratic Workers' Party was reformed, and Goebbels became manager of Gregor Strasser's office in the north Rhineland.

Goebbels left behind no record of a first meeting with Hitler, which probably took place around July 12, 1925, but he recorded his feelings about Hitler and his impressions of their early encounters and they make the early Goebbels diaries such fascinating reading.

In the entry for October 14, he is reading *Mein Kampf*: "I am finishing Hitler's book. Thrilled to bits! Who is this man? Half-plebeian, half God! Really Christ, or only John?"

On April 19, 1926, after a meeting with "the chief," he is euphoric: "Adolf Hitler, I love you, because you are both great and simple. A genius. Leave-taking from him. Farewell! He waves."

Nazi rally in Berlin, 1932. (Jay Lovestone Papers)

Goebbels diary entry for November 23, 1925.

"I arrive. Hitler is there. Great joy. He greets me like an old friend. And looks after me. How I love him! What a fellow! And he tells stories the whole evening. I could go on listening forever. A small meeting. He asks me to speak first. Then he speaks. How small I am! He gives me his photograph. With greetings from the Rhineland. Heil Hitler!"

Goebbels's handwriting is extremely difficult to decipher, a task made more challenging here by the poor condition of the diary, whose pages are in places burned, punctured, water damaged, and, in the final pages, in tatters.

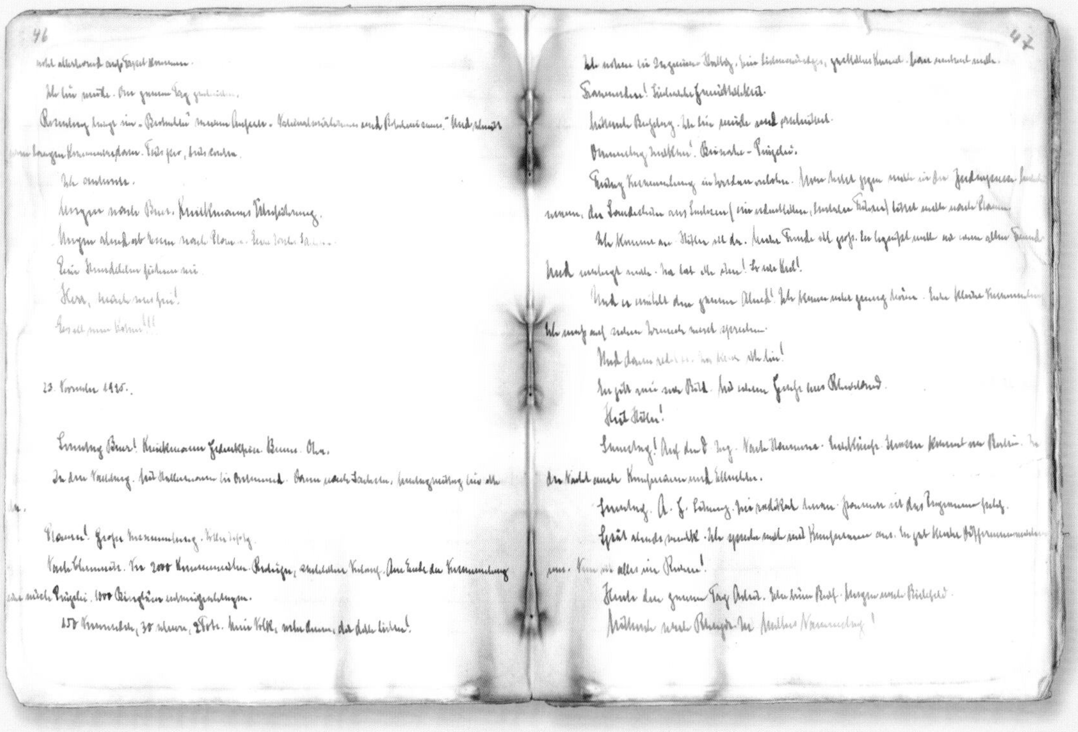

46

23. November 1925.

47

On his part, Hitler flattered Goebbels in order to win his loyalty and bring him over to the Bavarian wing of the National Socialists, seeing in him a valuable resource, and not only as a talented propagandist: as a spellbinder Goebbels was second only to Hitler. "Wherever he spoke," according to his biographer Ralf Georg Reuth, "he transformed halls and smoke-filled back rooms of taverns into bedlam."

Goebbels decided to hook his future to that of Hitler, even though it meant breaking old loyalties and compromising on his own beliefs, which were often more radical than Hitler's. At the end of 1926, Goebbels accepted Hitler's invitation to become Gauleiter (district boss) in Berlin. In 1930 he was made propaganda chief for the entire country, serving as "campaign manager" for the Nazis as they drove to power in a series of elections held between 1930 and 1933. Goebbels was the master propagandist for the Third Reich, even after the war began to go badly for Germany. He became what Craig calls "the first 'spin doctor,' transforming the shattering defeat at Stalingrad into a portent of future victory."

To the end, he remained a monster, regretting that the Nazi party had not wielded power more ruthlessly. In 1944 he wrote in his diary: "Only in the Jewish question did we pursue such a radical policy. It was correct, and today we are its beneficiaries. The Jews cannot do us any more harm. Even so, before we tackled the Jewish question, people said over and over again that the question could not be solved. One sees that it is possible, if one only has the will. But a bourgeois would naturally not be able to understand that."

The Early Diaries

The Hoover Institution has two original portions of the Goebbels diaries: a handwritten notebook covering the period 1925–26, and the typescript diary for 1942–43. They were rescued from the ruins of the Third Reich and came into the possession of U.S. Army Col. William Heimlich of the American occupation force, who gave them to Herbert Hoover in Frankfurt during Hoover's 1946 fact-finding tour to assess Europe's postwar relief needs.

Of the two diary sections, the later, wartime diary, though insightful, was written by a doomed man with an eye on posterity. The 192-page handwritten diary covering the period from August 12, 1925, to the end of October 1926 is a far more important document for judging Goebbels the man, his relationship with Hitler, and the foundations of the Hitler myth. The diary's most remarkable feature is its author's passion for self-dramatization. "As soon as one turns to the text," wrote Alan Bullock in introducing the first publication of the diary in 1963, "the first thing to strike the reader is the self-conscious, emotionally high-flown style in which Goebbels writes. At times it reads like a caricature of an adolescent's diary, although Goebbels was actually twenty-eight at the time he wrote it."

The entry for November 6, 1925, to take one example, contains a characteristically delirious passage:

> *We drive to Hitler. He is having his meal. He jumps to his feet, there he is. Shakes my hand. Like an old friend. And those big blue eyes. Like stars. He is glad to see me. I am in heaven. He retires for ten minutes. Then his speech is roughly finished. Meanwhile I drive to the meeting. And speak for two hours. Punctuated by applause. And then* Heils *and clapping. There he is. He shakes my hand. His big speech has quite finished him. Then he makes another half-hour speech here. Full of wit, irony, humor, sarcasm, seriousness and glowing with passion. That man has got everything to be a king. A born tribune of the people. The coming dictator.*

As Reuth observes, "Numerous diary passages written in the summer of 1926 show how far Goebbels's imagination could carry him; he not only transfigured Hitler into the new Messiah but also linked him with miracles and wonderful happenings in nature." One such passage appears in a lengthy entry for July 6, 1926: "Hitler speaks. On politics, the cause, organization. Deep and mystical. Almost like the Gospels. Shuddering we pass together with him along the edge of life's abyss. Everything is being said. I thank providence for having given us this man!" And at the end of the entry for July 24, providence makes a special appearance:

> *In the morning to the Hochlenzer. The chief talks about race questions. It is impossible to reproduce what he said. It must be experienced. He is a genius. The natural, creative instrument of a fate determined by God. I am deeply moved. He is like a child: kind, good, merciful. Like a cat: cunning, clever, agile. Like a lion: roaring and great and gigantic. A fellow, a man. He talks about the state. In the afternoon about winning over the state and the political revolution. Thoughts which I may well have had, but never yet put into words. After supper we go on sitting in the garden of the naval hostel, and he goes on for a long time preaching about the new state and how we are going to fight for it. It sounds like prophecy. Up in the skies a white cloud takes on the shape of the swastika. There is a blinking light that cannot be a star. A sign of fate?!*

As Bullock notes, by the time the entries in the early diary end, on October 30, 1926, Goebbels had made up his mind to switch allegiances from the Rhineland to the Bavarian branch of the Nazi party. Ten days later he accepted Hitler's invitation to go to Berlin.

Rendezvous

Among the Hoover rarities on the twentieth century's great tyrannies are albums of photographs that once belonged to Nazi leaders. These provide unusually intimate visual documentation of the diplomatic road to the Second World War.

Der Führer in Italy

In a speech in Milan in the autumn of 1936, Benito Mussolini described the connection between Rome and Berlin as "an axis round which all those European states which are animated by a desire for collaboration and peace can revolve." The word "axis" caught on around the world—as a source of pride in Germany and Italy and of apprehension in the Western democracies.

But there were stresses and strains in the relationship between the two Axis powers, which Germany's *Anschluss* of Austria in March 1938 did nothing to alleviate. Mussolini had acquiesced in the Nazi move, but now Hitler had his sights on Czechoslovakia, the chief topic of discussion during Hitler's state visit to Rome from May 3 to 9.

The city was festively decorated with flags and swastikas, and Hitler's itinerary outside the negotiating room was crowded with receptions and sightseeing excursions. These public aspects of the visit were captured in an album of photographs presented by the Italian government to Heinrich Himmler, head of the Gestapo and the SS. To judge from these images, Hitler was ill at ease during his Italian excursion, appearing impatient with all the pomp and splendor attending his visit. He is also said to have been irritated by the fact that King Victor Emmanuel III, rather than Mussolini, was his official host, and he felt that the king and queen and their circle did not treat him with appropriate deference.

Away from the cameras, the visit was a success for Hitler. He assuaged Italian fears by talking of a natural alpine border, in effect publicly renouncing any claim on South Tyrol, Austrian territory that had come into Italy's hands after the First World War. And he understood from Mussolini's comments that Germany was free to move against Czechoslovakia.

Upon his return to Berlin, Hitler began to tighten the screws on Czechoslovakia, threatening war and creating the crisis atmosphere that led to the agreement with the British and the French at Munich in September 1938. Czechoslovakia was forced to accept the loss of the Sudetenland, depriving it of a third of the population and its most important industrial region. British Prime Minister Neville Chamberlain returned to London declaring that he had secured "peace for our time," but of course this was not so. Hitler was bent on war with Poland.

Series of photographs from Heinrich Himmler's Italian photo album. (William R. Philp Collection)

Hitler and Mussolini

Front row, left to right: Joseph Goebbels (laughing), Hitler, Mussolini, Rudolf Hess, and Joachim von Ribbentrop.

Molotov signs the so-called nonaggression treaty with Germany, as von Ribbentrop and Stalin stand by. Pages from von Ribbentrop's photo album. (William R. Philp Collection)

The Nazi-Soviet Pact

Easily the most notorious treaty of the twentieth century was the Molotov-Ribbentrop Pact, also known as the Hitler-Stalin Pact and the Nazi-Soviet Pact. It was signed in Moscow on the night of August 23, 1939, between German Foreign Minister Joachim von Ribbentrop and his Soviet counterpart, Viacheslav Molotov. The public part of the treaty was a statement of nonaggression and friendship between the two countries. The treaty's secret protocols stipulated, among other things, that "in the event of a territorial and political rearrangement," the Soviet Union would be given preponderant influence in the Baltics and that Poland would be divided into German and Soviet spheres. On their part, the Soviets pledged to remain neutral in the event of a war between Germany and Poland or between Germany and the Western powers.

The shock produced by the announcement of the Nazi-Soviet Pact can hardly be exaggerated. The two powers were viewed as ideological opposites, yet here they were declaring their mutual friendship. The treaty would not last even two years before being dramatically nullified by the German invasion of the Soviet Union on June 22, 1941. For the time being, it gave Hitler the free hand he wanted for Germany to invade Poland, which it did on September 1. Two days later, Britain and France declared war on Germany. On September 18, German forces moving eastward into Poland met the westward-bound Soviet forces at Brest-Litovsk. Poland had disappeared from the map.

The Hoover Archives holds two albums of photographs taken during the visit of Ribbentrop to Moscow to sign the Nazi-Soviet Pact. The photographs, taken by Ribbentrop's private photographer, Gisela Pönzgen-Döhm, provide a unique record of the event. Because we know the aftermath, there is a surreal quality to the shots of the signing ceremony, the apparent good cheer of the participants a striking counterpoint to the enormous human misery about to be unleashed by the pact.

The albums came to the Hoover Archives in 1968 as a gift from Col. William R. Philp, a retired U.S. Army officer living in San Francisco. Philp was an intelligence officer on the Normandy invasion plans, served with General Patton on the continent, and was the chief of intelligence for the U.S. Army dealing with the prisoners awaiting trial at Nuremberg. As the story was told by Hoover librarian Kenneth Glazier in 1968 in announcing the gift:

> *A couple of weeks ago I received a phone call from a retired colonel in San Francisco saying that he had a few items that we might be interested in. A few days later I went to visit him in his apartment on Nob Hill. As he brought the material from various shelves and cupboards I couldn't believe my eyes. As an intelligence officer on the Normandy invasion plans and with General Patton he had found occasion to "liberate" many of these documents. After 25 years his wife had persuaded him that she would like him to clean house and get the stuff out of the apartment.*

The "stuff" included Hitler's marriage license and X rays of his head and teeth, taken after the failed attempt on his life on July 20, 1944.

Stalin smiles for the camera (above) and celebrates with von Ribbentrop, as Red Army Chief of Staff Boris Shaposhnikov (in uniform) and German SS officer Richard Schulze look on.

Winston Churchill, outside the Admiralty in London, in September 1939. At the outbreak of the Second World War, Churchill was appointed First Lord of the Admiralty, a post he had held from 1911 to 1915. He would become prime minister in May 1940. (World War II Pictorial Collection)

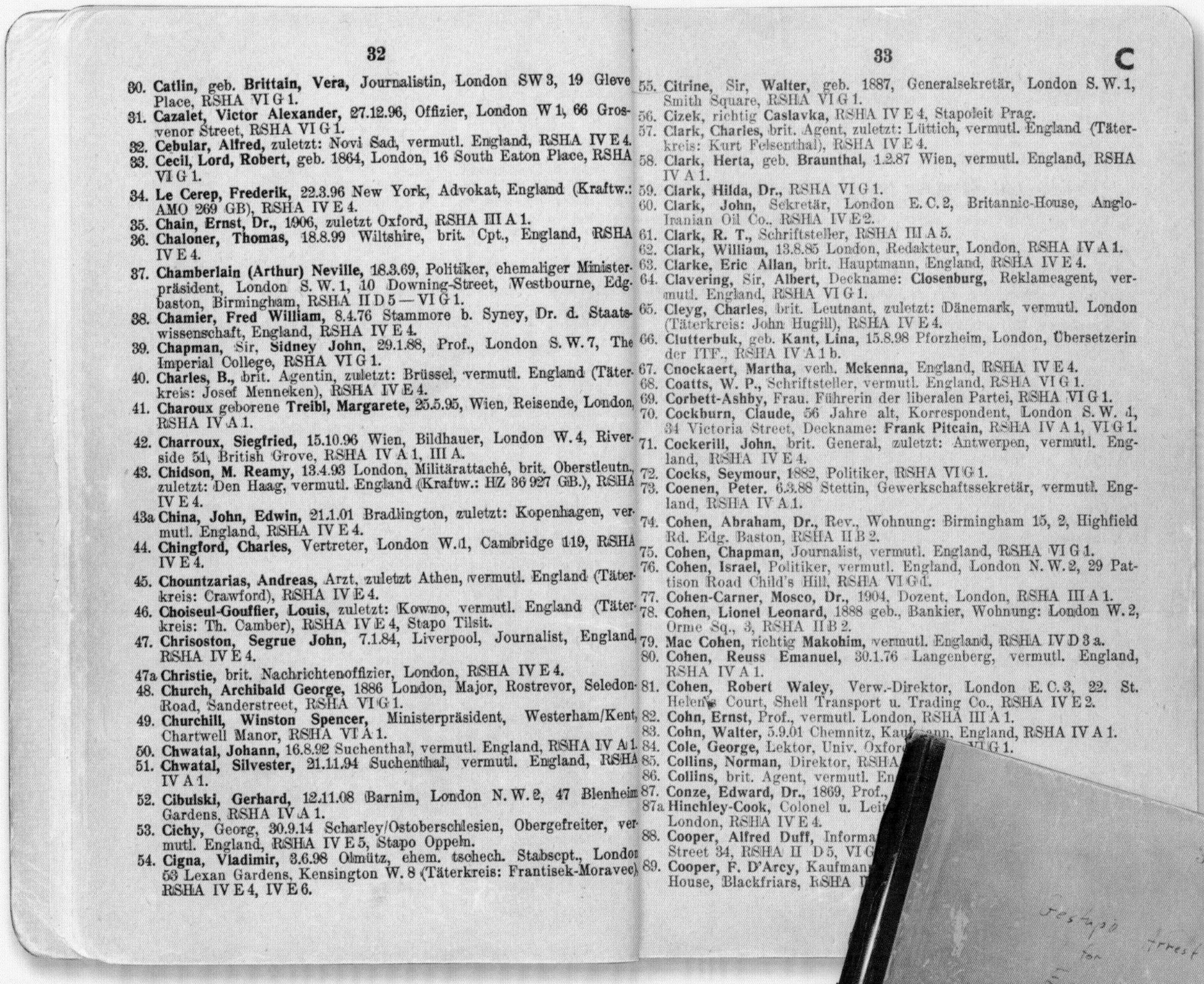
32

30. Catlin, geb. Brittain, Vera, Journalistin, London SW 3, 19 Gleve Place, RSHA VI G 1.
31. Cazalet, Victor Alexander, 27.12.96, Offizier, London W 1, 66 Grosvenor Street, RSHA VI G 1.
32. Cebular, Alfred, zuletzt: Novi Sad, vermutl. England, RSHA IV E 4.
33. Cecil, Lord, Robert, geb. 1864, London, 16 South Eaton Place, RSHA VI G 1.
34. Le Cerep, Frederik, 22.3.96 New York, Advokat, England (Kraftw.: AMO 269 GB), RSHA IV E 4.
35. Chain, Ernst, Dr., 1906, zuletzt Oxford, RSHA III A 1.
36. Chaloner, Thomas, 18.8.99 Wiltshire, brit. Cpt., England, RSHA IV E 4.
37. Chamberlain (Arthur) Neville, 18.3.69, Politiker, ehemaliger Ministerpräsident, London S. W. 1, 10 Downing-Street, Westbourne, Edgbaston, Birmingham, RSHA II D 5 — VI G 1.
38. Chamier, Fred William, 8.4.76 Stammore b. Syney, Dr. d. Staatswissenschaft, England, RSHA IV E 4.
39. Chapman, Sir, Sidney John, 29.1.88, Prof., London S. W. 7, The Imperial College, RSHA VI G 1.
40. Charles, B., brit. Agentin, zuletzt: Brüssel, vermutl. England (Täterkreis: Josef Menneken), RSHA IV E 4.
41. Charoux geborene Treibl, Margarete, 25.5.95, Wien, Reisende, London, RSHA IV A 1.
42. Charroux, Siegfried, 15.10.96 Wien, Bildhauer, London W. 4, Riverside 51, British Grove, RSHA IV A 1, III A.
43. Chidson, M. Reamy, 13.4.93 London, Militärattaché, brit. Oberstleutn., zuletzt: Den Haag, vermutl. England (Kraftw.: HZ 36 927 GB.), RSHA IV E 4.
43a China, John, Edwin, 21.1.01 Bradlington, zuletzt: Kopenhagen, vermutl. England, RSHA IV E 4.
44. Chingford, Charles, Vertreter, London W. 1, Cambridge 119, RSHA IV E 4.
45. Chountzarias, Andreas, Arzt, zuletzt Athen, vermutl. England (Täterkreis: Crawford), RSHA IV E 4.
46. Choiseul-Gouffier, Louis, zuletzt: Kowno, vermutl. England (Täterkreis: Th. Camber), RSHA IV E 4, Stapo Tilsit.
47. Chrisoston, Segrue John, 7.1.84, Liverpool, Journalist, England, RSHA IV E 4.
47a Christie, brit. Nachrichtenoffizier, London, RSHA IV E 4.
48. Church, Archibald George, 1886 London, Major, Rostrevor, Seledon-Road, Sanderstreet, RSHA VI G 1.
49. Churchill, Winston Spencer, Ministerpräsident, Westerham/Kent, Chartwell Manor, RSHA VI A 1.
50. Chwatal, Johann, 16.8.92 Suchenthal, vermutl. England, RSHA IV A 1.
51. Chwatal, Silvester, 21.11.94 Suchenthal, vermutl. England, RSHA IV A 1.
52. Cibulski, Gerhard, 12.11.08 Barnim, London N. W. 2, 47 Blenheim Gardens, RSHA IV A 1.
53. Cichy, Georg, 30.9.14 Scharley/Ostoberschlesien, Obergefreiter, vermutl. England, RSHA IV E 5, Stapo Oppeln.
54. Cigna, Vladimir, 3.6.98 Olmütz, ehem. tschech. Stabscpt., London 53 Lexan Gardens, Kensington W. 8 (Täterkreis: Frantisek-Moravec), RSHA IV E 4, IV E 6.

33 C

55. Citrine, Sir, Walter, geb. 1887, Generalsekretär, London S. W. 1, Smith Square, RSHA VI G 1.
56. Cizek, richtig Caslavka, RSHA IV E 4, Stapoleit Prag.
57. Clark, Charles, brit. Agent, zuletzt: Lüttich, vermutl. England (Täterkreis: Kurt Felsenthal), RSHA IV E 4.
58. Clark, Herta, geb. Braunthal, 1.2.87 Wien, vermutl. England, RSHA IV A 1.
59. Clark, Hilda, Dr., RSHA VI G 1.
60. Clark, John, Sekretär, London E. C. 2, Britannic-House, Anglo-Iranian Oil Co., RSHA IV E 2.
61. Clark, R. T., Schriftsteller, RSHA III A 5.
62. Clark, William, 13.8.85 London, Redakteur, London, RSHA IV A 1.
63. Clarke, Eric Allan, brit. Hauptmann, England, RSHA IV E 4.
64. Clavering, Sir, Albert, Deckname: Closenburg, Reklameagent, vermutl. England, RSHA VI G 1.
65. Cleyg, Charles, brit. Leutnant, zuletzt: Dänemark, vermutl. London (Täterkreis: John Hugill), RSHA IV E 4.
66. Clutterbuk, geb. Kant, Lina, 15.8.98 Pforzheim, London, Übersetzerin der ITF., RSHA IV A 1 b.
67. Cnockaert, Martha, verh. Mckenna, England, RSHA IV E 4.
68. Coatts, W. P., Schriftsteller, vermutl. England, RSHA VI G 1.
69. Corbett-Ashby, Frau. Führerin der liberalen Partei, RSHA VI G 1.
70. Cockburn, Claude, 56 Jahre alt, Korrespondent, London S. W. 1, 34 Victoria Street, Deckname: Frank Pitcain, RSHA IV A 1, VI G 1.
71. Cockerill, John, brit. General, zuletzt: Antwerpen, vermutl. England, RSHA IV E 4.
72. Cocks, Seymour, 1882, Politiker, RSHA VI G 1.
73. Coenen, Peter, 6.3.88 Stettin, Gewerkschaftssekretär, vermutl. England, RSHA IV A 1.
74. Cohen, Abraham, Dr., Rev., Wohnung: Birmingham 15, 2, Highfield Rd. Edg. Baston, RSHA II B 2.
75. Cohen, Chapman, Journalist, vermutl. England, RSHA VI G 1.
76. Cohen, Israel, Politiker, vermutl. England, London N. W. 2, 29 Pattison Road Child's Hill, RSHA VI G 1.
77. Cohen-Carner, Mosco, Dr., 1904, Dozent, London, RSHA III A 1.
78. Cohen, Lionel Leonard, 1888 geb., Bankier, Wohnung: London W. 2, Orme Sq., 3, RSHA II B 2.
79. Mac Cohen, richtig Makohim, vermutl. England, RSHA IV D 3 a.
80. Cohen, Reuss Emanuel, 30.1.76 Langenberg, vermutl. England, RSHA IV A 1.
81. Cohen, Robert Waley, Verw.-Direktor, London E. C. 3, 22. St. Helen's Court, Shell Transport u. Trading Co., RSHA IV E 2.
82. Cohn, Ernst, Prof., vermutl. London, RSHA III A 1.
83. Cohn, Walter, 5.9.01 Chemnitz, Ka[...], England, RSHA IV A 1.
84. Cole, George, Lektor, Univ. Oxfor[...] G 1.
85. Collins, Norman, Direktor, RSHA[...]
86. Collins, brit. Agent, vermutl. En[...]
87. Conze, Edward, Dr., 1869, Prof.,[...]
87a Hinchley-Cook, Colonel u. Lei[...] London, RSHA IV E 4.
88. Cooper, Alfred Duff, Informa[...] Street 34, RSHA II D 5, VI G[...]
89. Cooper, F. D'Arcy, Kaufman[...] House, Blackfriars, RSHA [...]

Gestapo arrest list, open to the page where Winston Churchill's name appears.

Cover of the arrest list, a small bound volume labeled "Geheim!" (Secret)

Gestapo Arrest List

After the fall of France in May 1940, the Gestapo prepared for the invasion of Britain by compiling an arrest list of more than 2,300 names that was printed in pocketbook size. The Hoover Archives holds one of the rare surviving copies. The list included most major figures in the British political establishment, from Winston Churchill and Neville Chamberlain on down, as well as prominent cultural figures and refugees who had fled the continent ahead of the Nazis, some of whom are explicitly identified as Jews. Among those slated for arrest were Lady Astor, Noel Coward, Virginia Woolf, H. G. Wells, Paul Robeson, Sidney Reilly, Heinrich Mann, Alexander Korda, Chaim Weizmann, Eduard Beneš, Oskar Kokoschka, Aldous Huxley, and Charles de Gaulle.

POLAND'S ORDEAL

The Katyn Massacre

On September 17, 1939, sixteen days after the German invasion of Poland from the west, the Soviet army invaded from the east. When Soviet troops crossed the Polish-Soviet border, many Polish units were ordered not to resist because it was believed (or at least hoped) that the Soviet Army was entering Poland to join the fight against the Germans. Of course, the action was in fact a joint endeavor between Germany and the Soviet Union.

Ten days after the Soviet invasion, the Poles surrendered and the Germans and Soviets divided Poland between them. In the months that followed, the Soviets arrested and deported hundreds of thousands of Poles from eastern Poland to remote regions of the USSR. Thousands of Poles were executed, on either Polish or Soviet territory, mainly those with ties to the Polish government and military.

The most infamous episode involving the Soviet executions of Poles has gone down in history as the Katyn Forest Massacre of spring 1940, in which more than 21,000 Polish officers and civilians were shot to death and buried in mass graves at three sites in the western USSR, including Katyn, near Smolensk in present-day Russia. The large majority of the officers came from intelligentsia circles: teachers, doctors, lawyers, and the like. They had been mobilized at the beginning of the war, mainly in the districts of eastern Poland, and had not succeeded in taking part in military activities. All were killed with a bullet to the back of the head.

The massacre was a secret to the world until April 1943, when Nazi Germany announced the discovery of some 4,500 Polish corpses in the Katyn Forest. Goebbels's propaganda machine set about making the most of the gruesome discovery, hoping to drive a wedge between the Western allies and the USSR. The Soviets cried foul and charged the Nazis with having committed the crime. Yet an investigation by an international team of experts in forensic medicine and other circumstantial evidence—most tellingly, the fact that nothing had been heard from the prisoners since the spring of 1940—pointed to Soviet culpability. More than 10,000 additional officers and civilians were believed to have been executed at the same time as the Katyn victims.

At the Nuremberg Trials, the Soviets attempted to include the Katyn Massacre in the indictment of the Nazi leaders, a move that Justice Robert Jackson strongly opposed. Not that Jackson had solid evidence exculpating the Germans: "I knew that the Nazis and the Soviets accused each other, that both were capable of the offense, that perhaps both had opportunity to commit it, and that it was perfectly consistent with the policy of each toward Poland." That policy was aimed at preventing the rise of an independent Poland,

Katyn. Unearthed mass grave. (Poland, Ministerstwo Informacji Records)

Single skeleton in a Polish major's uniform. (Poland, Ministerstwo Informacji Records)

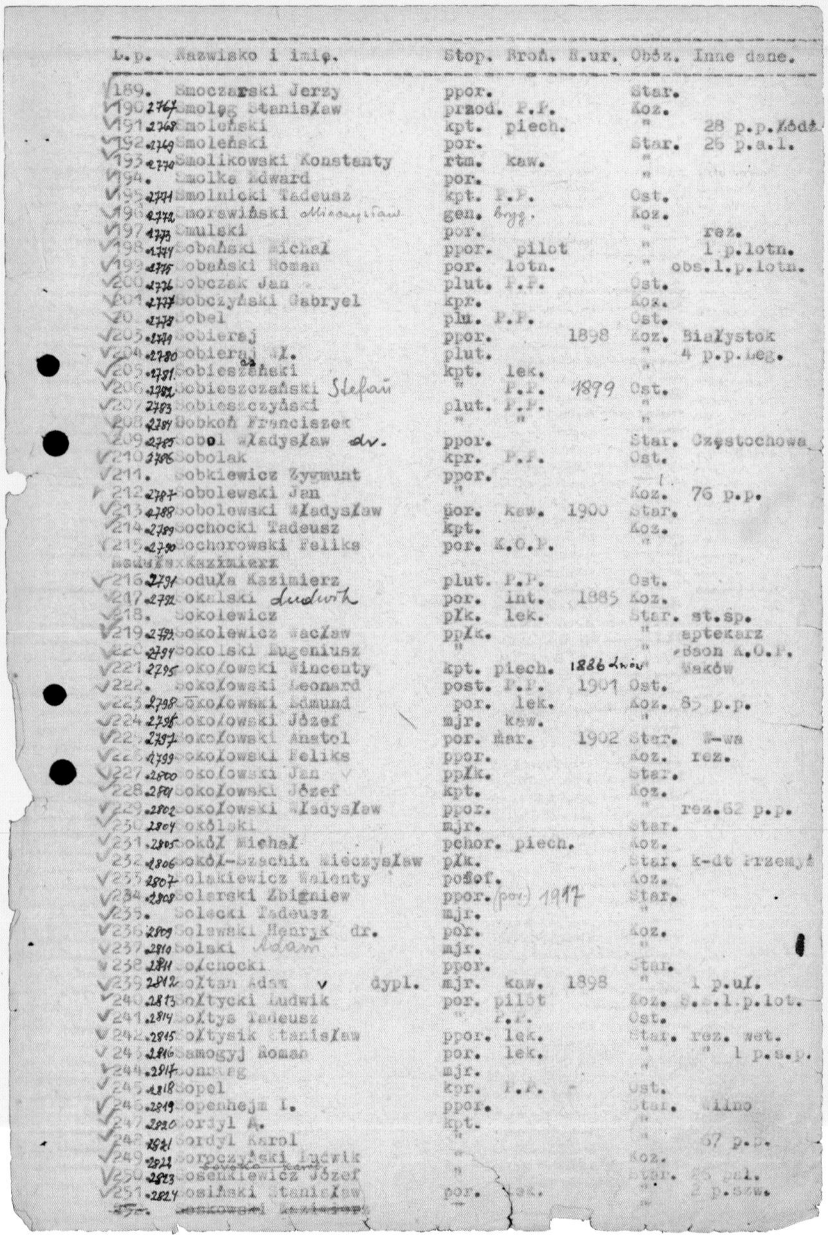

L.p.	Nazwisko i imię.	Stop.	Broń.	R.ur.	Obóz.	Inne dane.
189.	Smoczarski Jerzy	ppor.			Star.	
190	Smoląg Stanisław	przod.	P.P.		Koz.	
191	Smoleński	kpt.	piech.		"	28 p.p. Łódź
192	Smoleński	por.			Star.	26 p.a.l.
193	Smolikowski Konstanty	rtm.	kaw.		"	
194.	Smolka Edward	por.			"	
195	Smolnicki Tadeusz	kpt.	P.P.		Ost.	
196	Smorawiński	gen.			Koz.	
197	Smulski	por.			"	rez.
198	Sobański Michał	ppor.	pilot		"	1 p.lotn.
199	Sobański Roman	por.	lotn.		"	obs.1.p.lotn.
200	Sobczak Jan	plut.	P.P.		Ost.	
201	Sobczyński Gabryel	kpr.			Koz.	
202	Sobel	plut.	P.P.		Ost.	
203	Sobieraj	ppor.		1898	Koz.	Białystok
204	Sobieraj Wł.	plut.			"	4 p.p.Leg.
205	Sobieszański	kpt.	lek.		"	
206	Sobieszczański	"	P.P.		Ost.	
207	Sobieszczyński	plut.	P.P.		"	
208	Sobkoń Franciszek	"	"		"	
209	Sobol Władysław	ppor.			Star.	Częstochowa
210	Sobolak	kpr.	P.P.		Ost.	
211.	Sobkiewicz Zygmunt	ppor.				
212	Sobolewski Jan	"			Koz.	76 p.p.
213	Sobolewski Władysław	por.	kaw.	1900	Star.	
214	Sochocki Tadeusz	kpt.			Koz.	
215	Sochorowski Feliks	por.	K.O.P.		"	
216	Soduła Kazimierz	plut.	P.P.		Ost.	
217	Sokalski	por.	int.	1885	Koz.	
218.	Sokolewicz	płk.	lek.		Star.	st.sp.
219	Sokolewicz Wacław	ppłk.			"	aptekarz
220	Sokolski Eugeniusz	"			"	Bson K.O.P.
221	Sokołowski Wincenty	kpt.	piech.		"	Waków
222.	Sokołowski Leonard	post.	P.P.	1901	Ost.	
223	Sokołowski Edmund	por.	lek.		Koz.	85 p.p.
224	Sokołowski Józef	mjr.	kaw.		"	
225	Sokołowski Anatol	por.	mar.	1902	Star.	W-wa
226	Sokołowski Feliks	ppor.			Koz.	rez.
227	Sokołowski Jan	ppłk.			Star.	
228	Sokołowski Józef	kpt.			Koz.	
229	Sokołowski Władysław	ppor.			"	rez.62 p.p.
230	Sokólski	mjr.			Star.	
231	Sokół Michał	pchor.	piech.		Koz.	
232	Sokół-Szachin Mieczysław	płk.			Star.	k-dt Przemyśl
233	Solakiewicz Walenty	podof.			Koz.	
234	Solarski Zbigniew	ppor.			Star.	
235.	Solecki Tadeusz	mjr.			"	
236	Solewski Henryk dr.	por.			Koz.	
237	Solski	mjr.			"	
238	Sołchocki	ppor.			Star.	
239	Sołtan Adam dypl.	mjr.	kaw.	1898	"	1 p.uł.
240	Sołtycki Ludwik	por.	pilot		Koz.	[illegible] 1.p.lot.
241	Sołtys Tadeusz	"	P.P.		Ost.	
242	Sołtysik Stanisław	ppor.	lek.		Star.	rez. wet.
243	Somogyj Roman	por.	lek.		"	" 1 p.s.p.
244	Sonntag	mjr.			"	
245	Sopel	kpr.	P.P.		Ost.	
246	Sopenhejm I.	ppor.			Star.	Wilno
247	Sordyl A.	kpt.			"	
248	Sordyl Karol	"			"	67 p.p.
249	Sorczyński Ludwik	"			Koz.	
250	Sosenkiewicz Józef	"			Star.	25 p.l.
251	Sosiński Stanisław	por.	lek.		"	2 p.szw.

Katyn's victims. Single page from an alphabetical list of names of missing Polish prisoners who had been in the Soviet camps up to May 1940. The list was compiled by the Polish government-in-exile, on January 2, 1942. Most had been executed in spring 1940, on orders of the Politburo. (Poland, Ambasada [Soviet Union] Records)

which meant destroying its future leadership, and that included the men slaughtered at Katyn.

Katyn remained a major piece of unresolved business left over from the war, and uncovering the truth became a sacred cause for Poles everywhere. Despite the protests of the Polish government-in-exile in London, the Soviets fiercely insisted that Katyn was a German atrocity. In the decades after the war, the Kremlin made public discussion of the subject taboo and, behind the scenes, used its diplomatic muscle to squelch efforts to attribute the crime to Stalin's government. Only in the waning years of the Soviet era, under the pressures of the new "openness" initiated by Mikhail Gorbachev, would the Soviet government admit that its official story had been incorrect. Yet, it could never quite come clean on the matter. In an attempt at damage control as the mass graves of the remaining victims were being discovered in 1990, it sought to narrow responsibility for Katyn to "Beria and his henchmen," a reference to the head of the NKVD, the Stalinist secret police.

Only after the fall of the Soviet Union would the Russian government reveal the full truth about Katyn in the form of official documents implicating the entire Politburo in the massacre. These documents show that the executions were first suggested by Beria and then approved by the Politburo, which ordered the "supreme measure of punishment—shooting" for the captive Poles. The documents revealed that the total number executed was not 15,000, as had previously been thought, but rather 21,857 (the additional victims being civilians), and that the Politburo's intention had been to execute a total of 25,700.

Gorbachev and the last Soviet leaders wanted to blame Katyn on "criminals" such as Stalin and Beria, but in fact the Soviet Union under Stalin was a criminal regime and after Stalin was only less criminal. The Kremlin's special sensitivity about Katyn and its obsessive efforts to hide its responsibility for the massacre, right through the Gorbachev years, shows that it instinctively understood this point. Even more than the Nazi-Soviet Pact that made it possible, Katyn was the nexus between the two totalitarian regimes. When the Katyn file was made public in October 1992, Poland's president, Lech Walesa, stated the essential point: "The Katyn affair brought final condemnation of this inhumane system; its supporters simply no longer have—and could not have—arguments in its defense."

The Katyn Massacre is impressively documented in the archives and library of the Hoover Institution, which has enjoyed a special bond with Poland extending back to Herbert Hoover's food relief efforts after the Great War. The Hoover's collection of material on the Katyn Massacre includes original documentation from the Polish, Soviet, and German governments and comprehensive records on the victims. This information has been used by historians pursuing the truth about the massacre as well as by Polish citizens seeking information on the fate of those killed. The Hoover Institution has been collecting material on the massacre since the 1940s, when Hoover librarians catalogued the fraudulent report of the official Soviet investigation blaming the Nazis for the killings. In the 1990s, the Hoover Institution's arrangement with the Russian state archives to microfilm documents of the Soviet Communist Party made the official file on the Katyn Massacre and its cover-up available to scholars worldwide.

Exile

The Soviet occupation force in Poland in 1939 moved swiftly to arrest Poles whose social class, occupation, or political orientation marked them as innately "hostile elements" to the new Communist regime. They were convicted for alleged counterrevolutionary activities or as "enemies of the people" and, in four successive waves in 1940–41, were deported to a variety of locations in the USSR by the hundreds of thousands (the estimated total varies from as high as one million to as low as 320,000).

The Soviet attitude toward the Poles changed dramatically after the German invasion of the Soviet Union on June 22, 1941. Needing all the allies it could get, the Soviet government negotiated an agreement in July with the Polish government-in-exile based in London. The treaty, which restored diplomatic relations between the two governments, called for the formation of a Polish army on Soviet territory to help repel the Nazi attack. This force was to be set up under the command of Gen. Wladyslaw Anders, just released from a Moscow prison. A protocol attached to the treaty provided for an "amnesty to all Polish citizens who are at present deprived of their freedom on the territory of the USSR either as prisoners of war or on other adequate grounds."

This was the promise. In practice, as historian Katherine Jolluck recounts, "Some Poles received no notification of the amnesty, while others were barred from leaving their places of exile because local authorities denied them the documents necessary for departure and travel. Additionally, Soviet officials routinely diverted trains of Polish citizens in search of Polish delegations, routing them to collective farms in Kirghizia and Uzbekistan for continued forced labor."

Yet, despite these obstacles, by the late summer of 1941 thousands of Poles, often en route for months, began to make their way from all over the country to the southern regions of the USSR, either to offer their services to the embryonic Anders army or to seek the protection of Polish government officials. Relations between the Soviet and Polish governments began to sour, and in the spring of 1942 the Polish government sought and won Soviet approval to withdraw the Anders army from Soviet territory. The evacuations took place in two waves—in March–April and August 1942—and included military personnel with their surviving family members and orphaned children. Altogether, some 115,000 Poles made it out of the Soviet Union across the Caspian Sea to Iran, from where they dispersed to countries around the world.

This was a considerable achievement in view of the growing strain in relations between the Soviet and Polish authorities. Any hope for more evacuations was dashed after the discovery by the Nazis of the mass grave of Polish citizens at Katyn in April 1943. When the Polish government asked for an investigation of the Nazi claim that the massacre had

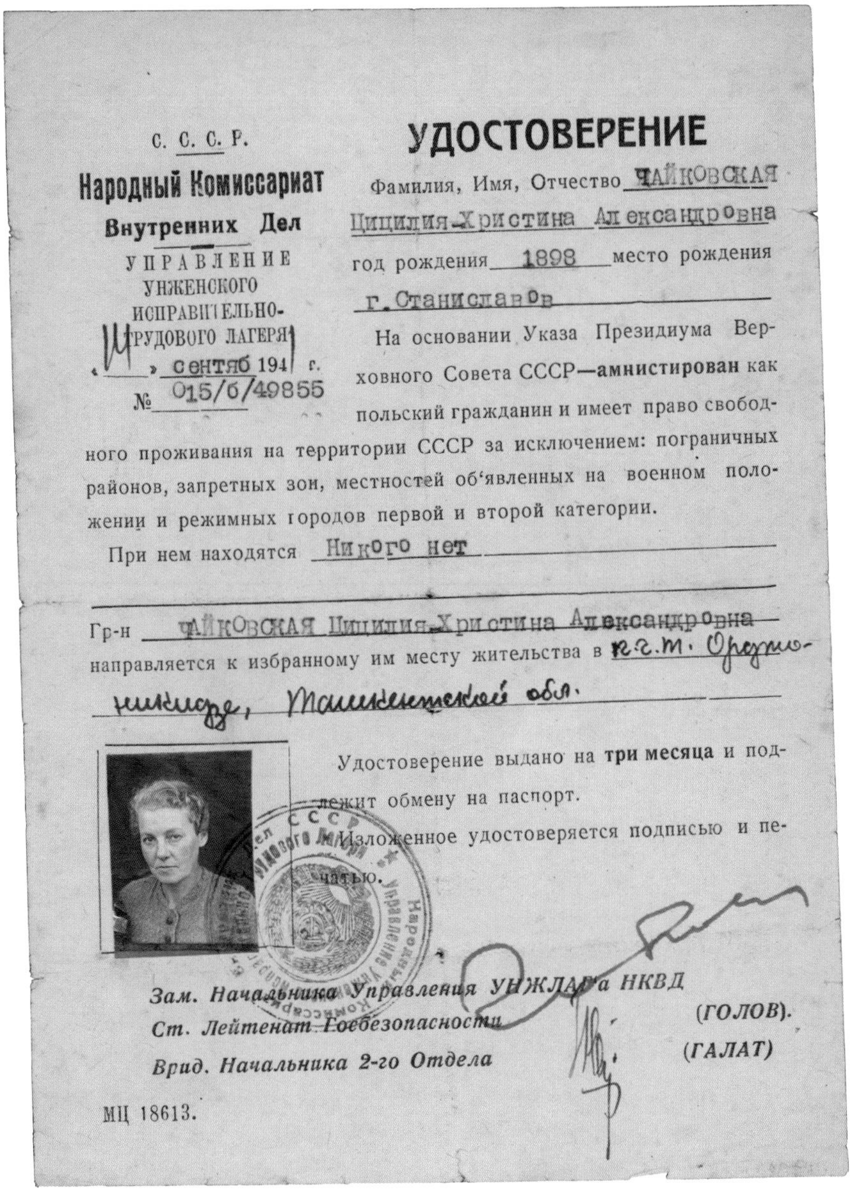
С. С. С. Р.
Народный Комиссариат
Внутренних Дел
УПРАВЛЕНИЕ
УНЖЕНСКОГО
ИСПРАВИТЕЛЬНО-
ТРУДОВОГО ЛАГЕРЯ
« » сентяб 1941 г.
№ 015/б/49855

УДОСТОВЕРЕНИЕ

Фамилия, Имя, Отчество ЧАЙКОВСКАЯ Цицилия-Христина Александровна
год рождения 1898 место рождения г. Станиславов

На основании Указа Президиума Верховного Совета СССР—**амнистирован** как польский гражданин и имеет право свободного проживания на территории СССР за исключением: пограничных районов, запретных зон, местностей об'явленных на военном положении и режимных городов первой и второй категории.

При нем находятся Никого нет

Гр-н ЧАЙКОВСКАЯ Цицилия-Христина Александровна направляется к избранному им месту жительства в к.г.т. Орджоникидзе, Ташкентской обл.

Удостоверение выдано на **три месяца** и подлежит обмену на паспорт.

Изложенное удостоверяется подписью и печатью.

Зам. Начальника Управления УНЖЛАГ'а НКВД
Ст. Лейтенант Госбезопасности **(ГОЛОВ).**
Врид. Начальника 2-го Отдела **(ГАЛАТ)**

МЦ 18613.

NKVD release certificate. The most valuable documents in the Ministry of Information collection are some 10,000 original certificates (*udostovereniia*) issued by the Soviet political police, the NKVD, in the second half of 1941 to Polish citizens released from camps. The Ministry of Information was the main information and propaganda unit of the Polish government-in-exile. (Poland, Ministerstwo Informacji Records)

been committed by the Soviets, Moscow accused it of collaborating with Germany and broke off relations. The Polish embassy in Moscow was closed down.

A large number of those Poles who managed to leave the USSR in 1942 were asked by Polish officials in Iran to write about their experience as exiles in the Soviet Union. Some 20,000 of these handwritten reports (collected from late 1942 through 1944) made their way to the Hoover Archives as part of the Anders Collection. This remarkable resource served as the basis for the book *Exile and Identity: Polish Women in the Soviet Union During World War II* (2002) by Stanford historian Katherine Jolluck.

These and many other valuable Polish documents ended up at the Hoover Institution as a result of diplomatic developments toward the end of the war, when the United States and Britain withdrew recognition from the London-based Polish government in favor of the Soviet-backed government in Lublin, Poland. With the writing on the wall, the Polish political and military authorities in the West decided to transfer some of the collections under their control to a safe location in the United States; they settled on the Hoover Institution.

Most of the Polish library and archival collections that were brought to the Hoover Institution after World War II came as part of three deposits: that of Poland's wartime ambassador to the United States, Jan Ciechanowski, in 1945, which included the archives of the Polish embassies in Washington, London, and Moscow-Kuibyshev; that of Gen. Wladyslaw Anders, in 1946; and that of Minister Aleksandr Zawisza, in 1959, the latter consisting of the archives of the Polish Ministry of Information and the Ministry of Foreign Affairs.

With these rich collections and other valuable holdings acquired before and since the Second World War, the Hoover Institution is home to the largest collection of twentieth-century Polish documents outside Poland.

Underground

The story of the Polish diplomat Jan Karski illuminates the horrors endured by Poland under the Nazi occupation and the international dimensions of Poland's ordeal. Karski had served as a diplomat before the war in Berlin, Geneva, and London. On the eve of the war he was commissioned as an officer in the Polish army. After the German *Blitzkrieg* attack on Poland on September 1, 1939, Karski fled in a boxcar to eastern Poland, where he was captured by the invading Soviet Army and moved to a prison camp inside the Soviet Union. He narrowly avoided the fate of the Katyn victims by hiding his officer's rank, thereby making himself eligible for a prisoner exchange. He later jumped from a German train that was carrying POWs to a Nazi labor camp.

Returning to Warsaw, he joined the Polish underground as a courier with the codename "Witold," conveying messages between Warsaw and the Polish exile government in Paris. Using his formidable skills in language and disguise, Karski was continually carrying out extremely dangerous missions. On one assignment he was captured and tortured by the Gestapo and survived a suicide attempt before managing to escape and resume his work in the underground. In August 1942 he was smuggled into the Warsaw Ghetto, with Jewish resistance leader Leon Feiner as his guide. As the two men toured what Karski later described as "a haze of disease and death," Feiner kept repeating to him, "Remember this."

Back outside the Ghetto, Karski witnessed scenes even more horrific. Donning the uniform of a Ukrainian militiaman, he was able to observe panic-stricken Jews being herded into boxcars lined with quicklime (calcium oxide). This was in the town of Izbica Lubelska,

German soldiers supervising the burial of a dozen corpses of civilians, seen dressed in winter clothes, hands tied behind their backs. (Jan Karski Papers)

Warsaw Ghetto. Wall across the middle of a Warsaw street blocking off the Jewish Ghetto. (Jan Karski Papers)

a holding point for the Belzec extermination camp, about forty miles distant, where 600,000 Jews and others would eventually be murdered.

It was now time for this witness to the unfolding Holocaust to become a messenger of a different kind. In October 1942, Karski managed to make his way to London, where he had talks with Foreign Minister Anthony Eden and other British officials before going to the United States, where he met with President Roosevelt, Secretary of State Cordell Hull, and other American leaders. In both capitals, his stories of the conditions in the Warsaw Ghetto and the extermination of the Jews were greeted with skepticism.

Karski's name is best remembered in this context for a conversation he had during his stay in Washington with Supreme Court Justice Felix Frankfurter, to whom he was introduced by Poland's ambassador to the United States, Jan Ciechanowski. Karski spent a half-hour recounting what he had witnessed of the Ghetto and the camps, but Frankfurter could not be moved. "Mr. Karski, a man like me talking to a man like you must be totally frank. So I must say: I am unable to believe you." Ambassador Ciechanowski was incredulous and asked if Frankfurter was calling Karski a liar. "Mr. Ambassador," Frankfurter replied in a tone of resignation, "I did not say this young man is lying. I said I am unable to believe him. There is a difference."

It was Karski's intention to parachute back into Poland in September 1943 to rejoin the underground, but his plans changed when an exiled Polish officer informed him that a Nazi radio broadcast had denounced him as a "Bolshevik agent in the service of American Jewry." Unable to return to Poland, Karski remained in America, delivering some 200 public lectures on what he had witnessed in Poland. In 1944 he published a book about the Polish underground, *Story of a Secret State*, which became a best-seller that year.

In April 1945 Karski was drafted by the Hoover Institution to help collect materials on Poland, on the strength of his excellent contacts with the Polish government-in-exile in London and the Polish embassy in Washington and other connections. He had great success in collecting documents from the underground press, photographs taken in Nazi-occupied Poland, and a large number of books and periodicals. In July 1945, when the United States withdrew recognition from the Polish government in London in favor of the Soviet-backed government in Lublin, the London office advised Ambassador Ciechanowski in Washington to turn over the embassy papers to the Hoover Library in the care of Karski.

Karski continued his collecting in Paris, Switzerland, and finally Rome, where he helped to secure the Wladyslaw Anders Papers for the Hoover Archives. Afterward he studied for a doctoral degree in international relations at Georgetown University, where he taught from 1952 to 1995.

"BLOODY SATURDAY" IN SHANGHAI

In the summer of 1937, after years of preparation and baiting, Japan launched a brutal full-scale invasion of China, beginning with bombing raids against Shanghai and Nanking, seat of the Nationalist government. The Chinese air force, such as there was, launched a counter-attack, with tragic results for the residents of Shanghai. On Saturday, August 14, one of the Chinese 550-pound bombs fell on the crowded Nanking Road, while another bomb fell on the busy Avenue Edward VII. More than 1,700 people were killed and some 1,800 injured. The gruesome scene of death and suffering was described by a British journalist:

> *The first bomb landed in Nanking Road between the Cathay and Palace Hotels. It created havoc. Hundreds of pedestrians of many nationalities simply disappeared in a whirling mass of dismembered bodies. Trams were set on fire. Motorists were burned to cinders in their blazing vehicles. The few who survived had not long to live. There was even greater devastation on Avenue Edward Seventh, where the second bomb dropped. This was the Chinese theatre district, an area of street stalls, of pavement sideshows, always thronged with sightseers. The carnage was appalling.*

The tragic accident that caused what came to be known as Bloody Saturday has never been explained. Some accounts blame the incompetence of the Chinese airmen, others their unreliable bombing racks, while the possibility that Japanese aircraft dropped one or both bombs has never been excluded. The next day and over the next weeks, Japanese bombers from Taiwan and Korea returned to inflict greater damage on Shanghai (and Nanking), but Bloody Saturday was the costliest single day of the invasion.

An American witness to the Bloody Saturday carnage was the journalist Randall Chase Gould, editor of the *Shanghai Evening Post and Mercury* from 1931 to 1941 and 1945 to 1949. Gould was also a news photographer, and the most valuable part of his collection in the Hoover Archives is five albums of photographs of China in the late 1930s, including candid shots of the Americans and other Westerners living in Shanghai when war came. By far the most arresting images are those of the Japanese terror-bombing of Shanghai, especially the scene in the city center on Bloody Saturday.

"Desultory shooting had started the previous day," Gould later recalled, "but it was Saturday which saw the beginning of the real hot stuff. Air bombs were dropping here and there, and while we could hear the explosions with painful clarity we had a terrible time locating the hits. . . . That afternoon a volunteer phoned in the information that an air bomb had dropped in Nanking Road half a block from the Bund [the promenade along the riverfront], between two of the leading hotels, which had received other bombs on their tops. It was so incredible that I dashed out to my car without my Leica, thereby learning an invaluable lesson, for I found that the report was all too true.

"At the office I was writing a few lines for an extra when I was interrupted by another report of a second bomb up our own street (Avenue Edward VII) at one of the busiest intersections. This time the Leica went along and I obtained some of the most remarkable, and horrible, pictures of a lifetime in a scene where 1,047 people were killed outright."

RED CHINA

After the Chinese Communists vanquished the Nationalist armies in 1949, China had a unified central government for the first time since the fall of the Manchu dynasty in 1911 (and effectively for considerably longer than that). Mao Zedong and the Communists had big plans and intended to act on them. The immediate goal was to rebuild the economy and eventually turn China, the most populous country in the world, into an industrial giant.

Despite Chinese communism's agrarian roots, Mao's government, relying on Moscow's technical and economic assistance, was guided by the Soviet economic model, with its emphasis on central planning, heavy industry, and collective agriculture. During the First Five-Year Plan, which began in 1953, large-scale agricultural cooperatives were formed throughout the country (740,000 in all, each comprising 200 to 300 households), while industrial production rose impressively across a number of sectors. The regime could claim a considerable success, though not all Chinese shared in the enthusiasm.

From the beginning, political repression and experiment were hallmarks of Communist rule in China, which witnessed a tumultuous series of campaigns and countercampaigns that produced unintended and costly consequences for the state and its citizens. "Let a hundred flowers bloom, let a hundred schools of thought contend," Mao proclaimed, encouraging intellectuals to openly criticize abuses within the party as a way of rejuvenating the revolution. And so they did, and with considerable vigor, for five weeks beginning on May 1, 1957.

What China's intellectuals had to say, however, was not what China's leaders expected to hear. As historian Jonathan Spence recounts, to Mao's surprise and great displeasure the intellectuals took aim at the authoritarian ways of the party, inveighing against its "control over intellectuals, the harshness of previous mass campaigns such as that against counter-revolutionaries, the slavish following of Soviet models, the low standards of living in China, the proscription of foreign literature, economic corruption among party cadres, and the fact that 'Party members enjoy many privileges which make them a race apart.'" An embar-

"Bloody Saturday," August 14, 1937, the accidental bombing of Shanghai. These photographs were taken at the intersection of Avenue Edward VII and Tibet Road. Gould wrote: "One of the most extraordinary snaps I ever made is lower right of a man whose garments had been blown off. Many ask 'What happened to him?' I don't know." (Randall Chase Gould Papers)

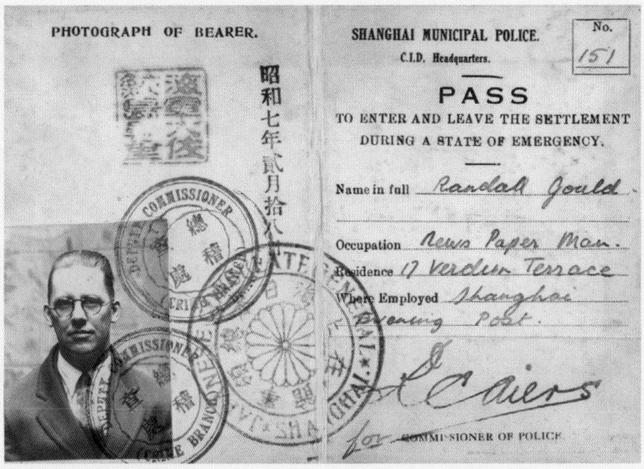
PHOTOGRAPH OF BEARER.

昭和七年貳月拾八

SHANGHAI MUNICIPAL POLICE.
C.I.D. Headquarters.

No. 151

PASS
TO ENTER AND LEAVE THE SETTLEMENT DURING A STATE OF EMERGENCY.

Name in full Randall Gould
Occupation News Paper Man.
Residence 17 Verdun Terrace
Where Employed Shanghai Evening Post.

for COMMISSIONER OF POLICE

Randall Gould's photo ID, issued by the Shanghai Municipal Police. (Randall Chase Gould Papers)

Chairman Mao Zedong and Premier Zhou En-lai, awaiting the arrival at Peking airport of Indonesian President Sukarno, October 8, 1956. (David Lancashire Photographs)

Chairman Mao's Little Red Book, second edition, published in 1966. Popularly known as Mao's Little Red Book, *Quotations from Chairman Mao* is a collection of Mao's aphorisms, such as "Political power grows out of the barrel of a gun." Millions of Red Army soldiers studied and memorized Mao's sayings, thereby magnifying his cult.

rassed leadership quickly silenced these critics, whom they now denounced as "bourgeois rightists." The abortive Hundred Flowers Movement landed many thousands of intellectuals in prison, labor camps, or exile to the countryside.

Meanwhile, the results of the First Five-Year Plan, announced in 1958, did not satisfy Mao. The rapid growth of heavy industry, the regime's top priority, could not be sustained without a radical improvement in agricultural production to provide the necessary capital. The solution was the Great Leap Forward, launched in the summer of 1958, which mobilized the rural population through moral exhortations and incentives and by amalgamating the cooperative farms into much larger "people's communes" (26,000 total). The goal was to develop rural industry and mechanize agriculture. Let a hundred tractor factories bloom, in other words. Peasants were compelled to melt down their farm tools to make steel in backyard foundries, one million of which sprouted up across China. Despite official enthusiasm, the peasants naturally resisted, and in any case they had no idea how to construct a functional foundry, let alone how to use one, with the result that the steel they produced was defective, much of it useless. Meanwhile, with the focus on steel, fertile rice fields were left untended. Before long, people began to starve.

The Great Leap Forward produced successive crop failures from 1959 to 1961, and this brought catastrophe in the form of what was possibly the worst famine in human history: at least 16 million people died of starvation and disease (this, according to the Chinese

Jolly Red Giant. The poster commands Chinese citizens, seen waving copies of Mao's Little Red Book, to get involved in affairs of state and carry out the Great Proletarian Cultural Revolution to the finish. (Janek Rowinski Collection)

Culture as a Weapon. The poster demands that literature and art be turned into a lethal weapon to destroy antirevolutionary "revisionists." The banner in the poster reads, "Long live the Great Proletarian Cultural Revolution." (Janek Rowinski Collection)

Communist government's own admission, twenty years later), though some estimates run as high as 30 million. With the economy on the brink of collapse, the government retreated. The collective farm system survived, but peasants were once again permitted to sell produce grown on private plots. Somehow, industrial production continued to move ahead. Like the Soviet Union, China was a selectively modernizing country: while its people starved by the millions, it armed itself like a great power. In 1964, China conducted its first successful test of an atomic bomb; in 1967 it exploded a hydrogen bomb.

But Mao was not finished revolutionizing China. Beginning in 1966, he and his closest comrades inaugurated the Great Proletarian Cultural Revolution, enlisting millions of high school students as Red Guards, charged with enforcing ideological purity by unmasking enemies of the people. Many factors contributed to the initiation of this new campaign, including factional politics, personal political rivalries, and an aging Mao's concern for the continued vitality of his revolution. Once again, the forces unleashed by the regime got dangerously out of hand.

The Red Guards went on a destructive rampage. In Peking and other cities, party officials and cultural and educational figures were subjected to public humiliation and cruel harassment for their "bourgeois ways." Across the country, entire schools, even entire universities, were shut down. Meanwhile, the upper reaches of the government and party were subjected to a massive purge, which eventually swept away two-thirds of the party's central committee. The Red Guards drew inspiration from the blossoming cult of Mao, who was heralded at the time as "our great teacher, great leader, great supreme commander and great helmsman." An indelible image from the period is of the Great Helmsman reviewing enormous parades of chanting Red Guards, each waving a copy of Mao's Little Red Book of sayings.

The chaos continued into 1969, when the army stepped in and restored order. The worst was over, though the Cultural Revolution could be said to have finally ended only with Mao's death in 1976. Hundreds of thousands had died, and millions were sent to labor camps or into the countryside to work the fields. China's educational system was all but destroyed, resulting in a "lost generation" of Chinese youth.

HUKAWNG
VALLEY
INDIA
(ASSAM)
Kohima
NAGA HILLS
Ukhrul
Pu-shing
Homalin
Uyu Riv
Chaunggyi R.
Maingkaing
Kawlum
River
Saingkyu
Magyigan
Mansi
Banmauk
Indaw
Meza
Katha
Bhamo
Namhkam
Sittaung
Pintebu
Wuntho
Pintha
Irrawaddy River
Lashio
Zigon
Ye-u
Hsipaw
Shwebo
Singu
Gokteik
Maymyo
Mandalay
BURMA
Stilwell's Route
from

Chapter Five

DIPLOMATS AND WARRIORS

The collections on the Second World War in the Hoover Archives happen to be exceptionally rich in their coverage of the Asian theater of operations. The papers of the American diplomat Stanley Hornbeck document the rising threat of Imperial Japan in the 1930s and the intricacies of U.S. diplomatic efforts to deter Tokyo and discern its intentions—right up through the disastrous attack on Pearl Harbor.

Two very dissimilar American soldiers, Joseph Stilwell and Albert Wedemeyer, each started out planning the American military campaign in Europe but for different reasons spent most of the war in the Far East. Stilwell, the superb tactician, was assigned the task of organizing an American offensive in North Africa and ended up fighting in the jungles of Burma. Wedemeyer, the supreme strategist, was on hand at the Allied diplomatic conferences to advocate an early invasion across the English Channel; he found himself directing the Chinese army's rebuff of a major Japanese offensive in the autumn of 1944.

Even as the settlement ending the war was being negotiated, it became impossible to ignore the fundamental incompatibilities of the Soviet and Western systems. In the papers of Ambassador Robert Murphy, political adviser to the American military occupation force in postwar Germany, we see American diplomats in Washington, Moscow, and Berlin wrestling with the question of how best to cope with the new threat to freedom.

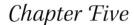

ALL THE NEWS ALL THE TIME

Los Angeles Times

IN THREE PARTS—42 PAGES

VOL. LX MONDAY MORNING, DECEMBER 8, 1941. DAILY, FIVE CENTS

JAPS OPEN WAR ON U.S. WITH BOMBING OF HAWAII

City Springs to Attention

F.D.R. Will Ask Congress Action Today

Berlin Says F.D.R. 'War Incendiary'

Honolulu Hit; Seven Die and

Fleet Speeds Out

Japanese Aliens Roundup Starts

ALL THE NEWS ALL THE TIME

Los Angeles Times

IN THREE PARTS—52 PAGES

VOL. LXI TUESDAY MORNING, DECEMBER 9, 1941. DAILY, FIVE CENTS

ENEMY PLANES ATTEMPT TO BOMB SAN FRANCISCO

Supreme Court Upholds 'Times'

Japan Troops Reported in Philippines

Japan Raid Spread Over Vast Sector

United States Declares War on Japanese

Searchlights Rout Raiders

Citizens Gird for Defense

Harbor Veiled

America under attack. *Los Angeles Times* page one headlines for December 8 and December 9, 1941. Copyright, 1941, Los Angeles Times. Reprinted with permission.

PEARL HARBOR

Japan's invasion of China in 1937 certainly caught America's attention, but it was the onset of the war in Europe that made Japanese military aggression a genuine concern for the United States. The fall of France in May 1940 and the Battle of Britain that summer changed the entire calculus in the Pacific. America's ambassador to Tokyo, Joseph Grew, remarked of War Minister Tojo and the Japanese imperialists that the Nazi Blitzkrieg had "gone to their heads like strong wine."

The U.S. goal was to take actions that would deter Japanese aggression in Southeast Asia yet not provoke Tokyo into war. Washington's most powerful instrument was economic sanctions, chiefly oil: the United States was the source of 80 percent of Japan's fuel supplies. But sanctions were a dangerous weapon, as Ambassador Grew warned Roosevelt in the autumn of 1939: "If we once start sanctions against Japan we must see them through to the end, and the end may conceivably be war. . . . [I]f we cut off Japanese supplies of oil [Japan] will in all probability send her fleets down to take the Dutch East Indies." In the protracted debate inside the U.S. government over policy toward Japan, Grew was part of the faction led by Secretary of State Cordell Hull that argued against sanctions. Their reasoning was that, far from moderating Japan's imperial ambitions, sanctions would only provoke the Japanese, driving them to seek alternative sources of supply, using military force if necessary, in the French, British, and Dutch colonies to the south, and even the Philippines. The United States, its attention focused on the European war, would be unable to prevent such an expansion.

Despite these fears, limited sanctions, not including oil, were introduced against Japan in the summer of 1940. This did nothing to deter the Japanese from moving into northern

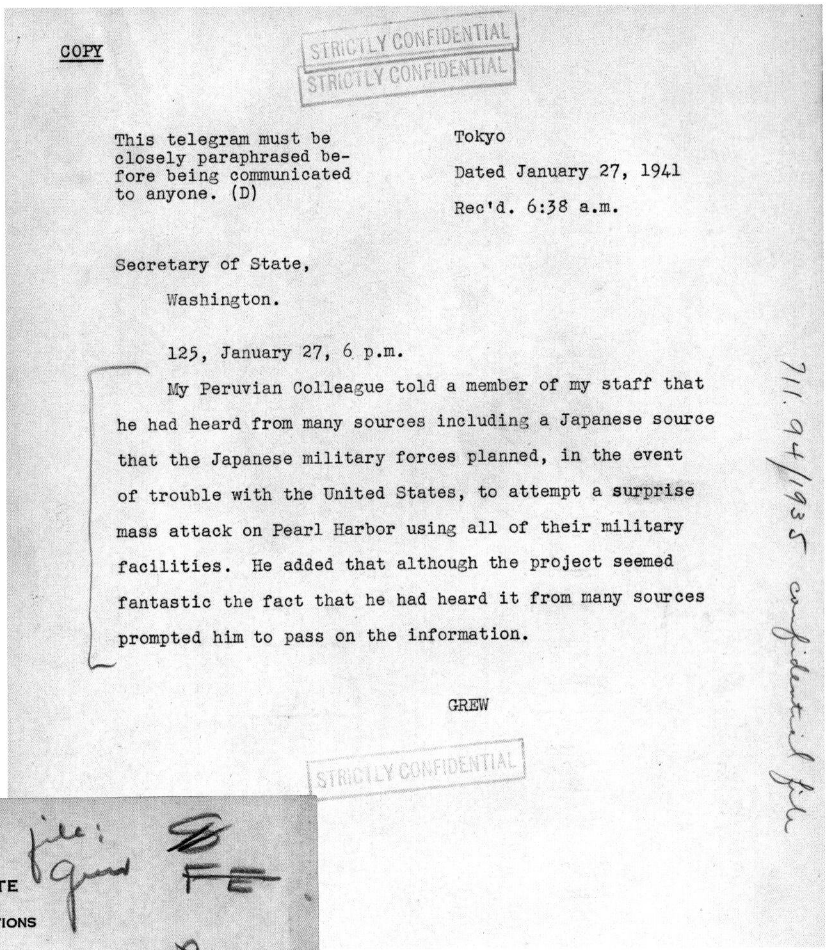

COPY

STRICTLY CONFIDENTIAL

This telegram must be closely paraphrased before being communicated to anyone. (D)

Tokyo

Dated January 27, 1941

Rec'd. 6:38 a.m.

Secretary of State,

Washington.

125, January 27, 6 p.m.

My Peruvian Colleague told a member of my staff that he had heard from many sources including a Japanese source that the Japanese military forces planned, in the event of trouble with the United States, to attempt a surprise mass attack on Pearl Harbor using all of their military facilities. He added that although the project seemed fantastic the fact that he had heard it from many sources prompted him to pass on the information.

GREW

STRICTLY CONFIDENTIAL

711.94/1935 confidential file

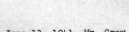

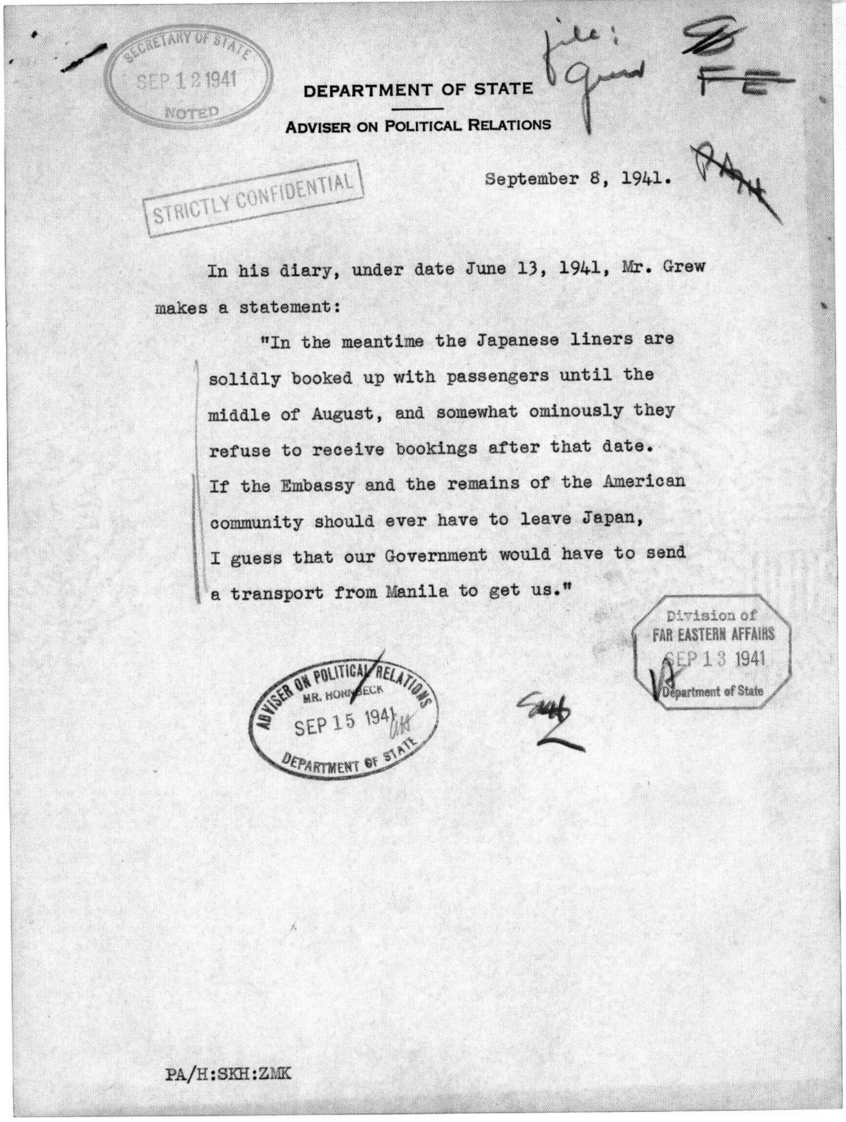

SECRETARY OF STATE SEP 12 1941 NOTED

DEPARTMENT OF STATE

ADVISER ON POLITICAL RELATIONS

STRICTLY CONFIDENTIAL

September 8, 1941.

In his diary, under date June 13, 1941, Mr. Grew makes a statement:

"In the meantime the Japanese liners are solidly booked up with passengers until the middle of August, and somewhat ominously they refuse to receive bookings after that date. If the Embassy and the remains of the American community should ever have to leave Japan, I guess that our Government would have to send a transport from Manila to get us."

Division of FAR EASTERN AFFAIRS SEP 13 1941 Department of State

ADVISER ON POLITICAL RELATIONS MR. HORNBECK SEP 15 1941 DEPARTMENT OF STATE

PA/H:SKH:ZMK

Paraphrased copy of confidential telegram from Joseph Grew to the secretary of state, January 27, 1941, regarding a report that the Japanese might "attempt a surprise mass attack on Pearl Harbor." (Stanley K. Hornbeck Papers)

Stanley Hornbeck note of September 8, 1941, relaying Grew diary excerpt of June 13, 1941, regarding Japanese government refusing to book liner passengers after the middle of August 1941. (Stanley K. Hornbeck Papers)

French Indochina in September, nor from becoming an Axis power that same month by joining Germany and Italy in the Tripartite Pact. American sanctions were ratcheted up over the course of the next six months, but Japan seemed undeterrable.

Germany's invasion of the Soviet Union in June 1941 emboldened the Japanese to act on their southward ambitions. On July 15, U.S. cryptographers learned the details of Tokyo's plans to occupy the rest of Indochina. On July 26, President Roosevelt placed a freeze on all Japanese assets in the United States. This was not yet a total trade embargo, but it became one thanks to Undersecretary of State Dean Acheson, a self-styled "hawk" on Japan who extended the embargo to cover oil while Roosevelt was away from Washington holding secret talks with Churchill in Newfoundland. The leverage offered by sanctions had now been used up. Although secret diplomacy would continue until December 7, Tokyo had already decided to launch a desperate strike against the United States.

Conspiracy theorists have long blamed Roosevelt for the Pearl Harbor disaster, charging that he used the Pacific Fleet to lure the Japanese into launching an attack so that he could bring the United States into the war. As historian David Kennedy explains in dismissing this idea, "Pearl Harbor was only one among many possible places where the first blow might fall, and arguably the least likely. Months, even years, of speculation about Japan's military intentions had focused on China, Soviet Siberia, Malaya, Singapore, Hong Kong, the Dutch East Indies, Thailand, Indochina, and the Philippines as possible Japanese targets—but rarely, if ever, Hawaii."

Researchers in the Hoover Archives can follow the events leading up to Pearl Harbor (as well as the diplomatic aftermath) in the papers of the American diplomat Stanley Hornbeck. In 1941, Hornbeck was the adviser on political relations to the secretary of state (one of three such advisers from 1937 to 1944). Prior to that, from 1928 to 1937, he was chief of the Division of Far Eastern Affairs. As an old Asia hand, Hornbeck enjoyed a close connection to Joseph Grew, the American ambassador to Tokyo since 1932. Grew kept an official diary, which he sent in installments to Hornbeck, who used them as the basis for communications to the secretary of state and other officials in Washington.

Despite Grew's overoptimism about the forces of moderation in Tokyo, Hornbeck's papers reveal that the ambassador continually warned of the danger of war, even sudden war, and that he made preparations for it by shipping home his private papers and destroying duplicate code books. Still, the *fact* of war, of a surprise Japanese attack on American territory, delivered a shock. Only after the news had been confirmed did Grew order the destruction of the embassy's codes and confidential files. Grew and his staff were interned in Tokyo from December 8 to June 25, 1942.

Above:
Walkout. Stilwell, second from right, leads the walk out of Burma, May 1942. (Joseph W. Stilwell Papers)

Left:
Return. Stilwell, with officers of the Chinese Army, in December 1943, at the start of the campaign to retake Burma. (Joseph W. Stilwell Papers)

STILWELL: EAGER FOR THE OFFENSIVE

"I'll Go Where I'm Sent"

On December 7, 1941, Maj. Gen. Joseph Stilwell was the Army's senior tactical commander in California assigned to the Third Corps with headquarters in Monterey, in charge of the defense of the sea frontier from San Luis Obispo to San Diego. Stilwell kept a diary, which documents the state of shock, confusion, and panic along the California coast in the aftermath of the Japanese attack on Pearl Harbor, with numerous false alarms about Japanese landings. On December 8 he wrote: "Disaster at Honolulu. Periscope at Cliff House—Periscope off Pt. Lobos."

Stilwell's next couple of weeks were spent securing the coast, before he was summoned to Washington to help plan the first major American offensive of the war. Upon arrival on Christmas Eve, he learned that he had been charged with organizing the operation that, a year later, would result in the American campaign in North Africa. At the time, however, there was considerable uncertainty and debate, especially between American and British officials, about where and when to launch the first Allied offensive.

Meanwhile, as the plans for North Africa were under discussion, the military situation in Asia was fast deteriorating. Japanese forces took Guam, Wake Island, and Hong Kong in the weeks after Pearl Harbor. They invaded Malaya and Thailand and seemed on the verge of making a clean sweep of every Allied defensive position north of Australia. Four years earlier, Japan had occupied much of China, driving the Nationalist government of Chiang Kai-shek from its capital, Nanking, to the inland city of Chungking. The Japanese controlled all the major Chinese ports, as well as all the major industrial centers and much of the most fertile agricultural land. China's only remaining surface link with the outside world was the sinuous Burma Road, running some 680 miles through jungle, swamp, and mountains from Lashio in Burma to Kunming in China's Yunnan Province.

From the American point of view, it was now vitally important to "keep China in the war." China's continued involvement would force Japan to maintain large and costly armies on the Asian mainland that could otherwise be used elsewhere. At the same time, China could provide the bases from which Allied air attacks would be launched against Japanese shipping, and from which the Japanese home islands might eventually be attacked. In Washington the consensus quickly developed that a high-ranking officer ought to be sent to Chungking. Joe Stilwell was a natural candidate.

Stilwell had had long prewar service in Asia as an Army language officer, battalion commander, and then military attaché. He could speak and read Chinese with facility, and he was regarded within the U.S. Army as its most knowledgeable Asia expert. Stilwell more than anything wanted a field command, and he was looking forward to leading the first American offensive operation of the war, but this was not to be. In January 1942 he was summoned to a private meeting with Secretary of War Henry Stimson, who asked him how he felt about the prospect of taking on the mission to China. Stilwell answered, "I'll go where I'm sent." Of course, this is what is expected of an officer, though as Stilwell summed up the matter in his diary, "the blow fell."

Promoted to lieutenant general, Stilwell was designated Commanding General of U.S. Army Forces in the China-Burma-India theater; Chief of Staff to the Supreme Commander of the China Theater, Generalissimo Chiang Kai-shek; and supervisor of American lend-lease aid to China. Essentially, Stilwell was assuming responsibility for the mainland front against the Japanese. His only requirement was that he be given genuine authority to command Chinese troops, which authority was promised by Chiang Kai-shek. On his part, Chiang had suggested that the senior military officer sent to China need not be an expert on Chinese affairs. As historian Jonathan Spence observes, "This rather suggested that the Chinese wanted a yes-man who would not be qualified to ask embarrassing questions."

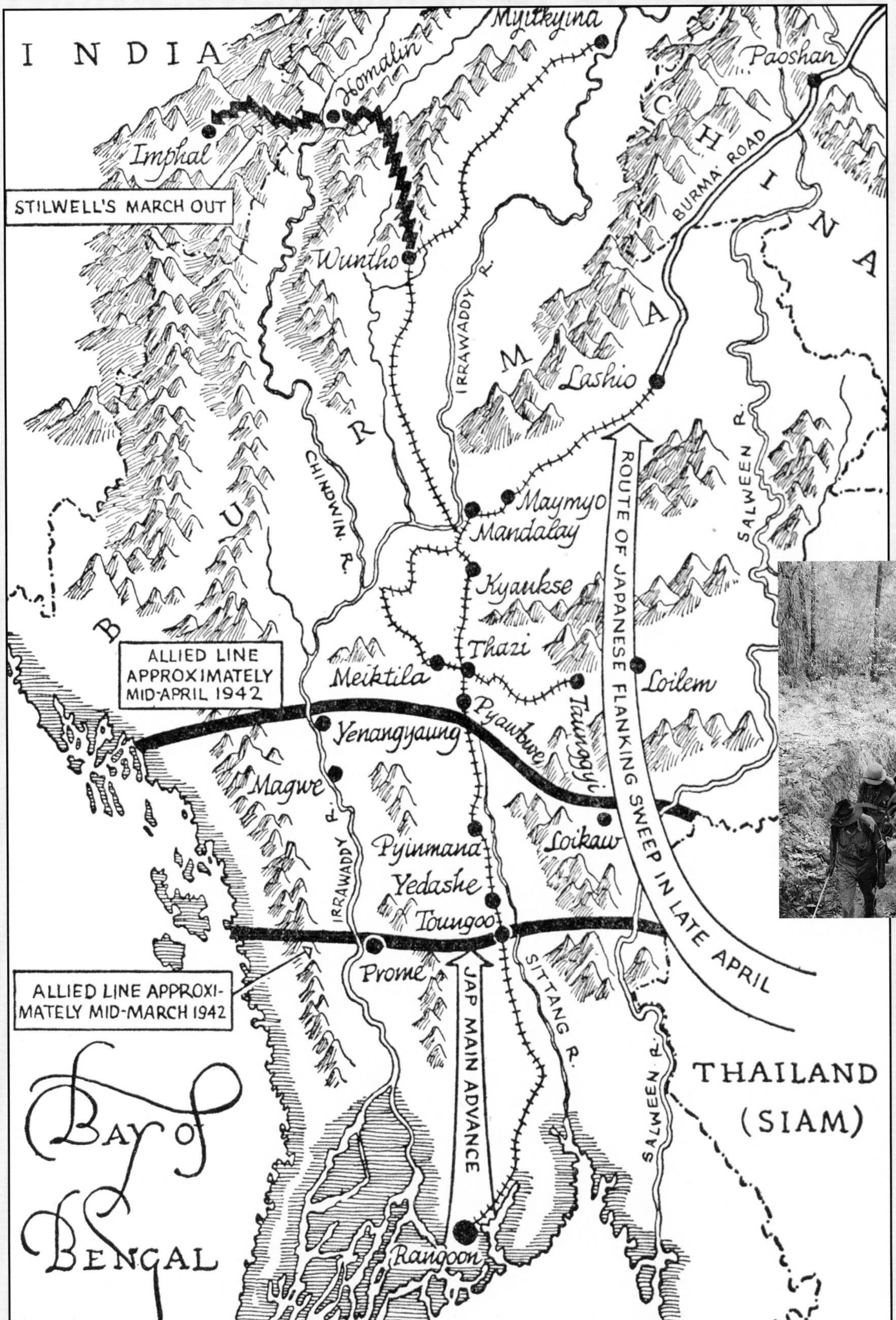

Map of Burma showing route of Stilwell's walkout in May 1942. From Theodore White, *The Stilwell Papers* (New York, 1948).

Inset: Stilwell, in foreground, leads his party out of Burma.

"A Hell of a Beating"

The news from Southeast Asia told of a further disaster. On February 15, two days after Stilwell flew from Miami, Singapore and its garrison of 85,000 British imperial troops surrendered to the Japanese. By the time Stilwell arrived in India on February 25, the East Indies and the Philippines had been lost, Java was being overrun, and Burma was crumbling. "Christ, what the hell is the matter?" Stilwell wondered in his diary. And a week later: "The world is crashing."

When Stilwell arrived in Chungking on March 4, the crucial question was whether Burma could be held and the door to China kept open. Stilwell had convinced Chiang to give him command of the Chinese Fifth and Sixth Armies to defend Burma, and one week after landing in China he left for the Burmese front to lead these troops in person. This was not supposed to be the primary purpose of his mission in China, but Chiang had placed two armies at his command and Stilwell knew where he was most needed. He arrived in Burma just as the British military position was collapsing. The Japanese had struck at the British flank, trapping and all but destroying the 1st Burmese Division. Stilwell rushed his Chinese forces to the rescue, but no sooner had they met the emergency than the Japanese smashed the Chinese line at Loilem, thoroughly destroying the Chinese 55th Division.

Now Stilwell's goal was to withdraw his Chinese troops to a new defensive alignment with the retreating British forces. Upon reaching Mandalay in the last days of April, however, Stilwell learned that the Japanese had seized Lashio, effectively cutting the Burma Road as an escape route to China. At this point, military discipline began to break down. From the beginning Stilwell discovered that Chinese army and division commanders often refused to obey his orders and were getting separate instructions directly from Chiang Kai-shek. Now, in the panic to flee the surging Japanese, Chinese generals failed to obey the orders of their own senior commanders.

With the Chinese formations dissolving, Stilwell's top priority became saving the American soldiers under his command. He hoped to move them by rail to Myitkyina, where one airfield still remained operational. But the single-track rail line was hopelessly jammed. The only alternative to capture by the Japanese was for Stilwell's party to make its way overland to India, which meant a long and difficult journey on foot. When the roads gave out, all vehicles had to be abandoned, including the radio truck, from which a last message was sent to Delhi informing headquarters of the intended route and advising that "we are running low on food with none in sight." Historian Barbara Tuchman describes the scene on the morning of May 7:

Standing on a truck at daylight to address the company, Stilwell explained the plan of march and laid down his rules. All food was to be pooled and all personal belongings discarded except for what each person could carry in addition to weapons and ammunition. A journey of some 140 miles lay ahead with a river and a mountain range to cross. The pass lay at 7,000 feet. They must make 14 miles a day; any slowing of progress would require more food than they had and would risk being caught by the rains. He warned that the party could only survive through discipline. Anyone who did not wish to accept his orders could leave now with a week's rations and make his own way. He looked around; no one moved. "By the time we get out of here, many of you will hate my guts but I'll tell you one thing: you'll all get out."

Stilwell's Story of Burma Battle:

'We Got Hell of a Beating'

By WILLIAM McGAFFIN.

NEW DELHI, India, May 25 (AP)—Still full of fight after a "hell of a beating" in Burma and a weary march of 140 miles through wild Burmese jungles, Lieut. Gen. Joseph W. Stilwell declared today that Burma can be—and must be—retaken from the Japanese.

The American came out of Burma the hard way. He refused a lift from a United States Army plane because he still had a job to do.

Then, when it became clear withdrawal was the only course, he and a group of soldiers and native nurses started from Wuntho May 4.

They made more than half of their 20-day trek afoot, hidden from aerial searchers by lush tropical forests while their food supplies dwindled. Gen. Stilwell flew here on the last leg.

He said he regarded Burma as a vitally important area for re-entry into China, now blocked from the Burma Road supply route. After conferring with Gen. Sir Archibald P. Wavell, British commander-in-chief in India, he is going back to China to talk to Gen. Chiang Kai-shek.

Here, in his own salty words, is what happened to the Allies in Burma:

"I claim we got a hell of a beating.

"We got run out of Burma and it is humiliating as hell.

"I think we ought to find out what caused it, go back and retake it."

"The Japanese are not supermen," continued Stilwell,

Burma Post-Mortem.

Authentically American.

THE EVENING BULLETIN PHILADELPHIA

WEDNESDAY, MAY 27, 1942

DOWN TO EARTH

Got Hell of Beating in Burma, Says Stilwell

LIEUT.-GEN. STILWELL

'Got Hell of Beating In Burma'—Stilwell

He Finds 'Japs Are Not Supermen'; Declares Area Must Be Retaken

Stilwell's Trek To India Marked By Daily Diet Of Rice, Rice, Rice

Diet Of Rice, Plain And Fancy, Marked Stilwell's Burma Trek

Page from Stilwell's scrapbook. (Joseph W. Stilwell Papers)

Stilwell's party, which numbered 114, consisted of twenty-six Americans and an assortment of British soldiers and civilians; Chinese guards; Burmese nurses; and Indian, Malayan, and Burmese cooks, porters, and mechanics. The walk out of Burma started on the dirt roads and jungle paths from Wuntho to the Uyu River, where the party made rafts and poled downstream for two days to the Chindwin River. After crossing the Chindwin, they spent eight days negotiating the rugged wooded mountains along the border with India. After a journey of 140 miles, on May 20 the party reached Imphal, where they were transported by truck, train, and plane to Delhi.

There, on May 24, Stilwell gave a press conference at which, resisting the encouragement of reporters to put a heroic face on his walkout of Burma, he uttered what would turn out to be his signature remark: "I claim we got a hell of a beating. We got run out of Burma and it is humiliating as hell. I think we ought to find out what caused it, go back and retake it." It was the kind of straight talk that had earned him the nickname "Vinegar Joe." A *New York Times* lead editorial, in commenting on Stilwell's bluntness, said of Churchill and Roosevelt that for all their inspiring speechmaking "each of them could learn something from General Stilwell."

"In the midst of catastrophe," Tuchman relates, Stilwell "drew up the plan that was to be his vehicle of return. It called for the transfer of Chinese troops to India where they could be trained and equipped under American direction as the task force for reconquest. He never proclaimed to the public, 'I shall return,' but this became a determination fixed in iron."

The Struggle

The fall of Burma closed the land route between India and China, leaving as the only lifeline for American lend-lease supplies the hazardous flights "over the Hump" of the Himalayas. Stilwell returned to Chungking, where he took up his primary responsibilities of building up Chinese military strength and sustaining Chinese-American relations. It was an assignment that brought him unending frustration.

The fact is, the China-Burma-India theater was not a high priority for the British and the Americans. This distressed Chiang, who wanted arms and supplies from the Allies and was always threatening to drop out of the alliance. Stilwell meanwhile kept badgering Chiang to be allowed to train and prepare to use Chinese soldiers to retake Burma. It was also Stilwell's idea to select the best of the Nationalist forces—thirty divisions in all—and properly equip and train them to defend unoccupied China and eventually take the offensive against the Japanese. But with only limited lend-lease supplies to dispense in China, he had little leverage with which to influence Chiang to act. Stilwell's diary records numerous rounds of raised and dashed hopes. As Theodore White recounts: "Again and again, Stilwell records with exuberant delight that he has finally wrung assent to a program of action from Chiang; and then the weeks spin by while the promise grows sterile, is forgotten, and its execution becomes a wretched process of bargaining."

A complicating presence on the scene for Stilwell was the American airman Maj. Gen. Claire Chennault, commander of the 14th Air Force, whose attacks were wreaking havoc on Japanese shipping. To Chennault, Stilwell's focus on reopening the Burma Road, and on constructing a new land route across Burma from Ledo in India, was proof that "Walking Joe" did not appreciate the potentially decisive influence of air power. On his part, Stilwell believed that Chennault's air assaults were bound to provoke the Japanese to move against China's defenseless air bases. Theirs was more than a difference of philosophy, as Stilwell,

Stilwell with the Chiangs, April 1942 (photograph by Clare Boothe Luce).
(Joseph W. Stilwell Papers)

Chennault, and Chiang clashed over how the precious tonnage coming in over the Hump ought to be put to use. Chiang, while hoarding lend-lease supplies for his own domestic purposes, supported Chennault's less expensive and, in Chiang's eyes, less politically costly air campaign, which also received the blessing of President Roosevelt.

Stilwell became convinced soon after he got to know Chiang that the Generalissimo cared less about expelling the Japanese from China than he did about keeping his powder dry for the decisive battle with Mao Zedong's Communists to the north, with whom the Nationalists had been engaged in a civil war off and on since 1927. Stilwell thought the Communists could be enlisted in the anti-Japanese cause, and he came to favor direct American aid to them, a proposition that exasperated Chiang.

Chiang's resistance to Stilwell's plans is also explained by the peculiar patchwork of alliances that constituted the Nationalist regime. When Stilwell proposed to remove incompetent Chinese commanders—or otherwise to reform the Nationalist armies—Chiang had to be concerned that such steps not threaten loyal supporters essential to his hold on power. As Spence observes:

> *Stilwell failed to see that his plans to slash back the number of divisions in the Chinese army, to redistribute arms and equipment among a select number, and to purge inefficient high commanders was not a simple matter of military reform; it would cut at the heart of the Generalissimo's power structure, and might well lead to his downfall, since Chiang's position depended on a delicate balance of personal loyalties and alliances.*

For Stilwell, the matter was more straightforward. In his diary, he referred to the Generalissimo as "Peanut" (or "the little bastard") and Madame Chiang as "Madamissima." (Only British military officers came in for harsher treatment.) Stilwell wrote in the summer of 1943 that the United States had been "forced into partnership with a gang of fascists under a one-party government similar in many respects to our German enemy."

The fact is, even had Chiang's government been united, efficient, and uncorrupt, Stilwell would nonetheless have met with frustration in Chungking. As journalist John Lardner, who was sympathetic to Stilwell's travails, wrote a few years after the war:

> *Stilwell wanted action, wanted battle, wanted to help the war effort in the manner he was trained for. In his job in Chungking, such activities were largely impossible. And the blame for this was by no means all on Chiang. It lay partly in the world situation, in the general strategy of the Combined Chiefs of Staff. Stilwell oversimplified. By his own admission, he was no diplomat, and he never really tried to be one. He accepted his job and, in a sense, refused to cope with it.*

Stilwell was able to convince Chiang to fly 45,000 troops from China over the Hump to Ramgarh, India, for training. Chiang eventually allowed Chinese divisions to be trained by Americans in Kunming as the so-called Yoke force. Stilwell was impatient for the reconquest of Burma to begin as soon as possible, with the Yoke force striking down the Burma Road from the east, and the Ramgarh Chinese forces striking from India. Yet he found Washington unable to commit the supplies and Chiang reluctant to commit the forces necessary for his projected Burma offensive.

Return to Burma

Finally, however, things seemed to turn in Stilwell's favor at the Cairo Conference of November 1943, where FDR, Churchill, and Chiang conferred together. The Allies agreed to launch a major offensive in Burma, with a large-scale British landing in the south joined by American troops, and with Chinese forces attacking from India and China. But on the heels of Cairo came the Teheran Conference, where Stalin insisted on a massive cross-Channel invasion in 1944. This meant an immediate change of plans for Burma, as it sharply curtailed the number of landing craft available for a British landing in the south. Roosevelt and Churchill returned to Cairo for further discussions and decided that the British would not participate in a Burma campaign. Stilwell, who remained in Cairo to await the result of the Teheran conference, had to return to Chungking and break the news to Chiang.

Stilwell persisted, attempting to convince Chiang to let him use the Chinese Yoke force to invade Burma from the east. When Chiang refused, Stilwell decided to use the Chinese troops he had been training in India and make a go of it, hoping to convince Chiang to permit the use of the Yoke force later on. For the first time, Chiang granted Stilwell complete command of the Ramgarh-trained forces. Two divisions were ready for action and had been moved to the India-Burma border in 1943; a third was completing its training. Stilwell headed back into Burma with a plan to drive as far as possible toward the Chinese border.

Afterwards, Stilwell was sharply criticized in some quarters for his personal involvement in the Burma campaign: a three-star general and the commander of a war theater had abandoned his headquarters to lead Chinese troops in the jungle. There can be little doubt that Stilwell, one of the Army's great specialists in infantry tactics, jumped into the Burma campaign as a way to escape the deskwork and dead-end diplomacy of Chungking. Yet Tuchman is certainly correct that "though he never put it on record it is probable that from the day he walked out of Burma nothing could have altered his determination to lead the way back." Moreover, Stilwell understood that only under his personal leadership would the campaign have any chance of succeeding.

Whatever his motivations, Stilwell was now eager for the offensive. He entered Burma with two Chinese divisions, the 38th and 22nd. Together with the third division in reserve they totaled about 50,000 men, accompanied by a small contingent of British forces and the American volunteer commandos known as Merrill's Marauders. They were opposed by an equal number of Japanese defenders, battle-tested and well dug in. Stilwell decided to force the issue by sending his Chinese forces ahead without maintaining supply lines to the rear, making them instead dependent on parachute drops of food and supplies along the way.

Stilwell would remain in the jungle, except for a couple of quick flights to Delhi and Chungking, from January to July 1944. He was sixty-one years old and he walked with his troops through rain, mud, heat, sickness, snakes, and hostile forces. All the while, by radio and courier, he pressured Chiang to deliver the Yoke force for the Burma campaign. In the face of an American ultimatum threatening to cut off lend-lease supplies, Chiang relented, and on May 11 the Yoke force began to move across the Salween into Burma.

After several months of fighting, in a bold stroke Merrill's Marauders, with attached Chinese troops, seized the airport at Myitkyina on May 17, and Stilwell flew in additional forces. The Japanese stubbornly hung on, and bloody battles ensued for several weeks before Stilwell's forces prevailed. In early August, the Japanese were forced to retreat. It was a costly victory, but Myitkyina was the first significant Japanese position to be retaken in Southeast Asia. Its capture shortened the Hump route, led to the eventual reopening of the Burma Road, and proved Stilwell's long-held contention that with proper leadership and supplies the Chinese soldier was the equal of any Allied soldier.

Stilwell in Burma, May 1942. Theodore White wrote of Stilwell's walk out of Burma: "He led the daily treks, counting cadence. He checked baggage and marching order. He inspected food and rationed the individual portions. He cursed, snarled, tongue-lashed his people—and brought every man through alive." (Joseph W. Stilwell Papers)

Stilwell's memorabilia at the Hoover Archives include his military cap, belt, and canteen, his government-issue Hamilton watch, and the patch of the China-Burma-India (CBI) Theater.

The Axe Falls

Stilwell's very success in Burma would be his undoing in China. In his absence, the Japanese launched an offensive that, just as he had predicted, overran Chennault's air bases and was threatening to inflict far worse damage. Comparing the military situation in China with Stilwell's victory in Burma, President Roosevelt, acting on a recommendation by the U.S. Joint Chiefs of Staff, demanded that Chiang Kai-shek make Stilwell commander-in-chief of the Chinese armies—in other words, that Stilwell be given direct command of Chinese armies in the field. To make his appointment less objectionable to Chiang, Stilwell was promoted to the rank of four-star general, a distinction he shared at the time only with Generals Marshall, Eisenhower, MacArthur, and Arnold. Chiang consented to this in principle, and negotiations ensued on the details, which would include increased lend-lease supplies and a substantial postwar aid package.

But Chiang temporized, and this prompted FDR to send a firm message to the Generalissimo, delivered in person by Stilwell on September 19, 1944. Stilwell called the president's message "Hot as a fire-cracker. 'Get busy, boy, or else.' '*Do it now.*' " Chiang's armies would have to do some real fighting, right away and under Stilwell's command, or American aid to the Nationalist government would cease. Stilwell handed Chiang the president's message and observed the effect: "The harpoon hit him right in the solar plexus, but although he turned green, he never batted an eye. He just turned to me and said 'I understand.' "

Stilwell tasted victory, but it was bound to be short-lived. In the opinion of historian Spence, the American proposal, however reasonable it seemed to American officials, was "completely unrealistic" in the Chinese context: "For anyone with any knowledge of Chinese history and politics it should have been clearly inconceivable that the Chinese would voluntarily put a Westerner in command of all their armed forces on their own soil, and obvious that doing so would bring about the fall of Chiang Kai-shek."

In the event, the results produced by Roosevelt's missive were exactly the opposite of what was intended. Chiang seems to have suspected that Stilwell himself had engineered the president's telegram; in any case, as Spence says, "Chiang could not forgive Stilwell for handing him such a message in such a way." Hardened in his determination to be rid of Stilwell, Chiang now demanded that he be replaced. Roosevelt, who put great stock in personal diplomacy, was ready to believe that much of the problem in Chungking stemmed from "Vinegar Joe" 's difficult personality. On October 19, 1944, Stilwell received a telegram from the chief of staff, Gen. George Marshall, informing him of his recall from China.

The Stilwell Diaries

Stilwell kept a diary for most of his life, including during the American occupation of the Philippines and the Great War in France, as well as during his extended service in China in the 1920s and 1930s. Taken together, the Stilwell diaries constitute one of the most important "documents" at the Hoover Archives. That he never intended the diaries to be published becomes obvious upon reading them. Selected parts were edited by Theodore White and published in 1948, and the diaries and other personal writings are the spine of Barbara Tuchman's Pulitzer Prize–winning 1971 book *Stilwell and the American Experience in China, 1911–45*. As Tuchman says, "Stilwell was always writing things down. In addition to diary, letters, essays and sketches, he wrote what he called 'Random Notes' or 'Odds and Ends' on sheets or scraps of paper dealing with thoughts, dreams, stray ideas, jokes, anecdotes, remarks, quotations or anything that was passing through his constantly ticking mind."

Any experienced researcher knows that one of the dangers of reading a historical subject's diary is that it can "get personal." Watching events from the perspective of the diarist makes it harder to maintain objectivity—especially when the diary is as remarkably engaging as Stilwell's. After one has walked out of Burma with him, it is almost impossible not to go the full distance, to follow the diaries to the end—which for Stilwell came in San Francisco, on October 12, 1946, shortly after he was diagnosed with liver cancer. In the penultimate entry, written on Tuesday, September 17, Stilwell undergoes a series of medical tests at Letterman Hospital, on the Presidio. Then, "as if in defiance," as Tuchman puts it, he set out on foot. "Walked miles," he wrote, and for the last time.

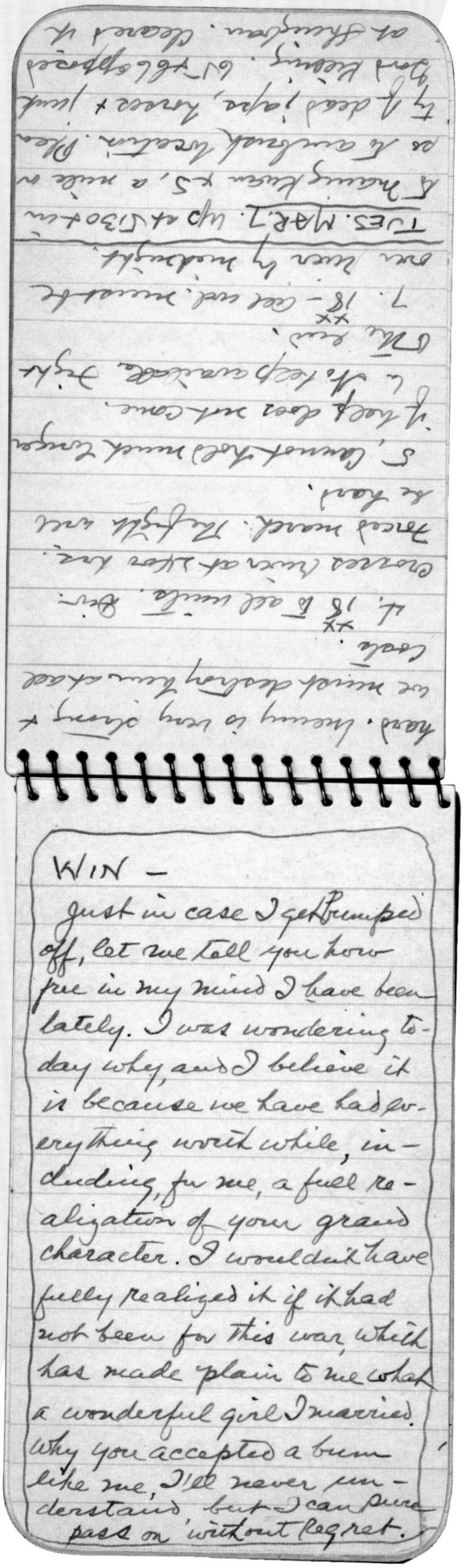
WIN –
Just in case I get bumped off, let me tell you how free in my mind I have been lately. I was wondering today why and I believe it is because we have had everything worth while, including, for me, a full realization of your grand character. I wouldn't have fully realized it if it had not been for this war which has made plain to me what a wonderful girl I married. Why you accepted a bum like me, I'll never understand but I can sure pass on 'without regret.'

Pages from Stilwell's diary. The upside-down (upper wing) entry is for Tuesday, March 7, 1944; the right-side-up (lower wing) entry (which is undated and comes immediately after the entry for February 9, 1944) is a personal note to his wife, Winifred, written in the heat of the campaign to retake Burma.

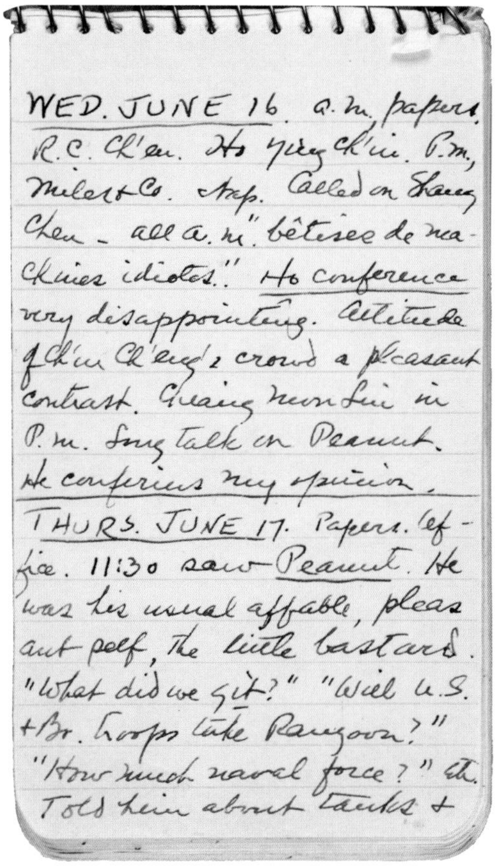
WED. JUNE 16. a.m. papers. R.C. Ch'en. Ho Ying Ch'in. P.m. Miles & Co. Nap. Called on Shang Chen – all a.m. "bêtises de machines idiotes." Ho conference very disappointing. Attitude of Ch'en Ch'eng's crowd a pleasant contrast. Chiang Meng-lin in p.m. Long talk on Peanut. He confirms my opinion.
THURS. JUNE 17. Papers. Left office. 11:30 saw Peanut. He was his usual affable, pleasant self, the little bastard. "What did we get?" "Will U.S. + Br. troops take Rangoon?" "How much naval force?" etc. Told him about tanks +

Stilwell diary entry (top) for Thursday, June 17, 1943: "Papers. Left office. 11:30 saw *Peanut.* He was his usual affable, pleasant self, the little bastard."

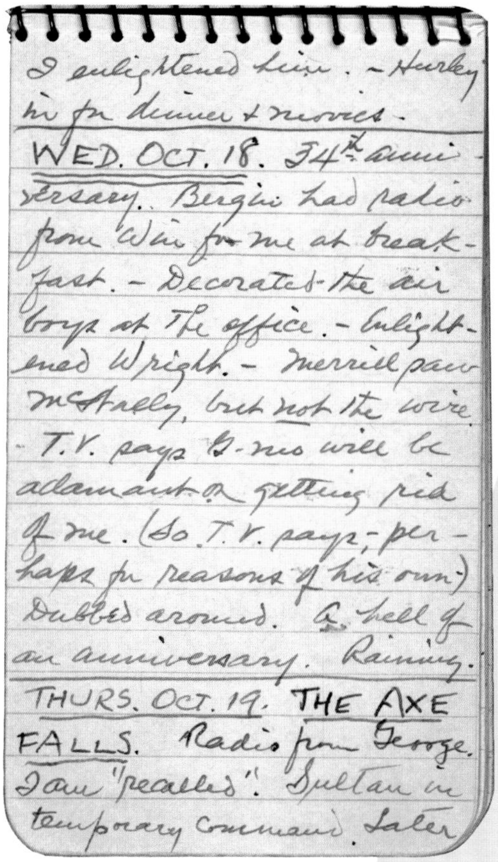
I enlightened him. – Hurley in for dinner + movies.
WED. OCT. 18. 34th anniversary. Bergin had radio from Win for me at breakfast. – Decorated the air boys at the office. – Enlightened Wright. – Merrill saw McNally, but not the wire. – T.V. says G-mo will be adamant on getting rid of me. (So T.V. says, – perhaps for reasons of his own) Dubbed around. A hell of an anniversary. Raining.
THURS. OCT. 19. THE AXE FALLS. Radio from George. I am "recalled". Sultan in temporary command. Later

Stilwell diary entry (bottom) for Thursday, October 19, 1944: "THE AXE FALLS." Stilwell had just received word from Chief of Staff Gen. George Marshall of his recall from China.

WEDEMEYER: GRAND STRATEGIST

Sixty years after Pearl Harbor, in the days following the surprise attack of September 11, 2001, as military planners met in Washington to figure out a response to the threat of global terrorism, they were conscious of a need to go beyond immediate counterterrorist measures and to think in strategic terms—in other words, to use what one of them called the "Wedemeyer Method."

Albert Coady Wedemeyer was one of the U.S. Army's greatest strategists and planners. As America followed the opening battles of the Second World War, Major Wedemeyer, serving in the War Plans Division of the General Staff, was assigned the task of designing a plan of mobilization to win the war in the event that the United States were drawn in. The result was the Victory Program, a document that, in the assessment of military historian John Keegan, "in large measure determined how the United States, and therefore the whole Western alliance, conducted its part in the Second World War." But Wedemeyer would become a vocal critic of how that victory was achieved, and to the end of his days he deplored what he saw as America's dangerous deficiencies in the practice of statecraft.

The Victory Program

Wedemeyer's road to grand strategist seems to have been to some extent a matter of personal temperament, yet it was also the direct product of his professional training and experience. He served tours in the Philippines in the 1920s and in China in the early 1930s, before entering the Army's Command and General Staff School at Fort Leavenworth, Kansas, in 1934, with the rank of lieutenant.

Albert C. Wedemeyer at his desk in Chungking, c. 1944. (Albert C. Wedemeyer Papers)

In the fall of 1936, the War Department sent Wedemeyer on a two-year tour as an exchange student at the Kriegsakademie, the German war college in Berlin. It sounds fairly preposterous—Hitler's Wehrmacht accepting foreign exchange students—but it was so, and Wedemeyer was able to observe firsthand the German army's rapid expan-

"Victory Program" cover. On December 4, 1941, only three days before Pearl Harbor, the most sensitive parts of the Victory Program were published in the American press, creating a sensation. The leak led to Wedemeyer's investigation by the FBI, which evinced a particular curiosity about Wedemeyer's German family background and the contacts he had made during his time at the war college in Germany. (Albert C. Wedemeyer Papers)

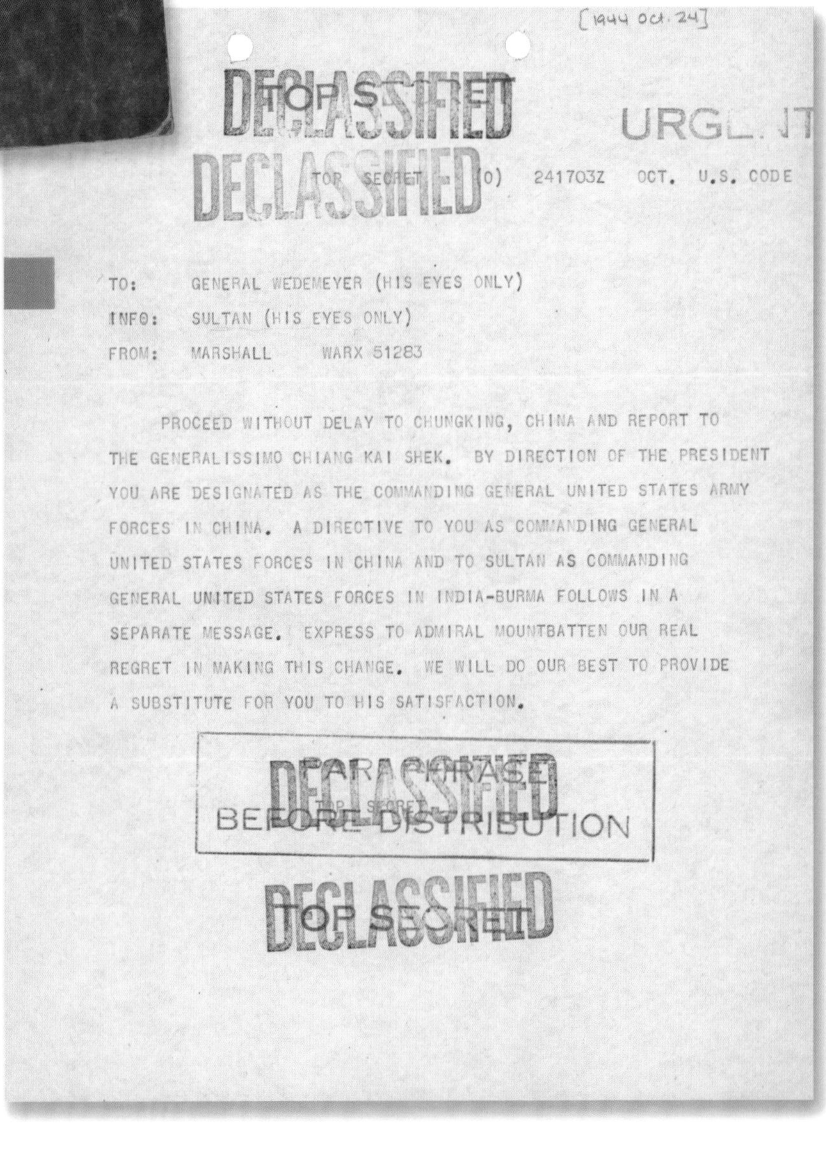

[1944 Oct. 24]

DECLASSIFIED TOP SECRET URGENT

DECLASSIFIED TOP SECRET (0) 241703Z OCT. U.S. CODE

TO: GENERAL WEDEMEYER (HIS EYES ONLY)
INFO: SULTAN (HIS EYES ONLY)
FROM: MARSHALL WARX 51283

PROCEED WITHOUT DELAY TO CHUNGKING, CHINA AND REPORT TO THE GENERALISSIMO CHIANG KAI SHEK. BY DIRECTION OF THE PRESIDENT YOU ARE DESIGNATED AS THE COMMANDING GENERAL UNITED STATES ARMY FORCES IN CHINA. A DIRECTIVE TO YOU AS COMMANDING GENERAL UNITED STATES FORCES IN CHINA AND TO SULTAN AS COMMANDING GENERAL UNITED STATES FORCES IN INDIA-BURMA FOLLOWS IN A SEPARATE MESSAGE. EXPRESS TO ADMIRAL MOUNTBATTEN OUR REAL REGRET IN MAKING THIS CHANGE. WE WILL DO OUR BEST TO PROVIDE A SUBSTITUTE FOR YOU TO HIS SATISFACTION.

DECLASSIFIED PARAPHRASE BEFORE DISTRIBUTION TOP SECRET

DECLASSIFIED TOP SECRET

Marshall telegram to Wedemeyer, October 24, 1944. Telegram from Gen. George Marshall to Wedemeyer informing him of his assignment to China to replace Gen. Joseph Stilwell. (Albert C. Wedemeyer Papers) sion, to learn of its new technologies, and to study its strategic and tactical doctrines, with their emphasis on achieving surprise through mobility and initiative. Upon his return from Berlin in 1938, he wrote a 147-page report about his experiences, describing "not only the organization and functioning of the German War College," he later recalled, but also "the German concepts of warfare involving the use of armored divisions, airborne divisions, and antitank units, none of which existed at that time in the United States."

The outbreak of the world war put a premium on Wedemeyer's experience in the German military. In September 1940 he was assigned to the War Department with the rank of major, and in spring 1941, at the initiative of the chief of staff, Gen. George Marshall, Wedemeyer was appointed to the War Plans Division of the General Staff. His opportunity came in July, after Nazi Germany invaded the Soviet Union. President Roosevelt directed the secretaries of war and the navy to draw up an estimate of the "over-all production requirements required to defeat our potential enemies," meaning Germany, Italy, and Japan. At the War Department, this daunting task fell on Major Wedemeyer. By late September he had produced an enormously detailed document that became known as the Victory Program, designed to serve, in the words of historian Keith Eiler, as "a broad blueprint for U.S. participation in a possible war against the Axis powers."

Wedemeyer understood, on the basis of his experience in Berlin, that an American victory could be achieved only by means of the total mobilization of the U.S. economy—its manpower, industry, and transport—in the service of the war effort. His program identified and prioritized requirements across a range of categories, from cargo ships, bombers, and tanks to rifles, binoculars, and blankets. It called for an expeditionary force of approximately five million men—a modern force with mechanized armor and air forces—within an overall total of almost ten million men in uniform. Wedemeyer's plan emphasized speed: Hitler had to be engaged and defeated "before he can liquidate or recoup from his struggle with Russia." This meant a "rapidly accelerated" development of industrial capacity to have America's military forces ready to fight by July 1, 1943.

After Pearl Harbor, Eiler relates, the Victory Program served as "the basic guide for mobilizing U.S. manpower and industry and for structuring and deploying the armed forces." In a note written to FDR shortly after the Japanese attack, Secretary of War Henry Stimson remarked that without Wedemeyer's timely and perceptive analysis of Blitzkrieg "we should be badly off indeed."

DECLASSIFIED

TOP SECRET

URGENT

EYES ALONE

DATE: 14 AUG 45

NO : CFB X 4580

TO : WARCOS FOR JOINT CHIEFS OF STAFF (EYES ALONE)

INFO: MACARTHUR AND NIMITZ (EYES ALONE)

1. Provision embodied in last paragraph of WARX 48625 is subject. I am sure that you recognize that MANCHURIA may properly be termed the critical area in connection with current and projected activities of Chinese Communists, and possibly Soviet Communists. If the General Order No. 1 to be issued by Japanese Headquarters provides for the surrender of Japanese Commander and of forces within China to the Generalissimo but excludes repeat excludes MANCHURIA insofar as the Generalissimo is concerned, following implications should be noted:

a. The attitude of Soviet Russia toward the Chinese Communists has never been determined accurately, nor have Soviet intentions in China been formalized to a degree that Americans can view the situation with equanimity. However it is not repeat not unreasonable to expect penetration of Soviet Communists ideologies in MANCHURIA with cooperation of Chinese Communists. If the General Order above referred to excludes MANCHURIA as now contemplated, there is extreme danger that Japanese equipment will become available surreptitiously or openly to the Chinese Communists in MANCHURIA. Further the Chinese Communist overall plans will be facilitated. If on the other hand the General Order clearly stipulates that Japanese Forces would surrender only repeat only to Soviet Russian Forces and/or the Generalissimo's Forces, the above dangers would be minimized perhaps obviated.

b. The ideas embodied in this message and in messages I have sent to you the past several days might suggest partisan leaning on my part. This is not repeat not the case. However, the United States policy has been and continues to be full support of the Generalissimo who heads the only officially and universally recognized constituted government in China. The Generalissimo is conceded at present to be the strongest Chinese leader and the only one capable of possibly accomplishing a modicum of stability during this period of uncertainty. It would therefore appear sound to create conditions by continued U.S. political, economic and military support (short of involvement in fratricidal war) which would strengthen the existing Central Government's position. This support should include iron clad stipulations designed to insure surrender of Japanese Forces and equipment to the Generalissimo throughout China including MANCHURIA, except in the immediate combat areas of the Russians.

c. I view Asia as an enormous pot, seething and boiling, the fumes of which may readily snuff out the advantages gained by Allied sacrifices the past several years and may also definitely preclude realization of the objectives of the Atlantic Charter, and the Teheran, Yalta and Potsdam agreements. In my CFB 526, 9 July, paragraphs 2 and 3, pertinent ideas and suggestions are expressed that have stronger and immediate application today.

- 1 -

DECLASSIFIED

Wedemeyer memorandum to Gen. Marshall, August 14, 1945. Page "three" (below) contains the text of a paragraph deleted from the copy sent to Marshall (as attested to in a handwritten addendum by Wedemeyer's assistant, James Boyle). (Albert C. Wedemeyer Papers)

TOP SECRET

c. I view Asia as an enormous pot, seething and boiling, the fumes of which may readily snuff out the advantages gained by Allied sacrifices the past several years and may also definitely preclude realization of the objectives of the Atlantic Charter, and the Teheran, Yalta and Potsdam agreements. America has unwittingly contributed to the trend of events in Europe which facilitate the substitution of Communism for Nazism, yet it is accepted that both forms of ism are equally abhorrent to Americans and diametrically opposed to the ideologies of democracy; both forms of ism abrogate the very principles for which we have made unstinted, astronomical sacrifices in lives and resources. The situation in Europe is a fait accompli: however we may still provide a frame work for realization of ideas and ideals for which I feel we are fighting. In my CFB 526, 9 July, paragraphs 2 and 3, pertinent ideas and suggestions are expressed that have stronger and immediate application today.

5/14/45 not sent this was contemplated as para c of foregoing message. JB

TOP SECRET

Wedemeyer's War

The Victory Program was not itself a strategic plan, but it was informed by strategy. Wedemeyer's two-year stay in Berlin, beyond the particular insights it offered him into the German way of war, gave him his education as a strategist. "Thanks to my assignment in Germany," he wrote two decades later, "I was afforded an opportunity to acquire a broad concept of strategy embracing political, economic, and psychological means for the attainment of war aims, in place of the narrower concept of strictly military science which I had studied at Leavenworth." This was "grand strategy," which took into account the influences on military affairs of geography, psychology, demography, economics, and politics.

Wedemeyer's training taught him the central importance for Germany's geopolitical ambitions of conquering Eastern Europe. He also strongly subscribed to the classic principle of military strategy that the most effective way to defeat an enemy was to concentrate one's forces for attack at the decisive point—in other words, to go for the enemy's jugular vein. What this prescribed in the circumstances of 1941, as the German armies advanced deep into Soviet territory, was a massing of forces in England for an early invasion of the continent and an offensive into the industrial heartland of Germany. Wedemeyer was an ardent proponent of a cross-Channel invasion in early summer 1943, or, should a victory by Hitler's armies on the Eastern Front appear imminent, of a diversionary attack across the Channel in 1942.

Wedemeyer was to discover, however, that America's British allies had a very different idea of how to prosecute the war. He was present at the early diplomatic conferences between the Americans and the British, there to assist General Marshall in presenting U.S. military proposals. At the conference table, the American negotiators were routinely outmaneuvered, their proposals for a cross-Channel invasion put aside in favor of the British preference to take the battle first into the Mediterranean, beginning with North Africa, later to Sicily, and then up the boot of Italy. It was a strategy of attacking Europe at its "soft underbelly," in Winston Churchill's phrase.

To Wedemeyer this was no strategy at all. Though he viewed Churchill as an inspiring leader (and a shrewd negotiatior), he found him to be a "pseudo strategist" with a "historically conditioned dread" of fighting in northern France after the experience of attrition warfare in the Great War. Yet, to Wedemeyer's increasing frustration, the British repeatedly won the argument. After the Casablanca Conference of January 1943, where FDR accepted Churchill's proposal to delay the cross-Channel campaign in favor of an invasion of Sicily, Wedemeyer wrote privately to a colleague in the United States: "We lost our shirts. . . . We came, we listened, and we were conquered."

Soon, Wedemeyer would not be on the scene to argue his case. At the Quebec conference in the late summer of 1943, Roosevelt and Churchill decided to establish a new Southeast Asia Command (SEAC), with headquarters in New Delhi, in order to better coordinate Allied efforts in the region. Wedemeyer, now a major general, was named deputy chief of staff to the SEAC commander, Lord Louis Mountbatten, and although he got along fine with Mountbatten he suspected that his transfer to the secondary theater was the work of the British. One year later, in October 1944, when Gen. Joe Stilwell was recalled from China, Wedemeyer took his place in Chungking. There he was given command of the newly established China Theater of Operations (a U.S. command) and made chief of staff to President Chiang Kai-shek.

Wedemeyer's basic assignment was the same as it had been for Stilwell: to keep China in the war. When he arrived at the end of October, the Japanese had launched a major offensive that threatened to overrun America's air bases and even the capital, Chungking, as well as the vital supply base at Kunming. To counter the threat, Wedemeyer airlifted two American-trained and -equipped divisions of Chinese troops from Burma to China. The Japanese offensive was repelled.

Like Stilwell before him, Wedemeyer learned quickly that his plans could be undermined by simple noncooperation and inefficiency on the part of the Kuomintang's civilian and military leaders. And yet, owing to several factors, relations with Chiang Kai-shek were much better than under Stilwell. For one thing, unlike his predecessor, Wedemeyer had outstanding diplomatic and organizational skills. Also, his assignment did not require him to control Chinese troops—the issue that ultimately brought the Chiang-Stilwell struggle to a head. Further, Chiang appreciated Wedemeyer's lack of enthusiasm for American proposals to supply Mao Zedong's Communists with military arms and training for the struggle against Japan. Moreover, having ousted Stilwell, Chiang understood that he needed to get along with Wedemeyer: the recall of a second American general might well snap America's patience and cut the lend-lease lifeline to Chungking.

With the Chinese Communist forces in the north gaining strength in the early months of 1945, Chiang and Wedemeyer shared the same basic goal of building up the Nationalist army as quickly as possible. Wedemeyer and his staff worked to improve the combat efficiency of thirty-nine specially selected Kuomintang divisions for a decisive battle with the Japanese. Wedemeyer was preparing for a Chinese offensive when the atomic bombs at Hiroshima and Nagasaki brought an abrupt end to the war in the Pacific.

Hiroshima and Nagasaki. These frames were made from film footage taken of the atomic explosion over Nagasaki, Japan, on August 9, 1945. Three days earlier, the *Enola Gay*, a U.S. Army B-29, had dropped an atomic bomb on Hiroshima. Original film footage of the Hiroshima and Nagasaki bombings—the only such film in existence—was donated to the Hoover Archives by Harold Agnew, a physicist who monitored the Hiroshima bombing from the *Great Artiste*, the instrument plane that accompanied the *Enola Gay* on its mission.

Wedemeyer and Marshall inspecting a Chinese honor guard on Marshall's arrival in China, December 1945. (Albert C. Wedemeyer Papers)

Debacle in China

Victory had come to the Allies, but not to China, which now threatened to descend into all-out civil war between the Nationalist and Communist forces. In the final years of the war, the United States had been working to achieve an accommodation between the two sides in the name of waging a common fight against Japan, but with the foreign enemy defeated the case for unity was harder to make.

Wedemeyer firmly believed that a Nationalist-Communist reconciliation was impossible, and that without strong U.S. support for Chiang's government a Communist triumph was inevitable. Most American officials saw Chiang as corrupt and devious (or worse), but although Wedemeyer found reason to be critical of Nationalist rule he was sensitive to Chiang's precarious political situation and believed that the Generalissimo was more sincere than his critics gave him credit for.

> *As I saw it the worst ills of China—corruption, maladministration, inefficiency, and the like—were the result not of the dictatorial nature of its government but of its lack of power and authority to get its orders carried out. And Chiang Kai-shek could to some extent, although not entirely, be excused for his failure to clean up his administration by having all along had his hands tied both by the endless war and his need to retain loyal cadres if China was not to fall apart. To call Chiang Kai-shek a fascist dictator, as was the fashion in America, was a ridiculous reversal of the truth, but was tragic in its consequences since it led to U.S. policy being based on a false premise. The powers of the Chinese Nationalist Government, far from being totalitarian, were much too limited.*

In any case, Wedemeyer tended to look beyond personalities to the level of ideology and strategy. The Kuomintang, though far from perfect, was the only alternative to the Communists under Mao, whom Wedemeyer saw as committed Marxist-Leninist revolutionaries—hardly the benign "agrarian reformers" they were portrayed to be by many in the West.

American policy after the defeat of Japan remained focused on arranging a coalition government of Nationalists and Communists, an idea that Wedemeyer regarded as unrealistic and increasingly perilous. This made it terribly awkward for him when President Truman sent General Marshall, recently retired from the Army, to China for the purpose of reconciling the two Chinese adversaries and integrating their armed forces. This led to tension between Marshall and his protégé, who regarded Marshall's mission as hopeless. Marshall arrived in December 1945 and shortly thereafter managed to secure a cease-fire, but beyond that he was unable to make genuine progress. By the end of 1946, the armed conflict resumed with a heightened intensity. It had been Marshall's intention to have Wedemeyer, now a lieutenant general, appointed U.S. ambassador to China as soon as the situation improved, but it never did, and in any case the Communists objected to the idea. Wedemeyer departed China in April 1946, returning to the United States, where he later was placed in command of the Second U.S. Army.

In July 1947, Marshall, now secretary of state, dispatched Wedemeyer to the Far East to assess the situation in China and Korea and to make policy recommendations to President Truman. In China, Wedemeyer's outspokenness about the "maladministration, corruption, and lethargy" he saw in the Nationalist government raised tensions between him and Chiang. Nonetheless, in the report he submitted to President Truman after his return, although conceding that Chiang's was "an unpopular repressive government," Wedemeyer advised that the United States provide military assistance to the Nationalist government. The offer of such aid, he wrote, contradicting the advice of State Department officials, need not be made contingent on Chiang Kai-shek's introducing key reforms; careful American supervision would suffice.

Wedemeyer's report was classified top secret and not released to the public until 1949, in the midst of the Chinese Communist victory and the bitter controversy in the United States over "Who lost China?"

Strategic Vision

Returning from China in 1947, Wedemeyer was assigned to the War Department's General Staff, where he served for a year as director of the Plans and Operations Division and for a further year as deputy chief of staff for plans and combat operations. In the early postwar years he was critical of his country for having failed to prosecute the war with an eye on its geopolitical outcome, in both Europe and Asia. As he wrote in a private letter from Washington in September 1946, "The picture of the world viewed objectively today reveals that we have substituted one totalitarian power or group of powers for another, and both were and continue to be equally abhorrent and unacceptable to the American people."

Wedemeyer's promotion record during the war had been nothing short of phenomenal—he would be made full general in 1953, by an act of Congress—and toward the end of the conflict he was widely regarded as a credible candidate for Army chief of staff. Yet in the postwar years his career stalled. "Wedemeyer was out of step philosophically with some of his army colleagues," historian Eiler explains, "and having incurred the displeasure of his old boss General Marshall (then secretary of state), he left the Pentagon in August 1949 to assume command of the Sixth U.S. Army headquartered in San Francisco." He retired from the military in 1951, but he was hardly finished. He went public in 1958 with *Wedemeyer Reports!*, a sharp and bitter critique of U.S. policy in the Second World War that became a controversial best seller. In it, he directly criticized Marshall for lacking strategic vision.

By allowing the delay of the cross-Channel invasion by a year, Wedemeyer wrote, and later by insisting on the unconditional surrender of Nazi Germany, the United States allowed the Soviet Union to capture the heartland of Europe and thus threaten the continent and the world.

> *After slaying one dragon, we found ourselves confronted in 1945 with a bigger and a more dangerous one. Having wanted to win at any cost, we insured the emergence of a more hostile, menacing predatory power than Nazi Germany, one which has enslaved more people than we "liberated." This fact became obvious when, only three years after her defeat, we started to resurrect the Germany we had sworn to destroy. We needed this Germany as our partner in the defense of Europe against our former ally, the Soviet Union.*

To the end of his days, Wedemeyer lamented America's poor grasp of the art and science of statecraft, and of the need to incorporate strategic vision and a sense of history, as interpreted by both civilian and military leaders, into the making of national security policy.

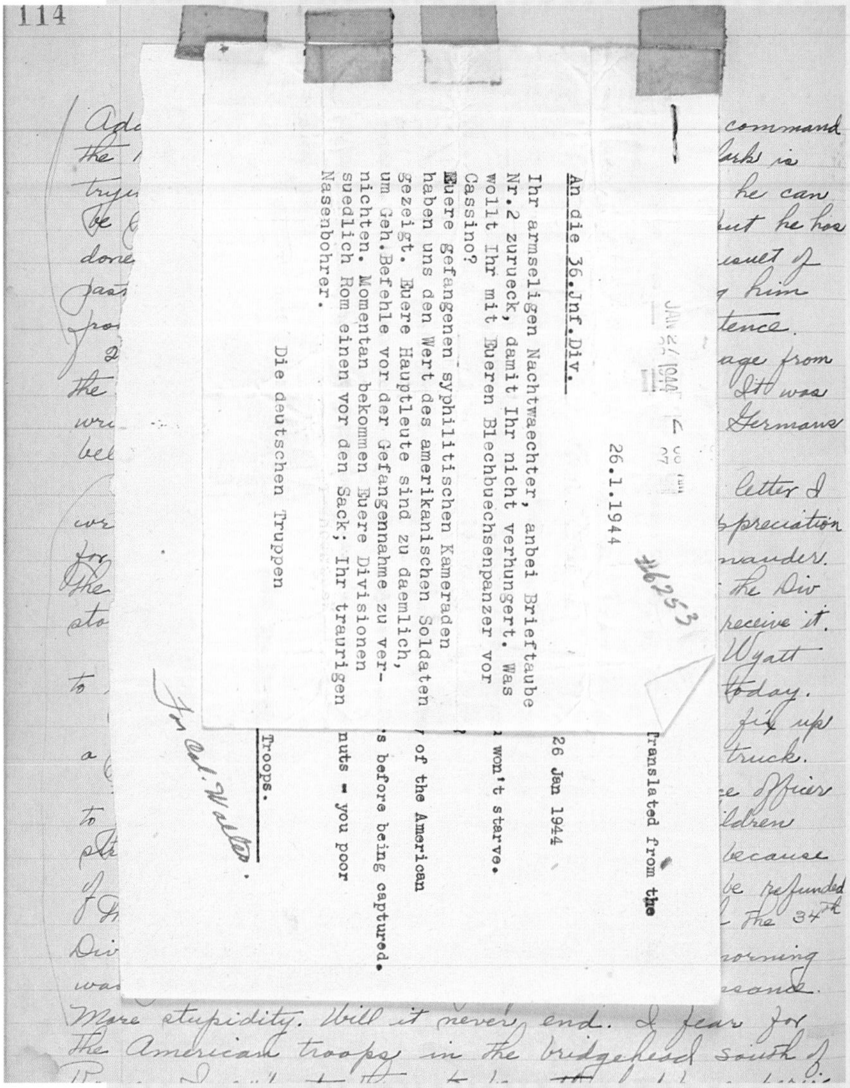

114

An die 36.Jnf.Div.

26.1.1944

Ihr armseligen Nachtwaechter, anbei Brieftaube Nr.2 zurueck, damit Ihr nicht verhungert. Was wollt Ihr mit Eueren Blechbuechsenpanzer vor Cassino?

Euere Gefangenen syphilitischen Kameraden haben uns den Wert des amerikanischen Soldaten gezeigt. Euere Hauptleute sind zu daemlich, um Geh.Befehle vor der Gefangennahme zu vernichten. Momentan bekommen Euere Divisionen suedlich Rom einen vor den Sack; Ihr traurigen Nasenbohrer.

Die deutschen Truppen

More stupidity. Will it never end. I fear for the American troops in the bridgehead south of

Page from Fred Walker's diary to which is affixed a message sent by German troops using a carrier pigeon that had been brought across the Rapido River by attacking American forces. The message, dated January 26, 1944, was translated for Walker as follows:

> To the 36 Infantry Division
>
> You poor nightwatchmen, here is pigeon #2 back so that you won't starve. What do you plan in front of Cassino, with your tin-can armor?
>
> Your captured syphilitic comrades have shown us the quality of the American soldier. Your captains are too stupid to destroy secret orders before being captured. At the moment your troops S of ROME are getting a kick in the nuts—you poor nosepickers!
>
> Signed *The German Troops*

(Fred Walker Papers)

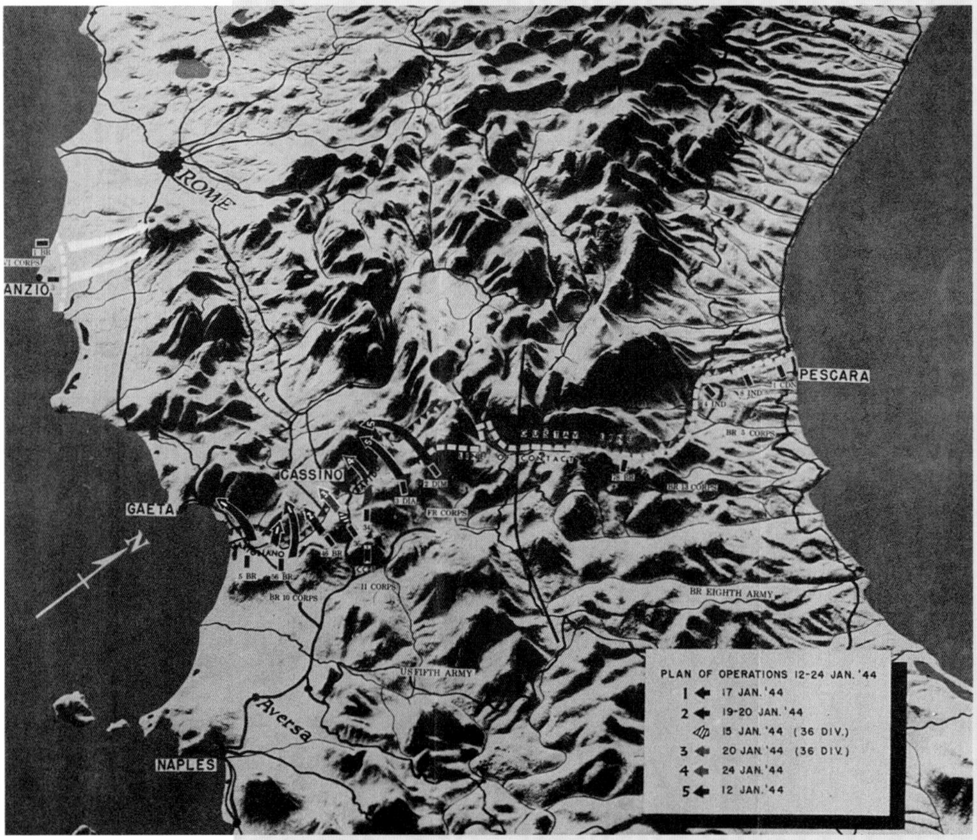

Map of midsection of Italy, showing Anzio and Cassino (from published Congressional hearings on the Rapido River crossing). (Fred Walker Papers)

MISSION IMPOSSIBLE AT CASSINO

"The first attack at Cassino in Italy on January 20, 1944, will rank high on any historical list of futile frontal assaults launched against fortified positions in the face of impossible odds." This was how Maj. Gen. Fred Walker, commanding officer of the American 36th Infantry Division, began his bitter account of the Cassino operation, one of the most controversial American battles of the Second World War.

The Battle of Cassino was in fact a series of four battles, from January to May 1944, fought against Field Marshal Albrecht Kesselring's forces dug in along what was known as the Gustav Line. Cassino was part of a larger campaign championed by Churchill as a strategy for advancing on the continent through its "soft underbelly." The Americans had never liked the idea—Wedemeyer called the British approach "periphery pecking"—and the costly battles up the boot of Italy during the autumn of 1943 turned American skepticism to anger. With the Italian campaign threatening to get bogged down in a World War I–style war of attrition, Churchill came up with an idea to break the deadlock by means of an Allied landing behind enemy lines at Anzio, thirty-five miles from Rome. The plans were approved at a Christmas conference between Churchill and Generals Eisenhower and Alexander. The date of the Anzio landing was set for January 22.

The basic idea was to make the Anzio landing after the main forces of the Fifth Army had advanced to Frosinone, a town in the Liri Valley twenty-five miles beyond Monte Cassino, the site of an ancient Benedictine monastery. What stood in the way of success were Kesselring's men, stretched out along a line running across Italy from coast to coast, most of it mountainous and bisected by fast-flowing rivers, a terrain that provided strong advantages for defending forces. The Germans were able to enhance these natural barriers by flooding the attacker's side of the rivers.

The plan was for one division—which turned out to be the American 36th—to break through the German defenses and enable the U.S. 1st Armored Division to drive into the Liri Valley. On January 16, Walker received his orders. His unit would cross the Rapido River south of Cassino on January 20 and establish a bridgehead three miles deep, in the process drawing German forces away from Anzio in time for the Allied landing on the 22nd. The Anzio force would meet up with the 1st Armored Division behind the Gustav Line for a lightning thrust at Rome.

Walker's men were supposed to cross the Rapido at two places, north and south of San Angelo, a town situated on a bluff forty feet above the water and dominating the stretches of the river where the crossings were to take place. Walker catalogued the enemy's formidable defenses, which included "houses with concrete bunkers and 88 millimeter guns concealed inside; steel pillboxes with periscopes and ball socket machine gun mounts;

undetectable wood 'schu' mines planted in profusion on all approaches; barbed wire laced with mines zigzagging across the entire front; a landscape denuded of vegetation and concealment." On both flanks, in the mountains rising behind the town—Monte Cassino (more than 1,700 feet) and Monte Maio—German artillery and observers enfiladed the river line, precluding a daytime crossing.

It was for good reason, then, that Walker had grave doubts about the planned offensive. In the First World War he received the Distinguished Service Cross for extraordinary heroism in the Marne defense of July 1918. In other words, he understood something about the difficulties of attacking a fortified river line. And the particular features of the Rapido River, with a depth of about ten feet and a current of eight to ten miles per hour, presented special challenges for an attacking force, especially its narrow width—fifty to sixty feet across—which reduced the chance for secrecy and surprise. Moreover, in the section near San Angelo the river had vertical banks rising two to three feet above the water, which was bound to impede the bridge-building efforts necessary in order for tanks to join the infantry on the other side. Also favoring the defenders, there were few roads in the approach to the river, and the river banks on both sides were clogged with thick winter mud.

The awesome task of breaking through these defenses now fell on the 36th, a one-time Texas National Guard division with little combat experience whose soldiers were extremely tired after fighting their way up from Salerno. All things considered, Walker felt that a frontal assault at San Angelo had little or no chance of success. He believed that a much better plan would be to bypass the Cassino defenses to the north where the Rapido was more fordable, the German defenses weaker, and the rocky terrain more favorable to the attacker than the mud and marshland at San Angelo. He suggested this option to the Fifth Army's commander, Gen. Mark Clark, and his corps commander, Maj. Gen. Geoffrey Keyes, but found them "disinterested and unresponsive." In an entry in his diary for January 20, Walker expressed despair:

> *Tonight the 36th Division will attempt to cross the Rapido River opposite San Angelo. Everything has been done that can be done to insure success. We might succeed but I do not now see how we can. The mission is poorly timed. The crossing is dominated by heights on both sides of the valley where German artillery observors [sic] are ready to bring down heavy artillery concentrations on our men. The river is the principal obstacle of the German main line of resistance. I do not know of a single case in military history where an attempt to cross a river that is incorporated into the main line of resistance has succeeded. So I am prepared for defeat. This mission should never have been assigned to any troops at this time, with our flanks exposed. Clark sent me his best wishes; said he was worried about*

our success. I think he is worried over the fact that he made an unwise decision when he gave us the job of crossing the river under such adverse tactical conditions. However, if we get some breaks we may succeed.

At 7:30 that evening, an Allied artillery barrage signaled the beginning of the attack. Historian John Ellis describes the action as the Germans replied in kind:

Many of their shells immediately found a target and the Texans scattered, some again blundering into uncleared clusters of mines, others trampling down the tapes that were to guide those following. Boats and makeshift bridges were abandoned so that almost 50 per cent of this equipment never even got to the river's edge. Just as the leading elements did get there, a thick mist descended, complicating yet further the task of those behind as they sought out the tapes and stumbled over abandoned boats, catwalks and corpses.

On the river, some of the assault boats sank in midstream, having been pierced by gunfire, while others capsized, pitching their occupants into the ice-cold water. Footbridges were shot to pieces and new ones had to be reconstructed from the parts that could be salvaged.

By daylight, only two battalions had managed to reach the far bank, and they had progressed just a few hundred yards. One of these battalions withdrew across its single remaining footbridge, while the other, cut off, was overrun. After a pause, Walker was ordered to make a second attempt—an order he resisted but was forced to obey—and this new assault met with similar results. A third assault was ordered but then called off; otherwise the losses to the 36th would have been more appalling still. As it was, according to the lowest estimate, the division had suffered 1,681 casualties, with 143 killed and 875 missing, out of approximately 3,000 men who had attempted to make the crossing. There was nothing to show for the effort; not one tank had been brought across the river. The Gustav line had held. Kesselring had not been forced to withdraw troops away from the coast. The landing force at Anzio was isolated.

Walker wrote in his diary for January 25: "The great losses of fine young men during the attempts to cross the Rapido to no purpose and in violation of good infantry tactics are very depressing. All chargeable to the stupidity of the highest command." In June the remains of the 36th fought their way to Rome. Some months later, after General Clark had reassigned the division's principal commanders and staff officers, Walker was eased out to a training command in the United States. After the war, the divisional association demanded and was granted a congressional inquiry, which ended up clearing Clark of responsibility for the disastrous crossing of the Rapido.

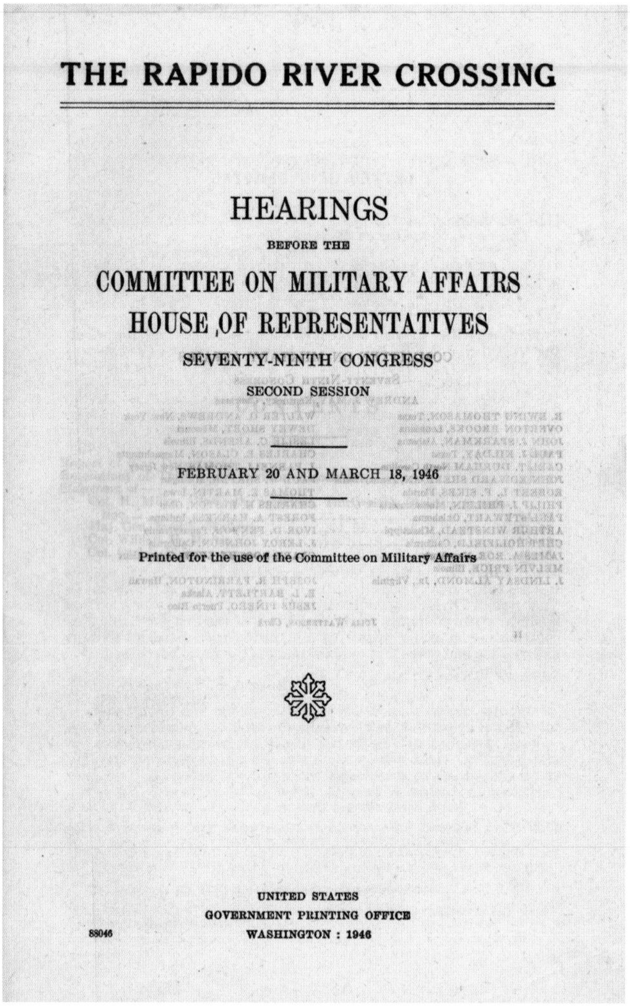
THE RAPIDO RIVER CROSSING

HEARINGS
BEFORE THE
COMMITTEE ON MILITARY AFFAIRS
HOUSE OF REPRESENTATIVES
SEVENTY-NINTH CONGRESS
SECOND SESSION

FEBRUARY 20 AND MARCH 18, 1946

Printed for the use of the Committee on Military Affairs

UNITED STATES
GOVERNMENT PRINTING OFFICE
WASHINGTON : 1946

88046

Cover page of congressional hearings on the Rapido River crossing. (Fred Walker Papers)

At the hearings, Walker's claim that he had voiced objections to the operation was sharply challenged. His corps commander, General Keyes, angrily testified that before the battle, "when I asked General Walker if he had any comments, he said, 'No, everything is all set and we'll take it—we'll do it.'" As Ellis remarks, despite the eerie "last will and testament" tenor of Walker's January 20 diary entry, quoted above, there is no proof that Walker protested publicly. "His diary might be a moving paean of praise to the 36th, as well as a bleak testament of one man's anguish, yet no diary entry would ever save a single life."

So controversy surrounds Walker's command, and much else about Cassino, though there is no disputing Clark's overriding obsession with capturing Rome, in itself a target of little strategic significance, and his paranoia that the British might arrive ahead of him and rob him of his glory. (In the event, Clark got there first, on June 4.) Ultimately, Cassino was taken, after successive battles of attrition lasting almost five months and involving American, British, French, Polish, New Zealand, Canadian, Indian, Moroccan, Algerian, Tunisian, and South African forces. Most of its German defenders had been able to escape and reestablish themselves north of Rome, along the Gothic Line. The ancient monastery on Monte Cassino, having been bombed from the air, was left in ruins.

Walker's judgment was that "Rome might have fallen in February instead of June,—if expediency had not bypassed sound doctrine; if time had been taken to marshal resources for a better prepared and more adequately supported offensive; if the priority had been to seize the high ground first; if the initial main effort had been directed against weakness instead of strength; if the high command had resisted the illusion that a straight line is the fastest distance to an object."

THE NEXT WAR

Three related pronouncements in early 1946 signaled the onset of a confrontation between the two principal victors of the Second World War. The first was Stalin's so-called election speech of February 9, in which he declared, true to the Marxist-Leninist tradition, that capitalism made war inevitable. Then came George F. Kennan's "long telegram," sent from the U.S. embassy in Moscow and arriving in Washington on February 22, which warned of a fundamental threat posed by the Soviet Union to the West. This was followed by Winston Churchill's speech at Fulton, Missouri, on March 5, in which he declared that an "iron curtain" had descended across Europe.

Postwar Berlin. (German Pictorial Collection)

ADDRESS OFFICIAL COMMUNICATIONS TO
THE SECRETARY OF STATE
WASHINGTON, D. C.

U. S. POLITICAL ADVISER
MAR 25 1946
BERLIN, GERMANY

DEPARTMENT OF STATE
WASHINGTON

March 12, 1946

AIR MAIL

SECRET

Dear Bob:

The Army recently sent to General MacNarney a copy of George Kennan's telegram no. 511 from Moscow. It was stipulated in the Army message that it be shown to you and it was on this basis that I agreed to its going. The telegram was a long and very thorough analysis of Soviet psychology, policies and methods of implementation, and concluded with some recommendations with regard to our policy. It constitutes to my mind the finest piece of analytical writing that I have ever seen come out of the Service. (It was in answer to a short telegram I sent George asking him, in the hope of drawing forth just such a message, how he felt the Soviets would proceed to implement the policy laid down in Stalin's electoral speech.) I thought it would be helpful for you to know that George's message has been received in the highest quarters here as a basic outline of future Soviet policy. That goes for the Secretary, the Secretaries of War and Navy, our highest Army and Navy authorities and also across the street. The telegram reached us, incidentally, just a day or so before the Secretary's recent speech - another document which I hope you have read with the greatest care - and although his speech had already been written, it served to confirm the advisability of putting in all it contained.

The Army asked my authorization to send the telegram to its top Commanders and it has gone accordingly to Marshall, Lee, Clark and MacArthur in addition to MacNarney. Also we have sent it in full summary as an

Info airgram

The Honorable
Robert D. Murphy,
United States Political Adviser on German Affairs,
Berlin.

AIR MAIL

-2-

Info airgram to many of our missions. (Yours was not included since you were receiving it through the Army.) It contains a lot of raw meat and in order to protect George we have had to seriously restrict its circulation.

I think you also ought to know that everyone here takes an extremely serious view of the present situation. You may or may not have seen reports of our Consul at Tabriz of the very substantial movements of Soviet troops and armor southward in Iran. The United Nations Security Council is scheduled to meet March 21. It seems clear that the Soviet Government will decline to withdraw Soviet troops from Iran, troops that are now there in direct violation of a treaty. The showdown will probably prove once and for all that the United Nations is not equipped to handle a dispute between the Big Three Powers. Its failure will then become a definite turning point in the future of the world with the Western Powers preparing as actively as possible against some ultimate conflict with the Soviet Union. I am convinced that only adequate strength will stop future Soviet aggression, at least until there have been internal changes visible signs of which are not yet evident. In our present deplorable condition of physical and moral demobilization, this is a pretty grim prospect.

This situation has, of course, very important implications with regard to our future policy toward Germany and I think certainly calls for some careful revision of both the letter and spirit of 1067.

Meanwhile, we keep more busy than ever here, as you may imagine and I look back with great pleasure on our very interesting and enjoyable motor tour through Germany last December.

With all good wishes,

As ever,

Doc

P.S. Gen. Hilldring is due to join us about April 8. – which is very good news.

Doc

Letter from H. Freeman "Doc" Matthews, director of the Office of European Affairs at the U.S. State Department, to Robert D. Murphy, U.S. political adviser on German affairs in Berlin, March 12, 1946. (Robert D. Murphy Papers)

The profound influence of these three moments can be seen from an interesting exchange of letters early in 1946 between H. Freeman "Doc" Matthews, director of the Office of European Affairs at the U.S. Department of State, and Robert D. Murphy, U.S. political adviser on German affairs attached to Gen. Lucius Clay's administration in Berlin. Matthews originated the exchange with a letter dated March 12, which revealed that it was he who had prompted Kennan's long telegram (here identified as #511) by sending a short one of his own. Matthews requested that Kennan offer some context for the speech Stalin had delivered on the eve of the elections to the Supreme Soviet in which he declared that "the development of world capitalism proceeds not in the path of smooth to even progress but through crisis and the catastrophes of war." Matthews's query ended up eliciting from Kennan an eight-thousand-word response, which laid the foundations for the strategy of containment that would guide American foreign policy during the Cold War.

Kennan's telegram identified both Russian and Soviet influences on the behavior of Stalin's Kremlin. A traditional Russian sense of fear and insecurity with respect to the outside world (now described, Soviet-style, as "capitalist encirclement") was magnified by ideological beliefs about the ultimate incompatibility of communism and capitalism. Kennan warned that Americans had to begin taking seriously the Soviet leadership's innate hostility toward the West: "We have here a political force committed fanatically to the belief that with the US there can be no permanent modus vivendi, that it is desirable and necessary that the internal harmony of our society be disrupted, our traditional way of life be destroyed, the international authority of our state be broken, if Soviet power is to be secure."

The effect of Kennan's telegram was immediate and enormous. It was must-reading within the Washington foreign policy establishment. "To say the least," Kennan wrote in his memoirs, "it went 'the rounds.' The President, I believe, read it. The Secretary of the Navy, Mr. James Forrestal, had it reproduced and evidently made it required reading for hundreds, if not thousands, of higher officers in the armed services."

A few weeks later came apparent substantiation of Kennan's warning as Moscow delayed the withdrawal of its troops from northern Iran. The Russians and the British had jointly occupied Iran in 1941 in order to prevent the oil fields from coming under the control of the Germans. However, when their agreed-on withdrawal date arrived, in early March 1946, the British alone removed their forces, while the Soviets stalled and played for time. An American consul at Tabriz reported large-scale troop movements, and Washington wondered whether this might not be a moment of truth.

The sense of threat inspired Washington to reconsider the document that guided U.S. policy toward postwar German reconstruction, JCS 1067 (the letters stand for Joint Chiefs of Staff). It was a very restrictive arrangement that forbade Americans of the occupation force from fraternizing with the German people. The document even insisted on separate toilets, which Murphy called "a sort of Jim Crow feature." More important, "it prohibited employment as executives or skilled workmen of any Germans who had been more than nominal members of the Nazi party." JCS 1067 bore the marks of the earlier Morgenthau Plan, which sought to perpetuate Germany's weakened economic condition. For example, it prohibited Germans in the American zone from producing more iron and steel than was minimally required for domestic consumption. As Matthews indicates, the effect of the February–March events was to reverse America's treatment of Germany as a conquered nation.

Matthews's letter was read by Murphy in Berlin, where the four powers were negotiating an arrangement for administering Germany and where, at that moment, things seemed to be going reasonably well. By the time Murphy responded to Matthews, on April 3, 1946, the Soviets had withdrawn their troops from Iran. Murphy congratulated Matthews for having prompted Kennan's telegram—"I think that you deserve a large bouquet of orchids for having engineered this process"—yet he registered a negative reaction to it among the military officers in Berlin. General Clay felt that the State Department action in passing along Kennan's telegram was "a sort of Pearl Harbor warning," designed to protect the department in case of a Soviet attack. Murphy, who shared the skepticism of his colleagues in Berlin, assured Matthews that General Eisenhower and Marshal Zhukov were getting along just fine, and that the last thing the Soviets wanted was renewed warfare: "I would like to make it quite clear that in our local innocence, we have never and still do not believe for a minute in imminent Soviet aggression."

This letter from Murphy provoked a firm response on April 18 from Matthews, who argued that whatever harmony might prevail among individual soldiers and diplomats in Berlin, the essential fact of relations between Russia and the West was a fundamental clash of worldviews. In this second letter Matthews used the term "Iron Curtain," which was absent from his earlier communication, written just one week after Churchill's Iron Curtain speech in Fulton, Missouri. In that speech, Churchill stated publicly what was being said privately among American officials. In his memorably dramatic formulation, "From Stettin in the Baltic to Trieste in the Adriatic, an iron curtain has descended across the continent." As Matthews's letters to Murphy attest, "Iron Curtain" quickly became part of official Washington's vocabulary.

A speech by Secretary of State James Byrnes in Stuttgart on September 6, 1946, took account of the changed political environment in announcing a new American approach to Germany: "It is not in the interests of the German people, or in the interests of world peace, that Germany should become a pawn or a partner in the military struggle for power between the East and the West. . . . The American people want to return the government of Germany to the people of Germany. The American people want to help the German people to win their way back to an honorable place among the free and peace-loving nations of the world." The Soviet Union and the United States would continue to call for a reunified Germany administered by the four occupation powers, but in fact the battle lines of the Cold War were now hardening within the borders of a divided Germany and a divided Berlin.

Berlin, 1946. General Dwight D. Eisenhower, U.S. Army Chief of Staff, and General Lucius D. Clay, deputy U.S. Military Governor in Germany. (Robert D. Murphy Papers)

On les aura !

Chapter Six

POSTERS AT WAR

The Hoover Archives poster collection is one of its best-known and most impressive resources. Yet this is not what was originally intended. In his first report on the Hoover War Collection, published in 1921, Director Ephraim Adams asserted that a decision had been made early on not to attempt a comprehensive collection of large-format posters and proclamations. His reasoning exemplifies an earlier era's lack of interest in social history:

> *They constitute, unquestionably, valuable historical material, though the usual display posters, urging war loans, etc, are of less value than official proclamations and orders. In either case it is difficult to preserve posters for use by students as they quickly fall to pieces on repeated folding and handling, and the size in itself prevents study and analysis by comparison.*

"Nevertheless," Adams reported, "the Hoover War Collection has several thousand posters from all the countries at war."

That was in 1921. Today, the Hoover's poster collection is one of the largest in the United States, with more than 33,000 catalogued political posters from around the world and more than double that number as yet uncatalogued. It ranges over the entire twentieth century and includes posters from more than eighty countries, the majority from Europe and America. The collection is a treasure trove for scholars and writers—and not just those looking for book illustrations. The posters themselves have become a subject of research, as visual evidence not only of artistic and aesthetic tastes but of social and political trends, as well as of the techniques of propaganda.

ARTISTIC PROPAGANDA

Political posters originated at least as early as the eighteenth century, but their heyday as a form of art and communication spanned the period from the last decades of the nineteenth century to the end of the Second World War. The most influential artistic developments took place in the first two decades of the twentieth century, a period marked by fruitful intellectual and artistic collaboration and influence across European borders. International exhibits showcased works from different countries so that both artists and the general public were exposed to various trends in poster art.

As in all artistic fields, innovation was not always immediately appreciated or understood. Part of the peculiarity of the poster as an artistic genre, particularly when used to sell products, promote causes, or inform the public, is the emphasis on its immediate impact. No matter how innovative the technique or daring the use of color or design, if the poster is

"Wake up, America!" USA, c. 1917. James Montgomery Flagg.

for some reason poorly understood or otherwise not well received by its target audience then it is considered a failure. Thus, when it comes to the business of selling, be it goods or ideas, the artists' aesthetic preferences have to be tempered by the cultural and aesthetic tastes of the intended audience.

Popular regard, on the other hand, did not necessarily translate into critical acclaim. Arguably, the most famous American poster images from World War I are James Montgomery Flagg's portrait of a severe Uncle Sam asserting "I want you" and Howard Chandler Christy's recruitment posters featuring sexy girls making provocative statements such as "I want you for the Navy" (page 207). One contemporary art critic, though admitting that "such designs appealed to certain intellects and thereby served their purpose," dismissed them as "poorly drawn sketches" and "not posters at all." These comments illustrate the precarious position posters occupied in attempting to bridge the elitist world of art, which is generally antagonistic toward commercialism, and the world of popular culture, in which the posters' target audience was situated.

Beyond these high-brow, low-brow tensions, evaluating the success or failure of posters poses an interesting challenge. It is often impossible to determine how influential individual posters were, how they were received by their intended audience, or even if they reached them at all. The "Christy girls" appear to have been quite popular in their day, yet it is difficult to document how they might have affected navy enlistment. As with all art forms, posters considered artistic failures in their day might be embraced by critics of later generations.

One of the few documented examples of a convergence of artistic and popular tastes comes out of Russia. There, during the first year of the Great War, Leonid Pasternak (father of the author of *Doctor Zhivago* and a prominent artist in his own right) was commissioned to produce a poster promoting relief for casualties of war. The resulting work, "Aid to war victims" (page 207), is better known as "The Wounded Soldier." The poster's design was minimal realist: against a plain backdrop, a uniformed Russian soldier, exhausted, leans against a wall, holding a bayonet rifle in one hand and applying a cloth to a bleeding head wound with the other. Its artistic merit aside, the poster proved to be a tremendous popular success. According to eyewitnesses, after the poster was displayed throughout Moscow crowds gathered before it and women wept. Postcard versions of the image were printed and sold in large quantities for fundraising campaigns. Interestingly, the one person on record as disapproving of Pasternak's poster was Tsar Nicholas II, who reportedly would have preferred to see more heroic Russian soldiers.

Few posters left behind such well-documented evidence of their popular reception. This, despite the fact that the governments that produced a steady stream of posters, particularly in times of war, placed a great deal of importance on their propaganda value. The information departments of various countries constantly monitored each other's poster production. Beyond the usual aesthetic and stylistic influences among artists across geographic borders, the political use of posters in wartime inspired a great deal of deliberate cross-border expropriation of images and themes. And because their themes involved, however indirectly, matters of life and death, most wartime posters have a sense of urgency about them. (In peacetime, only the posters of the totalitarian states of the 1930s—regimes that could thrive only in an atmosphere of perpetual crisis and vigilance against enemies—delivered this kind of forceful energy. As John Keegan has written, adapting Clausewitz, "Totalitarianism was the political continuation of war by other means.") This combination of competing and compelling images means that wartime posters offer the most fruitful material for contrasting national styles and messages.

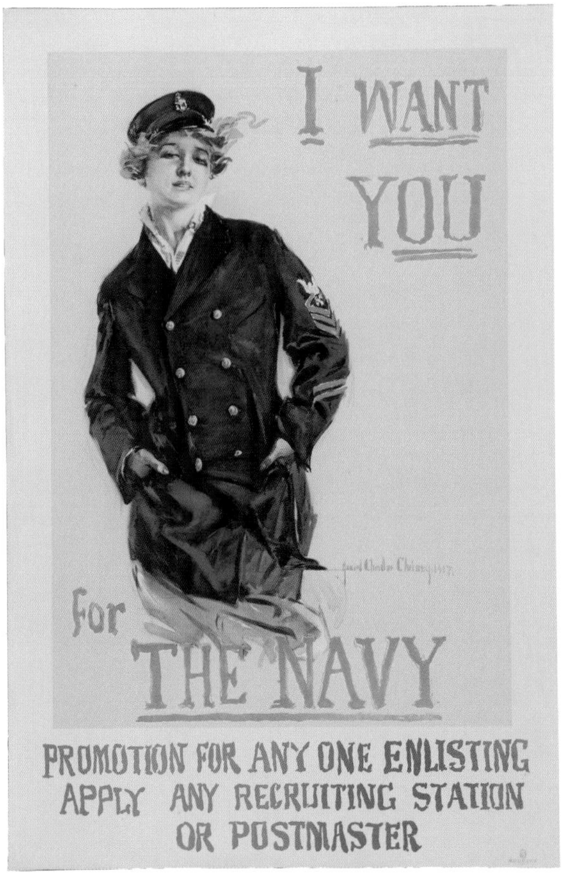

"I want you for the Navy." USA, 1917. Howard Chandler Christy.

"Aid to war victims." Russia, c. 1914. Leonid Pasternak.

THE FIRST WORLD WAR

The Great War witnessed an enormous expansion of the political role of the poster. By the time hostilities broke out in August 1914, the poster was already widely used for artistic and commercial purposes in Europe and the United States. Yet the transition to politics—the "mobilization" of posters—did not everywhere go smoothly.

France and Britain were both fairly prolific producers of wartime posters, in part because of the prewar popularity of the genre, which had created a large pool of prominent poster artists. In wartime Russia, on the other hand, posters were relatively underused. This was due in part to Russia's relatively undeveloped commercial culture, as well as the tsarist regime's general incompetence and its distaste for most manifestations of modernity. It also had a lot to do with the autocracy's inability to recognize the importance of popular mobilization, as well as its mistrust of it.

The United States entered the conflict late, in April 1917, but its poster artists had not been idle since 1914. In Washington, the Division of Pictorial Publicity, formed almost immediately after President Wilson brought the country into the war, mobilized some of the best-known artists and illustrators in America, most of whom supported the war and eagerly volunteered their talents and time. In the end, although the United States was at

"Enlist." USA, 1915. Fred Spear.

"Remember Belgium." USA, 1918. Ellsworth Young.

war for a comparatively brief eighteen months, its political posters left their artistic mark on the genre and may have substantially contributed to the American war effort.

In all countries during World War I, political posters were enlisted principally to help mobilize the population for military service (an especially urgent cause in the case of Great Britain, which still relied on volunteers) and encourage people to purchase war bonds and support war loans. Posters appealed to citizens' patriotism and a sense of duty, or played on their sense of guilt. Many used ethnic, racial, and cultural stereotypes to demonize the enemy. Poster designs could differ widely even within a country. Not all posters employed visual images; many relied exclusively on a text to get their point across. One American poster promoting war bonds, for example, delivered its message in black letters against a white background: "If you don't come across with your money, Kaiser Bill will come across with his army. Take your choice." Another textual poster played to feelings of patriotic duty: "The true American is the one who sticks by America in peace as well as in war. The coming Victory Liberty Loan will be a test of *your* Americanism."

As for visual images, a great deal of emphasis was placed on the bloodthirstiness and heartlessness of the German military, notably in the sinking of the *Lusitania* (and, more generally, German submarine warfare) and the mistreatment of civilians in occupied Belgium. Two of the most famous of these German-atrocity posters, both American, are in the Hoover collection. "Enlist," published in 1915, before America entered the war, shows a drowned mother and child sinking to the ocean's depths (page 208). The other shows a silhouette of a German soldier in spiked helmet dragging off a young girl against a backdrop of fiery destruction. The full caption reads, "Remember Belgium. Buy Bonds. Fourth Liberty Loan" (page 209).

In addition to playing upon sympathy and compassion for the embattled Europeans, U.S. Army recruitment posters appealed to the young American male's sense of adventure and masculinity. These posters sometimes give the impression of colorful travel advertisements for exotic vacation spots. Others take a more subdued approach, appealing to the young American's national pride and sense of duty. One poster seems intended to strike several chords at once: "And they thought we couldn't fight" shows an exuberantly macho doughboy standing in no-man's land after a battle, sporting a head wound and a collection of three spiked helmets, like so many German scalps (page 211).

One recruitment poster, James Montgomery Flagg's "The Navy needs you!" addressed differences of social class by juxtaposing a smartly dressed young man reading a newspaper and a muscular sailor in uniform. With a glamorous Columbia looking on, a sword and American flag in her outstretched hands, the sailor admonishes his dandified contemporary, "Don't *read* American history—*make it*!" This appeal to action takes place as a sea battle is under way behind them (page 211).

"And they thought we couldn't fight." USA, c. 1918. Clyde Forsythe.

"The Navy needs you!" USA, c. 1917. James Montgomery Flagg.

"If you sidestep *now* you will goosestep *later*." USA, c. 1917. Hager.

"We'll get them!" France, 1916. Jules Abel Faivre.

"One last effort and we'll get it." France, c. 1918. Eugène Courboin.

Humor was a device used frequently in America's wartime posters. This seems to have been in part a result of cultural disposition, but undoubtedly the country's great distance from the Western front had much to do with it. If other belligerents saved their humor—or satire, as was more often the case—for the enemy, Americans seem to have been more willing to smile at themselves, even when the subject was the risk to their freedom. An American poster from 1918 depicts a large goose in German uniform with the requisite spiked helmet; its message reads: "If you sidestep *now* you will goosestep *later*" (page 211).

One of the most famous French posters of the war, "We'll get them!" (1916) portrays the French infantryman as a picture of energy and confidence (page 211). By the time America's doughboys began arriving in Europe, the war had long before ceased to be an adventure for the British and the French, having settled down to a long stalemate in the trenches. Their posters reflect the evolution of the conflict into a battle of endurance and survival. Though the grim reality of war could not be captured within the genre of motivational propaganda, the posters gradually became more realistic. Determination to outlast the enemy became the dominant theme.

Two posters illustrate the point. One, promoting a French loan subscription, shows a gaunt soldier attempting to plant a battle-worn flag emblazoned with the word "Liberté" atop a bleeding globe (page 213). In another French poster from the last year of the war, a group of soldiers in the uniforms of the various Allied countries, with the Frenchman leading the way, is shown resolutely scaling a peak marked with the German iron cross and guarded by a ragged but still formidable German eagle. The text reads, "One last effort and we'll get it" (page 212).

Overall, French posters from this period, building on a strong poster-art tradition, are considered to be the most interesting artistically. British posters were deemed too practical and prosaic, with some art critics attributing this characteristic to the "taint" of commercialism. The British seem to have produced the largest share of textual posters, such as "Feed the guns with war bonds and help to end the war" (page 214). Among the best remembered visual posters produced in Britain during the First World War is "Step into your place," with its sober depiction of the road to uniformity (page 214).

"Liberté." France, c. 1917. Jules Abel Faivre.

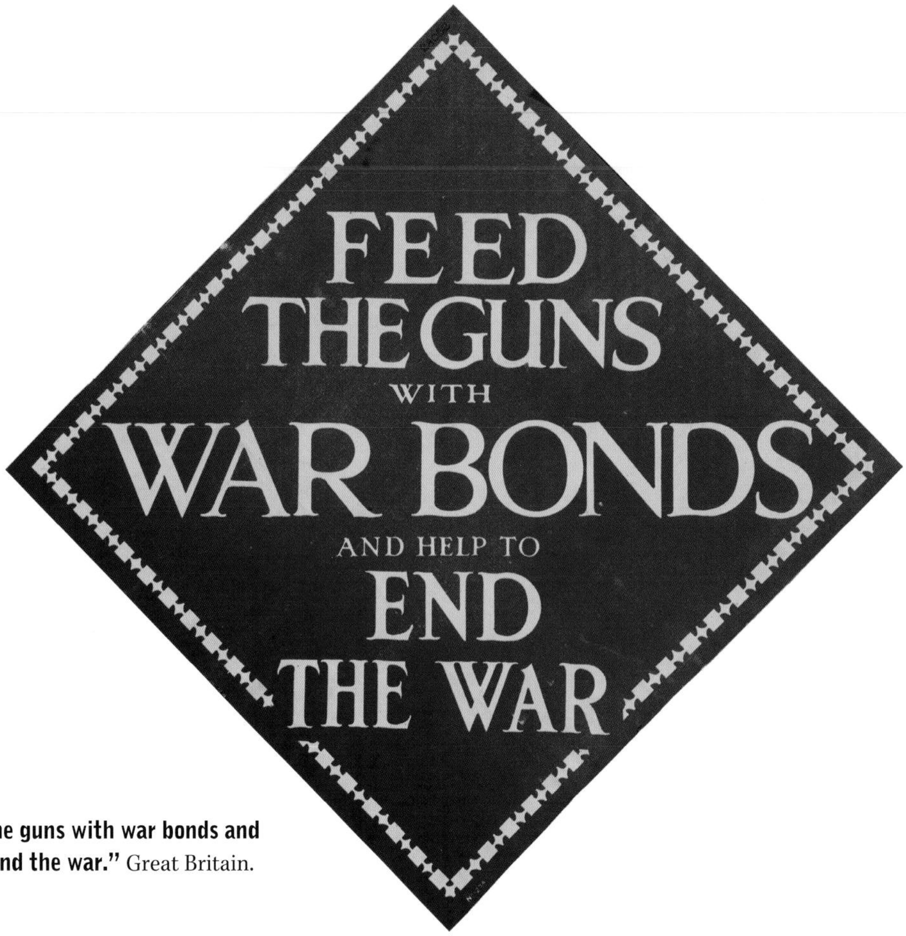

"Feed the guns with war bonds and help to end the war." Great Britain.

"Step into your place." Great Britain, 1915.

German posters from the Great War stand out in several ways. In part owing to technical obstacles, they were less colorful than the posters of other countries. The Germans relied rather more on internal images—allusions to the superiority of German history and culture—and rather less on demonizing the enemy. (Hitler later remarked on this distinction and how it worked to Germany's disadvantage in the war effort.) German artists were clearly aware of the way their country was depicted in propaganda posters in the Allied countries, most memorably as a rampaging ape in a spiked helmet. Their attempts to rectify Germany's image problem as the "bloodthirsty Hun" sometimes produced curious results. One poster portrayed Germany as a small hedgehog defending itself against the lion (Britain), the bear (Russia), and the rooster (France). The war, in other words, was not about German aggression but German self-defense (page 216).

In a similar vein there was the "Who is the barbarian?" series, which sought to demonstrate the cultural superiority of the Germans, as measured by such achievements as level of education and number of Nobel Prize winners. Here the English were the favorite point of comparison. One such poster shows a pudgy German boy wearing a spiked helmet and military coat and holding a toy sword; he looms over a puny English boy and his toy bulldog. Across the top is the six-syllable German word for population growth, which, as the numbers indicate, had strongly favored Germany since its formation as an independent state in 1871 (page 216).

Because the war did not take place on German soil, passionate calls for the defense of the homeland were not as prominent. Yet as the war dragged on and Germany's chances of victory diminished, German posters adopted a more stoical tone, even when the theme was self-defense. A mobilization poster, done in drab browns and yellows and depicting a soldier with his wife and child, encourages German men not yet in uniform to enlist for the Imperial Army (*Reichswehr*): "Defend your children! Defend your wives! Defend yourselves!" (page 216).

Russian posters in the Great War were a special case. Most employed a traditional folk style that makes them seem out of place alongside examples from most other countries. "The great European war" coopts a scene from a medieval legend to portray an embattled Russia. A medieval Russian knight faces off against a three-headed creature representing the Central Powers: Austria, whose head has been cut off; Germany, whose neck is wounded; and a vulnerable Turkey (page 217). Russian posters avoided realistic depictions of the war and often relied on crude mocking humor to ridicule the enemy. One poster shows a larger-than-life Russian peasant in winter clothing surrounded by tiny figures representing various members of the Entente, who are all trying to surrender and hide in the warmth of the Russian's winter coat. The magnanimous peasant's response is, "I understand that you all want to get warm; but why so many of you at once?" (page 216).

"Germany's hour of hardship." Germany. A. Franz.

"Defend your children! Defend your wives! Defend yourselves!" Germany, c. 1918. A. M. Cay.

"I understand that you all want to get warm; but why so many of you at once?" Russia, 1914. Iunak.

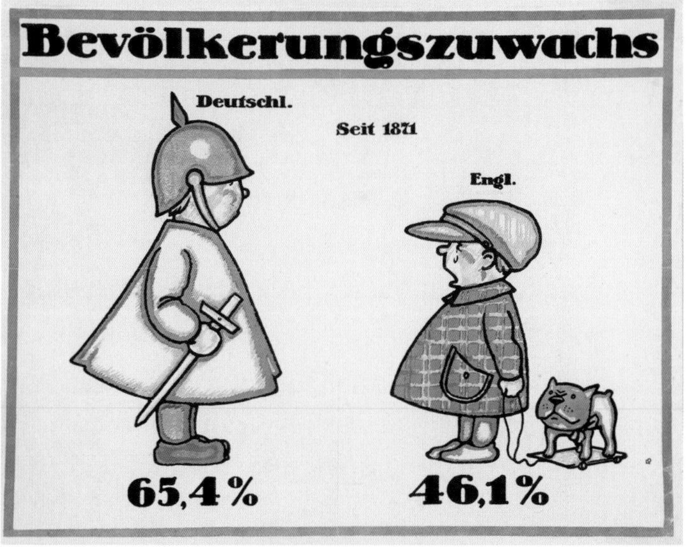

"Population growth." Germany, c. 1914.

"The great European war." Russia, c. 1915.

"1941." USSR.

"Ramming is the weaponry of heroes!" USSR, 1941. A. Voloshin.

"Hard times. Hard duties. Hard hearts." Germany, 1943.

"Light means your death!" Germany, c. 1944. Schmitt.

For all of the reasons noted—and despite notable exceptions such as Leonid Pasternak's "The Wounded Soldier"—Imperial Russia did not excel at the political poster. That this was more the result of politics than of culture became strikingly apparent shortly after the Bolsheviks took power. They found at their disposal a willing and able army of artists, both traditional and avant-garde. The Bolshevik regime proved to be especially adept at making innovative use of political posters to help consolidate their revolution and win a ferociously fought civil war against the White armies.

THE SECOND WORLD WAR

By the time of World War II, other propaganda outlets, such as radio, were becoming more widespread, and the poster lost the preeminence it had enjoyed in the First World War. The poster was no longer the cutting-edge genre, and because of this political posters made during the Second World War are, on the whole, less interesting from an artistic point of view. Perhaps because the stakes were so much higher in that war's total struggle to the death, artistic merit took second place to the force of the message.

Once again the essential themes of the posters were the same for all the belligerents—unity in a time of adversity, willingness to sacrifice for victory, total participation. As in World War I, the progress of the military conflict is reflected in each country's posters. The earliest Soviet war posters, for example, sound a note of alarm and even desperation. A poster made in the months after the Nazi invasion shows a Russian village on fire, with a ghostly "1941" written in red against the night sky (page 218). "Ramming is the weaponry of heroes!" proclaims another early Soviet World War II poster, promoting what is essentially a suicide mission by a defending pilot (page 218). As the tide of war shifted in the Soviets' favor, the tone of their posters became increasingly triumphal.

Nazi Germany's war posters followed the opposite trajectory: from the early assurances of easy victory to sullen desperation of the last years and particularly the final months of the war. The turning point was the defeat of the Germans at Stalingrad in early 1943. One poster from that year, "Hard times. Hard duties. Hard hearts," depicted the new sense not of guaranteed victory but of grim determination (page 218). By 1944, posters such as "Light means your death!" conveyed the sense of German vulnerability (page 218).

The most distinctive feature of the World War II posters as compared to their predecessors—aside from the glorification of the air war, which had played a lesser role in the earlier conflict—was what they revealed about ongoing social changes at the home front. Once again, the general theme was unity of purpose between the armed forces and the

"Let's *all* fight." USA, 1942.

"Be American!" USA, c. 1943.

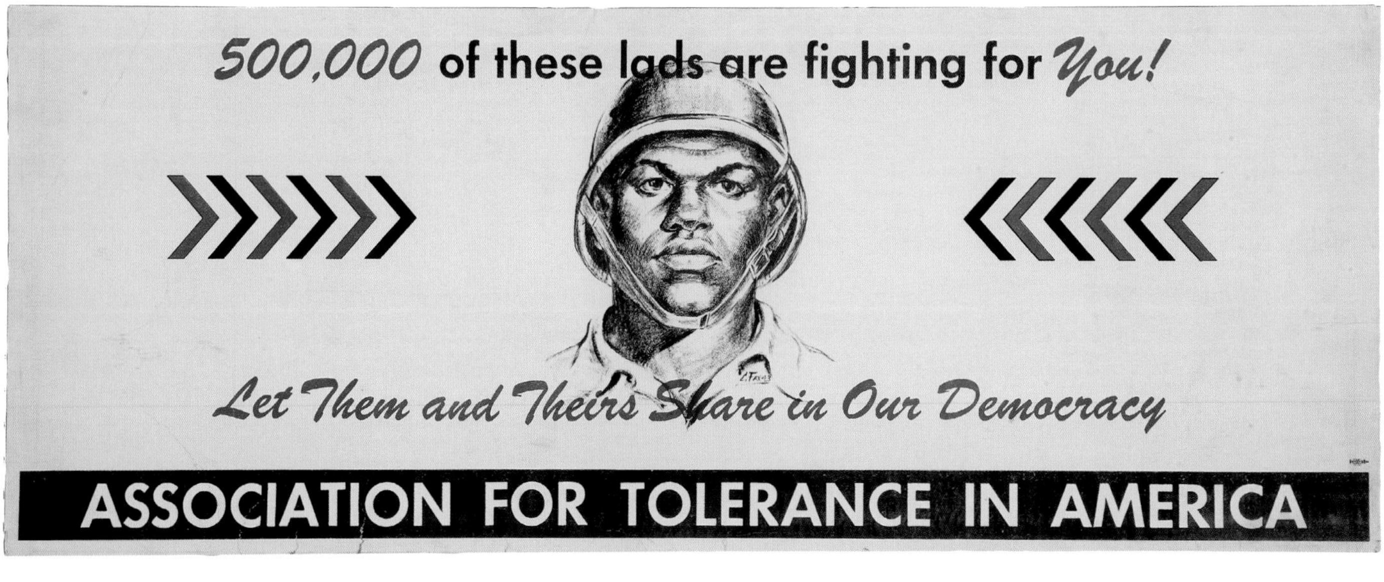

"500,000 of these lads are fighting for You!" USA, c. 1945. E. Fax.

"Soldiers *without* guns." USA, 1944. Adolph Treidler.

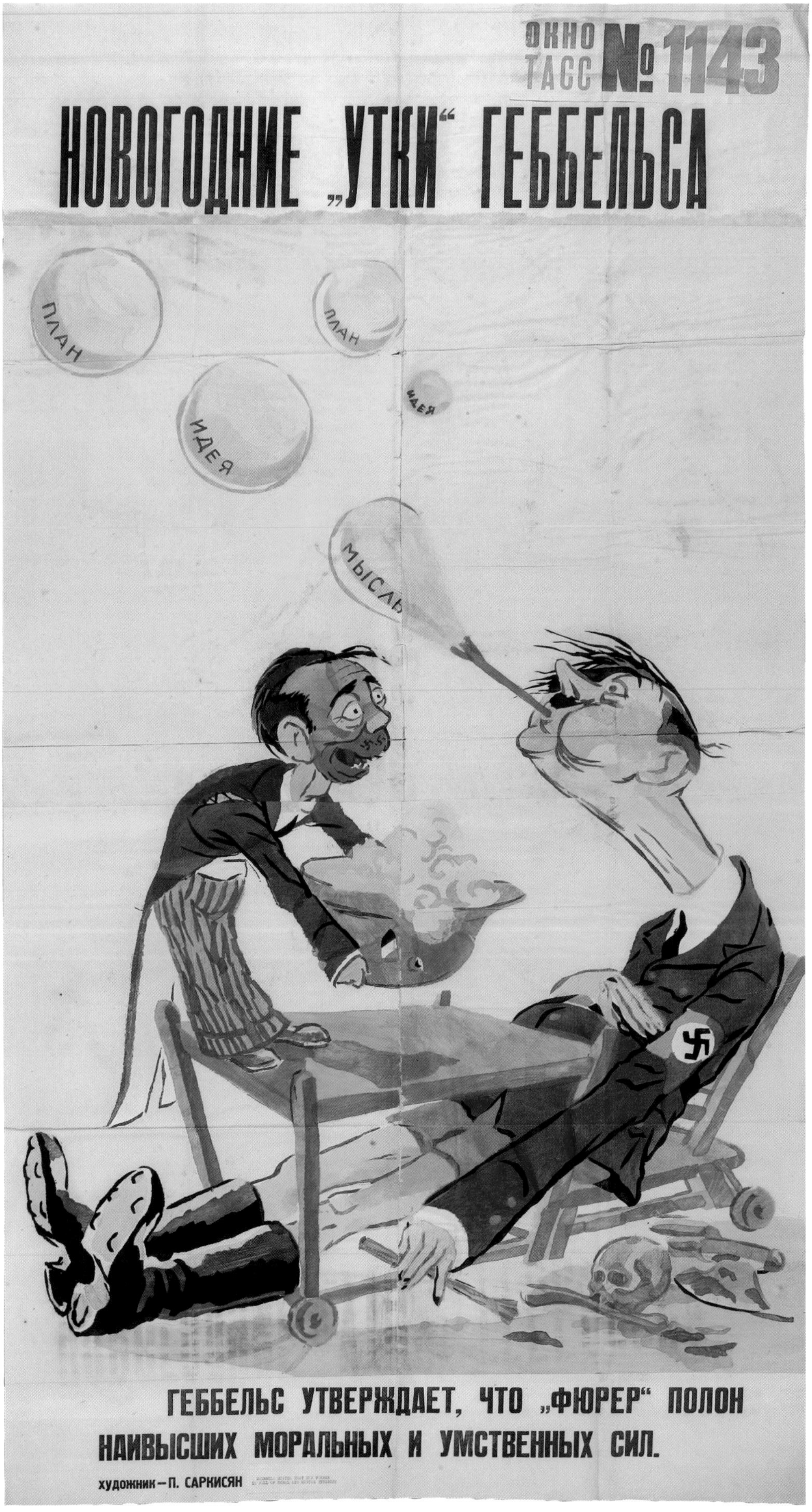

“Goebbels’s New Year’s ‘Canards.’ ” USSR, 1943. P. Sarkisian.

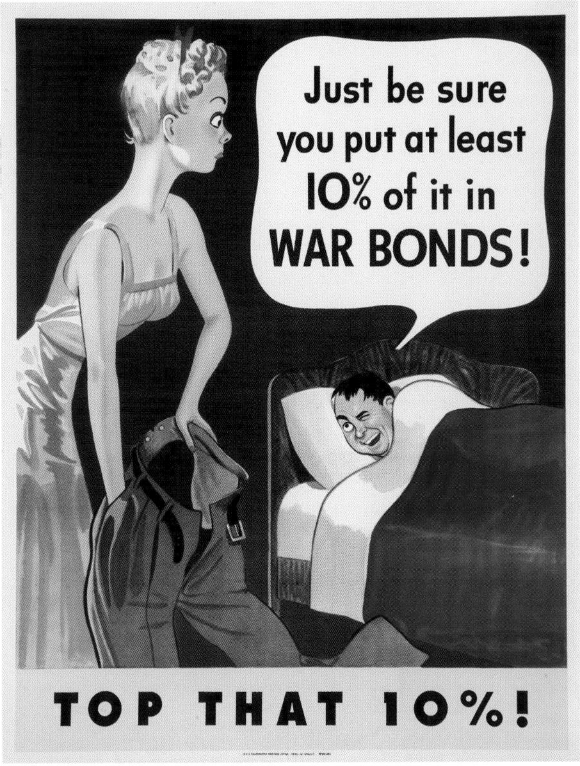

"Just be sure you put at least 10% of it in WAR BONDS!" USA, 1942.

"When you ride ALONE you ride with Hitler!" USA, 1943. Weimer Pursell.

"Wisht I was old enuf to be a marine!" USA, W. Willens.

civilian population. This time, however, more than civilians' money and discretion were required to achieve victory; in this total war victory required civilians to serve their country in factories and shipyards. "Let's *all* fight" shows a U.S. soldier going off to battle, propelled into action by the industrial workers in the rear (page 220).

American national unity is the theme of a poster depicting a military cemetery, where a cross in the foreground is labeled with a question mark. Was the unknown soldier's name "Smith? Kelly? Cohen? Svoboda?" (page 220).The answer, as the poster's text explains, was that it did not matter whether the dead soldier was a Protestant, Catholic, or Jew; the point is, he was an American. Posters recognizing the contribution of African American soldiers to the armed forces were issued by the Association for Tolerance in America. One of these used the force of numbers to make its argument: "500,000 of these lads are fighting for You! Let Them and Theirs Share in our Democracy" (page 220).

One of the most important social changes reflected in World War II posters is the mobilized status of women. In the posters from the First World War, women largely serve as images to beckon, seduce, shame, and otherwise recruit men into military service. The enduring image is the dreamy-eyed Christy girl in a military uniform striking a come-hither pose. Such flirtatiousness is generally absent from the posters of the Second World War, when women assumed a vital role in the workforce. An instructive counterpoint to the Christy girls are the three formidable women—two factory workers and a secretary—in "Soldiers *without* guns" (page 221).

Humor as a device in wartime posters once again distinguished the belligerent countries one from another. German posters seem utterly devoid of humor, even when the war was going well for the Axis powers. In the depiction of their enemies as well, the Germans preferred the grotesque to satire. In the Soviet Union, domestic themes were approached with gravity and pomposity, befitting the grandiose traditions of socialist realism. Satire was reserved for the enemy, as in "Goebbels's New Year's 'Canards,'" from late 1943, which showed a demented Hitler, slumped in his chair and blowing bubbles labeled "plan," "idea," and "thought." The caption at the bottom explains the double entendre of the title: "Goebbels confirms that 'the Führer' is at his moral and mental peak" (page 222).

In Britain and the United States, on the other hand, humor was used to further a wide range of domestic causes. A poster promoting war bonds shows a young blonde in a nightgown startled by her husband (or lover) who wakes up to find her going through his pants pockets. Her eyes are fixed on the text of his exhortation: "Just be sure you put at least 10% of it in WAR BONDS!" (page 223). A poster encouraging the economizing of gasoline shows a dapper young man at the wheel of a car, with an outline of a familiar figure seated alongside him and the admonition, "When you ride ALONE you ride with Hitler!" (page 223). Humor was used for recruitment posters too. "Wisht I was old enuf to be a marine!" says

"**Be smart: Act dumb! Loose talk can cost lives.**" USA, 1942. O. Soglow.

"**The enemy is listening in!**" Germany.

"**One word too many . . . one more death.**" Belgium.

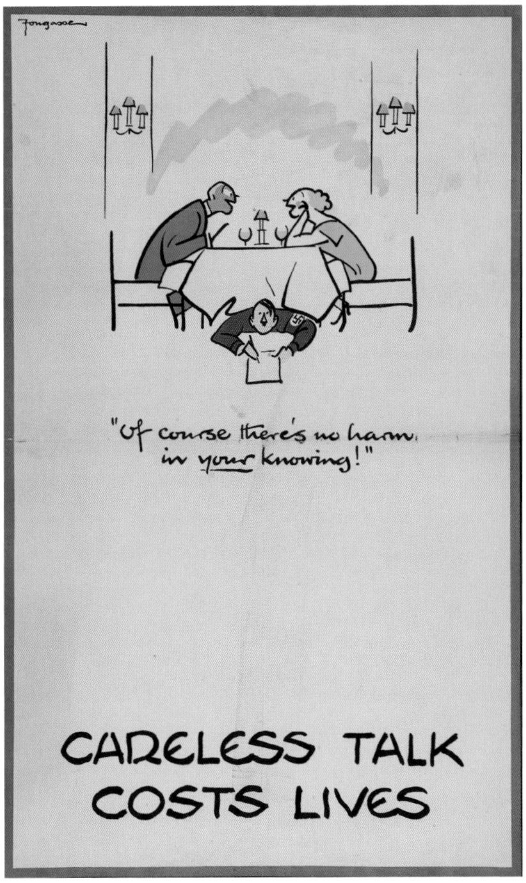

"**Careless talk costs lives.**" Great Britain. Fongasse.

"That liberty shall not perish from the earth." USA, 1918. Joseph Pennell.

one regretful little boy to another, as a marine takes advantage of one of the opportunities offered by enlistment in the corps (page 223).

A comparison of posters devoted to the importance of maintaining secrecy is also revealing of the varying national styles. Every belligerent country produced at least a few posters that sought to convey to the population the potential consequences of careless words. The continental European "Hush" posters tend to be deadly serious; American and British artists turned out both serious and humorous variations of the danger of loose lips sinking ships (page 225).

If our estimation of a poster's design can change over time as artistic tastes change, so can our reaction to its content under the force of intervening events. A striking case in point is the 1918 poster by Joseph Pennel depicting an air and submarine attack on New York City (page 226). "That liberty shall not perish from the earth," an enormously popular poster, was printed in two million copies. A horror fantasy designed to bring the war home to Americans, it invited them to imagine what it would be like to live in a European city under attack. For many Americans after the terrorist attack of September 11, 2001, the image reminds us of our profound sense of vulnerability and evokes a wistful nostalgia for a time when wars were fought "over there."

RFE
EDOM FO
ACHTUN
SIE VERLASSE
WEST BER

Chapter Seven

PHILOSOPHERS OF FREEDOM

The ideas of two intellectual giants, Sidney Hook and Karl Popper, illuminate the great struggles of the twentieth century between tyranny and freedom.

Hook, the philosopher and polemicist, underwent one of those dizzying conversions from dedicated Marxist to staunch anti-Communist once he came to recognize the threat to freedom posed by Communism. He did not, like many disillusioned radicals of the 1930s, simply drop out of politics but instead rushed to the intellectual barricades to combat the progressive image of Stalin's USSR among American liberals and leftists.

Popper was the century's greatest philosopher of science, the most formidable critic of Marxist doctrine, and one of the most effective advocates of the open society. Whereas Hook, the consummate New York intellectual, focused his energies on the defense of liberty in America, Popper, the exile from Central Europe, presented a more general argument in defense of freedom, securing his ideas a worldwide audience.

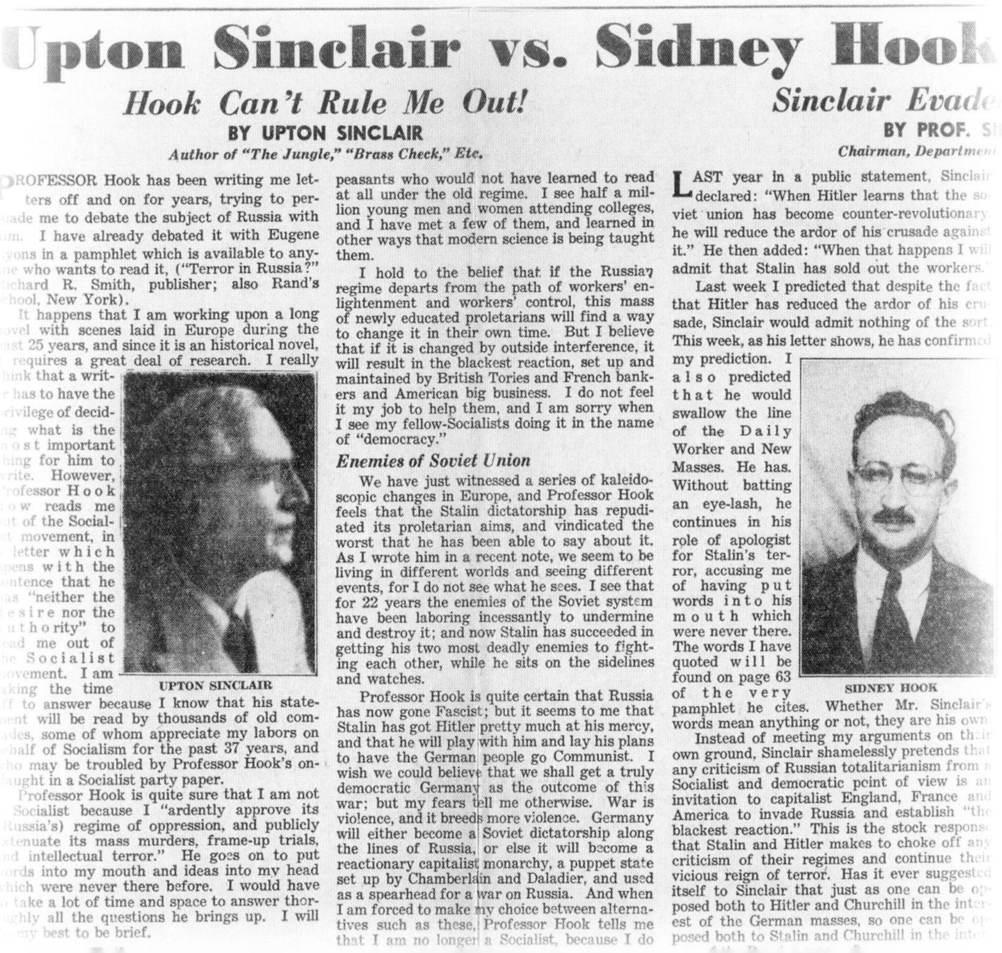

Upton Sinclair vs. Sidney Hook

Hook Can't Rule Me Out!

BY UPTON SINCLAIR

Author of "The Jungle," "Brass Check," Etc.

PROFESSOR Hook has been writing me letters off and on for years, trying to persuade me to debate the subject of Russia with him. I have already debated it with Eugene Lyons in a pamphlet which is available to anyone who wants to read it, ("Terror in Russia?" Richard R. Smith, publisher; also Rand's School, New York).

It happens that I am working upon a long novel with scenes laid in Europe during the past 25 years, and since it is an historical novel, it requires a great deal of research. I really think that a writer has to have the privilege of deciding what is the most important thing for him to write. However, Professor Hook now reads me out of the Socialist movement, in a letter which opens with the sentence that he has "neither the desire nor the authority" to read me out of the Socialist movement. I am taking the time off to answer because I know that his statement will be read by thousands of old comrades, some of whom appreciate my labors on behalf of Socialism for the past 37 years, and who may be troubled by Professor Hook's onslaught in a Socialist party paper.

UPTON SINCLAIR

Professor Hook is quite sure that I am not a Socialist because I "ardently approve its (Russia's) regime of oppression, and publicly extenuate its mass murders, frame-up trials, and intellectual terror." He goes on to put words into my mouth and ideas into my head which were never there before. I would have to take a lot of time and space to answer thoroughly all the questions he brings up. I will do my best to be brief.

peasants who would not have learned to read at all under the old regime. I see half a million young men and women attending colleges, and I have met a few of them, and learned in other ways that modern science is being taught them.

I hold to the belief that if the Russian regime departs from the path of workers' enlightenment and workers' control, this mass of newly educated proletarians will find a way to change it in their own time. But I believe that if it is changed by outside interference, it will result in the blackest reaction, set up and maintained by British Tories and French bankers and American big business. I do not feel it my job to help them, and I am sorry when I see my fellow-Socialists doing it in the name of "democracy."

Enemies of Soviet Union

We have just witnessed a series of kaleidoscopic changes in Europe, and Professor Hook feels that the Stalin dictatorship has repudiated its proletarian aims, and vindicated the worst that he has been able to say about it. As I wrote him in a recent note, we seem to be living in different worlds and seeing different events, for I do not see what he sees. I see that for 22 years the enemies of the Soviet system have been laboring incessantly to undermine and destroy it; and now Stalin has succeeded in getting his two most deadly enemies to fighting each other, while he sits on the sidelines and watches.

Professor Hook is quite certain that Russia has now gone Fascist; but it seems to me that Stalin has got Hitler pretty much at his mercy, and that he will play with him and lay his plans to have the German people go Communist. I wish we could believe that we shall get a truly democratic Germany as the outcome of this war; but my fears tell me otherwise. War is violence, and it breeds more violence. Germany will either become a Soviet dictatorship along the lines of Russia, or else it will become a reactionary capitalist monarchy, a puppet state set up by Chamberlain and Daladier, and used as a spearhead for a war on Russia. And when I am forced to make my choice between alternatives such as these, Professor Hook tells me that I am no longer a Socialist, because I do

Sinclair Evade

BY PROF. S

Chairman, Departmen

LAST year in a public statement, Sinclair declared: "When Hitler learns that the soviet union has become counter-revolutionary he will reduce the ardor of his crusade against it." He then added: "When that happens I will admit that Stalin has sold out the workers."

Last week I predicted that despite the fact that Hitler has reduced the ardor of his crusade, Sinclair would admit nothing of the sort. This week, as his letter shows, he has confirmed my prediction. I also predicted that he would swallow the line of the Daily Worker and New Masses. He has. Without batting an eye-lash, he continues in his role of apologist for Stalin's terror, accusing me of having put words into his mouth which were never there. The words I have quoted will be found on page 63 of the very pamphlet he cites. Whether Mr. Sinclair's words mean anything or not, they are his own.

SIDNEY HOOK

Instead of meeting my arguments on their own ground, Sinclair shamelessly pretends that any criticism of Russian totalitarianism from a Socialist and democratic point of view is an invitation to capitalist England, France and America to invade Russia and establish "the blackest reaction." This is the stock response that Stalin and Hitler makes to choke off any criticism of their regimes and continue their vicious reign of terror. Has it ever suggested itself to Sinclair that just as one can be opposed both to Hitler and Churchill in the interest of the German masses, so one can be opposed both to Stalin and Churchill in the inte

SIDNEY HOOK—AN EMBATTLED LIFE

Marxist Philosopher

Sidney Hook was born in 1902 in the Jewish slum of Williamsburg, a neighborhood of Brooklyn. He went to Boys High in Brooklyn and then to City College. As a Jew, he had to learn to fight and stick up for himself from an early age, with anti-Semitism endemic in the New York City school system and university administrations. Hook studied philosophy at Columbia under John Dewey, one of the great philosophers in American history, and went on to become chairman of the philosophy department at New York University.

Dewey was best known for his philosophy of education and for pragmatism, an eclectic, peculiarly American philosophy based on experience, broadly understood, rather than the fixed principles of classical philosophy. Hook became one of pragmatism's leading adherents, and Dewey's most effective defender against his critics. He might have gone on to become an important philosopher in his own right, but instead he became involved in the great political causes of the era.

Unsurprisingly for someone of his background, Hook became drawn to radical ideas and left-wing politics at an early age. "Sometime after my thirteenth birthday," he recalled late in life, "I discovered socialism." A critical influence in his development into a young communist philosopher was a year he spent studying in Europe in 1928–29, including a summer in Moscow at the Marx-Engels Institute. In Berlin he witnessed street confrontations between Nazis and Communists, and in Munich he observed Nazi rallies. He came away doubting the common wisdom that Hitler was strictly a marginal figure and that German fascism was a dead end.

The coming of the Great Depression completed his conversion to communism. Hook was never a member of the American Communist Party, but rather a devoted Marxist who interpreted Marx and tried to influence the Party from the outside. Leading Communists valued him as the most prominent American academic intellectual to embrace Marxism.

Hook's scholarship on the intellectual origins and meaning of Marxism took the form of lucidly and cogently written texts. His second book, *Towards the Understanding of Karl Marx: A Revolutionary Interpretation,* published in 1933, won respectful reviews even from nonsympathizers. Hook's thesis was that Marxism was not the *scientific* philosophy that it claimed to be, offering a guide to future social development; rather, it was a *social* philosophy aimed at creating a humane and just society through proper organization and activity. Here Hook thought he had found a way to harmonize Marx's social philosophy with basic American values.

Five decades later, the staunchly anti-Communist Hook wrote reflectively on his early

Cover of pamphlet *The Meaning of Marx,* 1934. (Sidney Hook Papers)

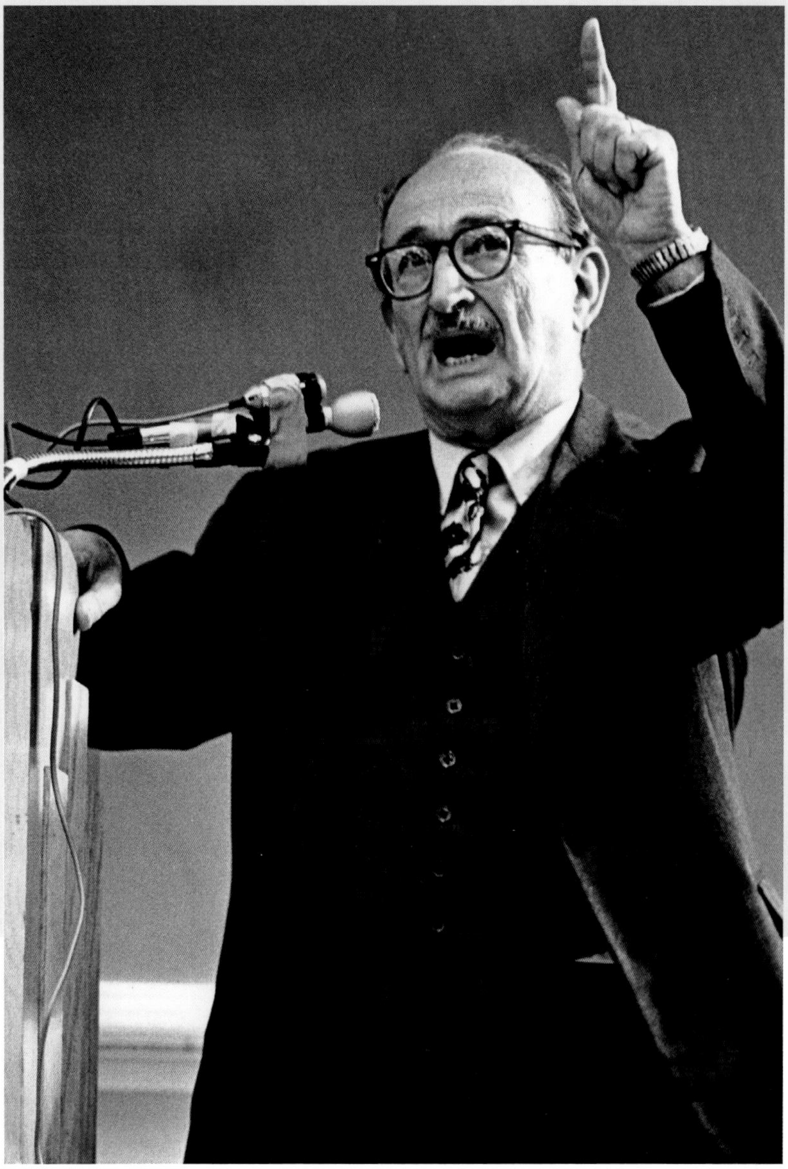

Sidney Hook, undated (1960s). (Sidney Hook Papers)

Marxist writings: "I cannot absolve myself from the guilt of failure to exercise critical responsibility toward my own radical ideals. I was guilty of judging capitalism by its operations and socialism by its hopes and aspirations; capitalism by its works and socialism by its literature." It is a statement that describes the mind-set of countless other critics of capitalism in the 1930s.

Hook cited three factors behind his earlier radicalism: an interpretation that blamed the First World War on the imperialist drives of capitalism, a genuine ignorance of what was really going on in the Soviet Union (and perhaps "a reluctance to find out"), and his sense that the only way to stop the Nazis from taking power was for the Kremlin to organize a revolution in Germany. The last factor fell away when Hitler came to power anyway in 1933 (with the assistance of Stalin's Comintern, which repudiated Germany's Social Democrats as "Social Fascists"), and it was at that point that Hook began to move away. By then, in any case, the discrepancy between the socialism practiced in the Soviet Union under Stalin and the socialist principles he had been devoted to since his teenage years became too big to ignore or explain away.

Nor did Hook have to look to Moscow for the evidence. The reception American Communists gave his book *Towards the Understanding of Karl Marx* was telling. As he recalled in his autobiography,

> *I prepared my volume on Marx in such a way as to go beyond the tired propaganda slogans and analysis of the Agitprop Division of the Communist Party, to stress the continuity between Marx's contributions and the intellectual tradition of the West, and to bring to a higher level the challenge of a democratic collectivist society to the capitalist order. . . . I did not compromise on any theoretical point in which I thought Marx, Engels, or Lenin were wrong, confident in my naïveté that these criticisms would be taken in the context of my new persuasive restatement of the social philosophy of Marxism as a whole. I did refrain from criticizing certain unhealthy developments in the Soviet Union, realizing already that I could get no hearing for my views among those I was trying to influence if I were to identify myself with any of the warring political factions. . . .*

As Hook soon realized, such tactfulness was lost on American Communists, who in all matters of ideology followed the Party line set in Moscow. Hook's purpose was to influence thinking in the American Communist Party, when in fact all of its thinking was done in the Kremlin. "Actually my expositions and reinterpretations of Marx and Communism had much more persuasive influence on persons *outside* the Communist Party than on those who were in it and whose beliefs about anything were bound by the discipline of the Party."

The more that "certain unhealthy developments" inside the USSR, notably political repression, became difficult to deny, the more ferocious was the Communist attack against independent thinkers such as Hook, who were routinely denounced as "bourgeois philistines." As Hook remembered, "The intolerance and suspicion of deviation from the Party line on any matter on which its leaders had spoken became much more intense as the pitch of domestic terror increased in the Soviet Union."

The Moscow Trials

In making his break with Soviet Communism in the middle years of the 1930s, Hook was moving against the grain. In Europe and America, the rise of Hitler had the effect of uniting liberal-to-left opinion in an antifascist common cause known from 1935 as the Popular Front. Hook called it "the heyday of respectable Communist fellow-traveling." The American Communist Party enjoyed a growing influence among intellectual and professional groups, while Communist front groups of intellectuals, artists, and writers took up the antifascist cause and pledged to defend the Soviet Union.

Before long, however, events in the USSR, in the form of the Great Terror, would intervene to undermine the unity of the Popular Front. The decisive moment was the Moscow Trials of 1936–1938, the most public face of the Terror. In three sensational show trials, key figures of the Bolshevik Revolution were accused of organizing and undertaking the most fantastical plots and crimes involving treason, sabotage, espionage, and assassination. Even more astoundingly, the defendants all confessed to their crimes. All were convicted and the principal defendants were executed, with the rest sent off to the camps. The only exception, for now, was Trotsky, in exile in Mexico, who was charged as a co-conspirator in all three trials.

It might be hard to fathom after so much time has passed, but the Moscow Trials were a turning point in the history of American liberalism, which was torn up in the controversies that arose over the guilt or innocence of the accused, some of whom had been Lenin's closest comrades. The most perplexing question was why the defendants would have confessed to their crimes if they were truly innocent. There were discrepancies among the various confessions (which were the only evidence submitted at all three trials), yet liberal-to-left publications such as the *New Republic* supported the credibility of the trials. (The larger picture of the Great Terror, the executions and exile to the growing Gulag of millions of Soviet citizens, as well as the thoroughgoing purge of middle- and lower-level Communist officials, was not yet understood at this time.) For many on the left, even if mistakes were made and some of the accused were in fact innocent the overriding concern was the defense of Stalin's USSR in the face of Hitler's Germany.

Hook later called the Moscow Trials "a decisive turning point in my own intellectual and political development. I discovered the face of radical evil—as ugly and petrifying as anything the Fascists had revealed up to that time—in the visages of those who were convinced that they were men and women of good will." Having written off the Communist Party faithful as a hopeless cause, Hook directed his polemical fire at the fellow travelers who were convinced that the USSR was a worthy democratic ally of the United States against the threat of fascism. This involved considerable courage and a thick skin.

"Seemingly, it required no great heroism to oppose communism in the U.S.," wrote Nathan Glazer, looking back on Hook's finest hour. "But that was true in the large. When it came to specifics, Mr. Hook was often in an embattled minority." And Hook was a master of the specifics, as he tirelessly worked to expose the trials as sham.

This led him to join forces temporarily with Trotsky, who in the late 1930s won the admiration of the anti-Stalinist left in America, as he single-handedly defied the Kremlin's executioners. Hook was never a Trotskyist, yet he understood that Trotsky was largely innocent of the preposterous charges made against him in the Moscow Trials, and he saw that the testimony of Trotsky could help expose the trials as a fraud. In the spring of 1937, he persuaded his mentor, John Dewey, to head an independent panel to investigate the charges against Trotsky.

The Dewey Commission, formally called the Commission of Inquiry into the Charges Made Against Leon Trotsky in the Moscow Trials, was carefully composed of intellectuals who could command respect in the liberal community, starting with Dewey. From the beginning, the enterprise was surrounded by controversy—for American Communists, as for Moscow, Trotsky had become a satanic figure—and a great deal of skepticism. Several prominent Americans, Albert Einstein among them, refused to serve on the commission. In order not to prejudice opinion against the commission, Hook remained behind the scenes (which did not stop the Communists from labeling him a "Trotskyist-Fascist").

The Dewey Commission sent a subcommission to Trotsky's place of exile, Coyoacan, Mexico, in April 1937. The subcommission, which was headed by Dewey, then almost seventy-nine years old, met at the home of the painters Frida Kahlo and Diego Rivera, where Trotsky and his wife Natalia were residing since their arrival in Mexico. The hearings opened on April 10, with the "defendant" delivering many hours of testimony (in English) over eight days, refuting the evidence used against him (and his son, Lev Sedov) at the Moscow Trials. The Dewey Commission took nine months to complete its work. It found that Trotsky and all those condemned in the trials were innocent victims of a monstrous Stalinist frame-up. Nonetheless, despite Dewey's solid liberal credentials, many American liberals refused to accept the commission's report absolving Trotsky.

It took an event more sensational than even the Moscow Trials to break apart the Popular Front: the announcement in August 1939 that the Soviet Union and Nazi Germany had signed a nonaggression pact. Stalin had made a deal with Hitler. The antifascism that had been the raison d'être of the Popular Front suddenly collapsed. Many left the Communist Party; others abandoned their sympathy for it. For some of them, however, all would be forgiven after June 22, 1941, when Nazi Germany invaded the Soviet Union. And after Pearl Harbor, for most Americans Stalin's USSR became a progressive democratic ally.

Trotsky in the study of his heavily guarded house in Coyoacan, a suburb of Mexico City, in 1939–40. (Alexander Buchman Collection)

Trotsky in exile in Mexico, months before he was killed by a Stalinist assassin wielding a pick-axe. He died on August 21, 1940. (Alexander Buchman Papers)

Cold War Liberal

After the world war came the Cold War, and the cause of American Communists and fellow travelers shifted to the maintenance of peace in the nuclear age, especially after the Soviets detonated their first atomic bomb in 1949. Hook organized a protest against the Communist-sponsored Waldorf Peace Conference in 1949, arguing that Americans were not, as a growing number seemed to believe, faced with a choice of being either red or dead. Hook's institutional base was an organization called the American Committee for Cultural Freedom, created with funding from the CIA in the wake of the Waldorf conference and counting in its ranks, at least initially, a number of respected liberals such as Arthur Schlesinger, Jr., and Richard Rorty.

Hook's influential 1952 pamphlet. (Sidney Hook Papers)

The Red Scare of the late 1940s and 1950s, which was punctuated by sensational espionage-related trials such as those of Alger Hiss (1949) and Julius and Ethel Rosenberg (1953) and which witnessed a hunt for Communists and their sympathizers inside and outside the government, tore at the fabric of liberal anti-Communism. The dilemma for Hook, as for many other liberals, was that his anti-Communism threatened to put him in league with those who now threatened American liberties. Were American Communists entitled to the same rights as all other citizens? Did the defense of liberty extend to those whose ideological convictions would cause them to deny it to others if they had the power?

Hook addressed these questions and attempted to rescue anti-Communism from Senator Joseph McCarthy's "cultural vigilantism" in an influential pamphlet published in 1952 called *Heresy, Yes—Conspiracy, No!* The defense of heresy, Hook argued, is an essential part of the American tradition and should be carefully distinguished from conspiracy, which refuses to play by the rules of the game, in politics, education, and other institutions. To Hook, the correct argument against Communism was not its heretical ideas but its conspiratorial nature. His pamphlet sought "to work out reasonable principles which will insure national security without creating hardships or injustice to the innocent." Hook believed that the best solution was a "tough-minded liberalism," as opposed to the "ritualistic liberalism" of those who could not distinguish between legitimate and threatening behavior.

> *This tough-mindedness is based upon the realization that the communist movement is an international conspiracy, and not a legitimate part of the liberal tradition which was the assumption of the Popular Front psychology. It is also based upon the realization that cultural vigilantism is a futile way of combatting communist influences. It defends a pluralistic approach to the question of democratic survival and proper functioning of democratic institutions, particularly the schools.*

McCarthyism, Hook saw, was providing cover for Communists, because it tainted all anti-Communism as hysterical. Thus was born the phenomenon of *anti*-anti-Communism: if you were an anti-Communist, then you had to be a McCarthyite. Hook sent a letter to the *New York Times,* published on May 8, 1953, in which he denounced McCarthy as a boon to Communism and called for the organization of a national movement to retire him from public life: "For the day Senator McCarthy leaves the political scene the Communists throughout the world will go into mourning." Hook was not the first prominent liberal to challenge McCarthy publicly in this way, but the private correspondence he received after his letter appeared in the *Times* indicates that it struck a chord.

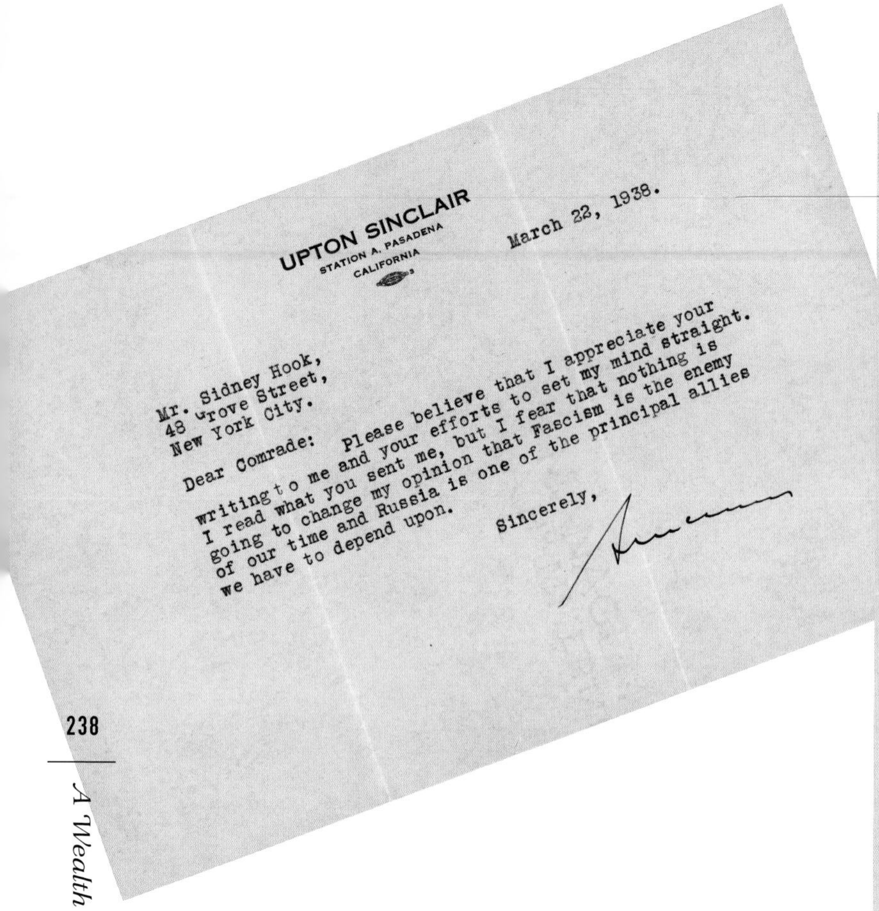

UPTON SINCLAIR
STATION A, PASADENA
CALIFORNIA

March 22, 1938.

Mr. Sidney Hook,
48 Grove Street,
New York City.

Dear Comrade: Please believe that I appreciate your writing to me and your efforts to set my mind straight. I read what you sent me, but I fear that nothing is going to change my opinion that Fascism is the enemy of our time and Russia is one of the principal allies we have to depend upon.

Sincerely,

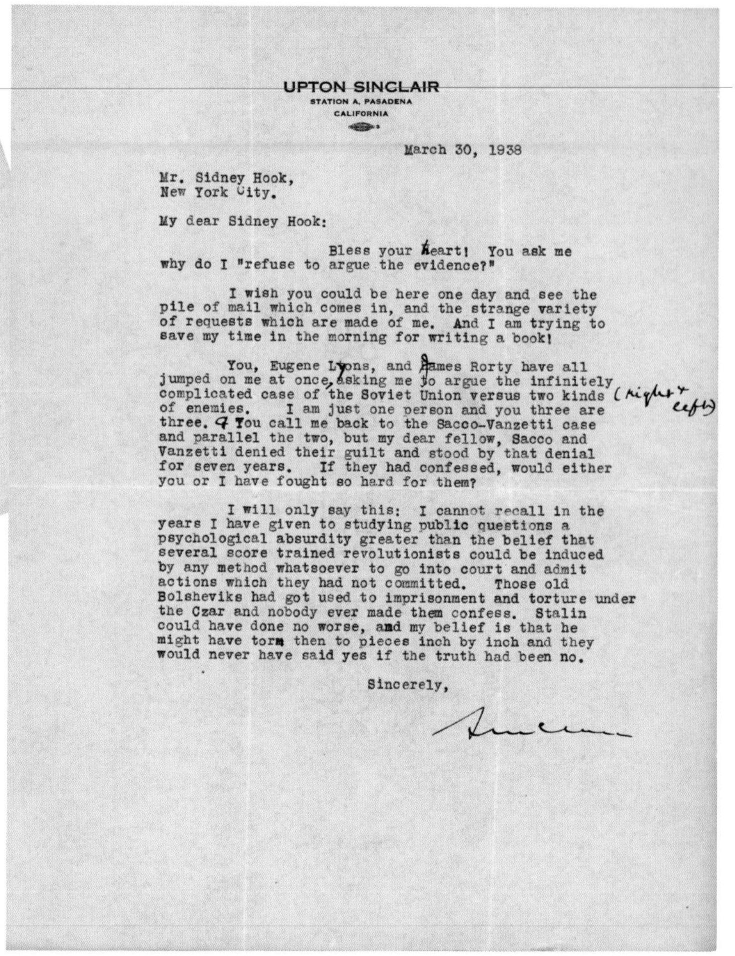

UPTON SINCLAIR
STATION A, PASADENA
CALIFORNIA

March 30, 1938

Mr. Sidney Hook,
New York City.

My dear Sidney Hook:

Bless your heart! You ask me why do I "refuse to argue the evidence?"

I wish you could be here one day and see the pile of mail which comes in, and the strange variety of requests which are made of me. And I am trying to save my time in the morning for writing a book!

You, Eugene Lyons, and James Rorty have all jumped on me at once, asking me to argue the infinitely complicated case of the Soviet Union versus two kinds of enemies. (right + left) I am just one person and you three are three. You call me back to the Sacco-Vanzetti case and parallel the two, but my dear fellow, Sacco and Vanzetti denied their guilt and stood by that denial for seven years. If they had confessed, would either you or I have fought so hard for them?

I will only say this: I cannot recall in the years I have given to studying public questions a psychological absurdity greater than the belief that several score trained revolutionists could be induced by any method whatsoever to go into court and admit actions which they had not committed. Those old Bolsheviks had got used to imprisonment and torture under the Czar and nobody ever made them confess. Stalin could have done no worse, and my belief is that he might have torn them to pieces inch by inch and they would never have said yes if the truth had been no.

Sincerely,

Letters from Upton Sinclair to Hook, dated March 22, 1938; March 30, 1938; and May 2, 1939. (Sidney Hook Papers)

"My Dear Upton Sinclair"

One of the most entertaining, as well as illuminating, exchanges of letters to be found among Sidney Hook's papers is his correspondence with Upton Sinclair in the late 1930s. Hook tried unsuccessfully to involve Sinclair in the Dewey Commission of Inquiry in 1937. Once Sinclair declared his reasons for declining the invitation (he thought Trotsky was guilty as charged), Hook went on the offensive. Sinclair was hooked, so to speak. Their correspondence—illustrated here with three of Sinclair's rejoinders—shows the forces buffeting the political left in the late 1930s, which was caught between Hitler's militarism and Stalin's terror. These pressures reached a kind of crescendo in March 1938, at the time of the third Moscow Trial, whose star defendant was Nikolai Bukharin. Sinclair found preposterous the notion that the elaborate confessions of these hard-bitten Bolsheviks, many of whom had endured years in tsarist prisons and exile, were somehow forced from them.

A year and several more epistolary engagements later, Hook once again berates "My Dear Upton Sinclair" for his naïveté about what was going on in Russia: "Do you not see what a position you are putting yourself in? You are a hundred percent apologist of Stalin's terror in Russia and out. The Stalinists throughout the world use you as a 'front' behind which to cover up their Hitlerian techniques in fighting socialists, syndicalists, anarchists and independent lovers of freedom everywhere, while in private they refer to you as 'a sap' (in the past they used to do this publicly!!)." In his reply, of May 2, 1939, Sinclair anticipates the Nazi-Soviet Pact of less than four months hence.

UPTON SINCLAIR
STATION A, PASADENA
CALIFORNIA

May 2, 1939.

Mr. Sidney Hook,
48 Grove St.,
New York City.

My dear Sidney Hook:

I am writing a long novel about Europe, and have to fight against entering into controversies. I can only say that it seems obvious to me that our one hope of overcoming Fascism lies in the military power of the Soviet Union, and it seems to me the apex of blundering for any radical to be sniping at it now. Of course if the infinite treacheries of the plutocracies should cause Russia to make a trade with Hitler, then my hopes are out, and both you and I can prepare our necks for the executioner's axe. I hope we won't be quarrelling when that happens.

Sincerely,

Page Four THE CALL Saturday, November 18, 1939

THE CALL
Published Every Week by the
Socialist Party of the United States of America
Published at 540 W. Juneau Ave., Milwaukee, Wis.
Address All Communications for Publication to:
Editorial Office
549 Randolph St., Chicago, Ill.
Telephone Number: State 3250
Subscription Rates:
$1 a Year; 50c for 6 Months; Foreign, $1.50 a Year
Advertising Rates Upon Request
Two Weeks Notice Required for Change of Address
Gerry Allard, Editor and Manager
Editorial Board:
Gerry Allard, Travers Clement, Judah Drob, Harry Fleischman, Arthur G. McDowell, Loren Norman
Entered as second class matter Jan. 17, 1939, at the Postoffice at Milwaukee, Wis., under the act of March 3, 1879.
Deadline for Copy: Thursday at Noon

A Statement of Policy

The recent right about face of the Communist party fools no one. This organization which formerly whooped it up for a holy war of the political democracies against Hitler today labels this war, which it helped to create, an imperialist war and unleashes its venom against England, France and the United States.

The Communist party is no more interested today in the welfare of the international working class in whose name it purports to speak than it was yesterday in democracy. It is interested in one thing alone—the nationalistic ambitions of its master, Joseph Stalin.

If tomorrow Stalin changes his mind and attempts once more to throw in his lot with the British and French, the Communists will again change their "line." Once again they will attempt to chain the workers to the chariot wheels of that same imperialism which they denounce so loudly today.

The Socialist party in 1917 maintained that the war then raging was not a war to save democracy, that it was an imperialist war and that its causes were not ideologic but economic. President Wilson, after the war, publicly admitted this fact, even though leaving Gene Debs to rot in jail for saying the same thing earlier.

The fact that at this moment the Communists are also saying it has no bearing on the case. They say anything that Stalin orders them to say, just as members of the German-American bund shout the slogans of Hitler.

The Socialist party repudiates all forms of totalitarianism—black, brown or red. It is a working class organization and its policies are determined democratically by its membership in this country. If Communists, or any one else, adopt any part of our program, there is no way we can prevent it. But let it be crystal clear that we shall never accept as allies representatives of any totalitarian dictatorship. Their aims and those of the Socialist party, which stands for industrial as well as political democracy, are irreconcilable.

A Government by Snoopers?

Last week we printed an item from Harlan Miller's Washington column stating that J. Edgar Hoover, head of the Federal Bureau of Investigation, was teaching young patriots lessons in Americanism by using the hysterical Mrs. Dilling's "The Red Network," a scurrilous book which has been discredited by its own words.

Now comes a report that Hoover is cooperating with the National Protective league

Upton Sinclair vs. Sidney Hook

The Debate on Russia Grows Warmer

Hook Can't Rule Me Out!

BY UPTON SINCLAIR
Author of "The Jungle," "Brass Check," Etc.

PROFESSOR Hook has been writing me letters off and on for years, trying to persuade me to debate the subject of Russia with him. I have already debated it with Eugene Lyons in a pamphlet which is available to anyone who wants to read it, ("Terror in Russia?" Richard R. Smith, publisher; also Rand's school, New York).

It happens that I am working upon a long novel with scenes laid in Europe during the past 25 years, and since it is an historical novel, it requires a great deal of research. I really think that a writer has to have the privilege of deciding what is the most important thing for him to write. However, Professor Hook now reads me out of the Socialist movement, in a letter which opens with the sentence that he has "neither the desire nor the authority" to read me out of the Socialist movement. I am taking the time off to answer because I know that his statement will be read by thousands of old comrades, some of whom appreciate my labors on behalf of Socialism for the past 37 years, and who may be troubled by Professor Hook's onslaught in a Socialist party paper.

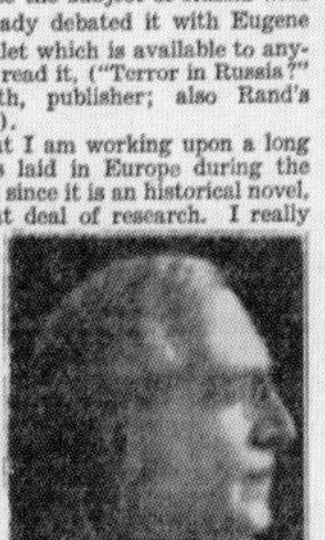
UPTON SINCLAIR

Professor Hook is quite sure that I am not a Socialist because I "ardently approve its (Russia's) regime of oppression, and publicly extenuate its mass murders, frame-up trials, and intellectual terror." He goes on to put words into my mouth and ideas into my head which were never there before. I would have to take a lot of time and space to answer thoroughly all the questions he brings up. I will do my best to be brief.

The Lesser Evil

Having been 61 years in this world, I have learned that what one wants and what one gets are not always the same thing. I have read a lot of history and learned that it is a cruel process. I would change it if I could. I set out with great determination more than 40 years ago to try. I have not succeeded—at least not to any extent so that I am able to measure the results. I have to look at the world as it is, and try to make discriminations in it. I have to choose among many evil things, and say: "This one is less bad." I have to try to understand the causes of social systems and social events, and also the tendencies, the goals towards which they drive. I have to say: "None of them suit me, but this one seems to me less promising of evil than the others."

All my life I have pleaded for democratic, peaceful and orderly social change. How hard I have worked for it is proved by more than 65 books and pamphlets, and God alone knows how many magazine articles, speeches, and let-

peasants who would not have learned to read at all under the old regime. I see half a million young men and women attending colleges, and I have met a few of them, and learned in other ways that modern science is being taught them.

I hold to the belief that if the Russian regime departs from the path of workers' enlightenment and workers' control, this mass of newly educated proletarians will find a way to change it in their own time. But I believe that if it is changed by outside interference, it will result in the blackest reaction, set up and maintained by British Tories and French bankers and American big business. I do not feel it my job to help them, and I am sorry when I see my fellow-Socialists doing it in the name of "democracy."

Enemies of Soviet Union

We have just witnessed a series of kaleidoscopic changes in Europe, and Professor Hook feels that the Stalin dictatorship has repudiated its proletarian aims, and vindicated the worst that he has been able to say about it. As I wrote him in a recent note, we seem to be living in different worlds and seeing different events, for I do not see what he sees. I see that for 22 years the enemies of the Soviet system have been laboring incessantly to undermine and destroy it; and now Stalin has succeeded in getting his two most deadly enemies to fighting each other, while he sits on the sidelines and watches.

Professor Hook is quite certain that Russia has now gone Fascist; but it seems to me that Stalin has got Hitler pretty much at his mercy, and that he will play with him and lay his plans to have the German people go Communist. I wish we could believe that we shall get a truly democratic Germany as the outcome of this war; but my fears tell me otherwise. War is violence, and it breeds more violence. Germany will either become a Soviet dictatorship along the lines of Russia, or else it will become a reactionary capitalist monarchy, a puppet state set up by Chamberlain and Daladier, and used as a spearhead for a war on Russia. And when I am forced to make my choice between alternatives such as these, Professor Hook tells me that I am no longer a Socialist, because I do not believe in democracy!

America's Problems

I can only tell him that I believe in democracy as much as I ever did, which is with my whole heart and soul. But I do not mean the Chamberlain-Churchill brand of democracy, nor yet the Daladier brand. I am still pleading for a democratic, peaceful, and orderly solution of our social problems in the United States. I will work for it up to the last hour, along with Professor Hook and anybody else who will help.

We in America have a long tradition of self-government behind us, and it is our duty to solve our problems under our constitution. But when we are passing judgment upon the different peoples of the earth, we have to read their history and know the traditions and standards which are a part of their being. To confuse our American problems with Russia's or Russia's with ours seems to me not according to the scientific method which Professor Hook and I agree in defending, even though we do not agree in applying it.

Sinclair Evades the Question!

BY PROF. SIDNEY HOOK
Chairman, Department of Philosophy, N. Y. U.

LAST year in a public statement, Sinclair declared: "When Hitler learns that the soviet union has become counter-revolutionary, he will reduce the ardor of his crusade against it." He then added: "When that happens I will admit that Stalin has sold out the workers."

Last week I predicted that despite the fact that Hitler has reduced the ardor of his crusade, Sinclair would admit nothing of the sort. This week, as his letter shows, he has confirmed my prediction. I also predicted that he would swallow the line of the Daily Worker and New Masses. He has. Without batting an eye-lash, he continues in his role of apologist for Stalin's terror, accusing me of having put words into his mouth which were never there. The words I have quoted will be found on page 63 of the very pamphlet he cites. Whether Mr. Sinclair's words mean anything or not, they are his own.

SIDNEY HOOK

Instead of meeting my arguments on their own ground, Sinclair shamelessly pretends that any criticism of Russian totalitarianism from a Socialist and democratic point of view is an invitation to capitalist England, France and America to invade Russia and establish "the blackest reaction." This is the stock response that Stalin and Hitler makes to choke off any criticism of their regimes and continue their vicious reign of terror. Has it ever suggested itself to Sinclair that just as one can be opposed both to Hitler and Churchill in the interest of the German masses, so one can be opposed both to Stalin and Churchill in the interests of the Russian masses?

Stalinazi Pact

This is so elementary that any one who professes to be a Socialist can easily see it. It is sometimes necessary in a trade union to criticize a corrupt leadership or demand that it be replaced. The more corrupt the leadership the more likely it is to reply that this is a plot to destroy the union and help the employers with whom as a matter of fact (like Stalin with Hitler) the leadership is actually leagued.

Notice the terms with which Sinclair seeks to justify the Stalinazi pact which let loose the dogs of war in Europe. "Stalin," says Sinclair, "has succeeded in getting his two most deadly enemies to fighting each other." To a Socialist, Mr. Sinclair, this means that Stalin has succeeded in getting the workers and peasants of Poland, Germany and France to slaughter each other. To what end? For Socialism? Sinclair has not yet brought himself to say this. But he will. Today, however, he apparently regards it as a feather in Stalin's cap that he has helped

my previous letter: The frame-ups, the artificially induced famines, the purge and liquidation of millions of innocent people including children. Insofar as he does essay a reply, it is twofold. All this may be true, but there are "a lot of other things" like the growth of literacy which allegedly I have never mentioned. (He is mistaken about this, cf. my "Reflections on the Russian Revolution," Southern Review, January, 1939). Secondly, these excesses may be deplored, but they were necessary. Let us reason about this together.

To begin with, notice how closely this defense parallels the defense which apologists of Hitler's terror make and which Sinclair does not accept. Does the fact of 100 per cent literacy in Germany justify Hitler's crimes any more than the absence of unemployment, the enthusiasm, the building of great engineering projects and plants for synthetic materials?

Why should, then, the growth of literacy and the building of factories in Russia serve as a justification for a terror even more ruthless than that of Hitler's? Besides what does the ability to read and write mean in a country in which people are free to read and write only what the government permits? Does progress consist in teaching people how to read litanies to Stalin instead of the czar?

Frame-ups in Russia

In 1927 when Sacco and Vanzetti were executed, America had reached the height of its power and prosperity. Suppose someone had reproached Sinclair at the time for not mentioning other aspects of American civilization like increase in health, wealth, and knowledge when he was denouncing the crime of their execution? He would have replied that even if true, these things did not make their execution any less of a crime. And so we reply to Sinclair! Granted that Russia and Germany have certain positive results to show from the rule of Stalin and Hitler, how do these justify or even extenuate their crimes? Why is it right to protest against frame-ups in America and Germany and not in Russia? Why is it that Sinclair never asks us to consider the history and traditions of Germany, Italy, and Japan when we condemn these countries but always speaks of peculiar Russian traditions as if the Russians were an uncivilized race of barbarians?

Sinclair's second answer to these questions seems to be that the things I listed in my previous letter were historically necessary, cruel to be sure, but an unavoidable part of the historical process. Outrages in capitalist countries, presumably, are not historically necessary: Outrages in Russia are. Very well, Mr. Sinclair, let us have the proof that any one of the things I mentioned was historically necessary in the interests of anything but Stalin's bureaucratic dictatorship.

We have a right to ask this proof of Sinclair. Last year in the New York Times (8/24/38) he admonished a critic and proclaimed "She is permitted to believe anything whatever that can be proved to be a fact but she must not believe anything that cannot be proved."

Regimentation of Art, Science

Is Sinclair prepared to prove that it was his-

"Upton Sinclair vs. Sidney Hook," *The Call*, November 18, 1939. The running battle between Hook and Sinclair was given a full page of coverage in *The Call* (New York) in November 1939. (Sidney Hook Papers)

"Firing Line." Hook on the set of the PBS series "Firing Line," July 24, 1987. In introducing his guest, William F. Buckley remarked that "anyone who knows Professor Hook or who has studied his polemical style knows instantly that when he calls his book *Out of Step,* he is referring to the rest of the world, not to himself." ("Firing Line" Broadcasts)

The Controversialist

Arthur Schlesinger, Jr., said of Sidney Hook, "In his day he performed great services in exposing the deceit, the fraudulence, the folly of Communists and fellow travelers." Yet Schlesinger was not alone in feeling that, over the post-McCarthy decades, Hook became obsessed with Communism. Part of this was Hook's combative style; he would not let go of an argument until others had confessed the errors of their past ways and, more than that, matched the fervor of his anti-Communism.

Hook's papers at the Hoover Archives provide abundant evidence of his trademark tenacity. He was a relentless polemicist, as a speaker and as an author of numerous books and many articles. He was also one of the great practitioners of the letter to the editor. "Sidney Hook Replies" is the title (in one or another variation) of dozens of newspaper clippings to be found among his files. Hook was equally persistent in private correspondence. Some of his epistolary battles, with both the famous and the obscure, lasted for decades. If you got into an argument with Sidney Hook, you had better be prepared to go the full fifteen rounds.

In his joy of combat, Hook was very much a product of his era and milieu; yet he was a special case. Nathan Glazer recalls, from his days as an editor of *Commentary,* attempting to convince Hook to submit to editing. "I tried to argue with him that an answer that was longer than the attacking letter lost a rhetorical advantage, but this had no effect on Mr.

Hook: Truth, answering every point, clearing up every element of illogic or irrationality, was more important than the polemical advantage to be gained by a brief dismissal."

Hook's causes and interests ranged far beyond communism, to encompass a variety of issues concerning politics, philosophy, education, ethics, and culture. Like Dewey, he took a special interest in the university and academic freedom. Here the student radicalism of the late 1960s, which he saw firsthand at New York University, left him feeling alienated. In his 1987 autobiography, *Out of Step,* he compared his own student generation to that of the sixties:

> *Ideas counted in a way that was hard to explain in terms of the historical materialism to which all of us uncritically subscribed. We would not have understood the anti-intellectualism of student radicals in the sixties, their rowdyism and violence. That was not because we thought of ourselves as "intellectuals"—the term always had a disparaging class connotation, in the labor and Socialist movement, of being an outsider—but because their pattern of violence was not ours.*

Hook brought his ideas and his fighting spirit with him to Stanford in 1973, where he was a senior research fellow at the Hoover Institution until his death in 1989. In his final years, Hook was called a conservative and a neoconservative, but he rejected those labels, and generally he resisted being put in a box. After Ronald Reagan awarded him the Presidential Medal of Freedom at the White House in 1985, he went out of his way to restate his credentials as a nonconformist.

> *I am an unreconstructed believer in the welfare state and in a steeply progressive income tax, a secular humanist, and a firm supporter of freedom of choice with respect to abortion, voluntary euthanasia, and other domestic measures to which he [Reagan] is opposed. My opposition to reverse discrimination and quota systems goes back to the days and words of Hubert Humphrey.*

And what of Hook the philosopher? In his autobiography, he recalled his promising early career in the study of philosophy, of how Dewey had seen him as his natural successor. Instead, he went off to fight the great ideological struggles of the twentieth century. Despite appearances, he wrote, "I am not conscious of having sought out these encounters. I engaged in them because most often no one else was willing to do so. Time and again after resolving to devote myself to the sweet uses of technical philosophy, I would be urged once more to enter the fray, often by the very people who had advised me previously that I ought to turn my back on politics and write books for eternity."

KARL POPPER—THE IMAGINATIVE LEAP

Skeleton in the Cupboard

Karl Popper was born in 1902 in Vienna to a middle-class Jewish family. He attended the University of Vienna, where in 1928 he received his Ph.D. in philosophy. In the interwar years, Popper came under the influence of the Vienna Circle, a group of philosophers and scientists who advocated a philosophical outlook known as "logical positivism." Logical positivists sought to differentiate between genuine empirical science on the one hand and religion and metaphysics on the other. Only theories that could be verified should be considered scientific. Popper began to question the Vienna Circle's demarcation between what is science and what is not, and in the process he ended up revolutionizing the way we think about the world.

Popper came of age at a time when modern physics was transforming the world of science. The boldness of Einstein's relativity theory excited his interest in the philosophy of science by raising doubts in his mind about the standard view of the way science worked. The hallmark of science was assumed to be *induction,* the method of arriving at general statements from the careful accumulation of observations and a long process of verification. Yet Einstein's discovery seemed positively reckless alongside this model of the scientific method.

It was David Hume, the eighteenth-century Scottish philosopher, who had first raised some awkward questions about induction. If an action is repeated many times over, Hume observed, the expectation that it will occur once again is a product not of logic but of psychology. The sun has risen every day for as long as we know, but as a matter of logic this does not mean that it will rise again tomorrow. In the textbook example, the statement "All swans are white" is based on centuries of counting white swans; yet we can still not be sure that all swans are white; a black one might show up someday.

Of course, to most working scientists "Hume's problem of induction" is one of those philosophical conundrums that have no real effect on the practical world or on how they practice science. Hume himself concluded that although there is no way to prove the theoretical validity of the inductive method, we go along with it because in practice it seems to work. But philosophers since Hume have puzzled over the problem. In 1926, the English philospher C. D. Broad characterized it as "the skeleton in the cupboard of philosophy." Then Popper came along and proposed a solution to Hume's problem, one that would challenge the standard view of science.

Karl Popper, Vienna, 1930. (Sir Karl Raimund Popper Papers)

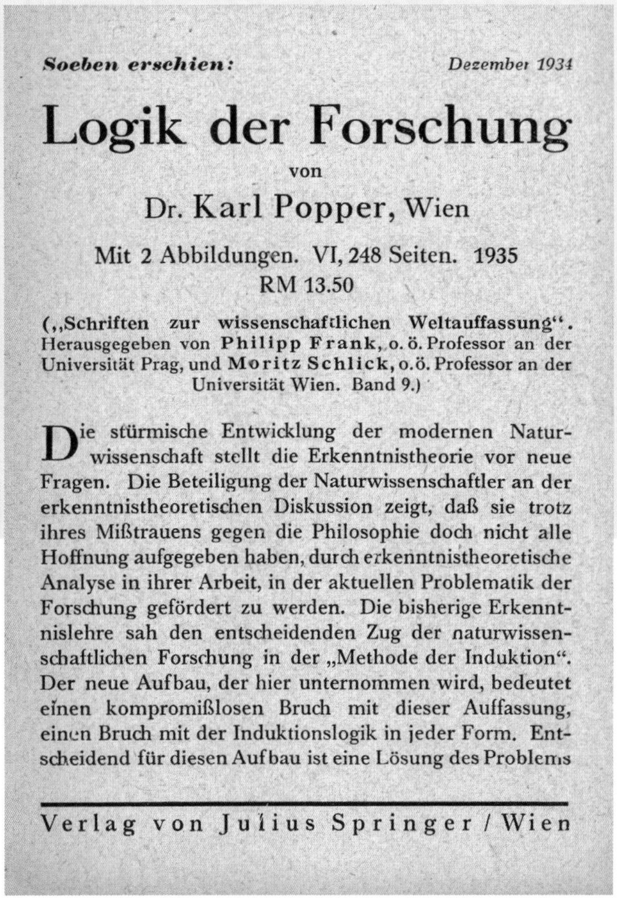

Soeben erschien: *Dezember 1934*

Logik der Forschung

von

Dr. Karl Popper, Wien

Mit 2 Abbildungen. VI, 248 Seiten. 1935
RM 13.50

(„Schriften zur wissenschaftlichen Weltauffassung". Herausgegeben von **Philipp Frank**, o. ö. Professor an der Universität Prag, und **Moritz Schlick**, o. ö. Professor an der Universität Wien. Band 9.)

Die stürmische Entwicklung der modernen Naturwissenschaft stellt die Erkenntnistheorie vor neue Fragen. Die Beteiligung der Naturwissenschaftler an der erkenntnistheoretischen Diskussion zeigt, daß sie trotz ihres Mißtrauens gegen die Philosophie doch nicht alle Hoffnung aufgegeben haben, durch erkenntnistheoretische Analyse in ihrer Arbeit, in der aktuellen Problematik der Forschung gefördert zu werden. Die bisherige Erkenntnislehre sah den entscheidenden Zug der naturwissenschaftlichen Forschung in der „Methode der Induktion". Der neue Aufbau, der hier unternommen wird, bedeutet einen kompromißlosen Bruch mit dieser Auffassung, einen Bruch mit der Induktionslogik in jeder Form. Entscheidend für diesen Aufbau ist eine Lösung des Problems

Verlag von Julius Springer / Wien

Book announcement for *Logik der Forschung*, 1934. (Sir Karl Raimund Popper Papers)

Trial and Error

Popper's breakthrough work was a book titled *Logik der Forschung (The Logic of Scientific Discovery),* published in Vienna in 1934 and considered by many to be the most important work of the 20th century on the philosophy of science (although it would remain little known until it was published in English nearly a quarter of a century later). Popper's proposed solution began by drawing a crucial distinction between verification and falsification. You could continue counting white swans in order to try to verify the statement "All swans are white," yet logically the statement could not be verified because the number of swans you counted would be finite. By contrast, the single observation of a black swan would enable you to make the logically sound statement "Not all swans are white." Empirical generalizations, in other words, though not verifiable, are *falsifiable.* Scientific laws, though not provable, can be tested by systematic attempts to refute them.

Popper was saying not merely that this is the way science *ought* to work but that it was the way science *actually* works. Hume's problem of induction was not really a problem for science, Popper argued, because science does not really use induction. It begins not with observation but with thought. Scientific theories are the product not of accumulated data

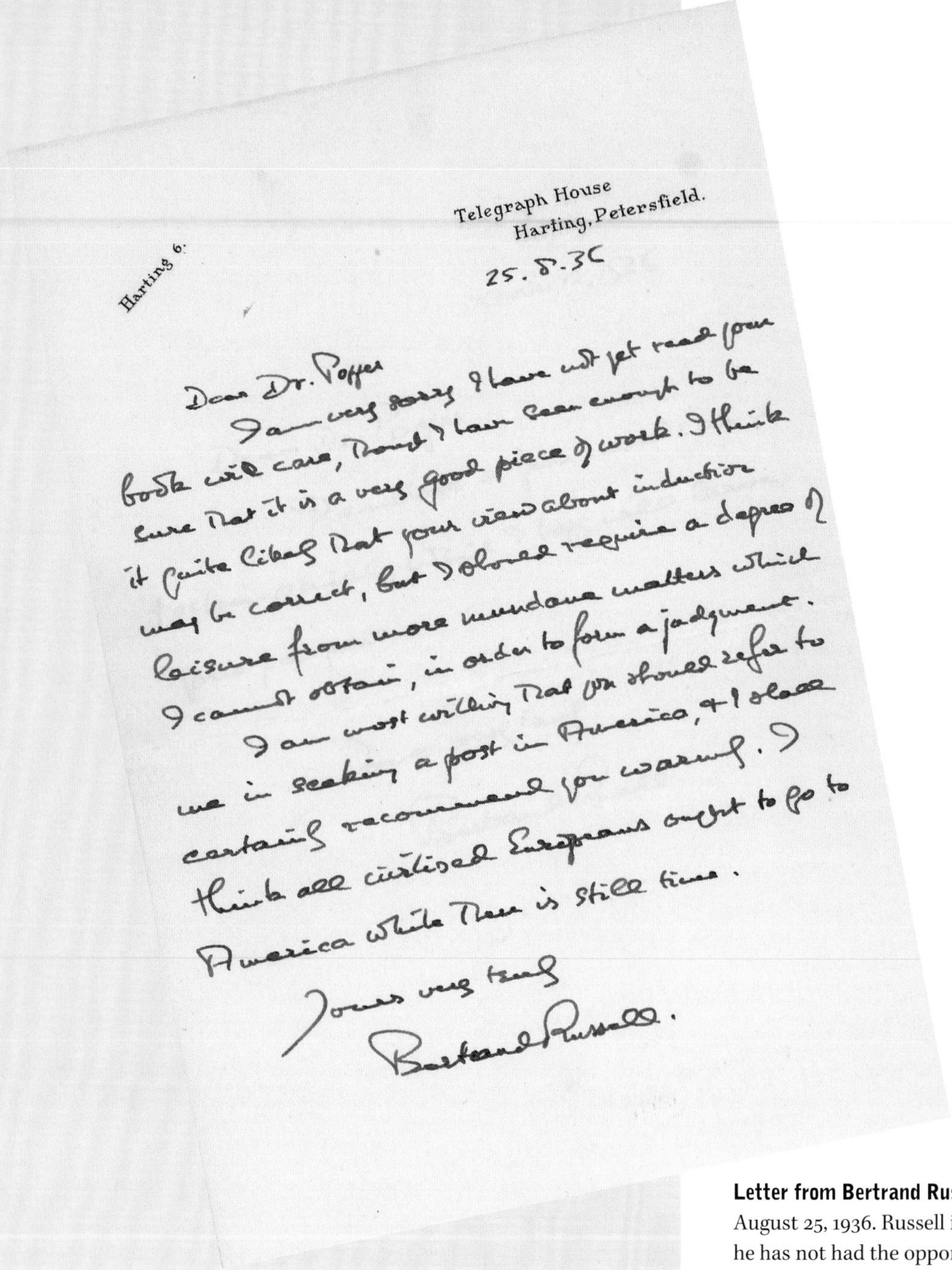

Telegraph House
Harting, Petersfield.

Harting 6.

25.8.36

Dear Dr. Popper

I am very sorry I have not yet read your book with care, though I have seen enough to be sure that it is a very good piece of work. I think it quite likely that your views about induction may be correct, but I should require a degree of leisure from more mundane matters which I cannot obtain, in order to form a judgment.

I am most willing that you should refer to me in seeking a post in America, & I shall certainly recommend you warmly. I think all civilised Europeans ought to go to America while there is still time.

Yours very truly

Bertrand Russell.

Letter from Bertrand Russell to Popper, dated August 25, 1936. Russell informs Popper that while he has not had the opportunity to give Popper's book *Logik der Forschung* a careful reading, "I have seen enough to be sure that it is a very good piece of work." Russell was sufficiently impressed to offer to help his Viennese colleague find a job in the United States. "I am most willing that you should refer to me in seeking a post in America, & I shall certainly recommend you warmly. I think all civilised Europeans ought to go to America while there is still time."

Of course for Jewish intellectuals like Popper escape from continental Europe was by then becoming a matter of some urgency. In 1937 Popper accepted a teaching position in New Zealand. The following year Russell moved from England to America, where he spent most of the Second World War teaching philosophy at leading universities and where he wrote his enormously popular *History of Western Philosophy.* He returned to England in 1944. Reproduced courtesy of the Bertrand Russell Archives at McMaster University. (Sir Karl Raimund Popper Papers) but of human creativity. Scientists do not attempt to verify generalizations, but rather to refute them. Again, the new physics showed the way. Einstein thought beyond the existing knowledge base and came up with his theory of relativity; he then daringly put it out there for the rest of the scientific community to attempt to refute. To Popper, this was just an outstanding example of the way all science worked.

And yet, in Popper's view of science, the best that could be said of Einstein's theory was that it had not been refuted. All swans are white, but only until someone proves otherwise. For Popper, falsifiability was the criterion of demarcation between science and nonscience. Only if some imaginable observation would refute it is a theory testable; and only if it is testable is it scientific. Thus Einstein's theory of relativity was science, whereas Freud's psychoanalysis was mere pseudoscience.

Popper's view of science left no room for dogmatism. As he once put it, following Socrates, "We know nothing—that is the first point. Therefore we should be very modest—that is the second. That we should not claim to know when we do not know—that is the third." The engine of progress was criticism, which would eliminate false theories and leave standing only those theories that had not yet been falsified. This was the best that science could do. A twenty-first century reader might find much of this rather obvious, yet as authors David Edmonds and John Eidinow observed in 2001, "Popper's idea that progress comes through trial and error was one of the truly great ideas of the twentieth century and, like many truly great ideas, it had the mark of utter simplicity."

The Sun Also Rises

Like many revolutionaries, Popper had a tendency to take things too far. He has been criticized for having exaggerated his insights, most notably his claim to have solved Hume's problem of induction. (It has been pointed out that Popper's own methodology relied on induction: the existence of a black swan would have to be verified through repeated observation.) In this same vein, he has been accused by some scientists and philosophers, among them Colin McGinn, of producing a distorted picture of how science works. "As Hume himself recognized, we use induction all the time, and it is hard to see how we could avoid using it: we assume that the future will be like the past, that the laws of nature will not change, that bread will nourish and fire burn. The sun will indeed rise tomorrow."

Or, to use the example of Imre Lakatos, if Popper was correct, then why not jump off the top of the Eiffel Tower? The inductive method of accumulated observation told you that the force of gravity was, in the past, implicated in countless accidents and suicides. Yet Popper was correct that logically one could not conclude from this that gravity would have its deadly effect the next time someone jumped. So why not give it a try? Clearly, this is a leap best left to the imagination.

Along these same lines, Popper's critics charge that he underestimated the role of observation in the scientific process. McGinn uses the example of the ebb and flow of tides as an observed phenomenon that inspired scientists to try to come up with an explanatory theory—in this case the moon's gravitational pull. "Observation poses a question of explanation, and creativity gets to work to produce the needed theory."

Nonetheless, Popper's insight into the role of the creative mind in the scientific process has been enormously influential. The critic Adam Gopnik cites the example of Bertrand Russell, who in 1945 could assume that whereas philosophy dealt with the unprovable, science was concerned with the realm of the definite. "A half century later, no philosopher (including Russell) would have written that. Everyone accepts that science centers on the hypothetical and the conjectural, the imaginative leap and the subsequent search for a significant test, and the questions turn on just what tests, and just what guesses, count. Popper was almost single-handedly responsible for this revolution."

The Open Society

Popper extended the power of his ideas beyond the realms of philosophy and science by applying his scientific theory to politics and society. These efforts would earn him worldwide fame and in the process help to win him belated recognition for his ideas about science.

In 1937, three years after the appearance of his *Logik der Forschung,* as Austrian anti-Semitism assumed ominous proportions in a rising tide of fascism, Popper accepted a university teaching position in New Zealand. At war's end, with the help of fellow Viennese exile Friedrich von Hayek, he was hired to teach philosophy of science at the London School of Economics, where he would remain for the next twenty-three years, until his retirement. Arriving in England in 1949, Popper was something of an intellectual celebrity, thanks to his 1945 book *The Open Society and Its Enemies,* a vigorous indictment of totalitarianism.

The dominant trend of thought going into the war was that the most rational, "scientific" organization of society was a centrally planned and ordered one—not least because it would prevent calamities such as the Great Depression. Popper showed that this notion was based on a mistaken conception of science. A truly scientific approach would support a society that is "open" and pluralistic, in which individuals and groups would be free to advocate competing solutions to society's problems; in which government policies could be changed in the light of effective criticism (in a word, falsified); and, ultimately, in which the government itself could peacefully be turned out of office. Only the democracy of trial and error could prevent tyranny and, as in science, ensure progress. Popper's idea is best summarized in his maxim "I may be wrong and you may be right, and by an effort, we may get nearer to the truth."

The "enemies" of a free society, as identified by Popper, were those who proposed inviolable ideologies. His book recounted how political philosophers, from Plato to Hegel to Marx, had tried to make their political philosophies rigorous by making them infallible. Popper argued that, just as there were no sacred and uncontestable scientific theories, so too were there were no inviolable ideologies. The most seductive of these ideologies claimed to be able to plot the future on the basis of the supposed laws of history. In fact, Popper argued, history has no plot. Nor is historical progress inevitable; only we human beings make it happen. The best way to achieve progress is through an open society.

It was in this context that Popper presented his devasting critique of Marxism. Marxists claimed that theirs was a scientific theory of history and society; indeed, beginning with Marx himself they had made a number of falsifiable predictions about capitalist society. In Marx's scenario, the middle class would disappear, as the rich got richer and the poor got poorer; capital would become concentrated in fewer and fewer hands; and class antagonism would become more acute as workers became more class-conscious. In fact, however, by the turn of the twentieth century none of these expectations had come to pass. The working class was better off; the middle class was growing, as was the number of capitalists; and class antagonism was becoming less acute. In general, the much anticipated contradictions of capitalism had not materialized. To use Popper's terminology, the theories of Marxism had been falsified.

Of course, this did not stop Marxists from wriggling out of these corners by clever use of the dialectic, by denying that the predictions had ever been made, or by denying reality. Theory and evidence were reformulated to keep the falsifiers at bay. When the ideology came to power, as in the Soviet Union, its guardians had other methods available for dealing with obvious failure, such as arrests, executions, and labor camps. When a black swan showed up, they simply denied it was a swan. If someone persisted in claiming it was a swan, he was shipped off to the Gulag.

Popper has been called Marxism's greatest critic, largely on the strength of *The Open Society and Its Enemies.* Isaiah Berlin wrote in 1963 that it contained "the most scrupulous and formidable criticism of the philosophical and historical doctrines of Marxism by any living writer." And yet, interestingly enough, the first edition of *The Open Society* offered only subdued criticism of the Soviet Union. Popper called the book "my war effort," a war being waged against the Axis powers, not the USSR, which was an ally. His primary target was not Marx but Plato and Hegel, whom he identified as the chief sources of inspiration for fascism.

Karl Popper, 1940s. (Sir Karl Raimund Popper Papers)

Not that Popper was biting his tongue. His book lauded Marx as a great liberator, despite the many failures of his philosophy; and Stalin was praised for "making bold and often successful experiments in social engineering." Such expressions of support for the Soviet experiment were quite common during the war, when the label "totalitarian" was typically reserved for Nazi Germany. The Marxists in power in Moscow might be mistaken about a lot of things, but the Soviet Union was one of the "progressive" powers fighting against the totalitarians. (One sees the same priorities, though less pronounced, in the first edition of Friedrich von Hayek's *The Road to Serfdom* in 1944.)

Looking back on his sympathy for Marx's egalitarian promise, which dated back to his teenage years, Popper wrote: "It took some time before I recognized this as no more than a beautiful dream; that freedom is more important than equality; that the attempt to realize equality endangers freedom. . . ." Under the influence of Hayek and the force of events, *The Open Society* was revised to cast the Soviet Union as a totalitarian nemesis. As his biographer, Haim Cohen, says of Popper and his most famous book, "He wrote it as a defense of democracy against fascism, but it quickly became, with his full support, a charter of cold war liberalism."

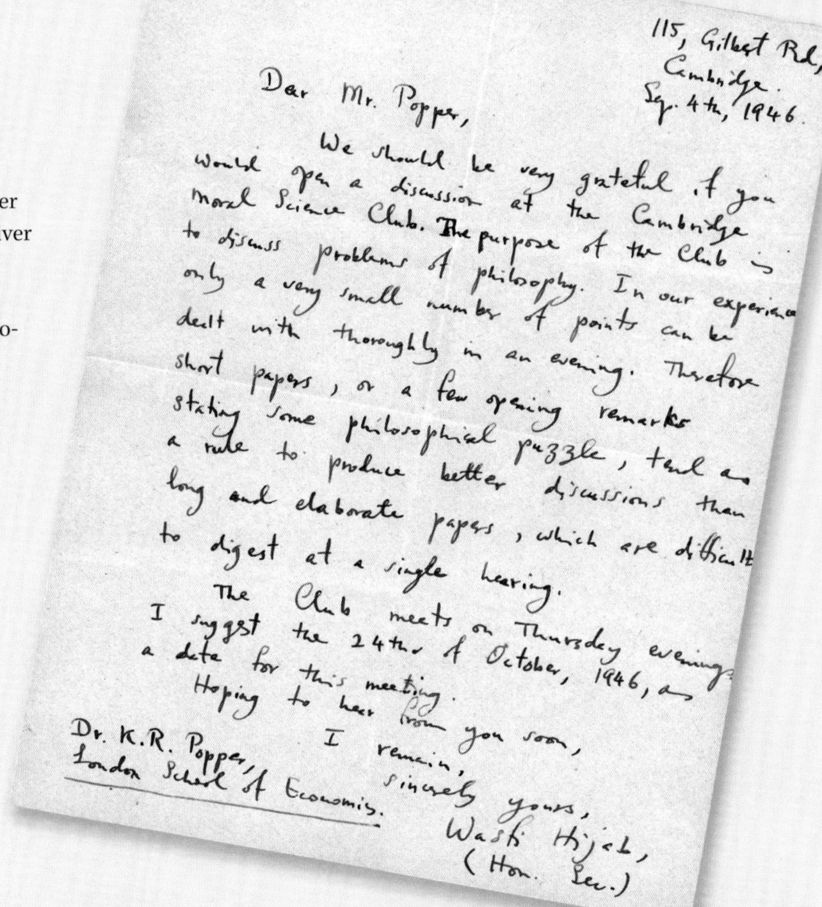

115, Gilbert Rd,
Cambridge.
Sep. 4th, 1946.

Dear Mr. Popper,

We should be very grateful if you would open a discussion at the Cambridge Moral Science Club. The purpose of the Club is to discuss problems of philosophy. In our experience only a very small number of points can be dealt with thoroughly in an evening. Therefore short papers, or a few opening remarks stating some philosophical puzzle, tend as a rule to produce better discussions than long and elaborate papers, which are difficult to digest at a single hearing.

The Club meets on Thursday evenings. I suggest the 24th of October, 1946, as a date for this meeting.

Hoping to hear from you soon,

I remain,
Sincerely yours,
Wasfi Hijab,
(Hon. Sec.)

Dr. K.R. Popper,
London School of Economics.

Letter of invitation to Popper, from Wasfi Hijab, secretary of the Moral Science Club, dated September 4, 1946. Note the suggestion that Popper should deliver "a few opening remarks stating some philosophical puzzle," the hallmark of Wittgenstein's Cambridge group. The session was held on a Friday to accommodate Popper's schedule. (Sir Karl Raimund Popper Papers)

Puzzles and Problems

Popper has become best known to a general audience not from his seminal work in philosophy and social science but from his role in a famous—and famously obscure—encounter with the Cambridge philosopher Ludwig Wittgenstein, another ex-Viennese living in Britain, considered the most brilliant philosopher of his generation. Wittgenstein and Popper held contrasting views of the role of the philosopher. Popper believed that he ought to concern himself with solving genuine theoretical problems, as philosophers had always done. Wittgenstein believed that there were no genuine philosophical problems, only conceptual puzzles resulting from the misuse or ambiguities of language. Popper found Wittgenstein's fixation on language frivolous and unworthy of a true philosopher.

The two men had a chance to debate these views on the evening of October 25, 1946, at a session of the Cambridge Moral Science Club, a weekly discussion group for the faculty and students of the university's Philosophy Department. The speaker that evening was Popper, who gave his paper the provocative title "Are There Philosophical Problems?" Presiding at the session was Bertrand Russell, who was an early influence on both men but who by then was becoming better known as a radical activist than as a philosopher.

What exactly happened that evening will always be open to debate, beyond the fact that Wittgenstein and Popper engaged in a brief, contentious exchange over the fundamental nature of philosophy before Wittgenstein abruptly left the room. Their ten-minute encounter is the subject of a lively book of ideas by Edmonds and Eidinow, called *Wittgenstein's Poker* (2001). The central dispute is whether Wittgenstein, who picked up a poker from the fireplace, used it to threaten Popper. That was how Popper remembered it. In his version of events, when Wittgenstein demanded a statement of moral principle, Popper replied, "Not to threaten visiting lecturers with pokers," prompting Wittgenstein to storm out of the room.

The Penalty of Success

The Open Society was an enormous success, published in numerous editions and translated into more than thirty languages. Popper lived to see the fall of the Berlin Wall and the collapse of the Soviet Union (he died in 1994). His advocacy of the open society was vindicated. George Soros, the Hungarian-born financier and philanthropist and a former student of Popper's, named his Open Society Foundation, which helped to speed the end of communism in Eastern Europe, in Popper's honor.

Yet the very success of his ideas, ironically, means that they are seldom attributed to Popper, whose name meanwhile slips into obscurity. His breakthrough ideas in science, notably the falsification method, have become common sense. Many of his political ideas—the critique of Marxism, the attack on authoritarianism, and the defense of the open society—have been widely embraced. As a political theorist, Popper did not produce a single, systematic worldview that would have attracted to him a group of committed followers, and his ideas have been interpreted variously across the political spectrum. Although he was embraced by conservatives, Popper remained a lifelong social democrat.

In the face of this success, Popper would have warned against complacency. The end of communism did not bring an end to history, but rather new challenges to the open society in the form of ethnonational intolerance, religious fundamentalism, and the threat to essential liberties posed by catastrophic terrorism and the defense against it. Nothing is guaranteed. Just as scientific discovery is an unending quest, so too is the struggle to maintain an open society.

FREEDOM IN THE AIR

The Cold War was fundamentally a contest of ideas. One way the West waged the contest was through Radio Free Europe and Radio Liberty, which broadcast news and features from Munich to countries behind the Iron Curtain starting in the early 1950s. The Radios tapped the resources and talents of émigrés from Eastern Europe to offer an alternative to the highly censored programming of the Radio Warsaws and Radio Moscows of the East Bloc. Despite continual Soviet jamming, threats to their funding during the detente of the 1970s, and even a Communist-sponsored terrorist attack at Munich headquarters in 1981, the Radios continued their broadcasts through the revolutionary year 1989 and the break-up of the Soviet Union two years later.

As a combined (since 1976) RFE/RL, at the end of the Cold War the operation was moved to Prague, at the invitation of former dissident-turned-president Vaclav Havel. In 2000, an agreement was signed to deposit all RFE/RL corporate and broadcast records up to 1995 in the Hoover Institution Archives. This immense collection of documents and broadcast tapes will provide scholars of the future with an extraordinarily rich record of the personalities, events, and developments inside the East Bloc during the Cold War and the years of transition to democracy.

Radio Free Europe. Czech and Slovak broadcasters record a radio play in a Radio Free Europe studio with assistance from U.S. Army personnel, undated (1950s). (RFE/RL Records)

Lech Walesa, Warsaw, February 6, 1989. "Without Western broadcasting, totalitarian regimes would have survived much longer. The struggle for freedom would have been more arduous and the road to democracy much longer. . . . From these broadcasting stations we gleaned our lessons of independent thinking and solidarity action."

Solidarity election poster, 1989. By 1989, after several years of reform Communism in Moscow, most Communist governments in Eastern Europe (Romania was the exception) began to follow Moscow's lead, some very reluctantly. Poland's transition to democracy was largely peaceful, with the once-banned trade union Solidarity evolving into the governing political party. This poster, which was designed by Tomasz Sarnecki, was created for the national election of June 4, 1989, which saw Solidarity win 99 percent of the freely elected seats in the Polish parliament—a landmark event in a landmark year. The poster employed an iconic image of American popular culture—Gary Cooper as the sheriff in the classic American film *High Noon*—to convey a sense of the gravity of the moment. Here Cooper's sheriff wears a Solidarity logo above his badge and carries a voting ballot where his holstered gun would normally appear. Poland's revolution was to be nonviolent; the call was to the ballot box, not the barricades.

Fall of the Wall. East and West Germans walking on the Berlin Wall, November 1989 (photograph by Christian Härtel). (German Pictorial Collection)

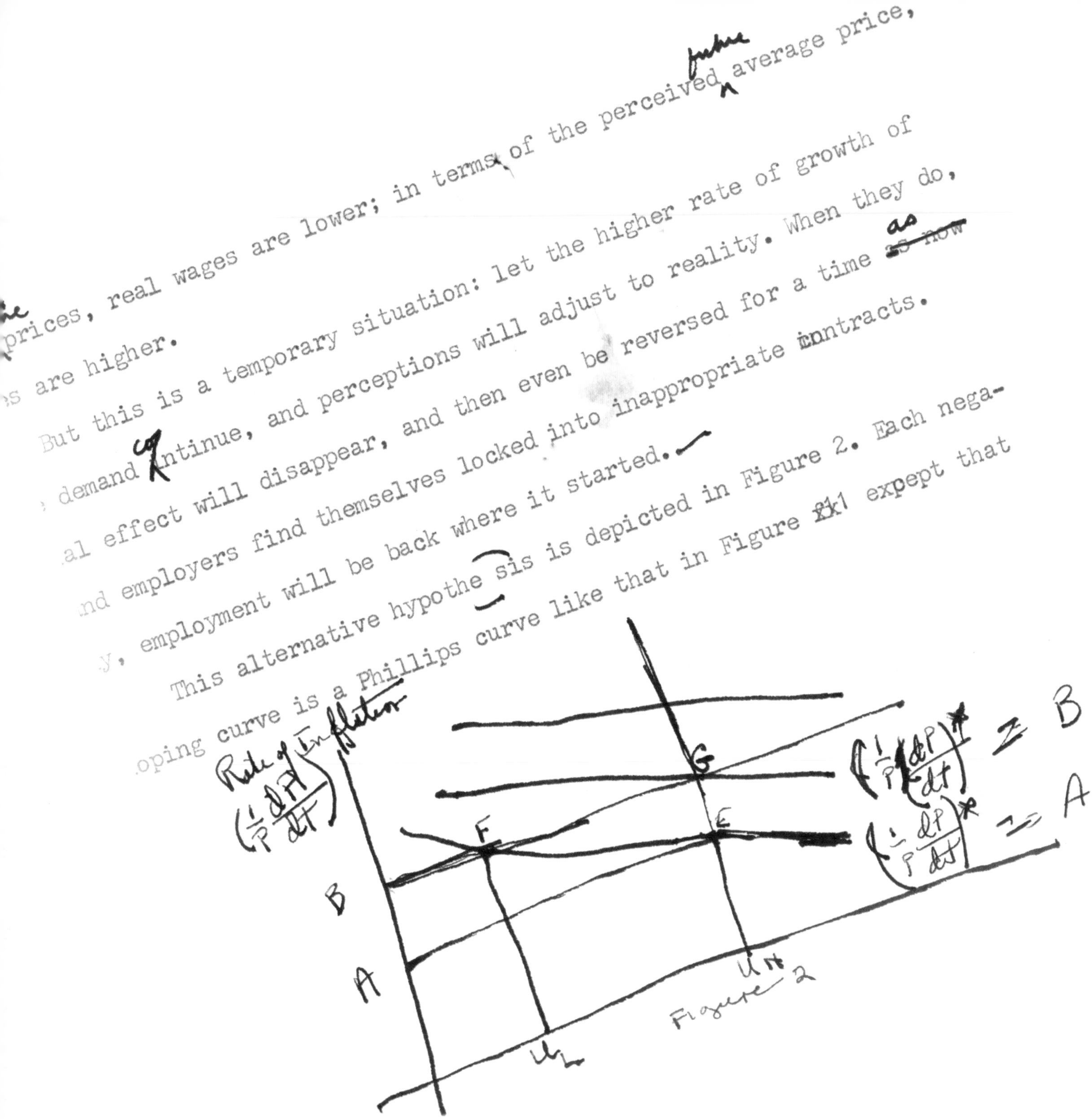
prices, real wages are lower; in terms of the perceived future average price,
s are higher.

But this is a temporary situation: let the higher rate of growth of
demand continue, and perceptions will adjust to reality. When they do,
al effect will disappear, and then even be reversed for a time as
nd employers find themselves locked into inappropriate contracts.
y, employment will be back where it started.

This alternative hypothesis is depicted in Figure 2. Each nega-
oping curve is a Phillips curve like that in Figure 1 expept that

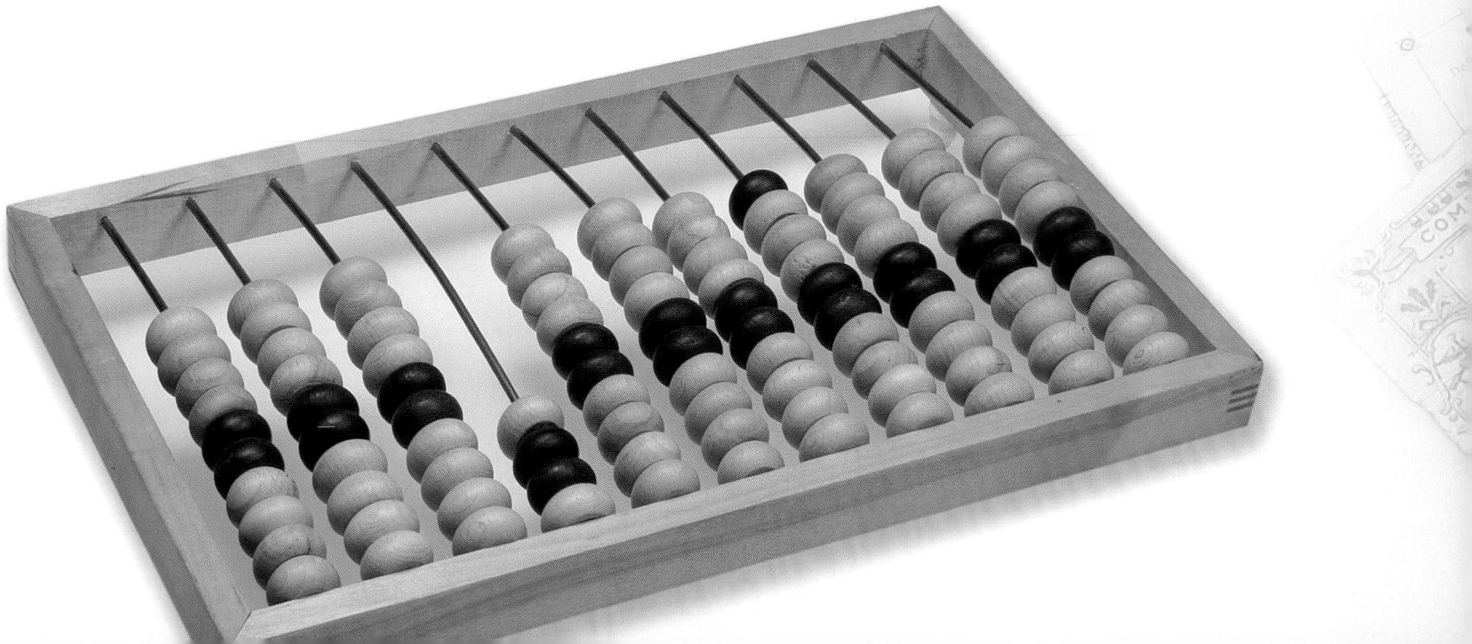

Chapter Eight

THE ECONOMISTS

One way to follow the major trends in economic thought and practice in the twentieth century is to trace the careers of three economists whose papers are in the Hoover Archives. All three were, in distinctive ways, counterrevolutionaries.

The Moscow agronomist Lev Litoshenko was an advocate of the free market in the Soviet Union in the 1920s. The Austrian economist Friedrich von Hayek, living in Great Britain in the 1930s and 1940s, resisted the growing popularity of economic planning and warned of the dangers of socialism. In the 1950s, the University of Chicago's Milton Friedman began his long quest to unseat Keynesian economics, which had prevailed in universities and bureaucracies since the onset of the Great Depression.

Hayek and Friedman became world-famous Nobel Prize winners, and they lived to see many of their most important ideas become accepted as the common wisdom. Litoshenko's promising career was cut short by Stalin's terror, and he died in obscurity in the Gulag.

LEV LITOSHENKO

Adam Smith under Lenin and Stalin

War Communism

When the Bolsheviks came to power in 1917, they had no program for building socialism. They had justified making their proletarian revolution in backward Russia, where more than 80 percent of the population was rural, with the argument that this act would trigger a revolution across Europe, starting with Germany. In the meantime, though, their anti-capitalist ideology pointed the way; one of their first economic steps was to nationalize the central bank.

Once the Bolsheviks were able to consolidate their control over Russia's urban centers, they were propelled forward by a heady combination of the exigencies of civil war and their ideological convictions. This led them to attempt, in the spring of 1918, to spread the class war to the countryside by turning the poorer peasants against the better-off "kulaks." This resulted in violence and economic chaos, which threatened to turn the entire peasantry against the regime just as the Civil War was getting under way. This brought an end, for now, to the experiment of "splitting" the peasantry, but Lenin's government nonetheless found it necessary to squeeze the peasantry as a whole.

As the Civil War intensified, in order to feed the Red Army and the cities (the strongholds of their support), the Bolsheviks had to rely increasingly on the forcible requisition of grain. Most of this work was done by armed food detachments, entering villages and uncovering grain "surpluses" at the point of a gun or bayonet—though by 1920, when the reputation of these units for ruthlessness had spread far and wide, it was said that their mere arrival on the scene was enough to make grain appear. Any peasant not cooperating by handing over his "surplus" grain was liable to be labeled a kulak and dealt with roughly. None of this caused the Bolsheviks to suffer pangs of ideological conscience; despite the spirit of collaboration implied in the emblematic hammer and sickle, the peasantry was never intended to be more than the junior partner in the revolutionary enterprise.

In industry too, the twin forces of circumstance and ideology encouraged a trend toward state control. In June 1918, the government nationalized all heavy industry and then proceeded from there incrementally to nationalize every other category—light industry, wholesale trade, retail trade, and cooperatives—until, near the end of 1920, state control had been extended to every enterprise hiring at least five employees. By then, there was so little industry in operation that such control existed mostly on paper, but the principle was clear. Taken together, these radical economic policies from 1918 to 1921 came to be known as War Communism.

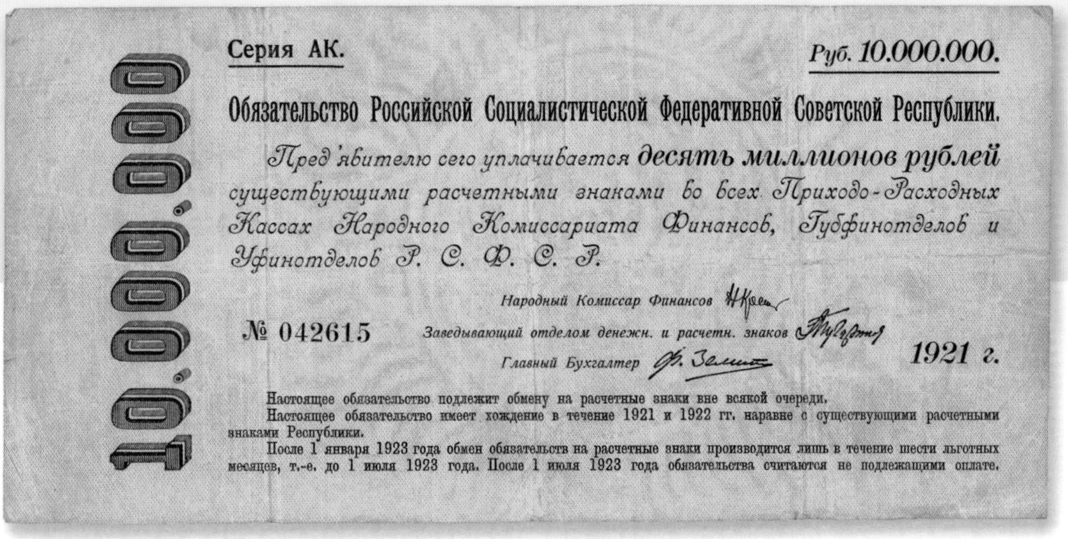
10.000.000
Серия АК.
Руб. 10.000.000.
Обязательство Российской Социалистической Федеративной Советской Республики.
Пред'явителю сего уплачивается десять миллионов рублей существующими расчетными знаками во всех Приходо-Расходных Кассах Народного Комиссариата Финансов, Губфинотделов и Уфинотделов Р. С. Ф. С. Р.
Народный Комиссар Финансов
№ 042615
Заведывающий отделом денежн. и расчетн. знаков
Главный Бухгалтер
1921 г.
Настоящее обязательство подлежит обмену на расчетные знаки вне всякой очереди.
Настоящее обязательство имеет хождение в течение 1921 и 1922 гг. наравне с существующими расчетными знаками Республики.
После 1 января 1923 года обмен обязательств на расчетные знаки производится лишь в течение шести льготных месяцев, т.-е. до 1 июля 1923 года. После 1 июля 1923 года обязательства считаются не подлежащими оплате.

useless. Barter replaced monetary transactions, as rubles were issued in denominations of millions. The Russians' cynicism about their ruble was reflected in their substitution of the word "lemon" *(limón)* for "million." At the time, radical Bolsheviks greeted this hyperinflation as a death blow for money, which they considered a vestige of dying capitalism. When the Soviet government returned to fiscal responsibility in 1921, it set about reining in this rampant inflation. (Currency Collection)

As the Red Army swept to final victory over the White Guard in 1920, and as private enterprise, money, and trade were increasingly outlawed, the Bolsheviks deluded themselves into believing that they were in fact close to achieving "communism." This, despite the utter ruin of Russia's industry, its transportation network, and its food supply and distribution system. These destructive policies contributed to the colossal famine of 1921–22, which took millions of lives.

By February 1921, the regime was faced with uprisings among hungry workers and peasants, and a rebellion of sailors at the Kronstadt naval base. At that point, Lenin convinced his colleagues of the need to retreat from communism to a limited market economy, an experiment that became known as the New Economic Policy, or NEP. This was a first-of-its-kind mixed economy. The government retained control of the "commanding heights" of heavy industry, railroads, utilities, and foreign trade, while allowing just enough private enterprise to rejuvenate industrial production, especially consumer industries, and just enough trade to restore the nexus between town and country. NEP was introduced as a kind of truce between the regime and the peasantry. To soothe the bitter disillusionment within the ranks of the Communist Party, Lenin called NEP a "breathing spell," implying that it was a holding operation until the day when the communist offensive could begin again.

Lev and Elena Litoshenko, Riga, Latvia, November 1925. This photograph was provided to the Hoover Institution in the 1990s by Elena Litoshenko's niece, Nathalie Brooke, whose mother, the Countess Maria Benckendorff, was living in exile in London in the 1920s and 1930s. She was the wife of Konstantine Benckendorff, son of Alexander Benckendorff, the former Russian Ambassador to the Court of St. James.

"A Radical Individualist"

The retreat to relative moderation in economic policy did not mean the end of political repression, however. Among the Revolution's "class enemies" after 1917 were non-Communist intellectuals and scholars, most of whom spent the civil war years preoccupied with the hunt for lifesaving food. Among the old-regime intelligentsia the economists fared best. They managed to stay professionally active because their expertise was needed by the government, which employed them as "specialists" to help run the economy. The coming of NEP, based on the idea of maintaining good relations with the peasantry and promoting agriculture through market incentives, seemed to make the position of the agrarian economists especially secure.

A maverick among the non-Marxist agronomists was Lev Nikolaevich Litoshenko, who was based at the Soviet government's Central Statistical Administration. A graduate of Moscow University (1909) and a professor of economics at the Timiriazev Academy, an agricultural research institute in the capital, Litoshenko had before the Revolution earned a reputation as a classical liberal. One colleague characterized him as "a thoroughgoing free-trader and a radical individualist." Under the Bolsheviks, Litoshenko had to be more circumspect, of course, and his publications after 1917 were largely statistical studies, mostly of peasant budgets, his particular specialty.

Yet this was hardly sufficient to occupy a mind like Litoshenko's. It was sometime in 1920, evidently, that he began secretly working on a comprehensive study of War Communism as it unfolded in the countryside. He drew on official decrees and policy statements, a wealth of agricultural statistics, and his own insider's knowledge of the policy makers and their work. As well, he incorporated eyewitness accounts to depict the economic effects and human toll of the Soviet government's agrarian policies.

Litoshenko's study, which he titled "The Socialization of the Land in Russia," laid bare the ideological urge behind the Bolshevik approach to the countryside, notably the coercion used to requisition food and suppress trade, which, in the author's view, surpassed serfdom under the tsars in its brutality. Moreover, toward the end of 1920 the Communists were preparing to nationalize agricultural production itelf. Only when their hold on power was threatened in the winter of 1921 did they give in and lift the ban on dreaded "free trade."

In his indictment of Bolshevik agrarian practices, Litoshenko invoked Adam Smith's four canons of taxation, expounded in *The Wealth of Nations.* Soviet taxes, he wrote, seemed designed with the intention of flouting all four of Smith's rules: they were unequal, arbitrary, inconvenient to pay, and uneconomical to administer. "This is aside from the brutalities worthy of the Middle Ages that accompanied the requisitions and taxes, aside from the 'militarization' of food supply, aside from the denial to all those considered 'work-bound' of their freedom as individuals. These aspects of a socialist taxation system could not have been envisaged in the humane age of Smith."

Obviously this was not a study of War Communism that could be published in Soviet Russia. In 1922, Litoshenko entrusted his work to Frank Golder, the Stanford historian who had entered Soviet Russia with Herbert Hoover's famine relief workers in order to collect documents for the new Hoover War Library. Golder shipped Litoshenko's manuscript back to Stanford, where it would help launch a most unusual and instructive experiment in U.S.-Soviet cultural relations.

A Year at Stanford

Professor Golder had come away from Soviet Russia convinced of the need for American scholars to study the Russian Revolution in all its political, economic, and social aspects, and he saw that the Hoover collections could serve as the foundation for a Russian research center. To this end, and with the help of the university president, in 1925 he won for Stanford a modest foundation grant, the first such award in support of Russian studies in the United States.

Golder called his project the Russian Revolution Institute, envisioning it as a permanent center for Russian studies at Stanford. He intended to use his network of contacts in Soviet Russia to enlist Soviet scholars and researchers in his endeavor, and through them to gain access to the Soviet archives. To accomplish this, he realized that he would need to secure the cooperation, or at least the noninterference, of the Soviet government. Negotiations between Stanford and the All-Union Society for Cultural Relations with Foreign Countries (VOKS) of the Soviet Foreign Ministry produced a general agreement in 1925.

Golder's idea was to invite Russian scholars to Stanford to work with American specialists; the Russians would perform the principal research using the Soviet archives, after which they would bring their materials to Stanford, where they would write their studies together with American scholars and have the resources of the Hoover Library at their disposal. The Russian Institute would then publish these studies in English in the United States.

The first fruit of this arrangement was the research visit to Stanford of Lev Litoshenko and his wife Elena, for the academic year 1926–27. Stanford President Wilbur appointed him Lecturer in History for the year; his wife took an administrative position in the Hoover Library. At Stanford, Litoshenko was reunited with his 1922 manuscript, which he now set about revising and bringing up to date. One year later, with the assistance of Berkeley economist Lincoln Hutchinson, Litoshenko completed a 593-page manuscript on Bolshevik agrarian policy from 1917 to 1927.

The enlarged manuscript was less harsh on the Bolsheviks than the 1922 original—not surprisingly since, according to Golder's arrangement with the Soviet government, it would have to meet with approval of the authorities in Moscow in order to be published. Nonetheless, the revised study presented the catastrophic collapse of Russian agriculture as the direct result of the Communist regime's economic policies in the period 1918–1920. Arbitrary food requisitions sanctioned by the central government induced the peasants to cut back their area of sown acreage, reducing output to the limit not subject to taxation. When a severe drought struck in 1920, the peasants had no reserve to fall back on; in 1921 they began to starve by the millions.

Litoshenko's study was careful to praise the return to moderation of the New Economic Policy, attributing it to Lenin's radical rethinking of the communist experiment and newfound desire for peaceful cooperation with the peasantry. Yet Litoshenko detected a fundamental contradiction within NEP, which, he determined, made it unsuitable as a program for achieving further economic growth in the USSR. Soviet government policy, he wrote, was geared toward hampering the stratification of the peasantry through heavily progressive taxation and controlled prices, both of which stifled the peasants' desire to expand production. As long as the state continued to direct its policies against the upper strata of the peasantry—that is, against the owners of large individual farms, the kulaks—it would perpetuate small-scale farming (or a small-scale farming mentality), thereby inhibiting the creation of marketable agricultural surpluses necessary for industrialization. In other words, NEP was a dead end.

The solution, as Litoshenko saw it, was to let the differentiation of wealth in the countryside take its course—that is, to let the market flourish. It was an option ruled out by Bolshevik ideology. Yet, Lenin's successors were committed to building socialism in Russia, which necessarily meant an emphasis on heavy industry. But by 1927, as Soviet industry

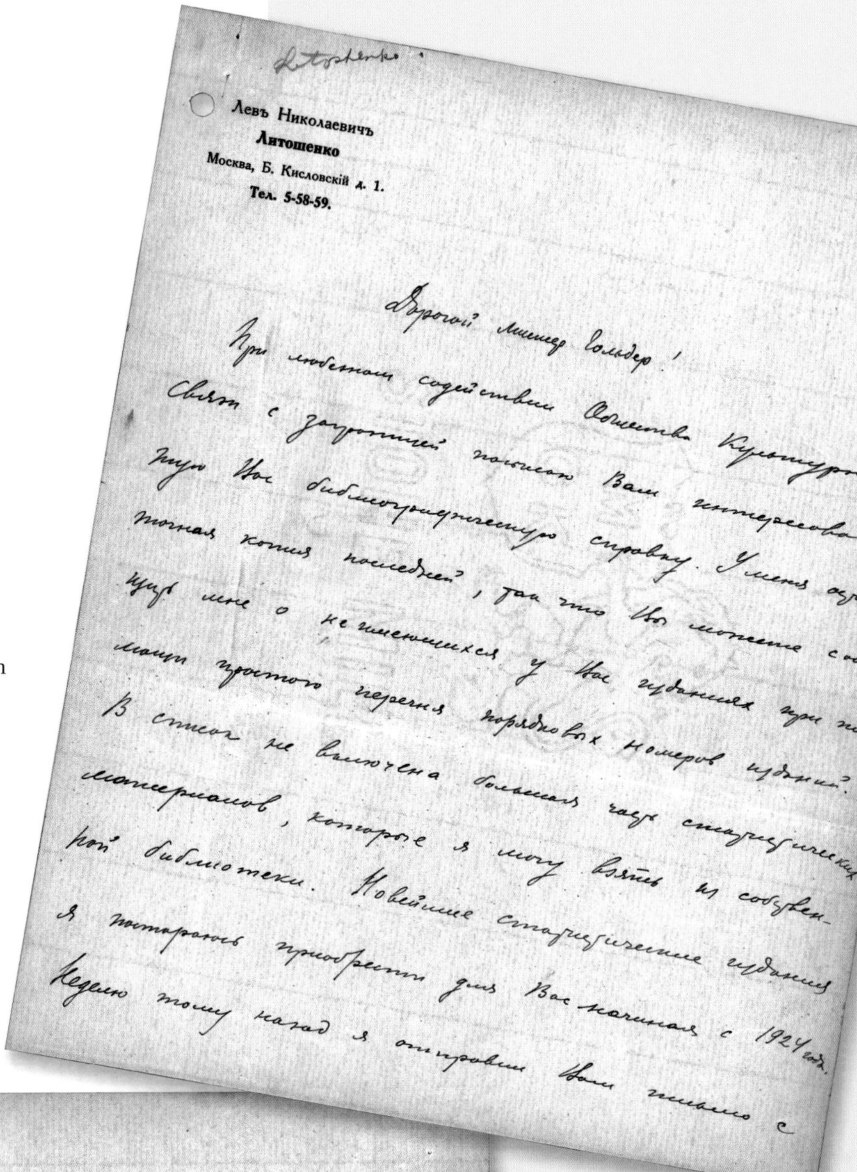

Litoshenko

Левъ Николаевичъ
Литошенко
Москва, Б. Кисловскій д. 1.
Тел. 5-58-59.

10

Дорогой мистер Гольдер!

При любезном содействии Общества Культурной Связи с заграницей посылаю Вам интересовавшую Вас библиографическую справку. У меня осталась точная копия последней, так что Вы можете сообщить мне о не имеющихся у Вас изданиях при помощи простого перечня порядковых номеров изданий. В список не включена большая часть статистических материалов, которые я могу взять из собственной библиотеки. Новейшие статистические издания я постараюсь приобрести для Вас начиная с 1924 год. Неделю тому назад я отправил Вам письмо с

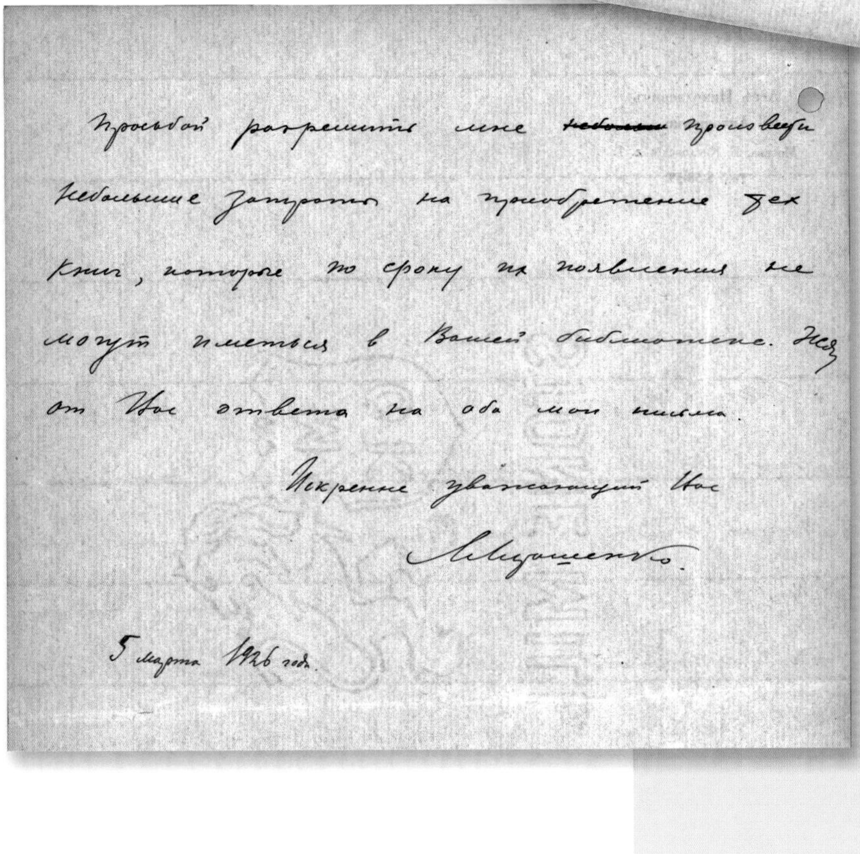

просьбой разрешить мне ~~небольшие~~ производить небольшие затраты на приобретение тех книг, которые по сроку их появления не могут иметься в Вашей библиотеке. Жду от Вас ответа на оба мои письма.

Искренне уважающий Вас

Л. Литошенко.

5 марта 1926 год.

Letter from Litoshenko (in Russian) in Moscow to Frank Golder, March 5, 1926. (Hoover Institution Records) completed its postwar recovery, largely on the basis of pre-1914 industrial plant, it was not clear where the capital necessary for further industrial growth could be found other than by "squeezing" the peasantry. An idea that had been raised in some Bolshevik circles ever since the Revolution was the wholesale forced collectivization of agriculture. This, Litoshenko wrote in his 1927 manuscript, was "an impossible dream."

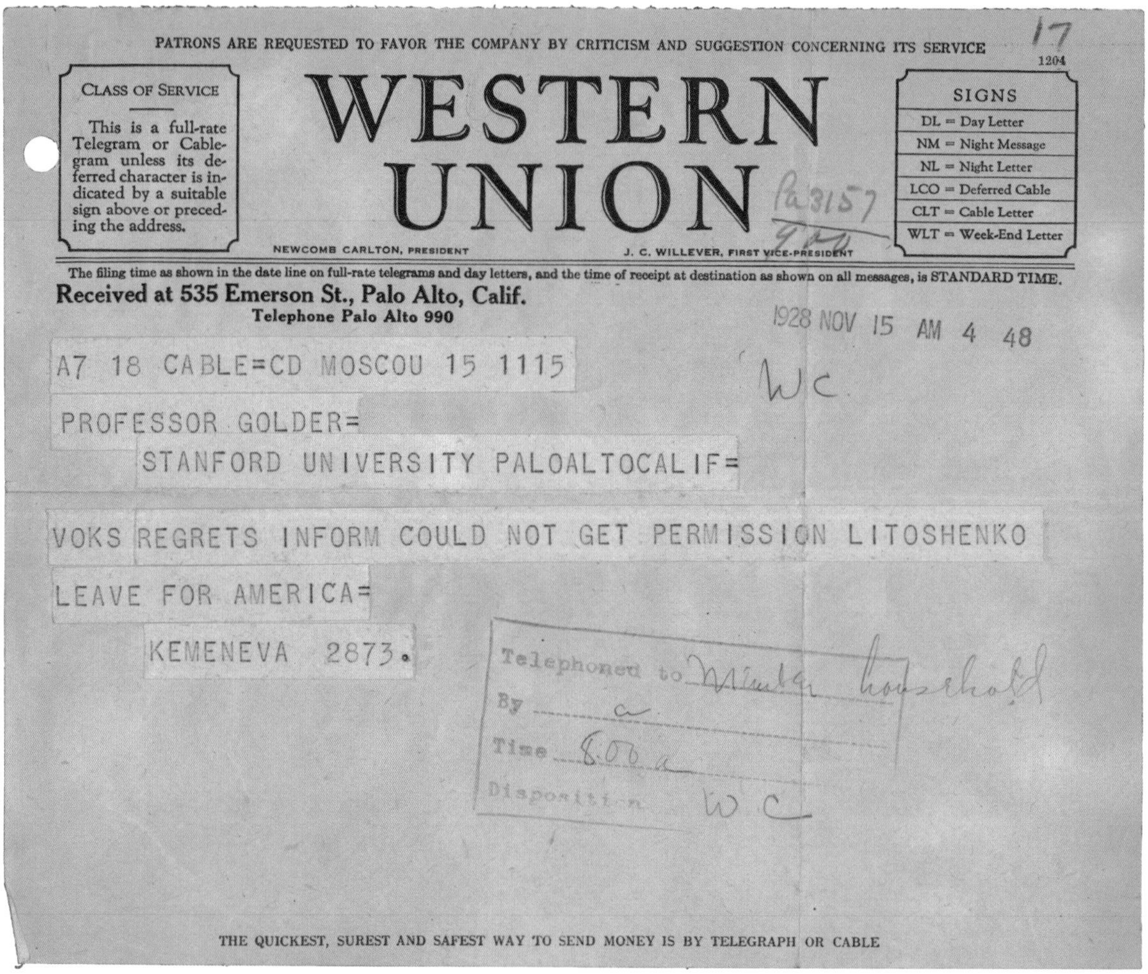

PATRONS ARE REQUESTED TO FAVOR THE COMPANY BY CRITICISM AND SUGGESTION CONCERNING ITS SERVICE

17
1204

CLASS OF SERVICE

This is a full-rate Telegram or Cablegram unless its deferred character is indicated by a suitable sign above or preceding the address.

WESTERN UNION

NEWCOMB CARLTON, PRESIDENT — J. C. WILLEVER, FIRST VICE-PRESIDENT

SIGNS
DL = Day Letter
NM = Night Message
NL = Night Letter
LCO = Deferred Cable
CLT = Cable Letter
WLT = Week-End Letter

The filing time as shown in the date line on full-rate telegrams and day letters, and the time of receipt at destination as shown on all messages, is STANDARD TIME.

Received at 535 Emerson St., Palo Alto, Calif.
Telephone Palo Alto 990

1928 NOV 15 AM 4 48

A7 18 CABLE=CD MOSCOU 15 1115

PROFESSOR GOLDER=
STANFORD UNIVERSITY PALOALTOCALIF=

VOKS REGRETS INFORM COULD NOT GET PERMISSION LITOSHENKO LEAVE FOR AMERICA=

KEMENEVA 2873.

Telephoned to
By
Time 8.00 a
Disposition W C

THE QUICKEST, SUREST AND SAFEST WAY TO SEND MONEY IS BY TELEGRAPH OR CABLE

Telegram from Olga Kameneva to Frank Golder, November 15, 1928. VOKS is the acronym for the All-Union Society for Cultural Relations with Foreign Countries. (Hoover Institution Records)

Stalin's Revolution-from-Above

Upon his return to Moscow from Stanford in the summer of 1927, Litoshenko discovered just how out of step his ideas were within the Bolshevik establishment. Golder learned this as well when he visited the Soviet Union that autumn to get Litoshenko's manuscript approved for publication and arrange for other Soviet scholars to come to Stanford. The atmosphere was politically charged as a major factional struggle was under way within the Communist Party, largely over the future of Soviet economic policy. Because of its criticisms of past Bolshevik agrarian policies, Litoshenko's manuscript would in any case have stirred controversy in Moscow; the fact that it prescribed the market as a way out of the current economic impasse made it political dynamite.

Golder found himself shuttling from office to office, trying to negotiate approval to publish Litoshenko's manuscript. Everywhere he went, Soviet officials were afraid to take initiative. The head of VOKS, Olga Kameneva, who was the wife of the Soviet leader Lev Kamenev and the sister of Leon Trotsky, both of whom had just suffered political defeat at the hands of Stalin, was in "deep trouble," as Golder understood it. At the same time, the Russian scholars Golder spoke with were afraid even to be associated with his project, let alone apply for permission to go to Stanford. Everywhere he turned, Golder could see that "fear had got the upper hand." He left the USSR empty-handed, and although in January 1928 the Politburo did vote to approve an expanded agreement with Stanford, Golder realized that the prospects for a fruitful Soviet-American joint enterprise were grim.

The year 1928 marked a full-scale assault on the non-Marxist agrarian scholars—part of the larger "cultural revolution" that began at the time. It also saw the first show trials against the technical intelligentsia, accused of sabotage and treason, the first in a series of such "plots" that were to become emblematic of the xenophobia of the Stalin years. Here the non-Marxist agrarian scholars were among the most vulnerable professionally because, more than most Soviet scholars, they placed a premium on professional contacts with foreign scholars and valued the good reputation of their work abroad. Such foreign connections were now suspect. By the second half of 1928, in every academic field "bourgeois specialists" were on the run.

Back at Stanford, Golder was becoming desperate to get Litoshenko out of the Soviet Union. Soviet archival documents show that Litoshenko's application to leave was discussed at the highest levels of the Kremlin, where it was placed before Stalin. A major concern was that, should Litoshenko be allowed to leave the country—and he insisted on bringing his wife along—he might decide not to return. The matter hung fire for several months until, on November 15, Kameneva sent a telegram to Golder informing him that VOKS "could not get permission [for] Litoshenko [to] leave for America."

Litoshenko's personal letters to Golder during this period fill in some of the political detail and document his descent into a state of despair, which only deepened when he learned of Golder's unexpected death in January 1929. Harold Fisher, Stanford professor of history and future director of the Hoover Institution, stepped in to try to salvage Golder's project, which before long amounted to trying to save Litoshenko's life. A trip to Moscow in August to clarify matters proved fruitless. The grip of fear had been further tightened. Litoshenko was now being openly denounced. A conference of Marxist-Leninist Scientific Research Organizations passed a resolution "On the Tasks of Marxist Science in the Field of Agriculture," which included this point:

> *The conference believes it necessary to conduct the most energetic struggle against bourgeois theoreticians (Kondratev, Litoshenko) who act as apologists of the capitalistic development of the countryside, depicting kulaks as the "carriers of progress" and resisting the offensive launched by the party against the capitalist elements of the countryside.*

In October, *Pravda* published an attack on Litoshenko that included a self-incriminating quote from a speech in the early 1920s:

> *The land will be in the hands of those who are stronger, who with hard work and love of property will be able to overcome all the disruptions brought about by the revolution. Our agrarian structure will be infinitely removed from all kinds of socialization.*

Toward the end of 1929 came Stalin's Great Turn in economic policy, a "revolution from above" that turned the industrial targets of the First Five-Year Plan into a crash industrialization campaign and introduced the forced collectivization of agriculture. Within a few years collectivization would turn twenty-three million peasant households into 250,000 collective farms—an outcome that Litoshenko had dismissed as an "impossible dream." What made it possible was a campaign of "dekulakization" involving the death or deportation to Siberia of hundreds of thousands of the country's most productive farmers. It was a return to the methods of War Communism, on a scale and with an effectiveness that would not have been possible a decade earlier, when Bolshevik authority barely penetrated the countryside. By 1932 the country experienced another major famine, this one centered in the Ukraine, which claimed millions more lives.

In the summer of 1930 Litoshenko was arrested on charges of conspiracy. At Stanford, Fisher and his colleagues felt helpless to act in his behalf, lest their appeals serve to further

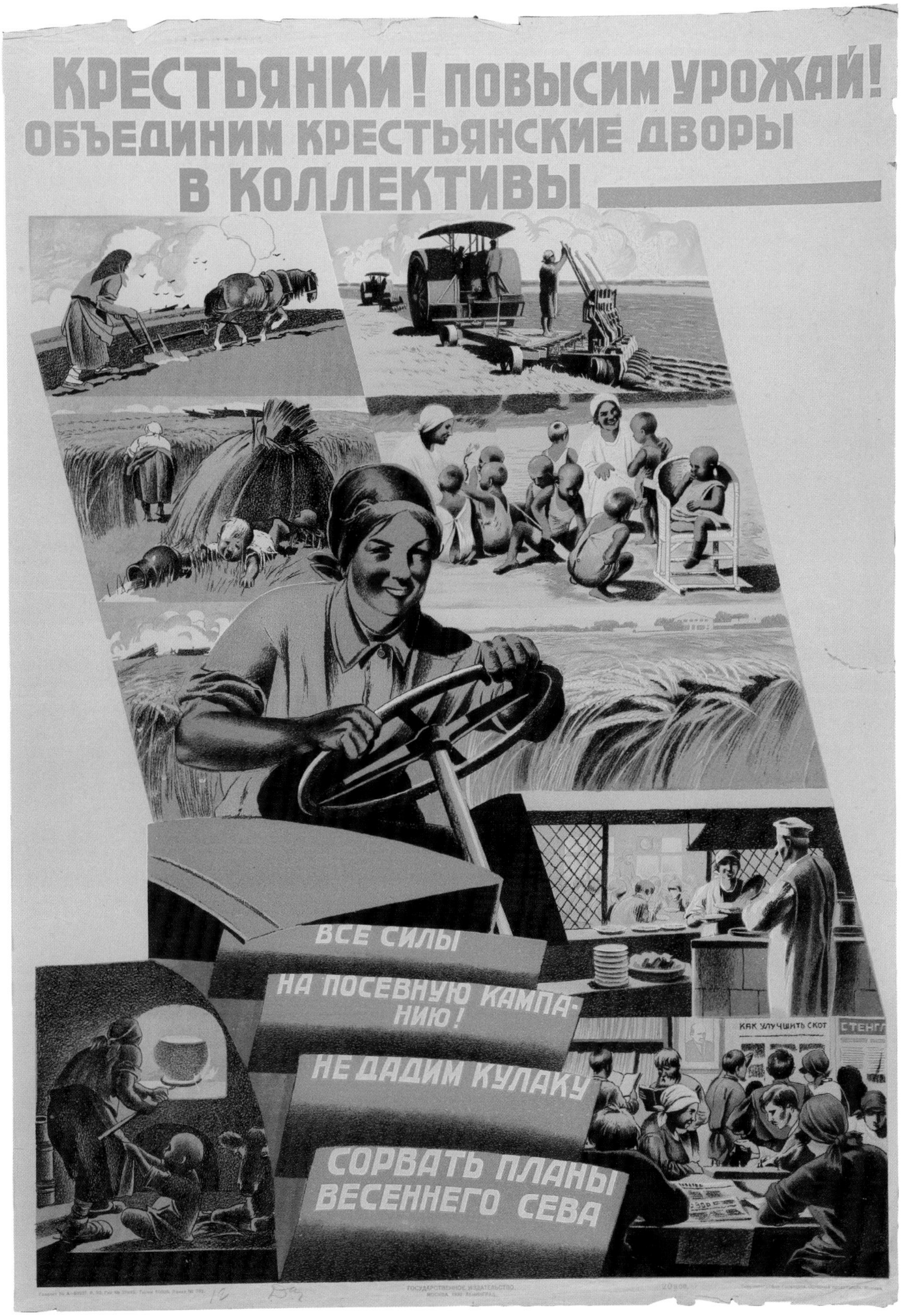

Soviet collectivization poster. The text in the foreground reads in part: "Don't allow the kulak to wreck the spring planting." USSR, 1930.

incriminate him. The last word received from Litoshenko arrived in the form of a brief note dated September 27, 1932, carried out by a Stanford historian visiting Moscow. It was devoted entirely to personal matters:

> *You will probably be glad to know that both of us, my wife and myself are still alive, staying in Moscow, working hard and always keeping the best memoirs of the University of Stanford and of our American friends. Out of the three last years I have spent 1½ years in jail perfectly innocent and accused of some dreadful doings which I never dreamed of. But everything that has a good end is good says a Russian proverb.*

He asked Fisher to have the Palo Alto Mutual Building and Loan Association not send him any further correspondence regarding the interest rate on the money in his bank account, a sum of $100 which he had left for Golder to buy him scholarly books.

> *. . . I ask them not to write to me anymore concerning this money. Otherwise I may be suspected of having "large funds" in foreign money and get in trouble again. . . . I would be awfully glad to get a letter from you, but I am afraid that even an entirely innocent correspondence as ours may prove to be perilous to its Russian partner.*

In January 1938, at the height of the Great Terror, Litoshenko was arrested, charged with engaging in counterrevolutionary activity. On April 9, 1938, he was sentenced to eight years in a labor camp. He died in a camp in Kolyma, in Siberia, on November 27, 1943.

In 1987, as the Soviet system began to reform itself into extinction, various individuals who had for decades been "nonpersons" began to be "rehabilitated," among them the "economists-professors" such as Litoshenko. Articles began to appear in the press detailing their professional biographies and scientific ideas. Their works began to be published. All at once, the enormity of Russia's loss in the field of economics during the decades of Soviet Communism became strikingly apparent.

In 2001, nearly eighty years after it arrived at the Stanford campus, Litoshenko's original 1922 manuscript, which remains unmatched as a study of War Communism in the countryside, was published in Russia. It is fitting that the publication was made possible by a joint undertaking of Russian and American scholars, in Moscow and at Stanford University.

FRIEDRICH VON HAYEK

The Vitality of Capitalism

Friedrich von Hayek's theories on free-market capitalism are today part of the common wisdom. The *New Yorker* magazine's John Cassidy observed in 2000 that "it is hardly an exaggeration to refer to the twentieth century as the Hayek century." Before the Second World War, Hayek was considered the only serious rival economist to John Maynard Keynes. After the war he was the most influential critic of socialism. And yet, today Hayek's name is barely known to the general public.

Friedrich von Hayek, 1944. (Fritz Machlup Papers)

Hayek Versus Keynes

Like many young intellectuals of his generation, Hayek, who was born in Vienna in 1899 and fought in the Great War, started out holding mildly socialist views. He shed them under the influence of the economists of the pro–free-market Austrian school of economics, especially his mentor Ludwig von Mises, who in 1922 published an influential critique of socialist economics.

Hayek's early area of expertise was money and business cycles, and his writings on these subjects brought him attention in academic circles beyond Austria, to the point where for a time he was seen as a possible contender against Keynes, the world-famous Cambridge economist and best-selling author of *The Economic Consequences of the Peace* (1919). Their theoretical dispute really began with the publication in 1930 of Keynes's *A Treatise on Money,* of which Hayek published a blistering review in the August 1931 issue of the journal *Economica.* Keynes fired back in response, and the game was on.

Their argument, which was often highly technical (with Keynes constantly complaining of not being able to understand Hayek's ideas or penetrate his German), can be boiled down to a basic disagreement. Keynes and his Cambridge disciples had developed a theory that economic recessions were the result of a shortage of demand, which could be prevented by reducing taxes and increasing government spending. Lionel Robbins and his team at the London School of Economics (LSE), meanwhile, upheld the traditional view that recessions were "Nature's cure" to an imbalance in the economy, as investment in the expansion of industrial capacity outstripped savings; the recovery could be accelerated by increased saving, but government intervention would likely make matters worse. Hayek's ideas were in harmony with those of Robbins and the LSE economists.

Keynes sharply criticized Hayek's position as set forth in his 1931 book *Prices and Production.* Replying to Hayek's harsh review of *A Treatise on Money,* Keynes used the occasion to attack Hayek's volume, which had just appeared in print:

> *The book, as it stands, seems to me to be one of the most frightful muddles I have ever read, with scarcely a sound proposition in it beginning with page 45, and yet it remains a book of some interest, which is likely to leave its mark on the mind of the reader. It is an extraordinary example of how, starting with a mistake, a remorseless logician can end up in Bedlam.*

All of this was very encouraging to Robbins, who invited Hayek to the LSE as a guest lecturer in 1931 and arranged for his full-time appointment the following year. Despite the continual volleys fired between Cambridge and London, on a personal level Hayek and Keynes enjoyed cordial personal relations. Keynes wrote to his wife in March 1933: "We get on very well in private life. But what rubbish his theory is—I felt to-day that even he was beginning to disbelieve it himself."

As the 1930s progressed, Keynes came out on top in the macroeconomic policy debate, as the deepening Great Depression led to the widespread acceptance of what would later be called "Keynesian economics." Keynesians were most closely identified with the fundamental lesson they drew from the Depression: namely, that the "invisible hand" of the market, if left unattended, could bring catastrophe. Government had to play a guiding role. This was a very popular notion at the time of capitalism's greatest crisis, when the Soviet Five-Year Plan captured the imagination of many Europeans and Americans.

Through a combination of these circumstances and Hayek's wide-ranging intellectual curiosity, he began to shift his attention from technical economics to social and philosophical problems related to economics. It was in this intellectual realm that he would have his greatest impact.

Updating Adam Smith

In the late 1930s, at a time when more and more people, especially Europeans, began to see some form of socialism as desirable and inevitable, Hayek stepped forward to challenge the consensus. He argued, against much evidence all around, the essential vitality of capitalism and the need to preserve it.

In November 1936, Hayek delivered a speech that was published as an article in February 1937 under the title "Economics and Knowledge." It attracted little attention when it

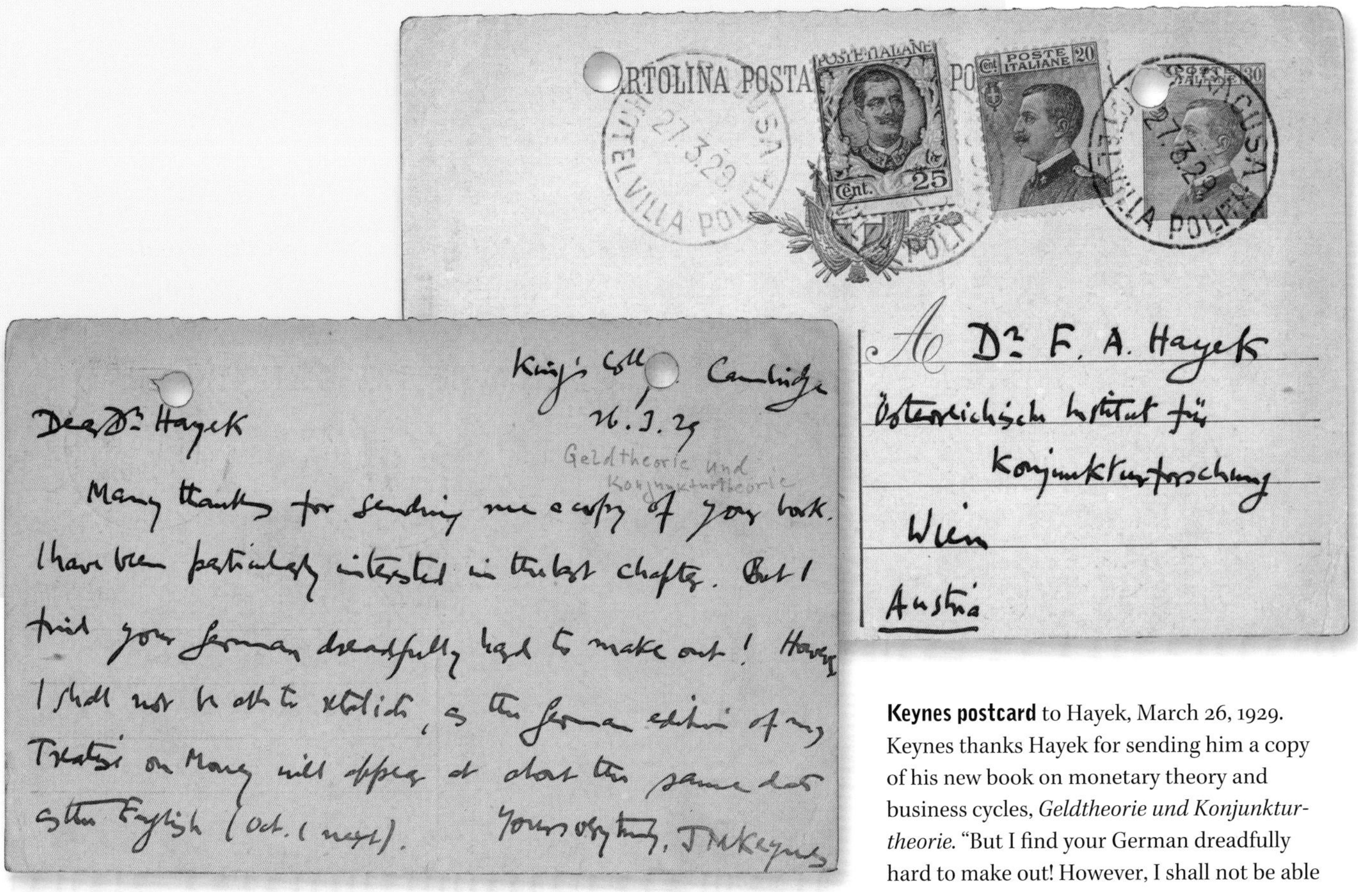
King's Coll. Cambridge
26.3.29
Dear Dr Hayek
Geldtheorie und Konjunkturtheorie
Many thanks for sending me a copy of your book. I have been particularly interested in the last chapter. But I find your German dreadfully hard to make out! However I shall not be able to retaliate, as the German edition of my Treatise on Money will appear at about the same date as the English (Oct. 1 next).
Yours very truly, J M Keynes

CARTOLINA POSTALE
POSTE ITALIANE
A Dr F. A. Hayek
Österreichisches Institut für
Konjunkturforschung
Wien
Austria

Keynes postcard to Hayek, March 26, 1929. Keynes thanks Hayek for sending him a copy of his new book on monetary theory and business cycles, *Geldtheorie und Konjunkturtheorie*. "But I find your German dreadfully hard to make out! However, I shall not be able to retaliate, as the German edition of my Treatise on Money will appear at about the same date as the English (Oct. 1 next)." (Friedrich von Hayek Papers)

appeared, yet in retrospect it was a turning point in Hayek's move away from technical economics and in the formulation of his general argument against socialism. It marked the origin of his most important contribution to economics: the idea that market prices are means of communicating information. At a time when central planning was increasingly viewed as the solution to capitalism's perceived irrational and inefficient distribution of resources and its chronic instabilities, Hayek pointed to a fundamental weakness of a centralized system: its inability to master the "division of knowledge" problem. As Cassidy explains,

> *In order to know where resources should be directed, the central planner needs to know both what goods people want to buy and how they can most cheaply be produced. But this knowledge is held in the minds of individual consumers and businesspeople, not in the filing cabinets (or, later, computers) of a government planning agency, and the only practical way for customers and firms to relay this knowledge to each other, Hayek argued, is through a system of market-determined prices.*

Because it is able to incorporate the private decisions of countless individuals, the market operates on the basis of vastly more information than any planner could possibly manage. Hayek called the end result of the market's information processing "spontaneous order." Here was a variation on Adam Smith's "invisible hand." As Cassidy writes, "This view of capitalism as a spontaneous information-processing machine—a 'telecommunications system' is how Hayek referred to it—was one of the great insights of the century. It may have been implicit in the work of some previous economists, notably Adam Smith, but Hayek was the first to spell it out."

This was a clear challenge to the proponents of planning. "However well-intentioned they may be," Hayek wrote, "the planners face a crucial deficit in information." As he expressed it in a 1939 essay, "Freedom and the Economic System," the "unconscious collaboration of individuals in the market leads to the solution of problems which, although no individual mind has even formulated these problems in a market economy, would have to be consciously solved on the same principle in a planned system." In strictly economic terms, then, a market economy is far superior to one that is centrally planned; it is likely to be far more productive and efficient, and more promising for technological progress because the market encourages innovation.

Yet Hayek's argument had a strong moral component as well, which, to him, trumped these economic advantages. Under socialism, the planners would unavoidably have to make choices about social ends, favoring some groups and individuals and disfavoring others. Yet they would do so in the absence of an agreed-on hierarchy of values to guide them. The planners themselves would have to decide upon and enforce a "detailed code of values." In Hayek's view, such choices are best left to individuals in a free society and not imposed by the state. Put simply, the free market is about not only creating wealth but maintaining freedom. Capitalism is essential to democracy.

Hayek's ideas reached a relatively small audience on the eve of the Second World War, a cataclysm that would strengthen the popularity of economic planning among intellectuals and the public. While others went into battle or otherwise went to war, Hayek (who, though a British subject since 1938, was not allowed to serve) made what he intended to be his contribution to the war effort, a book written for the general public on the dangers of collectivism.

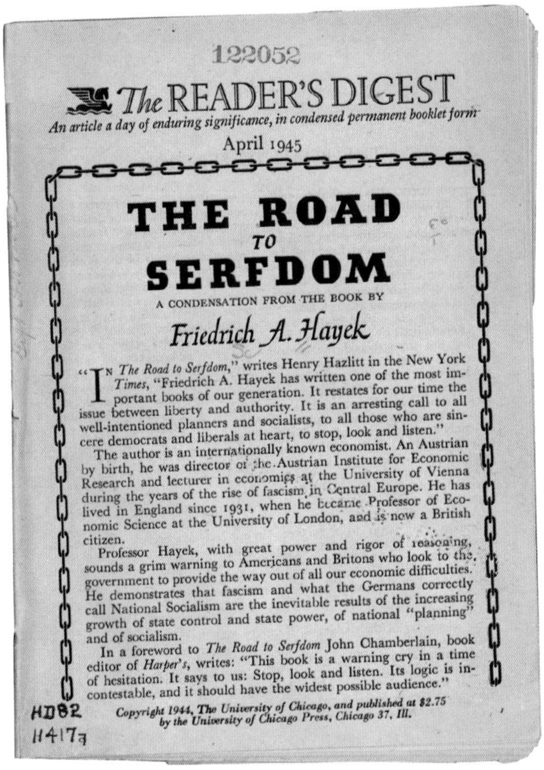
122052

The READER'S DIGEST

An article a day of enduring significance, in condensed permanent booklet form

April 1945

THE ROAD TO SERFDOM

A CONDENSATION FROM THE BOOK BY

Friedrich A. Hayek

"IN *The Road to Serfdom*," writes Henry Hazlitt in the New York *Times*, "Friedrich A. Hayek has written one of the most im- portant books of our generation. It restates for our time the issue between liberty and authority. It is an arresting call to all well-intentioned planners and socialists, to all those who are sin- cere democrats and liberals at heart, to stop, look and listen."

The author is an internationally known economist. An Austrian by birth, he was director of the Austrian Institute for Economic Research and lecturer in economics at the University of Vienna during the years of the rise of fascism in Central Europe. He has lived in England since 1931, when he became Professor of Eco- nomic Science at the University of London, and is now a British citizen.

Professor Hayek, with great power and rigor of reasoning, sounds a grim warning to Americans and Britons who look to the government to provide the way out of all our economic difficulties. He demonstrates that fascism and what the Germans correctly call National Socialism are the inevitable results of the increasing growth of state control and state power, of national "planning" and of socialism.

In a foreword to *The Road to Serfdom* John Chamberlain, book editor of *Harper's*, writes: "This book is a warning cry in a time of hesitation. It says to us: Stop, look and listen. Its logic is in- contestable, and it should have the widest possible audience."

Title page of *Reader's Digest* edition of *The Road to Serfdom.*

The Road to Serfdom

The defeat of Winston Churchill's Conservative Party in the general election of 1945 was in part due to the growing popularity of the idea of state intervention in the British economy. The victorious Labour Party was dominated by Fabian-socialist ideas of nationalizing major industry and utilities.

Fabian socialism was a leading intellectual current in Britain at the beginning of the twentieth century. The Fabians sought to put an end to the idea of *laissez-faire,* believing that only collective control of the economy—including collective ownership of the means of production—could bring the greatest good to the greatest number by creating a welfare state. The Fabians recommended nationalization of utilities and heavy industry, yet they were not Marxists. They insisted on the inviolability of private property and believed in nonviolent, gradual methods for introducing their program, to be brought about piecemeal by the votes of local electors. They wanted to rescue socialism from the barricades and did not much mind being called "gas and water socialists."

Their philosophy was best summed up in the phrase "the inevitability of gradualness," introduced by one of their leaders, Sidney Webb (incidentally, a founder of the London School of Economics, in 1895). The popularity of these ideas in Britain before World War I (the Fabians counted among their number such high-profile supporters as George Bernard Shaw and H. G. Wells) is best captured in the famous statement made at the turn of the twentieth century by Sir William Harcourt: "We are all socialists now."

Fabian-socialist ideas essentially came to power in Britain in 1945, when 230 Fabians (of a total 394 socialists) were elected to the House of Commons and 41 Fabians sat in the new Labour government. That government proceeded to nationalize the Bank of England, telecommunications, civil aviation, rail and road transportation, coal mines, electricity, gas, and medical services.

Thus Hayek was running against the tide with the publication in 1944 of *The Road to Serfdom,* which told of the dangers of socialism and state planning and explained the economic advantages and moral superiority of a free market. Writing his book in a language accessible to the general reader, Hayek warned that once a government starts out planning an economy, it runs the risk of becoming a dictatorship. There is no logical stopping point to planning; it has to work. If not, then the planners have to make it work by going further, introducing still more government involvement. This was the road to totalitarianism.

Hayek dedicated his book "To the Socialists of All Parties" and chose as its lead epigraph Hume's aphorism, "It is seldom that liberty of any kind is lost all at once." The road to serfdom, Hayek was saying, was paved with good intentions. His model for where the Western democracies might end up was not the Soviet Union but Hitler's Germany—which made his argument especially controversial because at the time Nazi Germany was considered the embodiment of evil. Hayek wrote:

> *Although few people, if anybody, in England would probably be ready to swallow totalitarianism whole, there are few single features which have not been advised by somebody or other. Indeed, there is scarcely a leaf out of Hitler's book which somebody or other in England or America has not recommended us to take and use for our own purposes.*

Within a short time, as the Cold War got under way, the Soviet Union replaced Nazi Germany in Hayek's analysis, a shift reflected in subsequent editions of his book.

The Road to Serfdom was a huge best-seller, especially in America, where the reactions both for and against the book were much more pronounced than in Britain. Although it took some effort to find an American publisher, the book sold more than 600,000 copies in the United States. *Reader's Digest* published a condensed version, and Hayek embarked on a speaking tour of the country.

Where to Draw the Line?

The Road to Serfdom made Hayek world-famous, though it was not universally popular with reviewers. One critic who expressed his views privately to the author was Keynes, who had a hand in creating postwar Britain's welfare state before his death in 1946. In a letter to Hayek of June 28, 1944, Keynes, though praising Hayek for having written a "grand book," chided him for basing his argument on "the very doubtful assumption that planning is not more efficient. Quite likely from the purely economic point of view it is efficient."

Otherwise Keynes claimed that his "only serious criticism of the book" was that Hayek had offered no guidance on the question of "where to draw the line" on government intervention in the economy. "It is true that you and I would probably draw it in different places. I should guess that according to my ideas you greatly underestimate the practicability of the middle course. But as soon as you admit that the extreme is not possible, and that a line has to be drawn, you are, on your own argument, done for, since you are trying to persuade us that so soon as one moves an inch in the planned direction you are necessarily launched on the slippery path which will lead you in due course over the precipice." For Keynes, as long as the planners shared basic moral principles the danger of dictatorship was negligible. "I should therefore conclude your theme rather differently. I should say that what we want is not no planning, or even less planning, indeed I should say that we almost certainly want more."

Over the years Hayek was especially sensitive about this question of drawing a line and establishing a point of no return. He often claimed that his ideas had been misunderstood, that he was talking about a degree of danger and not automaticity. In a response to his critics published in London's *The Spectator* on January 26, 1945, he attempted to clarify matters:

> *It is curious that the point which contemporary planners are so anxious to deny, that there is no stopping half-way on the road to a centrally planned society, used to be a favourite argument of the Socialists. The famous phrase about "the inevitability of gradualness" says precisely what I have been trying to say; and it has certainly worked, not only in the sense in which it was meant, of advancing to a given goal step by step, but also in the sense that it has driven its inventors by its ruthless logic from Fabianism to out-and-out Communism. The half-way house is as little an intellectual as a practical resting-place.*

Here Hayek was referring to the endorsement in the 1930s of Stalin's Soviet Union by several leading Fabians, notably Shaw and Sidney and Beatrice Webb.

> *All this is of course not meant to say that we are likely ever to put into practice either of the two great opposing principles in all its purity [that is, pure planning versus laissez-faire]. We are always on the move. All I am arguing is that the guiding principle which we adopt is likely to carry us far beyond the point at which we at first aim. Even Adam Smith thought that "to expect, indeed, that freedom of trade should ever be entirely restored in Great Britain is as absurd as to expect that an Oceana or Utopia should ever be established in it." Our planners are likely to be equally mistaken when they think they can stop the movement long before any of the horrors are reached which most of the more sensible among them admit that a completely planned society would involve.*

One of the problems with debating Hayek's ideas is the confusion surrounding the term "socialism," which has always carried many shades of meaning on either side of the Atlantic

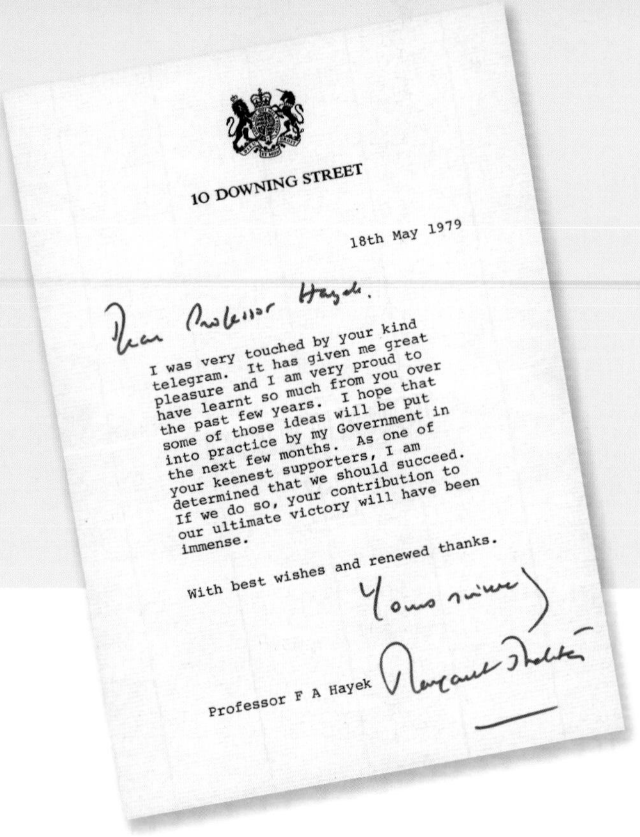
10 DOWNING STREET

18th May 1979

Dear Professor Hayek,

I was very touched by your kind telegram. It has given me great pleasure and I am very proud to have learnt so much from you over the past few years. I hope that some of those ideas will be put into practice by my Government in the next few months. As one of your keenest supporters, I am determined that we should succeed. If we do so, your contribution to our ultimate victory will have been immense.

With best wishes and renewed thanks.

Yours sincerely

Margaret Thatcher

Professor F A Hayek

Margaret Thatcher letter to Hayek, May 18, 1979. (Friedrich von Hayek Papers)

and within Europe. In retrospect, it is obvious that Hayek overestimated the dangers of social democracy as practiced in Western Europe after the Second World War. Whatever one might say in criticism of social democracy's efficiency and productivity, it did not produce dictatorships, let alone a Hitler or a Stalin.

Hayek's fundamental concern, in warning of the dangers of "socialism," was the centralized control of prices and wages. In his introduction to the 1976 edition of *The Road to Serfdom,* Hayek found Sweden to be less "socialist" than Britain or Austria because it had far less central planning and far less nationalization of the means of production. In other words, his objection was less to a "welfare state" than to an attempt to create "market socialism," a Third Way between capitalism and socialism that tried to combine government ownership of the means of production with market-determined prices. The key for Hayek was the interaction among competitive firms reacting to prices by innovating and redirecting resources.

Sea Change

Despite the immediate popularity of *The Road to Serfdom,* Hayek's views ran against the grain of economics as taught by academics and as practiced by Western policy makers. Hayek's ideas would be out of fashion for nearly three decades. In 1950 he accepted a position at the Committee on Social Thought at the University of Chicago, but after a while he longed for old Europe and in 1962 moved to Freiburg, Germany. In the meantime, he continued writing and produced important books on the liberal order, including, in 1960, *The Constitution of Liberty,* perhaps his greatest book, which stressed the importance of a legal framework for capitalism.

Inaugural meeting of the Mont Pèlerin Society. Hayek (center) chairs the first meeting of the Mont Pèlerin Society in April 1947. This is a composite of two photographs. Seated third from right (leaning forward) is Ludwig von Mises; at the far left are Milton Friedman and, to his left, Lionel Robbins. (Mont Pèlerin Society Records)

The Mont Pèlerin Society

In 1947, Hayek organized a conference of liberal intellectuals from various disciplines in a hotel on Mont Pèlerin near Montreux, Switzerland, above Lake Geneva. Hayek saw that socialists of all stripes were inspired by ideas, and he wanted to form a society as a way to energize liberals in the same way. His goal was nothing less than the "rebirth of a liberal movement in Europe." He wrote, "If we can regain that belief in the power of ideas which was the mark of liberalism at its best, the battle is not lost." For lack of an agreed-on name, the group called itself the Mont Pèlerin Society.

At the inaugural meeting, thirty-six participants gathered from ten countries; of these there were twenty professional economists (including Hayek's mentor, Ludwig von Mises), plus historians, lawyers, political philosophers, and journalists. Over the years, the society has met on average biannually at locations around the world. Hayek served as president of the society for 13 years, until 1960, and then as honorary president until his death in 1992. The records of the Mont Pèlerin Society are housed at the Hoover Archives.

But the audience for these works was never large. As Bruce Caldwell observes, "Although a small group of libertarians and conservatives always read him with enthusiasm, for much of the century Hayek was a subject of ridicule, contempt, or, even worse for a man of ideas, indifference." Cassidy is able to write, with only a bit of hyperbole, "If economic history had stopped when the Beatles split up, Hayek would have remained a museum piece favored mainly by right-wing cranks."

This is why it came as such a surprise when, in 1974, Hayek was awarded the Nobel Prize in Economics for his early writings on economic theory. Hayek, who was seventy-five years old at the time, shared the prize with Gunnar Myrdal, the left-wing Swedish economist; because of this, Hayek's award was seen as a sop to conservatives. By then, Hayek's reputation was based far more on his writings on political philosophy, so it seemed a bit curious to have his earlier, technical economic work receive such belated recognition.

And yet, as it happened, Hayek's Nobel Prize gave a boost to the counteroffensive against Keynesianism that was then under way in the field of economics. A few years later, with the Reagan-Thatcher "revolution" of the 1980s and its revolt against "big government," Hayek came into prominence. In the British press he was called Mrs. Thatcher's "guru," which certainly overstated the matter, although the Iron Lady made known her intellectual debt to Hayek.

The Nobel Prize seemed to rejuvenate Hayek, both physically and mentally, and he went on to write several more learned books on capitalism and the liberal order, including, at age eighty-nine in 1988, *The Fatal Conceit.* Hayek lived to see the collapse of the Soviet Union in 1991.

We are all Hayekians now, it would seem, though that depends on what one means by Hayekian. To the extent that his name is known at all outside academe, Hayek is usually thought of as an archconservative, the economist who opposed progressive taxation and proposed to privatize money supply. Yet, he once famously protested that he was not a conservative at all, but a classical liberal.

Like Adam Smith, Hayek was by no means antigovernment in principle. He rejected the term "laissez-faire," which to him seemed to imply that markets somehow sprang from nature. As he once wrote, "In no system that could be rationally defended would the state just do nothing. An effective competitive system needs an intelligently designed and continuously adjusted legal framework as much as any other." He believed that a certain amount of noncoercive government intervention was essential in order to maintain a system of equal opportunity and provide an economic safety net. What he resisted were attempts to turn legitimate forms of insurance into instruments of economic redistribution. As Caldwell puts it, "The safety net must not be allowed to become a hammock."

FREE TO CHOOSE
Nobel Economist Milton Friedman looks at the free market and the meaning of freedom in the new PBS series FREE TO CHOOSE. Big government, a phenomenon of the last fifty years, is not the answer to our problems. It *is* the problem. We must stop looking to government as the source of all good things. Watch Milton Friedman in FREE TO CHOOSE every ________ at _____ p.m. on Channel _____.

Milton Friedman, from the PBS series "Free to Choose" (1980). (Free to Choose Collection)

MILTON FRIEDMAN

The Power of Ideas

Milton Friedman has brought to the study of economics an extraordinary combination of theoretical depth, unparalleled policy influence, and enormous public influence through his pathbreaking books and articles, his long-running column in *Newsweek*, and a nationally broadcast Public Television series and its best-selling companion volume. An intellectual in the tradition of classical liberalism, Friedman has championed the virtues of a market economy and free trade and defended the freedom of the individual from government control.

Friedman's credentials as a pioneering economic scientist rest on his outstanding contributions to economic theory, particularly in the areas of consumption analysis, monetary history and theory, and stabilization policy. These achievements won him the Nobel Prize in 1976. More generally, Friedman led a counterrevolution against Keynesian economics that radically altered the way economists and policy makers perceive economic processes. Whereas Friedrich von Hayek in a sense went over Keynes's head in elucidating the fundamental advantages of the market and the dangers of planning, Friedman fought Keynes on the battlefield of macroeconomics.

Friedman's initial thrust was his watershed 1957 study of consumption analysis, *A Theory of the Consumption Function*, which overturned the Keynesian premise that expenditures on consumption by individuals and households reflect their *current* income. Friedman demonstrated that people's annual consumption is instead a function of their anticipated long-run, or *permanent*, income (a term he coined), meaning their expected lifetime earnings. Permanent income is not affected by short-term increases or decreases in income. Friedman first proposed the theory (which was developed independently by Franco Modigliani of MIT) and then tested it against family budget data, which confirmed

President Herbert Hoover in San Francisco on election day, November 8, 1932. Lou Henry Hoover is visible just behind the president. (Herbert Hoover Papers)

President-elect Franklin Delano Roosevelt, as shown on the cover of a dinner program in February 1933. (Raymond Moley Papers)

his hypothesis of the importance of long-term expectations in determining current consumption decisions.

This was the first blow Friedman struck at Keynesian economics, but it was in the area of monetary theory, especially the quantity theory of money, that he scored his greatest triumph against Keynes, whose ideas had reigned in the field since the 1930s.

The Keynesian Revolution

The Great Depression destroyed the naïve belief of the 1920s that the Federal Reserve, a twelve-bank system established in 1913, could manage the U.S. economy and "solved" its boom-and-bust business cycles. Indeed, opinion now swung in the other direction, that monetary policy could not have stemmed the Depression. The new assumption, to borrow imagery used by Friedman, was that monetary policy was a string: "You could pull on it to stop inflation but you could not push on it to halt recession." The Keynesian solution to depression and unemployment was fiscal policy: government spending to make up for insufficient private investment, and tax reduction to stimulate consumer spending.

The foundations of Keynesian economics were laid down in Keynes's landmark 1936 book *The General Theory of Employment, Interest, and Money,* which offered an interpretation of the Great Depression and made the case for government intervention through active use of fiscal policy, while minimizing the role of money. Despite mostly negative reviews of his book in the United States, before long Keynes's ideas were revolutionizing economic thought and policy, with the result that, as Friedman ruefully recalls, "For some two decades monetary policy was believed by all but a few reactionary souls to have been rendered obsolete by new economic knowledge. Money did not matter. . . ."

Friedman's Counterrevolution

It is not incidental that the man who would mount a challenge to Keynesianism was trained at the University of Chicago. As Friedman wrote in the 1950s, "Chicago was one of the few academic centers at which the quantity theory [of money] continued to be a central and vigorous part of the oral tradition throughout the 1930s and 1940s, where students continued to study monetary theory and to write theses on monetary problems." The theoretical approach taught at Chicago maintained that money does matter; any analysis of short-term economic activity that failed to account for changes in the supply of money was likely to be seriously flawed.

Friedman challenged the consensus of the academic establishment in his 1956 book *Studies in the Quantity Theory of Money.* In it he argued that, in the short run, increases in the money supply bring about an increase in employment and output, while decreases in the money supply have the opposite effect. "The key prediction of Friedman's quantity theory of money," as stated by his colleague Anna Schwartz, "is that, contrary to Keynesian doctrine, the demand for money is a stable function of a small number of variables." Friedman's book met with skepticism and resistance among economists, but he was just getting started.

Friedman then looked back in history in order to investigate the role of money in the United States during the decisive years 1929–1933. Keynes and most other economists of the era believed that the Great Depression had occurred despite aggressive expansionary policies by the Federal Reserve. Friedman was not convinced. Together with Schwartz, he examined the relations between changes in money supply and changes in prices and output from the Civil War to 1960. The results of their investigation were published as *A Monetary History of the United States, 1867–1960* (1963). Their findings demonstrated that the common wisdom about the role of monetary policy in the Depression stood reality on its head.

Friedman and Schwartz showed that from 1929 the Federal Reserve followed highly *deflationary* policies, failing to provide liquidity to the banking system as the quantity of money in the United States fell by one-third owing to bank failures. The Great Depression, it turns out, was a tragic mistake that could have been avoided had the Fed intervened in a timely and intelligent way. (The death in 1928 of Benjamin Strong, president of the Federal Reserve Bank of New York, the authors found, had left the Fed rudderless at a critical juncture.) Contrary to Keynes's belief, the Depression demonstrated the power of monetary policy, not its impotence.

As Olivier Blanchard recounts, "Friedman and Schwartz's challenge was followed by a vigorous debate and by intense research on the respective effects of fiscal and monetary policy. In the end, a consensus was reached. The truth was in between: Both fiscal and monetary policies clearly had effects. And if one cared about the composition of output and took into account the openness of the economy, the best policy was typically a mix of the two." Friedman's influence was soon felt in economics textbooks, which began to acknowledge the power of money as a macroeconomic tool and to recognize the importance of the Federal Reserve.

In the area of monetary *policy,* however, Friedman would claim only mixed success. Unlike Keynesian economists, Friedman and his fellow "monetarists" were proponents of limited government. They believed that policy makers would never have sufficient knowledge to enable them to fine-tune an economy, and that they could not be trusted to promote the general welfare without regard to their own political or ideological interests. Over time,

Friedman and his like-minded colleagues could claim success for their general argument in favor of less-active policy making. Yet, ironically, his call for restraint has been perhaps least successful in the realm of monetary policy.

In "The Role of Monetary Policy," the presidential address he delivered in Washington in December 1967 at the eightieth annual meeting of the American Economics Association, Friedman laid stress on what monetary policy *cannot* do (namely, control real variables, such as the real interest rate, the rate of unemployment, and the level and rate of growth of the real quantity of money), as much as what it *can* do (control nominal variables such as the rate of inflation or deflation). Judging by subsequent developments, however, Friedman's audience was not in complete agreement. Indeed, an observation Schwartz made twenty years later with respect to the influence of his monetary counterrevolution has only gained force in the intervening years, as the Federal Reserve Board has grown in stature: "To some extent, his success has backfired, since economists, in particular the Keynesians, now regard the central bank as a more potent instrument for controlling the economy than they had earlier believed."

Transforming the Phillips Curve

Throughout the 1960s, most mainstream economists believed that government faced a stable long-run trade-off between unemployment and inflation—an idea represented by the so-called Phillips curve, named after the economist A. W. Phillips. As Kevin Hoover writes, publication in 1958 of the Phillips curve "represented a milestone in the development of macroeconomics."

In researching the economy of the United Kingdom from 1861 to 1957, Phillips discovered clear evidence of a consistent negative relation between the rate of wage inflation and the rate of unemployment. When unemployment was low, inflation was high; when unemployment was high, inflation was low, even negative. The only important exception was the hyperinflationary period between the two world wars. Phillips portrayed this relationship by means of a graph, with the horizontal axis representing the unemployment rate and the vertical axis the rate of wage inflation; a negatively sloped Phillips curve depicted the relation between the two variables over the course of the business cycle.

The Phillips curve, as Blanchard explains, "appeared to imply that leaving aside such episodes as the Great Depression, countries could choose between different combinations of unemployment and inflation. They could achieve low unemployment if they were ready to tolerate higher inflation, or they could achieve price level stability—zero inflation—if they were ready to tolerate higher unemployment. Macroeconomic policy became focused

Two graphs from Friedman's 1976 Nobel lecture, "Inflation and Unemployment." The caption quotes are taken from Friedman's lecture. (Milton Friedman Papers)

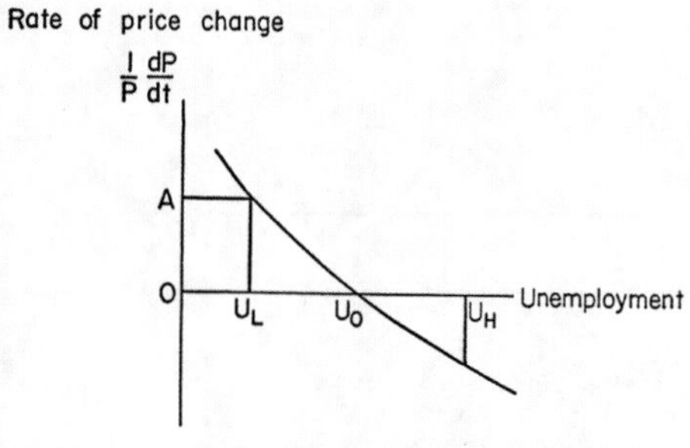

Figure I: Simple Phillips Curve

Simple Phillips Curve depicts a "causal relation that offered a stable trade-off to policymakers. They could choose a low unemployment target, such as U(L). In that case, they would have to accept an inflation rate of A. . . . Alternatively, the policymakers could choose a low inflation rate or even deflation as their target. In that case they would have to reconcile themselves to higher unemployment: U(O) for zero inflation, U(H) for deflation."

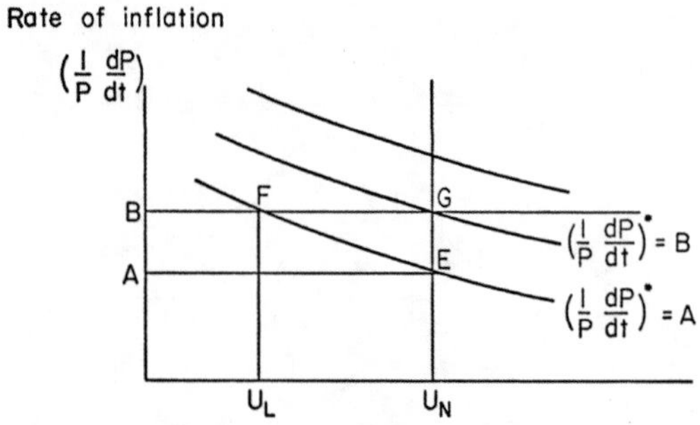

Figure 2: Expectations-adjusted Phillips Curve

Expectations-adjusted Phillips Curve: "Each negatively sloping curve is a Phillips curve like that in [the] figure [above] except that it is for a particular anticipated or perceived rate of inflation, defined as the perceived average rate of price change, not the average of perceived rates of individual price change. . . . Start from point E and let the rate of inflation for whatever reason move from A to B and stay there. Unemployment would initially decline to U(L) at point F, moving along the curve defined for an anticipated rate of inflation (1/P)(dP/dt)* of A. As anticipations adjusted, the short-run curve would move upward, ultimately to the curve defined for an anticipated inflation rate of B. Concurrently unemployment would move gradually over from F to G."

According to Friedman, this analysis, though oversimplified, highlights the key points: "What matters is not inflation per se, but unanticipated inflation; there is no stable trade-off between inflation and unemployment; there is a 'natural rate of unemployment' (U(N)), which is consistent with the real forces and with accurate perceptions; unemployment can be kept below that level only by an accelerating inflation; or above it, only by accelerating deflation."

-7-

will be entirely rational for him to interpret it as at least partly special and to react to it by seeking to produce more. He will be willing to pay higher nominal wages than he had been willing to pay before to attract additional workers because the real wage that matters to him is the wage in terms of the price of his product, and he perceives that price as higher than before. A higher nominal wage can therefore mean a lower real wage to him.

To workers, the situation is different: what matters to them is the purchasing power of wages not over the particular good they produce but over all goods in general. Both they and their employers are likely to adjust their perception of prices in general much more slowly—because they have less information about that—than their perception of the price of the particular good they produce. As a result, a rise in nominal wages may be perceived by workers as a rise in real wages and hence call forth an increased supply, at the same time that it is perceived by employers as a fall in real wages and hence calls forth an increased offer of jobs. Expressed in terms of the average of perceived future prices, real wages are lower; in terms of the perceived future average price, real wages are higher.

But this is a temporary situation: let the higher rate of growth of aggregate demand continue, and perceptions will adjust to reality. When they do, the initial effect will disappear, and then even be reversed for a time as workers and employers find themselves locked into inappropriate contracts. Ultimately, employment will be back where it started.

This alternative hypothesis is depicted in Figure 2. Each negatively sloping curve is a Phillips curve like that in Figure 1 except that

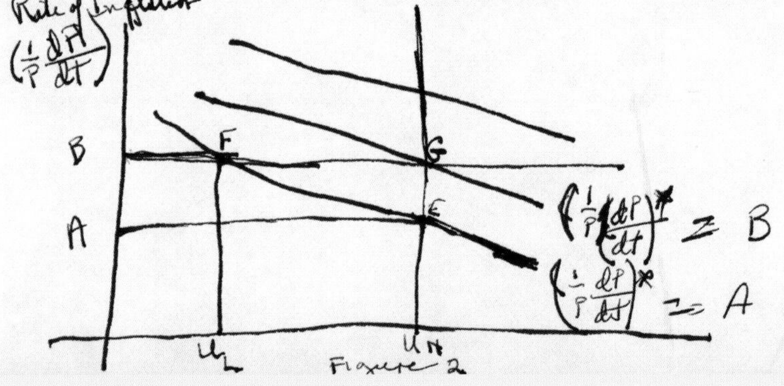

Page from the first draft of Friedman's Nobel lecture, "Inflation and Unemployment," showing an expectations-adjusted Phillips Curve drawn in his hand.

on choosing the preferred point on the Phillips curve." In other words, the Phillips curve came to be viewed as a kind of menu of policy trade-offs. In the 1960s, U.S. government policy makers aimed to maintain unemployment at a level consistent with moderate inflation. Indeed, throughout the decade the negative relationship between unemployment and inflation depicted in the Phillips curve proved to be a reliable guide to economic reality.

In the late 1960s, with the popularity of the Phillips curve at its height, Milton Friedman and Edmund Phelps, working independently, challenged its basis in theory. They argued, as a general proposition, that it was unrealistic to assume that *nominal* variables, such as the money supply or inflation, could permanently influence real variables, such as output or unemployment. In the long run, they maintained, the behavior of real variables is determined by real forces. Applying this general principle to the specific case of the Phillips curve, they argued that the existence of an apparently permanent trade-off between inflation and unemployment was illusory. What ultimately matters to companies and employees are real wages, the purchasing power of money wages adjusted to inflation. If the government pursued a long-term expansionary policy, sooner or later employers and workers would catch on and adjust, as Schwartz elaborates:

> *Once employers realized that there had been no increase in relative demand for their output but only an increase in the general price level, and once workers realized that they had been misled with respect to the purchasing power of nominal wages, unemployment would return to the level at which it stood before the unanticipated price rise.*

Friedman called this the "natural rate of unemployment"—meaning the lowest sustainable unemployment rate in the absence of *unanticipated* inflation. Expansionary policies could succeed in reducing the rate of unemployment for only very brief periods. Only unanticipated inflation would lead to lower unemployment. As Friedman phrased it in his 1976 Nobel Prize lecture, "Only surprises matter." The new understanding of the relation between inflation and unemployment is represented in a modified, or "expectations-adjusted," Phillips curve.

Like anything else that challenges the popular wisdom, this revision of the Phillips curve met with initial skepticism, and there was strong resistance to the very idea of a "natural rate" of unemployment. Then, in the 1970s, the theory put forward by Friedman and Phelps received striking confirmation in the form of "stagflation," higher inflation combined with higher unemployment. The explanation for this phenomenon went beyond the oil shocks of the decade. As Blanchard explains, stagflation was a manifestation of a long-term process that had begun around 1960:

The persistence of inflation led workers and firms to revise the way they formed expectations. When inflation is consistently positive, expecting that prices this year will be the same as last year becomes systematically incorrect, indeed foolish. People do not like to make the same mistake repeatedly. Thus, as inflation became consistently positive and more persistent, expectations started to incorporate the presence of inflation. This change in expectation formation changed the nature of the relation between unemployment and inflation.

The theory of Friedman and Phelps had anticipated such behavior. Most economists, including many Keynesians, were won over to their argument. The expectations-adjusted Phillips curve became, as it remains, the basic macroeconomic tool for analyzing the relationship between inflation and unemployment.

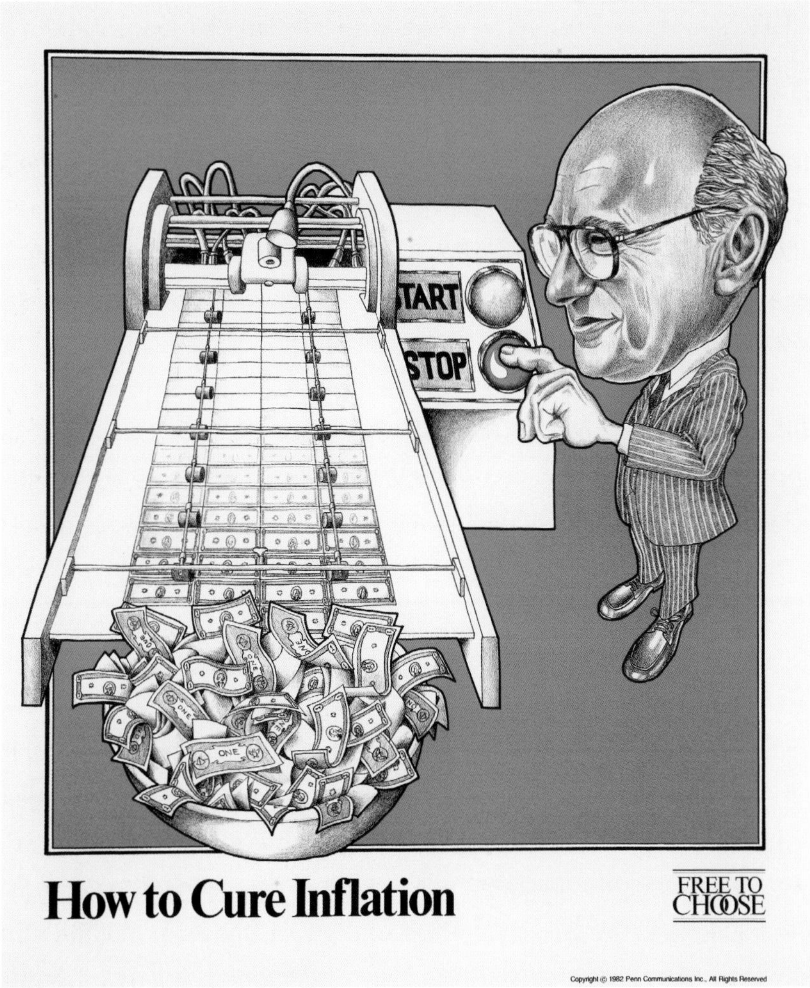

Publicity poster used for the PBS series "Free to Choose." (Free to Choose Collection)

Free to Choose

A dazzling economic scientist, Milton Friedman also became a great communicator of his ideas to the general public through his journalism and books. These ideas extended well beyond the narrow field of economics into the social-political arena. Friedman's point of departure—his fundamental message—is that economic freedom is as vital to a free society as is political freedom.

Friedman's first attempt to reach the general-interest book reader came in 1962 with *Capitalism and Freedom,* in which he argued in favor of a volunteer army, freely floating exchange rates, a negative income tax, and education vouchers, among other policy proposals. In the words of economist Thomas Moore, "At that time all of these ideas were considered radical and impractical. Now they all are either practiced or being experimented with. Even the negative income tax has in some sense through the earned income tax credit been accepted. It is a remarkable achievement."

In 1980, Friedman drew an audience of millions with his highly successful *Free to Choose* (coauthored with his wife, Rose Friedman), a lively exploration of the virtues of the free market and the vices of government control. It was written as the companion volume to a ten-hour television series by the same name that aired on Public Television. Individual programs in the series were devoted to Friedman's key concerns in the areas of market economics and a free society and gave him a platform to advocate favorite causes such as the earned-income tax credit, the flat-rate income tax, school vouchers, and the privatization of social security.

The PBS series was a hit, and *Free to Choose* became the top-selling nonfiction book of 1980. Television audiences saw why Friedman's reputation as a superb classroom teacher was richly deserved. And the timing of his enterprise was perfect: Americans were looking for answers to the seemingly incurable "stagflation" of the 1970s, and there was a growing reaction in the country against "big government," a movement that would help Ronald Reagan win the presidency in 1980.

The collapse of communism solidified the free-market consensus and elevated Friedman's status still further, as a number of his policy prescriptions, at one time regarded as highly unorthodox, entered the mainstream. It was, after all, a Democratic president, Bill Clinton, who declared that "the era of big government is over." To Friedman, of course, it was far from over, so long as the size of government continued to increase even as taxes decreased. Nonetheless, he could rightfully claim to have changed the terms of the debate. In the judgment of *The Concise Encyclopedia of Economics,* "No other economist since Keynes has reshaped the way we think about and use economics as much as Milton Friedman."

Friedman receives his Nobel Prize from King Carl XVI Gustaf of Sweden, December 10, 1976. The prize for economics, sponsored by the Central Bank of Sweden, was introduced in 1968 and is officially called the "Bank of Sweden Prize in Economics in Memory of Alfred Nobel." (Milton Friedman Papers)

"Knowledge wins." USA, c. 1918. Dan V. Smith.

SELECT BIBLIOGRAPHY

Adams, E. D. *The Hoover War Collection at Stanford University, California: A Report and an Analysis.* Stanford, [1921].

"Agents of the War on War." *Literary Digest.* August 1, 1914.

Baburina, N. I. *Russkii plakat: Vtoraia polovina XIX–nachalo XX veka.* Leningrad, 1988.

Bainbridge, John, and Maloney, Russell. "Where Are They Now? The Innocent Voyage." *New Yorker.* March 9, 1940.

Barrett, David D. *Dixie Mission: The United States Army Observer Group in Yenan, 1944.* Berkeley, CA, 1970.

Blanchard, Olivier. *Macroeconomics.* Upper Saddle River, NJ, 1997.

Bonnell, Victoria E. *Iconography of Power: Soviet Political Posters under Lenin and Stalin.* Berkeley, 1997.

Bull, G. V., and Murphy, C. H. *Paris Kanonen—The Paris Guns (Wilhelmgeschütze) and Project HARP.* Herford, Germany, 1988.

Burdick, Charles B. *Ralph H. Lutz and the Hoover Institution.* Stanford, 1974.

Cassidy, John. "The Price Prophet." *New Yorker.* February 7, 2000.

[Chang Kia-Ngau]. *Last Chance in Manchuria: The Diary of Chang Kia-Ngau* (ed., intro. Donald G. Gillin and Ramon H. Myers, trans. Dolores Zen). Stanford, 1989.

Craig, Gordon A. *Europe Since 1914* (3rd ed.). Fort Worth, TX, 1972.

———. "The True Believer." *New York Review of Books.* March 24, 1994.

Danielson, Elena S. "'Patriotic and Profitable': The World War I Postcards in the Hoover Institution Archives." *Popular Culture in Libraries,* vol. 3, no. 2, 1995.

———. *For Peace Alone Do I Ring.* Stanford, 2002.

de Basily, Nicolas. *Diplomat of Imperial Russia, 1903–1917: Memoirs.* Stanford, 1973.

Deutscher, Isaac. *The Prophet Armed. Trotsky: 1879–1921.* New York and London, 1954.

Dorn, Frank. *Walkout: With Stilwell in Burma.* New York, 1971.

Duignan, Peter (ed.). *The Library of the Hoover Institution on War, Revolution, and Peace.* Stanford, 1985.

Edmonds, David, and Eidinow, John. *Wittgenstein's Poker: The Story of a Ten-Minute Argument Between Two Great Philosophers.* New York, 2001.

Eiler, Keith E. (ed.). *Wedemeyer on War and Peace.* Stanford, 1987.

———. "An Uncommon Soldier." *Hoover Digest,* 2001, no. 4.

Ellis, John. *Cassino: The Hollow Victory.* New York, 1984.

Fleishman, Lazar. *Boris Pasternak: The Poet and His Politics.* Cambridge, Mass., and London, 1990.

Gallatin, A. E. *Art and the Great War.* New York, 1919.

Gilman, Rhoda R. "Zeppelin in Minnesota: A Study in Fact and Fable." *Minnesota History,* Fall 1965, vol. 39, no. 7.

———. "Count Zeppelin and the American Atmosphere." *Smithsonian Journal of History,* Spring 1968, vol. 3, no. 1.

Glazer, Nathan. "The Happy Warrior." *Wall Street Journal*, April 15, 1987.

[Goebbels, Joseph]. *The Early Goebbels Diaries: 1925–1926* (ed. Helmut Heiber). New York, 1963.

———. *Die Tagebücher von Joseph Goebbels: Sämtliche Fragmente.* pt. 1, vol. 1. Munich, 1987.

Gopnik, Adam. "The Porcupine: A Pilgrimage to Popper." *New Yorker*, April 1, 2002.

[Got'e, Iu. V.]. *Time of Troubles: The Diary of Iurii Vladimirovich Got'e, Moscow, July 8, 1917, to July 23, 1922* (trans., ed., intro. Terence Emmons). Princeton, 1988.

Hacohen, Malachi Haim. *Karl Popper—The Formative Years, 1902–1945: Politics and Philosophy in Interwar Vienna.* Cambridge, 2000.

Heinrichs, Waldo H., Jr. *American Ambassador: Joseph C. Grew and the Development of the United States Diplomatic Tradition.* Boston and Toronto, 1966.

"Henry Ford in Search of Peace." *Literary Digest*, December 11, 1915.

Hessen, Robert (ed.). *Breaking with Communism: The Intellectual Odyssey of Bertram D. Wolfe.* Stanford, 1990.

Hill, Cissie Dore. "Voices of Hope: The Story of Radio Free Europe and Radio Liberty." *Hoover Digest*, 2001, no. 4.

Hook, Sidney. *Out of Step: An Unquiet Life in the 20th Century.* New York, 1987.

Hoover, Kevin D. "Phillips Curve." *Concise Encyclopedia of Economics* (http://www.econlib.org/library/Enc/PhillipsCurve.html).

Huang Zhen. *Sketches on the Long March.* Beijing, 1982.

James, Robert Rhodes. *Gallipoli.* New York, 1965.

Jolluck, Katherine R. *Exile and Identity: Polish Women in the Soviet Union During World War II.* Pittsburgh, PA, 2002.

Keegan, John. *The First World War.* New York, 2000.

Kellogg, Vernon. *Fighting Starvation in Belgium.* Garden City, NY, 1918.

Kennedy, David M. *Freedom from Fear: The American People in Depression and War, 1929–1945.* New York, 1999.

Kershaw, Ian. *Hitler. 1889–1936: Hubris.* London, 1998.

Kraft, Barbara S. *The Peace Ship: Henry Ford's Pacifist Adventure in the First World War.* New York and London, 1978.

Lardner, John. "A Posthumous Blast at the Generalissimo." *New Yorker*, March 29, 1948.

Leube, Kurt R. (ed.). *The Essence of Friedman.* Stanford, 1987.

Lochner, Louis. *Always the Unexpected: A Book of Reminiscences.* New York, 1956.

Magee, Bryan. *Philosophy and the Real World: An Introduction to Karl Popper.* LaSalle, IL, 1985.

Majdalany, Fred. *Cassino: Portrait of a Battle.* London, 1957.

McGinn, Colin. "Looking for a Black Swan." *New York Review of Books*, November 21, 2002.

McInnes, Neil. "Popper's Return Engagement: The Open Society in an Era of Globalization." *National Interest*, Spring 2002.

Mirsky, Jonathan. "Message from Mao." *New York Review of Books*, February 16, 1989.

Morgan, Ted. *A Covert Life: Jay Lovestone. Communist, Anti-Communist, and Spymaster.* New York, 1999.

Murdock, Deroy. "Jan Karski, Freedom Fighter." *Hoover Digest*, 2000, no. 4.

Murphy, Robert D. *Diplomat Among Warriors.* New York, 1964.

Nash, George H. "Herbert Hoover and Belgium." [typescript; Hoover Archives] 1980.

———. *Herbert Hoover and Stanford University.* Stanford, 1988.

Nishiyama, Chiaki, and Leube, Kurt R. (eds.). *The Essence of Hayek.* Stanford, 1984.

Palmer, R. R., and Colton, Joel. A *History of the Modern World Since 1815.* New York, 1992.

Paret, Peter, Lewis, Beth Irwin, and Paret, Paul. *Persuasive Images: Posters of War and Revolution from the Hoover Institution Archives.* Princeton, 1992.

Paul, Gary Norman. "The Development of the Hoover Institution on War, Revolution and Peace Library, 1919–1944." Doctoral dissertation, University of California, Berkeley, 1974.

Perepiska B. Pasternaka c M. Baranovich. Moscow, 1998.

Rabinowitch, Alexander, Rabinowitch, Janet, and Kristof, Ladis K. D. *Revolution and Politics in Russia: Essays in Memory of B. I. Nicolaevksy.* Bloomington, IN, 1972.

Rawlings, John. *The Stanford Alpine Club.* Stanford, 1999.

Rawls, Walton. *Wake Up, America! World War I and the American Poster.* New York, 1988.

Reuth, Ralf Georg. *Goebbels* (trans. Krishna Winston). New York, 1993.

Romer, David. *Advanced Macroeconomics* (2nd ed.). Boston, 2001.

Salisbury, Harrison E. *The Long March: The Untold Story.* New York, 1985.

Savinkov, Boris. *Memoirs of a Terrorist.* New York, 1931.

Schapiro, Leonard. *The Communist Party of the Soviet Union* (2nd ed.). New York, 1971.

Sgovio, Thomas. *Dear America! Why I Turned Against Communism.* Kenmore, NY, 1979.

Skidelsky, Robert. *John Maynard Keynes: The Economist as Savior, 1920–1937.* New York and London, 1992.

———. *John Maynard Keynes: Fighting for Freedom, 1937–1946.* New York and London, 2000.

Snow, Helen Foster. *My China Years.* New York, 1984.

Spence, Jonathan D. *To Change China: Western Advisers in China, 1620–1960.* Boston and Toronto, 1969.

———. *The Search for Modern China.* New York and London, 1990.

Stilwell, Joseph W. *The Stilwell Papers* (ed. Theodore H. White). New York, 1948.

Sunstein, Cass R. "The Road from Serfdom." *New Republic,* October 20, 1997.

Tuchman, Barbara W. *Stilwell and the American Experience in China, 1911–45.* New York, 1985.

Turner, Piers Norris. "Remembering Karl Popper." *Hoover Digest,* 2001, no. 1.

Wedemeyer, Albert C. *Wedemeyer Reports!* New York, 1958.

White, Stephen. *The Bolshevik Poster.* New Haven, 1988.

Wolfe, Bertram D. *A Life in Two Centuries: An Autobiography.* New York, 1981.

Wood, E. Thomas, and Jankowski, Stanislaw M. *Karski: How One Man Tried to Stop the Holocaust.* New York, 1994.

INDEX

D

E

F

I

J

K

L

M

N

O

P

R

S

T

U

V

W

Y

Z

DISPLAY ILLUSTRATIONS

Front Endpapers

Russian troops in Petrograd during the February Revolution of 1917. (Russian Pictorial Collection)

Vernon Kellogg, *Fighting Starvation in Belgium*, 1918. (Hoover Library)

Medal by Belgian sculptor Godefroid Devreese, given to Vernon L. Kellogg for his work with the Commission for Relief in Belgium. (Medal Collection)

Letter from Wasfi Hijab to Karl Popper, September 4, 1946. (Sir Karl Raimund Popper Papers)

Abdication letter of Nicholas II, Emperor of Russia, 1917. (Nikolai Aleksandrovich Bazili Papers)

Special order from Chiang Kai-shek, issued by the National Government Military Committee, appointing Joseph W. Stilwell as the Chief Commander of the Chinese army in India, July 11, 1942. (Joseph W. Stilwell Papers)

Banner, n.d. (Robert D. Murphy Papers)

South African election ballot, 1994. (South African Subject Collection)

Back Endpapers

Fidel Castro in Havana, August 1970. (Elisabeth Burgos-Debray Papers)

Chinese medal. (Harry A. Mohler Collection)

Fidel Castro's business card, n.d. (Elisabeth Burgos-Debray Papers)

Frida Kahlo and Leon Trotsky, c. 1937. (Bertram D. Wolfe Papers)

Letter from Frida Kahlo to Bertram and Ella Wolfe, 1930s. (Bertram D. Wolfe Papers)

"Tina Modotti ha muerto," poem by Pablo Neruda, 1942. (Joseph Freeman Papers)

Woodblock print by David Alfaro Siqueiros, n.d. (Leo Eloesser Papers)

First edition of *Doctor Zhivago* in Italian translation, 1957. (Irwin Holtzman Papers)

Tina Modotti and Edward Weston in Mexico City, 1924. (Bertram D. Wolfe Papers)

Chapter One Opener (*right to left*)

Diary of Nobel Peace Prize winner Alfred Hermann Fried, August 7, 1914. (Alfred Hermann Fried Papers)

Peace buttons, n.d. (Alice Park Papers)

Polish medal and ribbon given to Hugh Gibson, c. 1920. (Hugh Gibson Papers)

Stereoscopic glass slide of a World War I trench. (World War I Pictorial Collection)

Announcement poster for an antiwar meeting, April 2, 1917. (David Starr Jordan Papers)

Chapter Two Opener (*right to left*)

Chinese Communist Party banknote, with image of Vladimir Lenin, 1933. (George W. Shepherd Papers)

Letter from Nicholas II, Emperor of Russia, to his mother, Mariia Feodorovna, Empress, consort of Alexander III, 1917. (Kseniia Aleksandrovna, Grand Duchess of Russia, Papers)

Alexei Nikolaevich, son of Nicholas II, Emperor of Russia, 1911. (Nikolai Aleksandrovich Bazili Papers)

Photograph by Tina Modotti of a hand and hammer, cover image for the journal *New Masses*, n.d. (Joseph Freeman Papers)

Chapter Three Opener

Hoover Library reading room in the Hoover Tower.

Chapter Four Opener (*right to left*)

Nazi booklet and pins, n.d. (Memorabilia Collection)

Nazi rally in Berlin, 1932. (Jay Lovestone Papers)

Photograph of Joseph Stalin on the front page of *Pravda*, August 18, 1933. (Hoover Library)

List of names of missing Polish prisoners who had been in the Soviet camps up to May 1940, compiled by the Polish government-in-exile on January 2, 1942. (Poland, Ambasada [Soviet Union] Records)

Chapter Five Opener (*right to left*)

Chinese tea set, n.d. (Albert C. Wedemeyer Papers)

Order of the White Sun and Blue Sky medal, China, n.d. (Albert C. Wedemeyer Papers)

Map of Burma showing route of Gen. Stilwell's walk-out in May 1942. (Frank Dorn Papers)

Joseph W. Stilwell diary, June 1943. (Joseph W. Stilwell Papers)

Joseph W. Stiwell's cap and watch, n.d. (Joseph W. Stilwell Papers)

Chapter Six Opener

Posters, including the French poster "On les aura!" by Jules Abel Faivre, 1916. (Poster Collection)

Chapter Seven Opener (*right to left*)

Issue of *The Call*, November 18, 1939. (Sidney Hook Papers)

Radio Free Europe microphone, n.d. (RFE/RL Records)

Photograph by Christian Härtel of East and West Germans walking on the Berlin Wall, November 1989. (German Pictorial Collection)

Karl Popper, 1940s. (Sir Karl Raimund Popper Papers)

Chapter Eight Opener (*right to left*)

Various coins and banknotes. (Currency collection)

Abacus, n.d. (Memorabilia Collection)

Page from the first draft of Milton Friedman's 1976 Nobel lecture "Inflation and Unemployment." (Milton Friedman Papers)

ACKNOWLEDGMENTS

This book could not have been assembled without the contributions of numerous individuals, beginning with the director of the Hoover Institution, John Raisian. The director of the Hoover Library and Archives, Elena Danielson, and her staff gave me generous and expert assistance throughout this project. I wish to thank Linda Bernard, Ronald Bulatoff, Carol Leadenham, Cissie Dore Hill, Dale Reed, Lisa Miller, Brad Bauer, David Jacobs, Aparna Mukherjee, Natalia Porfirenko, Anatol Shmelev, Polina Ilieva, Blanka Pasternak, Lora Soroka, Irena Czernichowska, Michael Gallagher, Lyalya Kharitonova, Gary McLerran, and Rayan Ghazal.

At the Hoover Library my research was greatly facilitated by the expertise and resourcefulness of Linda Ann Wheeler, Molly Molloy, Maria Quinonez, Kavous Barghi, Terry Gammon, Ramon H. Myers, Mark Tam, Joseph Dwyer, Maciej Siekierski, Zbigniew Stanczyk, William E. Ratliff, Jorge Machado, and Peter Duignan.

Norman Naimark deserves special thanks for a thorough and thoughtful critique of the entire manuscript. Ann Livschiz wrote a first draft of the posters chapter and made the initial poster selection. John Easterbrook and Keith Eiler were invaluable guides to the lives of, respectively, Stilwell and Wedemeyer. Terence Emmons, George Nash, Lazar Fleishman, Katherine Jolluck, Kurt Leube, and Thomas Moore read portions of the manuscript and rescued me from errors of fact and interpretation. Gloria Valentine allowed me access to Milton Friedman's uncatalogued papers.

Scanning and photography were executed by Jim Day, Steve Gladfelter, and MaryAnn Wijtman of Stanford's Visual Art Services, and Heather Wagner of the Hoover Archives. Tom Finnegan and Suzanne Chun helped shape and refine the text. Jean Mann is an incomparable indexer. Sarah Holmes, Connie Balsama, and Linda Huynh provided me with a cheerful and supportive writing environment.

At Stanford University Press this work was shepherded from proposal to publication by Norris Pope, Alan Harvey, Rob Ehle, Lowell Britson, and Mariana Raykov. The book owes its exquisite design to the unerring eye of Gordon Chun.